Brexit and the Northern Ireland Constitution

Brexit and the Northern Ireland Constitution

Lisa Claire Whitten

OXFORD
UNIVERSITY PRESS

Great Clarendon Street, Oxford, OX2 6DP,
United Kingdom

Oxford University Press is a department of the University of Oxford.
It furthers the University's objective of excellence in research, scholarship,
and education by publishing worldwide. Oxford is a registered trade mark of
Oxford University Press in the UK and in certain other countries

© Lisa Claire Whitten 2023

The moral rights of the author have been asserted

All rights reserved. No part of this publication may be reproduced, stored in
a retrieval system, or transmitted, in any form or by any means, without the
prior permission in writing of Oxford University Press, or as expressly permitted
by law, by licence or under terms agreed with the appropriate reprographics
rights organization. Enquiries concerning reproduction outside the scope of the
above should be sent to the Rights Department, Oxford University Press, at the
address above

You must not circulate this work in any other form
and you must impose this same condition on any acquirer

Published in the United States of America by Oxford University Press
198 Madison Avenue, New York, NY 10016, United States of America

British Library Cataloguing in Publication Data

Data available

Library of Congress Control Number: 2023940943

ISBN 9780198881940

DOI: 10.1093/oso/9780198881940.001.0001

Printed and bound by
CPI Group (UK) Ltd, Croydon, CR0 4YY

Links to third party websites are provided by Oxford in good faith and
for information only. Oxford disclaims any responsibility for the materials
contained in any third party website referenced in this work.

'For such a time as this'

NIV Bible, Esther 4:4

Acknowledgements

This book and the years of research that it represents would not have happened if not for the support of an exceptional collection of individuals. They include but are not limited to the following.

First and foremost to Professor David Phinnemore, my (long-suffering) primary PhD supervisor turned colleague, who has kindly read the majority of what follows more times than any one person ought to have had to—thank you. Closely followed by Professor Gordon Anthony KC, my secondary PhD supervisor, who lent his extensive knowledge of public and constitutional law to my novice-level understanding of the same. Then to the wider group of 'Brexperts' based at Queen's University Belfast and beyond—Professor Katy Hayward, Dr Billy Melo-Araujo, Dr Viviane Gravey, Professor Christopher McCrudden, Professor Lee McGowan, Professor Colin Harvey, Dr Jamie Pow, Professor John Garry, Professor Mary C. Murphy, Professor Mary Dobbs, Professor Nicola McEwen, Dr Jonathan Evershed, and Professor Michael Keating among many others. I am indebted to each one for their respective generosity in sharing expertise and graciousness in listening to my intermittent monologues on all things Brexit and Northern Ireland.

The years of research on which this book is founded have, primarily, been possible due to Economic Social Research Council funding, initially through the Northern Ireland and the North-East Doctoral Training Partnership programme and latterly through the 'Governance for a Place Between: the multi-levelled dynamics of implementing the Protocol on Ireland/Northern Ireland' project. I am (mostly) grateful to the ESRC for the opportunity to have spent a season of life in this manner—suffice to say it has been extremely intellectually stimulating if not, at times, just a little exhausting.

Then to the team at Oxford University Press, my sincere thanks for being willing to take the risk of supporting a first-time author proposing to publish on a not-yet-complete saga.

Finally, to the unrivalled crew that I am honoured to call family and friend—for your love, your support, your prayers, and your seemingly unending capacity to listen to politics-fuelled rants—I am more grateful than I could ever say.

Contents

List of Abbreviations — xii

1. Brexit's Northern Ireland Problem — 1
1.1 The Constitutional Fault Lines Exposed by Brexit — 3
1.2 The Constitutional Vulnerability of Northern Ireland to Brexit — 6
1.3 The Northern Ireland Constitution: In the Eye of the Brexit Storm — 8
1.4 The Northern Ireland Constitution as Significant, Overlooked, and Misrepresented — 10
1.5 Analytical Approach — 13
1.6 Book Structure — 14

2. The Northern Ireland Constitution: A History — 16
2.1 Northern Ireland: A (Brief) Constitutional History — 17
    2.1.1 Home Rule, Rebellion, and Compromise: 1800–1920 — 17
    2.1.2 An Accidental 'Mini-State': 1920–1972 — 21
    2.1.3 'Temporary' Direct Rule: 1972–1998 — 23
    2.1.4 Constructive 'Constitutional Ambiguity': 1998 present — 27
2.2 The Northern Ireland Blindspot in UK Constitutional Literature — 29

3. On Method and Approach — 34
3.1 Theoretical Assumptions — 35
3.2 Defining Terms — 37
    3.2.1 Research Definition of Brexit — 37
    3.2.2 Research Definition of the Northern Ireland Constitution — 38
3.3 Analytical Framework — 41

4. UK's EU Referendum — 44
4.1 UK's EU (Referendum) Act 2015 and the Referendum Campaign — 45
    4.1.1 The Story of the Referendum — 45
    4.1.2 The Referendum Result in Northern Ireland — 49
4.2 UK's EU Referendum and the Northern Ireland Constitution — 50
    4.2.1 Principle of Consent — 51
    4.2.2 Devolved Government — 53
        4.2.2.1 Northern Ireland: Placed Apart — 53
        4.2.2.2 Northern Ireland: A Place Apart — 56

4.2.3 North–South Dimension	59
4.2.4 East–West Dimension	61
4.3 Impact Assessment: UK's EU Referendum and the Northern Ireland Constitution	62
5. Triggering Article 50	**65**
5.1 The EU (Notification of Withdrawal) Act 2017 and Triggering Article 50	66
5.1.1 Conservative Leadership Election and UK Negotiating Position	67
5.1.2 Collapse of the Northern Ireland Executive and the Assembly Election	69
5.1.3 United Kingdom 'Constitutional Requirements' and the Miller Case	71
5.2 Triggering Article 50 and the Northern Ireland Constitution	72
5.2.1 Principle of Consent	72
5.2.2 Devolved Government	77
5.2.3 North–South Dimension	82
5.2.4 East–West Dimension	84
5.3 Impact Assessment: Triggering Article 50 and the Northern Ireland Constitution	86
6. UK–EU Withdrawal Agreement	**89**
6.1 The UK–EU Withdrawal Negotiations and UK–EU Withdrawal Agreement	91
6.1.1 Phase One of Withdrawal Negotiations: 'Flexibility and Imagination'	92
6.1.2 Phase Two of Withdrawal Negotiations: The 'Backstop' Protocol	95
6.1.3 Phase Three of Withdrawal Negotiations: The 'Front-Stop' Protocol	97
6.2 The UK–EU Withdrawal Agreement and the Northern Ireland Constitution	99
6.2.1 The Principle of Consent	101
6.2.1.1 Constitutional Status Reaffirmed	101
6.2.1.2 Self-Determination of National Identity and Citizenship Rights	103
6.2.1.3 Territorial Integrity and Territorial Waters	105
6.2.1.4 Democratic Consent Mechanism	107
6.2.2 Devolved Government	110
6.2.2.1 Applicable Union Law and CJEU Jurisdiction	112
6.2.2.2 Arrangements for Implementation and Representation	115
6.2.3 North–South Dimension	121
6.2.3.1 Defining the Border and Mapping Cross-Border Cooperation	122

		6.2.3.2	Cross-Border Trade in Goods	125
		6.2.3.3	Current and Future North–South Cooperation	128
		6.2.3.4	North–South as a Challenge to Northern Ireland in the UK Internal Market	131
	6.2.4	East–West Dimension		133
		6.2.4.1	'East–West' Provisions in the Withdrawal Agreement and Protocol	135
		6.2.4.2	Intergovernmental Relations: British-Irish Intergovernmental Conference	136
		6.2.4.3	Intra-UK and East–West Relations: British Irish Council	138
6.3	Impact Assessment: UK–EU Withdrawal Agreement and the Northern Ireland Constitution			139

7. Implementing the UK–EU Withdrawal Agreement in UK Law — 143

7.1	The UK's EU Withdrawal Act(s) and the Transition Period			146
	7.1.1	Key Political and Legislative Developments Prior to Transition Period		147
	7.1.2	Key Political and Legislative Developments During the Transition Period		152
7.2	UK Implementing Legislation and the Northern Ireland Constitution			159
	7.2.1	Principle of Consent		160
		7.2.1.1	New and Existing Legal Definitions of the '1998 Agreement'	160
		7.2.1.2	Self-Determination of National Identity and Citizenship Rights	163
		7.2.1.3	New and Existing Definitions of 'Northern Ireland'	165
		7.2.1.4	Legislating for a Democratic Consent Mechanism	166
		7.2.1.5	Legislative Consent	169
	7.2.2	Devolved Government		170
		7.2.2.1	Arrangements for Implementation	171
		7.2.2.2	Arrangements for Representation	176
	7.2.3	North–South Dimension		178
		7.2.3.1	Continued Development of North–South Cooperation	178
	7.2.4	East–West Dimension		182
		7.2.4.1	East–West Institutions in Implementing Legislation	183
		7.2.4.2	East–West Relations and Implementing Legislation	185
		7.2.4.3	Great Britain and Northern Ireland as 'East–West'	186
7.3	Impact Assessment: UK Implementing Legislation and the Northern Ireland Constitution			187

8. Brexit and the Northern Ireland Constitution — 190

8.1	Brexit and the Northern Ireland Constitution	192
8.2	Brexit and the Principle of Consent	195
8.3	Brexit and Devolved Government	197

8.4	Brexit and the North–South Dimension	201
8.5	Brexit and the East–West Dimension	205
8.6	Conclusion: What Impact Has Brexit Had on the Northern Ireland Constitution?	209

9. Northern Ireland's Brexit Problem — 212

- 9.1 Two Years of Implementation — 213
  - 9.1.1 Headline Events of the Protocol's First Two Years — 213
- 9.2 Constitutional Consequences Within and Beyond Northern Ireland's Borders — 222
  - 9.2.1 The New Protector: EU–NI Relations Post-Brexit — 222
    - 9.2.1.1 The Legal Dimension — 223
    - 9.2.1.2 The Political Dimension — 226
  - 9.2.2 Creation and Contestation: The Principle of Consent Post-Brexit — 227
  - 9.2.3 Exacerbating Fragility: Strand One Institutions Post-Brexit — 232
  - 9.2.4 Complex and Contingent: The North–South Dimension Post-Brexit — 234
  - 9.2.5 Tensions and Inventions: The East–West Dimension Post-Brexit — 238
    - 9.2.5.1 Interjurisdictional Relations and Institutions After Brexit — 238
    - 9.2.5.2 Intergovernmental Relations and Institutions After Brexit — 239
    - 9.2.5.3 Intra-UK 'East–West' *Relations* After Brexit — 240
- 9.3 Conclusion: Northern Ireland's Brexit Problem — 242

10. The Windsor Framework: An Addendum — 245

- 10.1 A (Surprisingly Comprehensive) Agreement in Principle — 245
- 10.2 The Windsor Framework: An Overview — 247
  - 10.2.1 Amendments and Provisions Related to Goods — 248
  - 10.2.2 Amendments and Provisions Related to Governance — 251
    - 10.2.2.1 EU–NI engagement — 252
    - 10.2.2.2 EU–UK Institutions — 252
    - 10.2.2.3 UK Unilateral Measures — 254
      - 10.2.2.3.1 Article 13(3): Stormont Brake on Amended or Replaced EU Acts — 254
      - 10.2.2.3.2 Article 13(4): Stormont Brake on New EU Acts — 255
- 10.3 Brexit, the Windsor Framework, and the Northern Ireland Constitution — 256
  - 10.3.1 EU–NI Relationship Consolidated — 256
  - 10.3.2 Democratic Deficit Mitigated — 257

10.3.3 Dual Divergence Guaranteed	258
10.4 An Inconclusive Conclusion	259
Table of Cases	261
Table of Legislation	262
Bibliography	269
Index	312

List of Abbreviations

1998 Act	Northern Ireland Act 1998
1998 Agreement	Belfast/Good Friday Agreement
1914 Act	Government of Ireland Act 1914
BBC	British Broadcasting Cooperation
BIA	British Irish Agreement
BIC	British Irish Council
BIIC	British Irish Intergovernmental Conference
CAP	Common Agricultural Policy
CI	Constitutional Issues
CJEU	Court of Justice of the EU
CTA	Common Travel Area
DARD	Dept for Agriculture and Rural Development
DExEU	Dept for Exiting the EU
DUP	Democratic Unionist Party
ECA	European Communities Act
ECHR	European Convention on Human Rights
ECNI	Equality Commission Northern Ireland
EEC	European Economic Community
EU	European Union
EUWA	EU Withdrawal Act 2018
EU(WA) Act	EU (Withdrawal Agreement) Act
FCO	Foreign Commonwealth Office
FTA	Free Trade Agreement
GATT	General Agreement on Tariffs and Trade
GB	Great Britain
HC	House of Commons
HL	House of Lords
HMG	Her Majesty's Government
HMRC	HM Revenue and Customs
JCHRC	Joint Committee of Human Rights Commissions of Ireland and Northern Ireland
JCWG	Joint Consultative Working Group
LCM	Legislative Consent Motion
MLA	Member of Legislative Assembly
MOU	Memorandum of Understanding
MP	Member of Parliament
MPA	Multi-Party Agreement
NDNA	New Decade New Approach
NI	Northern Ireland

NIAC	Northern Ireland Affairs Committee
NICS	Northern Ireland Civil Service
NI(EFEF)	NI (Executive Formation and Execution of Functions)
NIHRC	NI Human Rights Commission
NILT	Northern Ireland Life and Times
NIO	Northern Ireland Office
NISRA	NI Statistics and Research Agency
NSMC	North South Ministerial Council
ONIEB	Office of NI Executive in Brussels
PM	Prime Minister
PUP	Progressive Unionist Party
RHI	Renewable Heat Incentive
RSE	Rights Safeguards Equality of Opportunity
SDLP	Social Democratic Labour Party
SI	Statutory Instrument
SNP	Scottish National Party
SPS	Sanitary and Phytosanitary
Supreme Court	UK Supreme Court
Taxation (CBT)	Taxation (Cross Border Trade)
TCA	Trade and Cooperation Agreement
TEU	Treaty on the European Union
TFEU	Treaty on the Functioning of the EU
TUV	Traditional Unionist Voice
UDP	Ulster Democratic Party
UK	United Kingdom
UKCG	UK Coordination Group
UKG	UK Government
UKIM	UK Internal Market
UKIP	UK Independence Party
VAT	Value Added Tax
VIR	Validation Implementation and Review
WA	Withdrawal Agreement

1
Brexit's Northern Ireland Problem

> Wherever green is worn ... changed, changed utterly: A terrible beauty is born.
>
> W. B. Yeats, September 1916[1]
>
> It's as if there's a tidal wave coming; it just hasn't quite hit yet.
>
> Senior Northern Ireland Civil Servant, 28 June 2016[2]

One hundred years after W. B. Yeats' poetic prediction, the poet's words seemed once again apt. In the aftermath of the United Kingdom's (UK) referendum on European Union (EU) membership, a tidal wave of disruption was triggered, and the force of the surge seemed set to cause irrevocable change on the island of Ireland. Based on a broad understanding of constitutions as the fundamental political principles and established legal precedents of government, this book traces the nature and extent of the change catalysed by the UK's EU referendum in 2016 on the unique constitution of Northern Ireland.

Although often used as a singular noun, 'Brexit'[3] was not a singular moment or event but a complex and multifaceted process, one with domestic and international aspects, that resulted in substantive political and legal changes in the structure of the UK, the nature of UK–EU relations, and the UK's international status. Brexit was also an inherently constitutional process. Article 50(1) of the Treaty on the European Union (TEU), that the UK government invoked in March 2017 to begin the formal withdrawal process, provides that any EU Member State can decide to leave the EU 'in accordance with its own constitutional requirements' (*Official Journal*, 2016: 68). Following the UK's EU referendum and prior to triggering Article 50,

---

[1] Reproduced from: W. B. Yeats, *The Collected Poems of W. B. Yeats* (Wordsworth Editions Limited, Hertfordshire 1989).
[2] This comment was made by a senior civil servant at a meeting during a Northern Ireland Civil Service (NICS) delegation official visit in the week after the UK's EU Referendum to the Office of the Northern Ireland Executive in Brussels (ONIEB) in which the author was working at the time.
[3] Short for '[Great] British + Exit', the neologism 'Brexit' is arguably somewhat of a misnomer insomuch as the term implicitly excludes Northern Ireland. While this linguistic inaccuracy is notable, the term Brexit is used here to refer to the process of the UK's withdrawal from the EU as it has come to be understood in common parlance and as it is defined in Chapter 3 (see 3.2.1). For analysis of the development and spread of the term, see (Fontaine, 2017); for a critique of its use, see (O'Leary, 2017).

Brexit and the Northern Ireland Constitution. Lisa Claire Whitten, Oxford University Press.
© Lisa Claire Whitten (2023). DOI: 10.1093/oso/9780198881940.003.0001

conversations about what exactly the 'constitutional requirements' of the unwritten, uncodified constitution of the UK were, in the unprecedented scenario of an EU Member State deciding to withdraw, dominated UK politics. Disagreements that resulted led to a prolonged period of political upheaval, ground-breaking legal judgments, and, ultimately, to a series of substantial changes in the UK's legal order. As a *constitutional* process, therefore, Brexit catalysed a new level of interest in the UK constitution, sparking extensive discussions regarding its nature, its legitimacy, and its longevity. Alongside the substantive legal changes arising from Brexit, the outcomes of Brexit-related political debates about the UK constitution can also be expected to shape the future development of the UK polity.

In the rhetorical maelstroms catalysed by Brexit, Northern Ireland often took centre stage. Given that it is the only region of the UK to share a land border with another EU Member State, Northern Ireland could reasonably have been expected to play an important part in any UK–EU withdrawal negotiations and resulting agreement(s). However, as the region of the UK with the most unique political and constitutional structure, and one whose history is defined by constitutional conflict, the impact of the complex, multifaceted, and *constitutional* process of Brexit was always going to be most difficult, and most potentially transformative, for and in Northern Ireland.

Unlike the rest of the UK, the constitution of Northern Ireland is largely codified in one statute. Prior to 2016, the *Northern Ireland Act* of 1998 (hereafter 'the 1998 Act') had been judicially recognised to be 'in effect a constitution' for the region (in the case of *Robinson v Secretary of State for Northern Ireland* 2002: 11) that is to be interpreted in line with the principles laid down in the historic Belfast 'Good Friday' Agreement, also of 1998 (hereafter 'the 1998 Agreement').[4] The signing of the 1998 Agreement brought an end to three decades of internecine conflict between communities with different national identities and opposing visions for the constitutional future of Northern Ireland. In pursuit of peace, the 1998 Agreement relied on a 'constructively ambiguous' compromise between previously warring parties on the contested issues of nationality and statehood. Crucially, this meant that the 1998 Agreement did not solve the constitutional conflict in Northern Ireland but rather allowed it to be 'managed differently' (Phinnemore and Hayward, 2017: 22) through a series of interdependent and

---

[4] The Agreement is referred to as both the 'Belfast Agreement' and the 'Good Friday Agreement' in academic literature and political discourse. In Northern Ireland, typically, the 'Belfast Agreement' is associated with unionism and the 'Good Friday Agreement' with nationalism, but the choice of term does not always imply political preference. For the purpose of brevity and to avoid implication in favour of any particular political affiliation, 'the 1998 Agreement' is used here and throughout to refer to the Belfast 'Good Friday' Agreement signed on 10 April 1998.

overlapping institutions providing for: devolved government in Northern Ireland; cooperation between the two jurisdictions on the island of Ireland; and intergovernmental cooperation between Ireland and the UK, including its devolved administrations and Crown Dependencies. In the years since the signing of the 1998 Agreement, Northern Ireland's political and constitutional development had been slow, stuttering, but steady; Brexit and its consequences threatened, and continue to threaten, that development. On this premise, the purpose of this book is to consider the intersection of the two processes so far mentioned: the steady yet fragile development of Northern Ireland's unique post-1998 constitution; and the complex, multifaceted, and constitutional process of Brexit.

To set the context for the discussion, this introductory chapter sets out the key features of the environment in which the Northern Ireland constitution and Brexit intersect before briefly outlining the methodological approach and consequential structure of the book.

1.1 The Constitutional Fault Lines Exposed by Brexit

Brexit was a destabilising force for the UK political establishment. The 51.9% majority vote in favour of leaving the EU shocked the cadre of politicians in power at the time and led to the immediate resignation of Prime Minister David Cameron (see Oliver, 2016; Shipman, 2016). In the (dramatic) Conservative Party leadership election that followed, substantially different interpretations of the meaning and implications of the Leave Vote became clear (see Jeffery et al., 2018). Related disagreements among politicians of all parties dominated domestic political discourse for at least three years after the UK's EU referendum; as a consequence, Brexit became the defining issue on which political representatives were judged and categorised.

Alongside party political disruptions, the process of Brexit exposed previously under-acknowledged complexities in the constitutional structure of the UK state. Prior to the UK's EU referendum, the uncodified constitution of the UK had been characterised as 'multi-layered' (Elliott, 2015: 39), 'unsettled' (Walker, 2014: 2), and possessive of 'divided sovereignty' (*Jackson v Attorney-General*, 2005: 102) due to it having multipolar sources of authority. Constitutional plurality and instability were understood to have originated in a series of constitutional reforms introduced from 1973 onwards. Joining the European Economic Communities (EEC now EU) in 1973, incorporating the European Convention on Human Rights (ECHR) into UK law in 1998, the creation of the Scottish Parliament, Welsh Assembly, and Northern Ireland

Assembly, also in 1998, were all considered to have variously altered core features of the 'Traditional British Constitution' (see, for example, Norton, 2014; King, 2001).[5] Importantly, however, the extent of unsettlement caused by these constitutional changes had not received that much public or political attention prior to June 2016 (Walker, 2014; Bell, 2014). Brexit changed this. When the prospect of initiating the UK's withdrawal from the EU 'in accordance with its own constitutional requirements' (TEU, Article 50(1)) arose, the depth of divergence over what precisely the UK's unsettled, uncodified, constitution required became clear. In resultant debates two major fault lines emerged: disagreement over (1) the balance of executive power vis-à-vis parliamentary sovereignty; and disagreement over (2) the authority of central government vis-à-vis devolved administrations.

The first fault line was prominent in the landmark case of *Miller v Secretary of State for Exiting the EU* (2017) wherein the United Kingdom Supreme Court (hereafter 'Supreme Court') ruled against the government by recognising that its position relied on an antiquated understanding of the royal prerogative that did not adequately account for the constitutional impact of the UK's EU Membership (*Miller*, 2017: 88). While in *Miller* (2017) the Supreme Court ruled that the government needed parliamentary approval prior to triggering Article 50, the judgment did not fully resolve underlying questions about the limits of executive powers in a constitutional order premised on the sovereignty of Parliament. Disagreement about the extent and legitimate use of executive power vs parliamentary power became a persistent theme of efforts to ratify a UK–EU Withdrawal Agreement during Prime Minister May's tenure and continued into Prime Minister Johnson's premiership. Following the seeming return to comfortable majority governments after the landslide victory for Boris Johnson's Conservative Party in the 2019 general election, major political disputes along this constitutional fault line are less likely in the near future. This does not, however, remove the existence of the executive vs parliamentary fault line that Brexit served to expose.

---

[5] The traditional British constitution is generally understood to have had four principal features: (1) a singularly sovereign Parliament; (2) the rule of law, an essentially procedural doctrine whereby laws must be interpreted and applied by an impartial judiciary; those charged under the law are entitled to a fair trial, and no one can be imprisoned outside the due process of law; (3) a unitary state whereby formal power resides exclusively in the national authority (Parliament and the Crown) with Parliament able to confer powers on other bodies, which remain subordinate to Parliament; (4) 'parliamentary government under a constitutional monarchy' refers to the form of government established since the seventeenth century wherein Ministers are legally answerable to the Crown but politically answerable to Parliament; a government is returned by general election and depends on the confidence of a majority of Members of Parliament to pass law and continue in office (see Norton, 2014: 253–4). Literature on the historical British (and/or English) constitution and its core features is extensive; introductory overviews can be found in Norton (2014), Parpworth (2018) or Thompson and Gordon (2017); see also Chapter 2, section 2.1.

The second constitutional fault line exposed by Brexit related to the authority of central government vis-à-vis devolved administrations. Despite central governments' initial determination 'that the devolved administrations *should* be fully engaged' in the Brexit process (May, 2017: *emphasis added*), accusations of an attempted 'power grab' by central government were made repeatedly by devolved representatives during the Brexit process (Sturgeon and Jones, 2017; Elliott, 2017). The nature of devolved administrations' authority also featured in the *Miller* (2017) case. The Supreme Court took the view that 'most' of the 'devolution issues' addressed whether or not the government was obliged under the Sewel Convention to seek the consent of devolved administrations before triggering Article 50, given that withdrawal would impact the type and scope of devolved competencies (*Miller*, 2017: 5; 6).[6] The Supreme Court adopted an orthodox view on the matter by employing a 'power-hording' approach to central government's powers (Anthony, 2018; King, 2001)[7] that relied on the creation of a false dichotomy between the legal and political world; while simultaneously overlooking questions of a 'constitutional nature' specific to Northern Ireland (*Miller*, 2017: 6; see also McCrudden and Halberstam, 2017; Anthony, 2018). As scholars have since argued, and subsequent political events arguably suggest (see Elliott, Williams, and Young, 2018), the Supreme Court's reassertion of constitutional orthodoxy in this instance may have created more constitutional complexities than it clarified.

To summarise, rifts that emerged on the political and legal landscape following the UK's EU referendum exposed a dormant lack of settlement in the UK constitution and ignited debates about the extent to which the UK was, is, or will be a constitutionally plural state. In the (often heated) constitutional conversations catalysed by Brexit, Northern Ireland played something of a starring role.

---

[6] The Sewel Convention refers to the UK Government's stated policy on legislation concerning devolved matters; it is named after Lord Sewel who set out the terms of the policy during the passage of the *Scotland Bill 1997–98*. Lord Sewel stated: 'we would expect a convention to be established that Westminster would not normally legislate with regard to devolved matters in Scotland without the consent of the Scottish parliament' (HL 21 Jul 1998 vol. 592 c. 791). Broader application of the convention was later embodied in the Memorandum of Understanding (MoU) drawn up between central UK Government and all of the UK devolved administrations, first in 1999, then revised and superseded by subsequent MoUs (for the most recent see Cabinet Office, 2012; for contect and discussion see Bowers, 2005).

[7] Reference to 'power-hoarding' here follows the 'power-sharing' vs 'power-hoarding' archetypes proposed in King (2001). According to King, in a power-sharing constitutional order 'there exists, within the governmental system itself, autonomous centres of political power ... institutions of government are to a considerable extent pluralist and fragmented. There is no single Hobbesian "sovereign"' (*ibid*.: 7). By contrast, in a power-hoarding constitutional order 'political power is concentrated in the hands of the government, and the government is usually a single-party government' (9), noting further that a power-hoarding regime is usually associated with a 'political culture that legitimises and reinforces the hoarding of power' through a guiding normative principle of 'winner takes all' (*ibid*.: 10).

1.2 The Constitutional Vulnerability of Northern Ireland to Brexit

Northern Ireland was, at best, a byline during the UK's EU referendum campaign. It was rarely mentioned by proponents of either Leave or Remain and subsequent insider accounts suggest it was far from the minds of those directing UK-wide campaigns (see Oliver, 2016; O'Toole, 2017; Shipman, 2016; Banks, 2016). The referendum campaign within Northern Ireland was lacklustre and failed to gain much traction with voters or politicians (Northern Ireland Affairs Committee (NIAC)), 2016; Burke, 2016; Murphy, 2018) as was reflected in a turnout of 62.7%, the lowest of the UK regions.[8] Yet, as the withdrawal process progressed, Northern Ireland became central.

From early on, all parties characterised Northern Ireland as an exceptional case. Prior to triggering Article 50, it was described as a 'unique' region by the joint leaders of its devolved, power-sharing government (The Executive Office, 2016a) and its 'specific interests' and 'particular circumstances' were recognised by the Prime Minister as an 'important priority for the UK' (The Prime Minister, 2016). Once formal notification was given by the UK to the EU, the latter made clear that the 'unique circumstances and challenges' UK withdrawal presented on the island of Ireland (European Commission, 2017a: 14) would be a negotiating priority. The EU suggested 'flexible and imaginative solutions' would be required to continue to 'support and protect the achievements, benefits and commitments' of the peace process in Northern Ireland, an aim it deemed 'of paramount importance' (European Council, 2017a: 11). As UK–EU withdrawal negotiations proceeded, it became clear that arrangements for Northern Ireland and its border with Ireland post-Brexit would be the most difficult issue for UK and EU negotiators to resolve. The situation was not helped by Prime Minister May's reliance on ten Democratic Unionist Party (DUP) MPs for her slim parliamentary majority. Political dissent regarding the Ireland/Northern Ireland 'backstop' Protocol derailed attempts to ratify the UK–EU Withdrawal Agreement agreed in 2018, and ultimately ended May's premiership. Arrangements agreed in the revised Ireland/Northern Ireland Protocol

---

[8] The percentage turnout by UK electoral region was: South East 76.8%; South West 76.7%; East 75.7%; East Midlands 74.2%; West Midlands 72%; Wales 71.7%; Yorkshire and The Humber 70.7%; North West 70%; London 69.3%; North East 69.3%; Scotland 67.2% and Northern Ireland 62.7%. This also meant that the only three electoral regions to return Remain majorities—London, Scotland, and Northern Ireland—were among the bottom four for turnout (The Electoral Commission, 2019).

(hereafter 'the Protocol') contained in the UK–EU Withdrawal Agreement, (re)negotiated and successfully ratified by Prime Minister Johnson in 2020, substantially differentiate Northern Ireland from the rest of the UK through an unprecedented set of provisions. As the content of this book demonstrates, the requirements of the Protocol and its implementation have, and will, profoundly impact the economic, political, and constitutional structure of Northern Ireland going forward.

The centrality of Northern Ireland in the Brexit process is a consequence of its particular and multifaceted vulnerability. Foremost, and rather obviously, it is the only region of the UK to share a land border with another EU Member State, making it the most visible physical canvas for any change in UK–EU relations. Relatedly, and less obviously, it was also the most economically exposed part of the UK due to the scale and scope of cross-border economic cooperation on the island of Ireland (see Brownlow and Budd, 2019) as well as its reliance on the 'uniquely vulnerable' agri-food sector (see The Executive Office, 2016a), its position as a net recipient of EU regional development funding, and the importance of dedicated EU PEACE funding (see Hayward and Murphy, 2018; MacFlynn, 2016; Oxford Economics, 2016). Even more fundamental to its geography and economy, however, Northern Ireland was uniquely vulnerable because of the crucial facilitative role that joint EU membership of the UK and Ireland had played on its path to peace. Since the accession of the UK and Ireland to the European Communities together in 1973, the EU's shared legal, economic, and political framework had provided the 'essential context' for Northern Ireland's still-in-process peace (Phinnemore and Hayward, 2017: 7; see also Hayward and Murphy, 2018; Murphy, 2019); the creation of the EU Single Market in 1993 was particularly significant in this regard. Furthermore, shared EU frameworks made the legally innovative aspects of the 1998 Agreement feasible, meaning that Northern Ireland was also the region of the UK whose legal and judicial structure was most clearly premised on the assumption of continued UK membership of the EU (see McCrudden, 2017; Anthony, 2017).

Taking these factors together, in view of its geographic position, its economic structure, and its political and legal order, Northern Ireland was, by some margin, the most vulnerable part of the UK in the face of Brexit. Every facet of this vulnerability can be traced back to, and ought to be understood in light of, Northern Ireland's unique constitutional arrangements, the contested constitutional history from which they arose, alongside a tendency amongst many political actors on the UK stage to overlook or underplay the same.

1.3 The Northern Ireland Constitution: In the Eye of the Brexit Storm

Since it was created in 1921, Northern Ireland has been a place of constitutional contestation. De-stabilisation of a union that had existed between Great Britain and Ireland since the Acts of Union of 1800 led to the creation of two new constitutional settlements on the island of Ireland in the 1920s—a devolved Parliament under the authority of Westminster in Northern Ireland, and an independent Irish Free State south of the newly created land border (Calvert, 1968; Hadfield, 1989). Partition of the island of Ireland into Northern Ireland and what became the Republic of Ireland developed as a means of solving Great Britain's so-called 'Irish Question' (Adelman, 1996). For Northern Ireland, however, the 'solution' of the 1920s did not ultimately last.

The governing architecture set up in Northern Ireland was designed to facilitate indefinite rule by the Unionist, largely Protestant, majority at the expense of a Nationalist, largely Catholic, minority. In the words of the first Prime Minister for Northern Ireland, it was 'a Protestant Parliament and Protestant State' (Craig, 1934: 1091–5). Prolonged discrimination and intermittent clashes between members of the minority Nationalist community and representatives of the Northern Irish state led to the outbreak of violence in the late 1960s following a series of civil rights protests. Following various interventions from Westminster, the first era of self-rule in Northern Ireland, and first experiment in devolved governance in the UK, ended in March 1972 with the collapse of the Stormont Parliament amid a seemingly inexorable slide into civil war. Life in Northern Ireland for the next three decades was characterised by internecine conflict between communities defined by their opposing visions for Northern Ireland's constitutional future—Nationalists who sought a united Ireland and Unionists committed to staying part of the UK.

Then, in April 1998, the circumstances in, and constitutional arrangements of, Northern Ireland changed. With the signing of the 1998 Agreement, the societal, political, and constitutional development of Northern Ireland entered a new era, one from which it has since progressed in a steady yet fragile manner.

The 1998 Agreement has two parts—a political agreement, agreed between and signed by political parties in Northern Ireland (the 'Multi-Party Agreement' (MPA)), and an international treaty between the governments of the

UK and Ireland (the 'British-Irish Agreement' (BIA)), who act as 'guarantors' to the substance of the Multi-Party Agreement. Underpinning the 1998 Agreement are a series of statements regarding the constitutional status of Northern Ireland; these are affirmed by all parties and set out in the opening sections of both the Multi-Party Agreement and the British-Irish Agreement. Signatories recognise 'the present wish of the majority of the people of Northern Ireland' is to remain in the UK (MPA, *Constitutional Issues*, 1(iii); BIA, Article 1(iii)) but, if that wish changes, 'it is for the people of the island of Ireland alone ... to exercise their right of self-determination on the basis of consent ... to bring about a united Ireland' (MPA, *Constitutional Issues* 1(ii); BIA Article1(ii)). The two guarantor governments agreed: to exercise any sovereign power held at any time in respect to Northern Ireland with 'rigorous impartiality' (BIA Article 1(v)); to recognise the birthright of people in Northern Ireland 'to identify themselves and be accepted as Irish or British, or both' regardless of the constitutional status of Northern Ireland (BIA Article 1(vi)); and to introduce legislation necessary to recognise the constitutional status of Northern Ireland in the event of any future change in that status. This series of commitments are normally referred to collectively as the 'principle of consent'.

Based on the principle of consent, the 1998 Agreement set out an innovative, multi-levelled system for government in Northern Ireland through the 'three strands' of the Multi-Party Agreement. Strand One provided for the creation of new democratic institutions—the Northern Ireland Assembly and the Northern Ireland Executive—to which powers were devolved on the basis of a consociational system for power-sharing between Nationalists and Unionists, underpinned by rights-based guarantees. Strand Two provided an all-island or North–South dimension through the North South Ministerial Council (NSMC) and North/South Implementation Bodies that enable cooperation between the Irish Government and the Northern Ireland Executive. Strand Three provided an intergovernmental or East–West dimension through the creation of the British-Irish Council (BIC), designed to facilitate relations between Ireland, the UK, and its regions; and the bilateral, British-Irish Intergovernmental Conference (BIIC) to preserve and strengthen relations between the governments of the neighbouring states.

In the British-Irish Agreement, the two governments 'affirm[ed] their solemn commitment to support, and where appropriate implement, the provisions of the Multi-Party Agreement' (BIA, Article 2). As such, and according to the terms of the 1998 Agreement, the Irish Government proposed an amendment to remove the territorial claim to Northern Ireland still contained in the Constitution of Ireland at the time; this was subsequently approved by referendum.[9] Following a concurrent, confirmatory referendum in Northern Ireland, the principal content of the Multi-Party Agreement was transposed into UK law via the *Northern Ireland Act 1998*. The explicit purpose of the 1998 Act is 'to make provision for the government of Northern Ireland' (*Long Title*); it remains the primary statutory source of the Northern Ireland constitution. The 1998 Act was judicially recognised to be 'in effect a constitution' for Northern Ireland, the content of which 'must be construed against the background of … the principles laid down by the Belfast Agreement for a new start' (in *Robinson*, 2002: 11; 25). In view of the explicit aim of the 1998 Act and in keeping with the judicial recognition it received, the substance of Northern Ireland's constitution is here taken to reside in the legal provisions and political principles dually enshrined in the 1998 Act and the 1998 Agreement, including the commitments and affirmations made by Ireland and the UK in the British-Irish Agreement.

1.4 The Northern Ireland Constitution as Significant, Overlooked, and Misrepresented

Northern Ireland's constitution, and the history from which it developed, sets it apart as constitutionally unique within the UK and internationally; this fact has, however, often been overlooked, or under-appreciated in the domestic political context.

According to conventional understandings, the essence of the uncodified UK constitution is its ongoing capacity to adapt to change without overt rupture (Bell, 2014: 2). The adaptability of the uncodified UK constitution is claimed as continuity; flexibility is its defining feature and the cornerstone of its constitutional legitimacy (*ibid.*: 8). The predominance of this

---

[9] The 1937 Constitution stated: 'The national territory consists of the whole island of Ireland, its islands and the territorial seas.' After the 1998 Agreement, the text was amended to recognise that '[i]t is the entitlement and birth-right of every person born in the island of Ireland, which includes its islands and seas, to be part of the Irish nation …' (Article 2) and that while '[i]t is the firm will of the Irish nation, in harmony and friendship, to unite all the people who share the territory of the island of Ireland … a united Ireland shall be brought about only by peaceful means with the consent of a majority of the people, democratically expressed, in both jurisdictions in the island' (Article 3(1)). Under Article 47(1) of the constitution, amendments can only be made if 'approved by the people' via referenda; following a 94.4% vote in favour of doing so on 22 May 1998, the 19th Amendment to Constitution was made on 3 June 1998 to accept the BIA and the amendments to Articles 2 and 3 outlined.

understanding of the UK constitution has meant that the reigning narrative of constitutional history in the UK is one of gradual change, the slow accumulation and evolution of constitutional precedent. The constitutional history of Northern Ireland contradicts this.

Constitutional rupture is generally required to enable the signing of peace agreements. Consensus is predicated on breaking with a past that was unacceptable to at least one involved party and a commitment by all parties to some newly formed constitutional architecture. The political and legal process that led to the 1998 Agreement and its subsequent translation into law typified the kind of constitutional rupture expected in peace negotiations. It marked a 'constitutional moment' for Northern Ireland (Harvey, 2012). The process conforms to the idea of a constitutional moment (proposed by Ackerman, 1993 and 1998) in that its ratification required the collective agreement of the citizenry—North and South of the land border—to principles beyond those of normal politics, thereby engaging a higher form of law associated with nationally existential questions. Northern Ireland's constitutional moment of 1998 therefore augmented a novel approach to constitutional development in the UK. In contrast to the traditional 'pragmatic empiricist' approach of British constitutionalism which relies on precedent to guide a gradual constitutional development, the 1998 Agreement is 'ideological', meaning it relies on normative principles agreed by specific parties at specific times to guide constitutional development (McCrudden, 2004: 198). Yet, notwithstanding the importance of Northern Ireland's constitutional moment in 1998, and the widespread heralding of this as a political victory that introduced a new era for Northern Ireland (Blair, 2010; Obama, 2013), the creative significance of the 1998 Agreement in the context of UK constitutional development is consistently overlooked.

Attempts to fit the 1998 Agreement (and the 1998 Act) into a 'straightjacket of devolutionary thinking' are common (Campbell et al., 2003: 319). These characterisations fail to capture the complexity of its provisions for multi-levelled governance and its use of innovative law that exceeds the boundaries of a conventional definition of devolution. The provisions for North–South and East–West cooperation, established under Strand Two and Strand Three of the 1998 Agreement, introduced (quasi)confederal and inter-governmental requirements for governance in Northern Ireland with facilitating institutions whose existence is underpinned by international law (O'Leary, 1998: 3; Anthony, 2017: 4). In addition, employing *sui generis* international law, under the 'principle of consent', the 1998 Agreement contains a unique, open-ended provision for a potential change in the future sovereignty of Northern Ireland if agreed by democratic means (Donohue, 2016; Campbell et al., 2003), and incorporates an exceptionally malleable concept of nationality by enabling those born in Northern Ireland to choose British citizenship, Irish citizenship, or both. Through its three-stranded, multi-layered structure, and the uniquely fluid definition of nation and statehood, the 1998 Agreement embodies 'constructive ambiguity' regarding the constitutional future of Northern Ireland and the national identities of its citizenry (Bell and Cavanaugh, 1999; Mitchell, 2009). In this respect, as already stated, the peace agreement did not solve the constitutional conflict in Northern Ireland but rather enabled it to be 'managed' (Phinnemore and Hayward, 2017: 22) through this imaginative set of cross-community, cross-border, and inter-governmental institutions and a universal commitment in Northern Ireland to democratic means.

In UK politics, Northern Ireland is predominantly characterised as a 'devolved administration' and the 1998 Agreement as a 'devolutionary settlement' (see UK Government, 2018a). Such descriptions are not wholly inaccurate, but they are incomplete; they omit the unique provisions regarding consent and cross-border, cross-jurisdictional cooperation. Use of the devolution 'straight-jacket' nonetheless persisted with scholars of UK constitutional history tending to subsume Northern Ireland into a pure devolutionary model to which, they posit, the UK 'clearly adheres' (Elliott, 2015: 40; see also Norton, 2014). These reductionist depictions of the UK, and by proxy Northern Ireland, have been possible because of the minimal analysis generally given to the constitutional character and history of Northern Ireland in UK-wide analyses (Campbell et al., 2003). Northern Ireland has frequently been portrayed as 'oddly detached' or a 'place apart' (King, 2009: ix) without much justification as to how, why, or the manner in which this might be true.

In the context of Brexit, this blindspot as regards the significance of Northern Ireland's constitutional history, and the exceptional, innovative, and multi-layered nature of Northern Ireland's post-1998 constitution, became problematic in that the centrality of Northern Ireland in the Brexit process was premised on a legacy of successive UK governments, parliamentarians, and constitutional scholars overlooking the contested constitutional history of the polity and the constructively ambiguous constitutional (un)settlement of post-1998 Northern Ireland in UK-wide analyses. The central position of Northern Ireland in the Brexit process arguably therefore disrupted a well-established historical norm whereby the political and constitutional status of Northern Ireland had been marginalised in UK-wide discussions. This being so, the impact of Brexit on Northern Ireland's constitutional future could be expected to be even more significant than its unique vulnerability alone would suggest.

1.5 Analytical Approach

To summarise the contextual factors set out thus far: (1) Brexit exposed a previously under-studied lack of settlement in the UK constitution and, as a result, fault lines emerged between parties with differing views of what the UK constitution requires; (2) the significance and vulnerability of Northern Ireland facing Brexit was multifaceted and derived from its constitution and its constitutionally contested history; (3) the Northern Ireland constitution is unique in the UK and internationally; (4) the high profile granted Northern Ireland in the context of Brexit marked a shift away from an established norm in UK politics of paying minimal attention to the constitutional particularities of the place. Taking these collectively, the importance of the intersection between the complex and multifaceted Brexit process and Northern Ireland's unique 'constructively ambiguous' constitution was clear, but the outcome was not. On this basis, the purpose of this book is to answer the seemingly simple question: *What impact did Brexit have on the constitution of Northern Ireland?* This central research question can be broken down into a series of sub-questions each of which addresses the specific impact of different stages of the Brexit process—the UK's EU referendum, the triggering of Article 50, the UK–EU Withdrawal Agreement, and the relevant UK implementing legislation—on different aspects of the Northern Ireland constitution, namely, the principle of consent, devolved government (Strand One), the North–South dimension (Strand Two), and the East–West dimension (Strand Three). Chapter 3 discusses this approach in more detail and develops an analytical framework to help us consider the progressive impact of elements of the Brexit process on the core components of the Northern Ireland constitution.

The primary method underpinning the research presented here is content analysis of political and legal texts produced by the Brexit process regarding Northern Ireland. Brexit produced a wealth of texts with constitutional significance for the UK including new international agreements, a large amount of new domestic legislation, and important legal judgments alongside a myriad of political discourse, official correspondence, and policy papers. A sustained analysis of the progressive impact of these texts on the unique constitution of Northern Ireland has not yet been published.

1.6 Book Structure

This book is structured as follows: Chapter 2 provides an historical grounding for the analysis by setting out a brief constitutional history of Northern Ireland; based on this historical overview, in the concluding subsection, this chapter identifies a 'blindspot' that pervades literature on the UK-wide constitution in respect to Northern Ireland and its unique backstory. Having set the historical and intellectual scene, Chapter 3 then addresses questions of method and presents an analytical framework from which flows the structure of subsequent chapters. Working definitions for Brexit and the Northern Ireland constitution are outlined and used as the basis for a framework through which to analyse their interaction.

Chapters 4 to 7 are the most important of the book. Each one analyses the impact of a specific element of the Brexit process on the constitution of Northern Ireland: Chapter 4 is focused on the UK's EU referendum; Chapter 5 on the triggering of Article 50 TEU; Chapter 6 on the UK–EU Withdrawal Agreement, and Chapter 7 on the impact of domestic legislation that implements UK withdrawal in general and the UK–EU Withdrawal Agreement in particular. Each of these four empirical chapters follows the same structure: an introduction followed by an overview of relevant events; then, mirroring the structure of the 1998 Agreement and 1998 Act, the main body sets out the impact of events on the four components of the Northern Ireland constitution: (A) the principle of consent; (B) devolved government in Northern Ireland (Strand One); (C) North–South relations and institutions (Strand Two); and (D) East–West relations and institutions (Strand Three); with a final section summarising key findings. While repetitive, this structure allows us to capture the *progressive* impact of Brexit in Northern Ireland; it enables comparison between the various stages of the process and helps to explain why, seven years on from the 2016 referendum when the final chapter of this book was written, Northern Ireland was still at the centre of Brexit-related debates.

Based on the key findings identified in Chapters 4 to 7, Chapter 8 concludes the empirical section of the book by providing a summative analysis of the overall impact of the Brexit process on the Northern Ireland constitution. Among the most important findings are that Brexit: led to a new formulation of the principle of consent; strengthened the powers of the UK government over the Northern Ireland Executive and Assembly beyond the balance of competencies envisaged in the 1998 Agreement; rebalanced the 1998 Agreement by prioritising North–South cooperation above its other component parts; resulted in a new understanding of 'East–West' relations that now includes relations between Great Britain and Northern Ireland; and established the EU as a 'protector' of those aspects of the 1998 Agreement explicitly covered by the Withdrawal Agreement and Protocol.

To conclude, Chapters 9 and 10 bring the discussion up to the contemporaneous political moment by reviewing the impact of Brexit on the Northern Ireland constitution so far from the perspective of, respectively, January 2023 and March 2023. Initially intended to be the final chapter of the book—Chapter 9—incorporates analysis of the results of the Northern Ireland Assembly elections of May 2022, and the tumultuous first two years of the Protocol's implementation. The actual and potential implications of the Brexit process on the constitutional future for those living in Northern Ireland are discussed as are some of the repercussions for all those looking on from beyond its recently (in)famous borders. The book then actually finishes with an addendum Chapter 10 written in the immediate aftermath of the UK and EU agreeing the package of measures known as the 'Windsor Framework' concerning arrangements for implementing the unique post-Brexit arrangement for Northern Ireland previously agreed under the Protoocol. Chapter 10 reviews the substance of the Windsor Framework texts and provides a preliminary analysis of their possible and likely repercussions.

2
The Northern Ireland Constitution: A History

To contextualise analysis of Brexit and the Northern Ireland constitution some familiarity with the history of Northern Ireland is necessary. This chapter is therefore devoted to a high-level account of Northern Ireland history. By setting out a specifically constitutional history this chapter elaborates on the idea that Northern Ireland's vulnerability in the face of Brexit derives from its unique constitutional arrangements, its evolving constitutional structure, and the contested history from which they developed. What is consistently evident from even a brief historical account is that Northern Ireland is, and always has been, a constitutionally unique part of the UK. Indeed, Northern Ireland has often played the part of the constitutional exception that disproves, or at least challenges, those constitutional rules and norms that apply elsewhere in the UK. It follows that Northern Ireland has also frequently been depicted as 'a place apart' in analyses of and debates about the UK constitution. While perhaps understandable, this 'placing apart' trend can be problematic if and when it prevents the constitutional particularities of Northern Ireland from being recognised and accommodated in UK-wide discussions and developments. A tendency to blindspot the Northern Ireland case in debates about, or narratives of, the UK constitution, and how it relates to UK withdrawal from the EU, is explored more fully in the second section of this chapter (2.2) and in subsequent chapters. But before getting to blind spots and Brexit, let us first ground this discussion in an account of how contemporary Northern Ireland came to be.

2.1 Northern Ireland: A (Brief) Constitutional History

2.1.1 Home Rule, Rebellion, and Compromise: 1800–1920

In 1800, the Acts of Union of Great Britain and Ireland joined two separate polities[1] into one and provided that all legislative power would reside in the Houses of Parliament in Westminster.[2] The governing arrangement that resulted continued in relative peace until towards the end of the 19th century when dissatisfaction on the island of Ireland inspired a series of constitutionally innovative legislative initiatives that sought to establish a new legislature in Dublin to which Westminster would transfer some powers while retaining sovereignty (see Quekett, 1928: 9). This policy of 'Home Rule' for Ireland was contentious. Debate over the so-called 'Irish Question' and how to answer it dominated parliamentary business for much of the first two decades of the 20th century. After several failed attempts, the *Government of Ireland Act 1914* (the 1914 Act) made provision for a new devolved Dublin legislature and was passed alongside a *Suspensory Act 1914* to delay its implementation until one year after the end of World War I.[3]

During the debates on Home Rule for Ireland, a supplementary 'Ulster Question' had arisen as a specific point of dispute. With its majority Protestant, Unionist population and industrial economy, the nine-county, Northern province of Ulster was an outlier in the predominantly Catholic, Nationalist, and economically agrarian island of Ireland (see Quekett, 1928; Lawrence, 1965; Hadfield, 1989). There was therefore concern at the prospect of coercing Ulster into a Home Rule governing arrangement that many of its people and, more significantly, its Unionist political representatives, did not want.[4] The 1914 Act did not include differentiated arrangements for Ulster,

---

[1] Up until 1800, Britain and Ireland had existed as separate states, albeit with a degree of interdependence. The earliest definitive record of a Parliament in Ireland is from 18 June 1264. Ireland had a functioning Parliament for over 500 years thereafter; this had various iterations, including: the General Assembly of the Confederation of Kilkenny (1642–1649), the 'Patriot Parliament' (1689–1782), and 'Grattan's Parliament' (1782–1800).

[2] Although often referred to in the singular, three acts were passed to achieve the same purpose: the *Union with Ireland Act 1800* c. 67 passed in Westminster; the *Act of Union (Ireland) 1800* c. 38 passed in Dublin; and *An Act for the Union of Great Britain and Ireland 1800* which was signed by both Parliaments.

[3] A *Government of Ireland Bill* was first introduced in 1186 and a second in 1893. The first was rejected by the House of Commons and the second by the House of Lords. By the time the third *Government of Ireland Bill* became law on 18 September 1914, the Lords' power of veto had been removed (by the *Parliament Act 1911*) and the World War I had begun.

[4] The first legislative initiative for the differentiation of Ulster came in the form of an amendment to the 1914 Act during its parliamentary stages. The Marquis of Crewe and Lord Privy Seal tabled an amendment which would have allowed for a poll to be held in any of the nine counties of Ulster if a tenth of the electorate requested as such with the proposed question—*Are you in favour / are you against the exclusion of your county from the operation of the Government of Ireland Act 1914 for a period of six years?* The amendment was rejected when the Bill returned to the Commons in July 1914 (see Hadfield, 1989: 26–7).

but during its parliamentary process, the government said they would 'hold themselves free to make changes [to the 1914 Act] if it becomes clear that special treatment must be provided for the Ulster counties' (*British Cabinet*, 1912 in Mansergh, 1936: 219). The means by which the need for 'special treatment' might become evident was, however, unstated—Ulster's Question remained unanswered.

At the same time as legislation to facilitate devolution was debated, defeated, revised, and agreed at Westminster, tensions were growing on the streets of Ireland. There was strong opposition to Home Rule among Unionists in Ulster who would have preferred direct rule to continue. Ten days after the 1914 Act received royal assent, 450,000 men and women in Belfast signed the 'Ulster Covenant' and 'Ulster Declaration' in which they (respectively) pledged to use 'all means which may be found necessary' to defeat the 'conspiracy to set up a Home Rule parliament in Ireland' (see *Public Records Office Northern Ireland*, 2021). Two years later, an attempted rebellion in Dublin—the 1916 'Easter Rising'—on the part of Irish Nationalists was met with a strong response from the British Government. Although the rising was supressed militarily, the violence compelled the government to revisit the 'Irish Question'. On 21 May 1916, British Prime Minister Herbert Asquith assigned Lloyd George the task of reaching a settlement between Unionists and Nationalists on the question of Home Rule.

Lloyd George held separate talks with Unionist MPs—Edward Carson and James Craig[5]—and Nationalist MPs—John Redmond, Joseph Devlin, and Thomas Power O'Connor[6]—on a proposal to bring forward the implementation of the 1914 Act except in the six counties of what is now Northern Ireland which would form an 'excluded area' and remain under the direct authority of Westminster (HM Government, 1916: 2).[7] The proposed exclusion was to apply for a set period with the possibility of extension and an inbuilt mechanism for review. It was, however, ambiguously drafted (Hadfield, 1989: 30).[8]

---

[5] Representing the Irish Unionist Party.
[6] Representing the Irish Parliamentary Party.
[7] In *Headings of a Settlement as to the Government of Ireland* the 'excluded area' was 'to consist of the six counties of Antrim, Armagh, Down, Fermanagh, Londonderry, and Tyrone, including the parliamentary boroughs of Belfast, Londonderry and Newry' (HM Government, 1916: para. 2). The same language was later used to define 'Northern Ireland' in the 1920 Government of Ireland Act (s1(1)); this remained the legal definition for Northern Ireland until the 1920 Act was repealed by the *Northern Ireland Act 1998* which offers no replacement definition.
[8] The disagreement centred on diverging interpretations of the intended duration and provisions for review. The *Headings for a Settlement* text stated that the 1914 Act would 'remain in force during the continuance of the war and a period of twelve months thereafter' with the proviso that 'if Parliament has not by that time made further and permanent provision for the government of Ireland, the period for which the [Act] is to remain in force is to be extended by Order in Council for such a time as may be necessary in order to enable Parliament to make such a provision' (HM Government, 1916: para. 14). The text also suggested that a 'permanent settlement for Ireland' would be considered at an 'Imperial

Disagreement over its intended duration—Nationalists perceiving it to be temporary and Unionists permanent—led to the breakdown of talks and the erosion of support for a political settlement through existing structures.

The British Government's response to the 1916 Rising—in particular the killing of prisoners convicted for their part in the rebellion—had bolstered support for the Nationalist movement in Ireland. After the failure on the part of Irish Parliamentary Party MPs to reach an acceptable compromise in negotiations with Lloyd George, the already growing support for their Republican political rivals—Sinn Féin—increased further. The 1918 general election was a Sinn Féin landslide. Despite winning 73 of the 105 parliamentary constituencies in Ireland the abstentionist party did not take their seats in Westminster. Instead, in January 1919, Sinn Féin set up a breakaway parliament—Dáil Éireann—and passed a declaration of independence which reaffirmed the declaration made during the 1916 Rising. A period of guerrilla warfare ensued—known as the War of Independence—between the British Forces and the Irish Republican Army. Legislative attempts to end the conflict were undertaken. In an effort to reconcile the desires of Irish Nationalists and the fears of Ulster Unionists, a revised plan for Home Rule passed in the form of the *Government of Ireland Act 1920*. The 1920 Act differed from its predecessors in one crucial respect—instead of one Parliament in Ireland there would to be two: the Parliament of Northern Ireland in Belfast and the Parliament of Southern Ireland in Dublin. The 1920 Act also set out the first iteration of 'the consent principle'. Under its terms, the two new Parliaments would exist indefinitely unless and until, 'by identical Acts agreed to by an absolute majority of members' in *both* the Northern Ireland Parliament *and* Southern Ireland Parliament, they decided to establish a 'Parliament for the whole of Ireland' (1920 Act: s3(1)). Such a requirement for concurrent consent to any change in the constitutional and legislative arrangements for, in particular, Northern Ireland reassured Unionists in Ulster who, reluctantly, accepted Home Rule on these terms.

The 1920 Act received royal assent on 23 December 1920. The new Parliament of Northern Ireland was officially opened on 22 June 1921 by King George V who spoke of his hope that this 'may prove to be the first step towards an end of strife' on the island of Ireland (see *BBC News*, 2021). Despite regal hopes, strife continued.

Conference' proposed to be held at the end of WWI (*ibid.* para. 15). For Unionists, the provisions were thought to enable an indefinite prolongation of the agreed arrangement—Home Rule excluding six Ulster counties—while for Nationalists, the provisions were thought to confirm the 'exclusion' of what became Northern Ireland as a temporary stopgap to be reviewed soon after the war.

After nearly three years of warfare, peace talks resulted in the 'Anglo-Irish Treaty' which was signed on 6 December 1921 by the British and Irish delegations led, respectively, by then British Prime Minister Lloyd George and Irish Secretary of State for Foreign Affairs, Arthur Griffith.[9] In the 1921 Treaty the British Government recognised the legitimacy of a nascent Irish Free State and granted it Dominion status in the British Empire (1921 Treaty: Sch 1). The status of the six Ulster counties had featured prominently in the negotiations. Irish Nationalists were passionately opposed to any partitioning of the island of Ireland and Lloyd George was sympathetic. The Prime Minister believed 'grave difficulties would be raised for both parts of Ireland if the jurisdiction over the reserved subjects were not conferred upon a common authority' (Lloyd George, 1921a) yet, resolved 'that there should be no coercion of Ulster'. Lloyd George instead sought 'to persuade Ulster to come into an All-Ireland Parliament' (1921b in *Hansard*); he was not successful.

Regarding Northern Ireland, the provisions of the 1921 Treaty set out a compromise. Article 1 of the Treaty granted 'Ireland' dominion status—the choice of language has since been termed a 'legal fiction' (see Hadfield, 1989: 34) because it reflected a belief, on the part of negotiators, that the 1921 Treaty could (or ought to) apply to the whole island of Ireland. Article 12 of the Treaty, however, provided the six counties of Northern Ireland—as defined by the 1920 Act—with an opt-out of the new arrangements for the governance of 'Ireland'—via an address requesting as much to His Majesty—within one month of its ratification. Two days after the statutory date of ratification, both Houses of the Parliament of Northern Ireland unanimously supported the exercise of the Article 12 opt-out; the six counties were thus excluded indefinitely and the (still new) Northern Ireland institutions were retained according to the terms of the 1920 Act.

Although perhaps not directly relevant to the constitutional development of Northern Ireland, it is important to recognise how divisive the 1921 Treaty was in the Irish Free State it created. Between June 1922 and May 1923 an Irish Civil War was fought between 'anti-Treaty' Irish Republican Army forces—who believed the Treaty to be a betrayal of the Irish Republic—and 'pro-Treaty' Provisional Government forces who—with the help of weapons supplied by the British Government—claimed the victory. From a Northern

---

[9] Signatories to the 1921 Treaty on the British side were: Prime Minister David Lloyd George, Lord Privy Seal Austen Chamberlain, Lord Chancellor Lord Birkenhead, Secretary of State for the Colonies Winston Churchill, Secretary of State for War Sir Laming Worthington-Evans, Attorney General Sir Gordon Hewart, and Chief Secretary for Ireland, Sir Hamar Greenwood; signatories on the Irish side were: Secretary of State for Foreign Affairs Arthur Griffith, Secretary of State for Finance Michael Collins, Secretary of State for Economic Affairs Robert Barton, and two other Sinn Féin TDs (MPs), Eamonn Duggan and George Gavan Duffy.

Ireland perspective, it is worth noting that internecine conflict, just south of its newly formed land border, was the backdrop for its first few years of existence.

2.1.2 An Accidental 'Mini-State': 1920–1972

The 1920 Act was not designed to be implemented in Northern Ireland alone. In its original form, the legislation had an all-Island logic. If it had been fully implemented, the 1920 Act would have established a Council of Ireland to allow for 'harmonious action . . . [and] the promotion of mutual intercourse and uniformity' between the two new legislatures in matters affecting the whole Island with 'a view to the eventual establishment of a Parliament for the whole of Ireland' (1920 Act s2(1)). As already discussed, (see 2.1.1), the 1920 Act also provided a route for the integration of the two legislatures it proposed to create on the basis of mutual and concurrent parliamentary consent (1920 Act, s3). In hindsight, the all-Island, integrationist design of the 1920 Act sits in tension with the effect of its partial implementation which was to augment partition and enable a novel regional administration in Northern Ireland to actively pursue divergence from their would-be counterparts in 'Southern Ireland', then the Irish Free State, then Éire, and later the Republic of Ireland. This tension between the original design and the historical effect of the 1920 Act is worth noting because it underlines the extent to which the governing arrangement introduced to Northern Ireland in 1921 arose more from incident than intent.

Under the 1920 Act, the UK Government retained supremacy over Northern Ireland (s6) and excepted powers in a stated list of areas that included matters of the Crown, the military, and foreign relations (s4).[10] Outside of explicitly excepted matters, the new legislature was given 'power to make laws for the peace, order and good government' of Northern Ireland (*ibid.*). In practice, competencies of the new bicameral Northern Ireland Parliament and Government included education policy, planning, local government, law and order, civil and criminal law, minor taxation, appointment of local magistrates and judges, and in health and social services. Executive powers were located in the Prime Minister for Northern Ireland—leader of the largest (invariably Unionist) party—who presided over a same-party Cabinet.

---

[10] The full list of areas under the 1920 Act included: the Crown and related matters (succession and property); the Lord Lieutenant; the making of peace and war; the military; treaties or any relations with foreign states; dignities or honours; treason; foreign trade; submarine cables; wireless telegraphy; arial navigation; lighthouses, buoys, or beacons; coinage, legal tender, and weights or measures; trademarks, copyright, and patent rights (see 1920 Act s4).

As originally enacted, the 1920 Act set up electoral systems to safeguard the minority Nationalist/Catholic community in Northern Ireland; these were, however, substantially revised in the first decade of devolved government. Before the 1920 Act passed in December of that year, local elections had been held across the island of Ireland in January and June under a single transferable vote (STV), proportionally representative, electoral system; the electoral outcomes yielded notable gains for Nationalist candidates in what became Northern Ireland.[11] It followed that one of the first significant actions of the new Unionist Northern Ireland Government was to bring in a *Local Government Bill* to change local government elections to a 'first-past-the-post' (FPTP) system, thereby securing Unionist majorities at local level. Introduced on 31 May 1922, the bill was unopposed in Stormont and completed its passage by 5 July, at which point it was forwarded to the Lord Lieutenant who—under the 1920 Act (s12)—wielded the power to grant or withhold royal assent to any bill passed by the new devolved legislature. Assent to the *Local Government Bill* was, initially, withheld due to British Government concerns, and those in the Irish Free State administration, that the proposed change would disenfranchise the Nationalist/Catholic community in Northern Ireland. After several months of (fierce) debate between Belfast, London, and Dublin, royal assent was granted. The Northern Ireland Government had threatened to resign if what became the *Local Government (Northern Ireland) Act 1923* did not pass (see Buckland, 1980; Hopkinson, 1990) and the British Government acquiesced. Throughout the next 50 years of devolved government, the Lord Lieutenant never again withheld royal assent to a bill passed by the Northern Ireland Parliament, which thus enjoyed considerable autonomy from Westminster. Some years after the 1923 Act, a similar change was made to the system for elections to the Northern Ireland Parliament. Initially, seats in the Northern Ireland Parliament were returned under a proportional representation system (as according to the 1920 Act s14(3)); this changed in 1929 when the Northern Ireland Government again exercised powers to alter 'the law relating to elections' (s14(5))[12] by passing the *House of Commons (Method of Voting and Redistribution of Seats) 1929* which changed what

---

[11] A PR system of single transferable vote for Irish local elections had been introduced in 1919 by the *Local Government (Ireland) Act 1919*. In the six counties of would-be Northern Ireland, Ulster Unionists returned 75 seats, Sinn Féin returned 28 seats, and Irish Nationalists returned 22 seats. Although Unionists retained a clear majority across the region, the strength of support for their Nationalist/Republican rivals unsettled the Unionist political establishment of the day (see *Department of Planning, Housing and Local Government*, 2020).

[12] Under section 24(5) of the 1920 Act the exercise of powers to amend 'law relating to elections' in either jurisdiction was not possible until three years after the first meeting of the Parliament of Southern or Northern Ireland.

was an STV electoral system to FPTP.[13] The effect of these changes to election laws in Northern Ireland soon after its creation was to enable indefinite rule by the Unionist, largely Protestant, majority often at the expense of the Nationalist, largely Catholic, minority. In the words of the first Prime Minister for Northern Ireland, this was 'a Protestant Parliament and Protestant State' (Craig, 1934: 1091–5).

Throughout the 50-year period of its existence, scrutiny of the Unionist Northern Ireland Government on the part of Westminster was almost non-existent. This arose from two conventions that developed early in the life of the new legislature. In 1923, the Speaker of the House of Commons ruled with regard to 'those subjects which have been delegated to the Government of Northern Ireland' any 'questions must be asked of Ministers in Northern Ireland, and not in this House [Westminster]' (*Hansard*, 3 May 1923: vol. 163, cc. 1625). Alongside this, by convention, Acts of the Westminster Parliament dealing with matters delegated to the Stormont Parliament did not extend to Northern Ireland without the express consent of the subordinate legislature; this was an early form of what is now referred to as the 'Sewel Convention'. The extent of powers granted under the 1920 Act, the early amendments to laws governing local and regional elections, and the conventions that developed in Westminster regarding devolved matters combined to give the Unionist Northern Ireland Government a degree of autonomy unprecedented in the history of UK devolution, before or since. In possession of a Prime Minister, a Cabinet, a Parliament and subject to almost no scrutiny from Westminster, Northern Ireland operated from 1920 to 1972 with all the trappings of 'a mini-state' (Hadfield, 1989: 88). Its status was without parallel in the British Commonwealth at the time, being neither a dominion nor a colony; Northern Ireland was an integral part of the United Kingdom yet had a separate legislature and executive that derived from, and operated in accordance with, one codified constitutional text: the 1920 Act.

2.1.3 'Temporary' Direct Rule: 1972–1998

Government in Northern Ireland continued in a state of relative stability under the terms of the 1920 Act until 1968 (see Lawrence, 1965; Hadfield, 1992). When a series of civil rights demonstrations, organised

---

[13] The 1929 Act also subdivided nine of the ten multiple-seat constituencies established by the 1920 Act thereby creating 48 single-seat constituencies; the only exception was the Queen's University constituency that stayed STV until it was abolished in 1969. For analysis, see Pringle (1980).

that year, led to clashes between largely Catholic/Nationalist demonstrators, largely Protestant/Unionist counterdemonstrators, and the Royal Ulster Constabulary (RUC) police force, the relative stability started to break down.

In view of violence and unrest that was catalysed by the civil rights movement, the Governor of Northern Ireland commissioned a parliamentary inquiry to look into the causes of the protests and reactions to them. The 'Cameron Commission Report' ('the 1969 Report') that followed found that a widespread 'sense of political and social grievance' had been 'long unadmitted' and therefore gone 'un-redressed' by successive Governments of Northern Ireland (Cameron, 1969: 6). The Report highlighted a 'rising sense of continuing injustice' among large sections of the Catholic population in Northern Ireland due to: the inadequacy of housing provision and (at least) perceived misuse of discretionary powers of allocation on the part of (perpetually) Unionist local authorities (*ibid.* para. 128–31; 139); discrimination against Catholic/Nationalist individuals in the making of local government appointments (*ibid.* para. 128; 138); deliberate manipulation of local government electoral boundaries with the aim of maintaining Unionist majorities (*ibid.* paras 133–7); resentment due to the existence of the partisan and paramilitary Ulster Special Constabulary (the 'B Specials') recruited exclusively from the Protestant/Unionist community (*ibid.* para. 145); alongside resentment, particularly in the Catholic/Nationalist community, about the continuance in force of the *Civil Authority (Special Powers) Act 1922* (Cameron, 1969: para. 144) that empowered the Minister of Home Affairs to 'take all such steps and issue all such orders as may be necessary for preserving the peace and maintaining order' in Northern Ireland including the (potential) imposition of curfews, use of internment and/or sanction of capital punishments. The findings of the Report, alongside further instances of sporadic civil unrest, led to greater involvement of the UK government in Northern Irish affairs.

On 14 August 1969, British Army troops were deployed to Northern Ireland in an effort to keep the peace, but the security situation continued to deteriorate. In 1970, the Provisional Irish Republican Army (IRA) began a bombing campaign in Belfast. In September 1971, the Reverend Ian Paisley announced the formation of the DUP, and the Ulster Defence Association (UDA) emerged as a coordinating body for several loyalist (paramilitary) bodies. On 9 August 1971, internment without trial was introduced under the Special Powers Act and subsequently used disproportionately against members of the Catholic/Nationalist community (see *Civil Authorities (Special*

Powers) 1971).[14] On 30 January 1972, the infamous killing of thirteen people in Derry/Londonderry by the First Parachute Regiment on 'Bloody Sunday' led to widespread disaffection and a campaign of civil disobedience by members of the Catholic/Nationalist community.

Throughout this time, relations between Stormont and Westminster were increasingly strained. To the ire of Northern Ireland's (Unionist) Government, talks between British Prime Minister Edward Heath and Irish Taoiseach Jack Lynch about the situation in Northern Ireland began in February 1972. Talks between British Prime Minister Heath and Northern Ireland Prime Minister Brian Faulkner followed in March 1972. The outcome of the latter was a UK Government insistence that all powers for law and order be removed from the Northern Ireland Government. Prime Minister Faulkner and his Cabinet responded with the threat of collective resignation. On 24 March 1972, a bill was introduced in Westminster to suspend the Parliament and Government of Northern Ireland after Faulkner and his colleagues had been forced to fulfil their threat.

The *Northern Ireland (Temporary Provisions) Act 1972* suspended the Northern Ireland institutions and vested its previously held powers in the newly created office of the Secretary of State for Northern Ireland which would be supported by the, also new, Northern Ireland Commission and Privy Council. As its title indicated, the 1972 Act provisions were not designed to last. In 1973, new arrangements for government were established under the *Northern Ireland Assembly Act 1973* and the *Northern Ireland Constitution Act 1973* (the '1973 Acts') which together abolished the suspended (under the 1972 Act) Parliament, established a new assembly to be elected by PR, provided for devolved government on the basis of power-sharing between Unionists and Nationalists, and made arrangements for North–South cooperation between the Northern Ireland Executive and the Irish Government if/when agreed.

The provisions of the 1973 Acts were controversial. Within a year of their ratification, Unionist reaction to the 'Irish dimension' of the proposed new governing architecture had brought an abrupt end to Northern Ireland's first experiment in power-sharing government.[15] Despite a compromise being reached on the 'Irish dimension' issue at cross-party talks

---

[14] Between August 1971 and December 1975 when internment was practised, 1,981 people were detained without trial, 1,874 of which were from the Catholic/Nationalist community and only 107 from the Protestant/Unionist community.

[15] For reasons of space, the events between May 1973 and May 1974 are not here covered in detail. For further analysis of the Sunningdale Agreement, see Gillespie (1998); for more detail on the Ulster Workers' Strike, see Aveyard (2014); and for an account of the relationship between Sunningdale and the 1998 Agreement, see Tonge (2000).

held in Sunningdale, England, in November 1973, grassroots Unionist and Loyalist opposition to the implementation of what became known as the Sunningdale Agreement (implemented in the 1973 Acts) withheld. Following a strong electoral result for Unionist candidates in the February 1974 UK general election, an umbrella Unionist/Loyalist organisation—the Ulster Workers Union—called a general strike in May 1974. The strike lasted two weeks. Food and electricity supplies were badly affected across Northern Ireland, instances of serious violence and bombings took place. On day fourteen of the strike, the resignation of the moderate Unionist leader of the new power-sharing government, Brian Faulkner, sparked a series of resignations which collapsed the Executive and thus, in effect, ended the first iteration of power-sharing devolution in Northern Ireland.

In the wake of the Executive collapse, the UK government brought in a system of 'interim' direct rule under the *Northern Ireland Act 1974*. Section 1 of the 1974 Act made provision for 'temporary' direct rule in an 'interim period' (s1(4)) until the next devolutionary scheme of government for Northern Ireland was agreed at the 'constitutional convention' established under section 2 of the 1974 Act. Elections to the constitutional convention took place in May 1975 but, in the context of escalating violence, its proceedings were marred by political divisions and abstentions. The conventions' summative report, laid before Parliament in November 1975, reflected the views and preferences of the powerful United Ulster Unionist Council. The report was rejected by the Secretary of State for Northern Ireland on the grounds that its proposals did not 'command sufficiently widespread acceptance' from all communities in Northern Ireland (Rees in *Hansard*, 1976). The constitutional convention was dissolved on 4 March 1976.

As failure to reach consensus for a new form of devolved government became a recurring theme, the 'direct rule' provisions in section 1 of the 1974 Act became the new normal. Under these provisions, legislation for Northern Ireland was passed by Order in Council for all matters previously reserved or transferred under the terms of the 1920 Act. In practice, therefore, under direct rule the majority of laws that applied in Northern Ireland were made in the form of delegated legislation via a procedure that did not allow for amendment, and which left almost no room for parliamentary scrutiny (see Hadfield, 1989: 130–5). Under these direct rule provisions, the power to determine the political direction of new legislation in Northern Ireland was vested in the Secretary of State for Northern Ireland and five junior British Government Ministers; scrutiny of their powers happened in Westminster on a limited basis and with almost no input from Northern Irish representatives.[16] This system of direct rule that had been justified by the UK Government on the basis of (granted) an exceptional circumstance and with the intention that it would not last yet thus became the blueprint for the governance of Northern Ireland for more than two decades.

2.1.4 Constructive 'Constitutional Ambiguity': 1998 present

In 1998, the circumstances in and constitutional arrangements of Northern Ireland changed. Following prolonged talks between previously warring parties, the Belfast 'Good Friday' Agreement, which was signed on 10 April 1998, heralded a new era of peace for Northern Ireland, one from which it has since progressed, albeit in a fragile manner.

As outlined in Chapter 1 (see 1.3) the signing of the 1998 Agreement brought an end to the decades-long conflict between communities with different national identities and opposing visions for Northern Ireland's constitutional future. In pursuit of peace, the 1998 Agreement relied on a 'constructively ambiguous'[17] compromise on issues of nationality and statehood by setting up interdependent and overlapping institutions providing for: devolved government in Northern Ireland (Strand One); cooperation between the two jurisdictions on the island of Ireland (Strand Two); and intergovernmental cooperation between Ireland and the UK, including its devolved administrations and Crown dependencies (Strand Three), all underpinned by rights-based guarantees and a unique provision for constitutional change conditional on popular consent. In the years since the 1998 Agreement was signed, Northern Ireland's political and constitutional development has been slow, stuttering, but steady.

The first elections to the newly established Northern Ireland Assembly were held on 25 June 1998 and its inaugural meeting took place on 1 July 1998, albeit in 'shadow' form until full powers were formally devolved on 2 December 1999. Since established, the 1998 Agreement Strand One institutions have proven vulnerable to collapse. Prior to 2016, the Northern Ireland

---

[16] There was no Select Committee on Northern Irish Affairs during direct rule; there existed a Northern Ireland (Standing) Committee which could choose to deliberate on any Northern Ireland matter; deliberation was its sole power. Otherwise, Northern Ireland received the same treatment as any other issue of government, being on a rota for Oral Questions supplemented by Written Questions if/when submitted.

[17] 'Constructive ambiguity' refers to 'the deliberate use of imprecise language in the drafting of an agreement on a sensitive issue' (Berridge and James, 2003: 51). The term is of particular relevance in peace negotiations and agreements wherein it can be used as a strategy to achieve consensus between opposing parties through constructive vagueness in the hope that this 'will encourage further and more substance steps towards an agreement' (Berridge and James, 2003: 51). For an account of constructive ambiguity in Northern Ireland, see Bell and Cavanaugh (1999).

Assembly had been suspended on four separate occasions following related collapses of the power-sharing Executive. Three of these suspensions were brief but the most significant lasted nearly five years. Strand One institutions were not fully operational between October 2002 and May 2007 after Unionist politicians had withdrawn from the Executive in protest following police raids on Sinn Féin offices as part of an investigation into allegations of intelligence gathering on behalf of the IRA by members of the party in Stormont Buildings.

The Northern Ireland devolved government was only re-established in 2007 when multi-party talks between political parties resulted in the signing of the St Andrews Agreement in October 2006. The St Andrews Agreement is the most significant of the numerous 'successor' agreements that build on the commitments and provisions of the 1998 Agreement because the revisions contained within it were sufficient to bring the DUP on board. Under the leadership of Ian Paisley Snr., the party has previously (and vociferously) opposed the 1998 Agreement; however, with the changes agreed in St Andrews, primarily regarding procedures for nominating First and deputy First Ministers, the DUP consented to the mandatory power-sharing structure of post-1998 government for the first time (for details and analysis, see Anthony, 2008). St Andrews also contained a commitment from Sinn Féin to support the Police Service of Northern Ireland (PSNI) and provided for a 'Transitional Assembly' to be established which began preparations for the return of devolution in advance of elections to a fully restored Assembly. Elections were held on 7 March 2007, and, for the first time, saw the DUP returned as the largest Unionist party and Sinn Féin as the largest Nationalist party; the two thus agreed to enter power-sharing government together under the respective leaderships of First Minister Ian Paisley and deputy First Minister Martin McGuinness.

Strand Two and Strand Three of the 1998 Agreement have been somewhat more resilient than Strand One. During periods of Assembly suspension, the work of the North–South Implementation Bodies, established under Strand Two, and the work of the East–West bodies, established under Strand Three, have continued, albeit on a slightly less regular basis during the 2002–2007 suspension. It is, however, also the case that the tripartite structure was designed to ensure that the nature and extent of (in)operation of any one strand impacts the nature and extent of (in)operation of the other two. The clearest demonstration of this inherent mutuality is between Strand One and Strand Two where the ministerial body of the latter—the North–South Ministerial Council—cannot meet if the ministerial body of the former—the Northern Ireland Executive—is not functioning; the NSMC was not operational during the five-year hiatus in devolution.

There have been various other 'successor' agreements that build on the provisions and principles of the 1998 Agreement. Three of these have been agreed since St Andrews and are worth briefly noting. The *Hillsborough Castle Agreement*, reached in February 2010, laid the ground for the devolution of justice and policing to the Northern Ireland institutions later that year (see Northern Ireland Office, 2010). The *Stormont House Agreement*, reached in December 2014 following inter-party talks chaired by US diplomat Richard Haas, made recommendations to deal with (contested) issues of flags, identity, culture, and tradition as well as setting out a process for the resolution of so-called legacy issues—meaning unsolved atrocities committed during the Troubles and compensation to victims and survivors of the same—and making some proposals regarding the Irish language (see Northern Ireland Office, 2014). Difficulty implementing aspects of the 2014 Stormont House Agreement led to more inter-party talks the following year which resulted in the conclusion of *A Fresh Start: the Stormont Agreement and Implementation Plan*, reached in November 2015, that addressed a range of issues including provisions for tackling paramilitarism alongside procedures for implementing its 2014 predecessor and some measures to deal with more 'normal' policy problems such as tax, welfare, and financial stability.

While much more could be said about the previous constitutional epochs in Northern Ireland and its development in the post-1998 era, the account presented so far provides enough historical background to begin to consider how the Northern Ireland case fitted (or did not fit) into broader narratives of UK constitutional history and constitutional arrangements prior to 2016 and why this is important for understanding the Brexit process. By way of conclusion, the final subsection of this chapter picks up the discussion from this point.

2.2 The Northern Ireland Blindspot in UK Constitutional Literature

Historically, analyses of the constitution of the UK concerned the 'English constitution' (see Bagehot, 1867; Freeman, 1873; Dicey, 1915); later work progressed to the more inclusive '[Great] British constitution' (see Greaves, 1938; Harvey and Bather, 1963; Jennings, 1971), but these generally excluded the 'special' case of Northern Ireland. From 1920 onwards, analysis of the 'Northern Ireland constitution' that underpinned its 1920–1972 devolved government was subject of a separate, specialist area of scholarship (see Quekett, 1928; Lawrence, 1965; Hadfield, 1989; 1992) and excluded from 'British' constitutional literature. Although it may seem superfluous to note divisions in antiquated literatures, this is an important legacy because there remains a clear trend in more recent literature on the UK constitution whereby the particularities of the Northern Ireland constitution and its constitutional history are excluded and/or subject to partial analysis. Take, for example, King (2009) who justifies the omission of Northern Ireland from his book, *The British Constitution*, on the premise that its politics and the constitution 'are oddly detached' from those of the rest of the UK and, to include 'a Northern Ireland dimension' would have 'greatly lengthened' and made the study 'incredibly complicated and indigestible' (ix). Characterisations of Northern Ireland as overly complex and difficult are not uncommon; Bogdanor (2007), for example, describes the UK as a 'multinational state comprising not one nation but four or three-and-a-half nations, however you call the Northern Irish'. The 'complex' case of Northern Ireland is often treated to minimal analysis. Norton's (2014) account of the development of UK devolution, for example, fleetingly refers to the 'other unique constitutional arrangements' that accompanied the creation of the Northern Ireland Executive and Assembly (260); Norton is, presumably, referring to everything in the 1998 Agreement outside of the section on Strand One, while also omitting its novel structure for mandatory power-sharing. On other occasions, Northern Ireland is excluded entirely from the analysis. Consider, for example, Loveland (2012) who describes the creation of Great Britain in the Act of Union 1707 but provides no equivalent description of the creation of the UK following the Act of Union 1801 (see 43); this otherwise comprehensive textbook on *Constitutional Law, Administrative Law and Human Rights* offers a full chapter on the 'Governance of Scotland and Wales' (421–42) but nothing on Northern Ireland. While not a comprehensive review, instances such as these are indicative of the prevalence of a blindspot in literature on the UK constitution when it comes to the complex and unique case of Northern Ireland.

As a consequence of the largely separate development of 1920–1972 literature on 'the Northern Ireland constitution' vis-à-vis the '[Great] British constitution', the particular position of Northern Ireland has rarely been considered in some of the central debates in UK constitutional scholarship that are relevant for analyses of Brexit's constitutional effects. The debate about the political and/or legal constitution of the UK is an important example.

Since an influential lecture on the 'The Political Constitution' of the UK by J. A. G. Griffith in 1979, constitutional scholars have debated, often sharply, the extent to which the UK constitution ought to be characterised as either 'political' or 'legal'. The concept of the political constitution rests on a recognition of the inherently political nature of law. For Griffith and his supporters, law is not and cannot be separate from politics because 'law is politics carried on by other means' (1979: 20). On this basis, political constitutionalists foreground political processes and institutions in their analysis of constitutions and constitutional change whereas legal constitutionalists foreground legal processes and legal institutions. While the political vs legal binary is somewhat artificial (see Kavanagh, 2019), the debate relates to our topic for several reasons. Notwithstanding some legal constitutional critics, following Griffith, the UK constitution is widely characterised as a political constitution because it is not codified in a legal text, has relied on gradual evolution rather than revolution, and is understood to centre on the principle of parliamentary sovereignty (see in particular Gee and Webber, 2010; Bellamy, 2007). Within this broad understanding of the UK constitution as a political constitution, the particular history of Northern Ireland is largely overlooked. The fact that from 1920 to 1972 the *Government of Ireland Act 1920* was, in effect, a codified constitution for Northern Ireland and described as such in dedicated literature (see Quekett, 1928; Lawrence, 1965; Hadfield, 1989; 1992) challenges orthodox narratives about the *political constitution* of the UK in history. Furthermore, the 'constitutional moment' that resulted in the 1998 Agreement (Harvey, 2012) conflicts with accounts of the 'pragmatic empiricist' (McCrudden, 2004: 193) evolutionary development of the UK political constitution (Bell, 2014). One of the aims of this research is to begin to address the Northern Ireland 'blindspot' in debates about the political (vs legal) UK constitution by drawing on political constitutionalist theory when analysing the impact of Brexit on post-1998 Northern Ireland.

Alongside a 'Northern Ireland blindspot' in academic debates on constitutional theory, depictions of the 'devolution settlement' and narratives of constitutional 'unsettlement' from the 1970s onwards have also tended to overlook and/or under-analyse Northern Ireland. As mentioned already in Chapter 1 (see 1.4), the innovative features of the 1998 Agreement— namely, the principle of consent and its quasi-confederal (Strand Two) and intergovernmental (Strand Three) institutions—sit uncomfortably with any conventional understanding of devolution (Campbell et al., 2003; Harvey, 2012). Yet, in academic and official government literature, the UK generally and Northern Ireland in particular are predominantly characterised as a devolved state and devolved administration respectively (see Elliott, 2015:

40; Hazell, 2000: 1; Cabinet Office, 2011: 8.13–8.16).[18] In prevailing narratives of constitutional development in the UK, scholars mark a substantive change from the 1970s onwards, citing the combined effect of joining the EEC (EU) in 1973 (via the *European Communities Act 1972*), the 'creation' of devolved administrations in 1998, and domestic incorporation of international human rights law (via the *Human Rights Act 1998*); it is argued that the 'Traditional British Constitution' has been transformed into one that is 'multi-layered' (Elliott, 2015: 39) and 'unsettled' (Walker, 2014: 2–4) due to its possessing a 'divided sovereignty' (Steyn in *R (Jackson)* 2005: 102). While not seeking to question the legitimacy of the academic consensus as regards the (relative) accuracy of prevailing characterisations of devolution, or the transformative significance of reforms introduced in 1972 and 1998, it is important for this analysis to emphasise the extent to which the constitutional particularities of Northern Ireland are overlooked in both cases. By subsuming the contemporary Northern Ireland constitution into a devolution 'straight-jacket' (Campbell et al., 2003: 317) and portraying the devolution of powers in 1998 as a wholly new chapter in UK constitutionalism rather than 'another step' (Tierney, 2013: 144) in a longer history that began with the *Government of Ireland Act 1920*, scholarly discourses on the constitution prior to the UK's EU Referendum in 2016 arguably had a blindspot in respect to Northern Ireland.

In addition to widespread omission of the empirical differences in the constitutional history of Northern Ireland, post-1998 analyses of the UK constitution have also tended to overlook or underplay the specific significance of the 1998 Agreement. As an international treaty, underpinned by the exercise of popular consent on the part of the citizenry of Northern Ireland and Ireland, the contents of which are largely transposed into one codified piece of 'constitutional' legislation (the 1998 Act, as per *Robinson*, 2002: 25), the 1998 Agreement presents a challenge to what is generally understood as '*the* fundamental principle' of the UK constitution, namely, parliamentary sovereignty (Gordon, 2019: 126 *emphasis in original*; see also Gordon, 2015; Goldsworthy, 2010). While the UK parliament retains sovereignty over the devolved institutions in Northern Ireland (see 1998 Act s5(6)), the origins of the 1998 Agreement, the 1998 Act, and the relationship between the two, sit awkwardly with the idea that the UK Parliament could 'unmake' either

---

[18] The Cabinet Manual (2011), for example, references the '1998 Belfast Multi-Party Agreement' but makes no mention of the principle of consent, Strand Two relations or institutions, or the inter-governmental dynamic of Strand Three (8.13–8.16). Elsewhere, the assessment by Hazell (2000) of the 'first year' of devolution in the United Kingdom inaccurately cites this as '1999–2000' without acknowledging the 50-year history of devolution in Northern Ireland from 1920 to 1972 (1).

(Dicey, 1985). This creates a rarely acknowledged tension between the codification of the majority of the 'constitutional laws of Northern Ireland' (as per *Interpretation Act (NI) 1954*: s7) in the 1998 Act with characterisations of the inherent adaptability of the political constitution of the UK, founded on parliamentary sovereignty, that prevail in the literature. In view of these omissions, and as the next chapter reiterates, by using a political constitutionalist approach to analyse the impact of Brexit on the UK constitution *in respect of Northern Ireland* this book contributes to an under-developed area in the literature. Before entering fully into the analysis, the next chapter contains some short but necessary notes on method, structure, and approach.

3
On Method and Approach

In considering the constitutional impact of Brexit on Northern Ireland, this analysis adopts a broad understanding of constitutions as a body of fundamental principles and established precedents according to which a polity is acknowledged to be governed. The process of Brexit is inherently constitutional in that it involves, and requires, making substantive changes to fundamental legal principles and established political precedents according to which the UK is governed. At an EU level, although the process does not require making any changes to EU Treaties, it was a precedent-setting process for EU internal governance, as the first use of the Article 50 of the Treaty on the European Union provision for a Member State to withdraw from the Union, and one that led to a new frontier in EU external relations between previous Member State, now third country, UK; analysing the impact of this constitutionally novel process through the lens of constitutional theory is *prima facie* justified.

The research undertaken was interdisciplinary. It drew on literature and approaches used in the disciplines of law and politics, and thereby contributes to ongoing debates about the nexus of the two 'worlds' of law and politics. The approach taken to analysing the impact of Brexit on the Northern Ireland constitution intersects with broad areas in political and legal theory and is reliant on several theoretical assumptions. These can be summarised as follows: that law is constructed, and its enforcement depends on the 'rule of recognition' by institutions and individuals who practice it (Hart, 2012 [1961]); that constitutions are changeable and constitutional law is shaped by, and reliant upon, the ongoing processes of politics (Griffith, 1979; 2001; Bellamy, 2007; Gee and Webber, 2010; King, 2001); that European integration is a constitutional process with domestic constitutional implications (de Búrca and Weiler, 2012; MacCormick, 1999; Walker, 2016); and that political language and rhetoric are powerful, contestable, and, therefore, worthy of study (Foucault, 1999 Finlayson, 2004; 2006; Barker, 2000; Rose, 1999; Aristotle, *Rhetoric*). Before setting out research definitions and an analytical framework, some of these foundational assumptions are explained in more detail with reference to relevant areas of scholarship.

3.1 Theoretical Assumptions

This analysis presupposes the understanding that law and politics are interdependent. This theoretical starting point aligns with a political constitutionalist (see 2.2) concept of the primacy of politics in the construction and practice of constitutional law (see Griffith, 1979; Bellamy, 2007; Gee and Webber, 2010). The assertion of political constitutionalism whereby law is neither separate from nor superior to politics but rather 'law is politics carried on by other means' (1979: 20) is apt for the study of the self-evidently legal *and* political process of Brexit. Additionally, and as outlined in the previous chapter, by conducting an interdisciplinary study of the impact of Brexit on the Northern Ireland constitution, the findings of this research contribute to an under-developed area in literature on the political and/or legal UK constitution *in respect to Northern Ireland*.

Grounded in political constitutionalism, this research also aligns with the definitional framework of King (2001) regarding the 'small-c constitutions' and 'capital-C Constitutions'. The former, King posits, are 'the set of the most important rules' regulating relations within government, and between the government and citizenry (*ibid.*: 1), with the latter being those same most important rules in written or codified form, developed in a particular place and time. As such, small-c constitutions and capital-C constitutions are always overlapping and interrelated, but the degree of overlap is unique to each country and era but 'is *never* total' (*ibid.*: 3, *emphasis in original*). While the distinction between small-c and capital-C constitutions therefore sits awkwardly with a binary understanding of legal vs political constitutionalism, it also provides a helpful basis on which to enter the debate as, following King, one can understand the codified, legal, capital-C constitution as dependent upon the uncodified, political, small-c constitution; the debate therefore becomes a question of degrees of overlap rather than an (artificial) question of either, or.[1] In view of the particularities of Northern Ireland's post-1998 constitution sitting uncomfortably with dominant accounts of 'the UK' political constitution (see 2.2), King's framework used in tandem with the political constitutionalist approach that it favours provides a sound theoretical basis for this analysis.

---

[1] In his work, King (2001: 4) distinguishes between written (Constitution) and unwritten (constitution); here, this is changed to codified and uncodified aspects of a given constitution as these are more accurate categories in the context of the contemporary constitution of the UK and Northern Ireland which, in both cases, do not have one coherent capital-C constitutional document; aspects of constitutional law exist in written form in various aspects of legislation.

In studying a process of constitutional change—Brexit—an understanding of the contingency of law, beyond the boundary of constitutional theory, on the 'ultimate rule of recognition' whereby a rules-based legal system depends on its own internal criterion of validity (Hart, 2012 [1961]: 110) is useful. In this respect, this book draws on the seminal work of Hart, *The Concept of Law*, wherein he argues that the central 'rule of recognition' that legitimates any law as a law exists only to the extent that it is practised, stating that all law depends on its recognition in the 'complex, but normally concordant practice of the courts, officials and private persons' (*ibid.*). In the UK context, using the language of Hart, the Supreme Court has expressly adhered to the view that the doctrine of the sovereignty of the Westminster Parliament is the ultimate rule of recognition for domestic law (in *Pham*, 2015: 80 and *Miller*, 2017: 60); the implications of such a view in and for the case of Northern Ireland facing Brexit are explored in detail in the empirical chapters of this book, most particularly in Chapter 5 (see 5.2).

By analysing the constitutional impact of formal *dis*integration from the EU, this research also relates to the (expansive) existing literature on the constitutional implications of EU integration, in particular to the idea of its 'pluralising' effect. As a political and legal entity, the EU has 'long defied easy categorization' either in the language of constitutional law or international organisations (de Búrca and Weiler, 2012: 3). While broad scholarly consensus can be found for the idea of the EU as an international community of states under law (or *rechstgemeinschaft*), the effect that EU membership does, or ought, to have on domestic constitutional arrangements is still a source of dissent. Related debates have given rise to the concept and language of 'constitutional pluralism' as a means of describing the existence of competing sources of normative authority—local, regional, national, and supranational—in EU Member States as a consequence of membership. Originating in the work of MacCormick and Walker, the central tenets of constitutional pluralism posit that by creating multiple sources for the development of laws—supranational and national—both with an independent claim to constitutional authority and which exist in a non-hierarchical relationship to each other, EU membership fundamentally disrupts the domestic constitutional orders of Member States (MacCormick, 1999; Walker, 2016). This idea of the 'pluralising' effect of EU membership is of important contextual relevance for this research because, *if* constitutional pluralism is an accurate description of the effects of EU membership, the process of UK withdrawal from the EU can be expected to expose divisions *within* the UK constitution that have resulted from over 40 years of 'pluralised' constitutional authority. In view of the research findings, Chapter 8 returns to the applicability or otherwise of the concept of constitutional pluralism to the case of Brexit and Northern Ireland.

3.2 Defining Terms

The central question of this research concerns the impact of Brexit on the constitution of Northern Ireland. Before setting out the method, these two key terms and the phenomena to which they relate ought to be defined.

3.2.1 Research Definition of Brexit

Arguably, 'Brexit' is a misnomer. Being short for 'Britain's exit from the EU', the connotation of the term excludes Northern Ireland. It is unlikely that the linguistic in-exactitude of the term 'Brexit' was intended. It is, however, significant, as an emblematic demonstration of a tendency to overlook or omit Northern Ireland in dominant popular and political discourses. Nonetheless, Brexit became the term of reference for the process by which the UK revoked its status as an EU Member State. Yet, in the fast-growing field of literature, there is often little space afforded to defining its precise meaning which is presumed to be self-evident. In the (in)famous words of Prime Minister May, 'Brexit means Brexit' (May, 2016). Although an interesting piece of rhetoric, May's epithet and the ubiquitous use of the term is not sufficient to operationalise Brexit for the purpose of systematic research (see Bruschi, 2017: 2219).

In this research, Brexit is used to refer to the events involved in the process of the UK's withdrawal from the EU, the legal and political texts that this process produced, and their legal, political, and societal consequences. Although often used as a singular noun, Brexit cannot be reduced to one moment or a single event but is rather a complex and multifaceted process, one with overlapping domestic and international aspects which resulted in a series of substantive political and legal changes in the domestic structure of the UK, the nature of UK–EU relations, and the status of the UK internationally. To study the effects of this complex, multifaceted process, it is useful to break it down into constituent elements. First, the UK's referendum on EU membership in June 2016, its origin, the substance of the campaign, and what its result demonstrated. Second, the UK Government's triggering of Article 50 of the TEU in March 2017, the process that led to this, and its consequences. Third, the UK–EU withdrawal negotiations that

Table 3.1 Constitutive Elements of 'Brexit'

Constitutive Brexit Element	Time Period	Associated Legal Text
UK's EU Referendum	JAN 2016–JUNE 2016	European Union Referendum Act 2015
Triggering of Article 50	JULY 2016–MAR 2017	European Union (Notification of Withdrawal) Act 2017
UK–EU Withdrawal Agreement	MAR 2017–JAN 2020	Agreement on the withdrawal of the United Kingdom of Great Britain and Northern Ireland from the European Union and the European Atomic Energy Community 2020
UK Implementing Legislation	MAR 2017–JAN 2020	European Union (Withdrawal) Act 2018; European Union (Withdrawal Agreement) Act 2020

resulted in the UK–EU Withdrawal Agreement, signed in 2019 and ratified in 2020. Fourth, the development of legislation to deal with the repatriation of law-making powers from the EU and the domestic implementation of any Withdrawal Agreement, including in particular the *European (Withdrawal) Act 2018* and the *European Union (Withdrawal Agreement) Act 2020*. Although not an exhaustive list of all involved in the process, these four elements correspond to key points of change in the overall process of change associated with Brexit; each one also corresponds to critical pieces of domestic or international legislation. For this reason, as evidenced in Table 3.1, these four elements can be used as the basis for an operational definition of Brexit and one that underpins this research.

3.2.2 Research Definition of the Northern Ireland Constitution

The 'Northern Ireland constitution' is made up of those constitutional norms that apply across the UK and those that relate specifically to Northern Ireland—this research is focused on the latter. Unlike the rest of the UK, the principal content of the constitution of Northern Ireland derives from a single document—the 1998 Agreement. Concluded on 10 April 1998 (Good Friday), the Agreement is the result of multi-party negotiations between the UK Government, Irish Government, and Northern Ireland political parties. Its provisions reflect an historic compromise between communities defined by their opposing visions for Northern Ireland's future—Nationalists who sought a united Ireland and Unionists committed to staying part of the UK.

As outlined in Chapter 1 (see 1.3), the 1998 Agreement has two parts—the Multi-Party Agreement (MPA) between political parties in Northern Ireland[2] and the British-Irish Agreement (BIA), an international treaty between the governments of the UK and Ireland who act as 'guarantors' to the Multi-Party Agreement. Underpinning the 1998 Agreement are a series of statements agreed by all parties as to the constitutional status of Northern Ireland, set out in the opening sections of both the Multi-Party Agreement and British-Irish Agreement. In both instances, signatories recognise that 'the present wish of the majority of the people of Northern Ireland' is to remain in the UK and that Northern Ireland's continued status as part of the UK 'reflects and relies upon that wish' (MPA, *Constitutional Issues* (CI) 1(iii); BIA, Article 1(iii)); the parties recognised 'that it is for the people of the island of Ireland alone ... to exercise their right of self-determination on the basis of consent ... to bring about a united Ireland, if that is their wish' (*ibid.* 1(ii); *ibid.* 1(ii)). The two guarantor governments also commit to introducing legislation necessary to support any future change in the constitutional status of Northern Ireland; to exercise any sovereign power held at any time in respect to Northern Ireland with 'rigorous impartiality' (*ibid.* 1(v); *ibid.* 1(v)); and to recognise the birthright of people in Northern Ireland 'to identify themselves and be accepted as Irish or British, or both' regardless of the constitutional status of Northern Ireland (*ibid.* 1(vi); *ibid.* 1(vi)). This series of commitments is generally referred to as the 'principle of consent', although there is some differentiation in how this principle is interpreted and applied.

For those who adopt a narrow interpretation of the principle of consent, the commitments set out in the first section of the Multi-Party Agreement and British-Irish Agreement relate only to the constitutional position of Northern Ireland within the UK and the possibility of that position changing to 'bring about a united Ireland' according to the procedure set out (MPA, CI 1(ii); BIA, Article 1(ii)). A narrow interpretation gives primacy to legal provisions for the exercise of consent rather than political commitments to it. For those who adopt a broad interpretation, the principle of consent applies to 'any change in the [constitutional] status of Northern Ireland' (*ibid.* 1(iii); *ibid.* 1(iii)). Moreover, proponents of the broad interpretation tend to see consent

---

[2] Eight political parties or groups signed the 1998 Agreement: on the Unionist side, the Ulster Unionist Party (UUP), the Progressive Unionist Party, and the Ulster Democratic Party (UDP); on the Nationalist side, the Social Democratic Labour Party (SDLP) and Sinn Féin; and the non-aligned Alliance Party and the Northern Ireland Women's Coalition. Only seven parties signed on 10 April 1998 as Sinn Féin only did so after the text was approved at an Ard Fheis (party conference) on 11 May, backed by 331 of 350 party delegates (see *Associated Press*, 1998).

as a multifaceted principle by linking the requirement for popular consent to any change in constitutional status to the requirement for cross-community consent on 'key decisions' in the power-sharing Northern Ireland Executive and Assembly, and to the so-called Sewel Convention whereby the UK government ought to obtain the consent of devolved institutions—including in Northern Ireland—prior to legislating in areas of devolved competence. A broad interpretation gives primacy to political commitments to the principle of consent rather than (merely) to legal provisions for its exercise. The tension between narrow and broad understandings of consent in the Northern Ireland context came to the fore at various points of the Brexit process; these are detailed in Chapters 5 to 7 and the tensions discussed again in Chapter 9.

Based on the principle of consent—broadly or narrowly understood—the 1998 Agreement sets out an innovative system of multi-levelled government for Northern Ireland, contained in the three strands of the Multi-Party Agreement. Strand One provides for democratic institutions in Northern Ireland, the Northern Ireland Assembly, and power-sharing Northern Ireland Executive; Strand Two provides for a North–South Ministerial Council (NSMC) and North–South Implementation Bodies; Strand Three provides for East–West institutions (a British Irish Council and British Irish Intergovernmental Conference). Most of the substance, particularly as it relates to institutions and rights, of the Multi-Party Agreement was transposed into UK law by the 1998 Act. The explicit purpose of the 1998 Act is 'to make provision for the government of Northern Ireland' (*Long Title*); as amended, the 1998 Act remains the primary statutory source of constitutional norms in Northern Ireland.

In accordance with the terms of the 1998 Agreement, the 1998 Act set out the rules of procedure for the newly established Northern Ireland Assembly and power-sharing Northern Ireland Executive, and the distribution of powers and responsibilities between the UK Parliament and Government in London and the new institutions in Belfast.[3] Certain areas of policy are 'excepted'—meaning the UK Government retains power in those areas indefinitely—or 'reserved'—meaning the UK Parliament and Government retains power in these areas unless and until there is agreement to add these to those already 'transferred' to the devolved government (see 1998 Act s4–6; Sch2; Sch3). The establishment of North–South institutions agreed under Strand Two of the 1998 Agreement and East–West institutions agreed

---

[3] The Assembly was created by s1 of the *Northern Ireland (Elections) Act 1998* which received royal assent on 7 May 1998, six months prior to the 1998 Act which contained the detailed rules for the functioning and competencies of the new institutions.

under Strand Three of the 1998 Agreement are provided for in Part V of the 1998 Act.

While the 1998 Act does not provide for those UK-wide constitutional norms applicable in Northern Ireland as a consequence of its position as a UK region, it does include all of those constitutional norms that are uniquely applicable in Northern Ireland. The 1998 Act has been judicially recognised, by Lord Bingham in the case of *Robinson* (2002), to be 'in effect a constitution' for Northern Ireland, the provisions of which should be 'interpreted generously and purposively, bearing in mind the values which the constitutional provisions [of the 1998 Act] are intended to embody' (11). Speaking in the same case, Lord Hoffman stated unequivocally, 'the 1998 Act is a constitution for Northern Ireland' (*ibid.*: 25) that exists in the context of the 1998 Agreement, meaning 'the Act must be construed against the background of […] the principles laid down by the Belfast Agreement for a new start' (*ibid.*: 33).[4] In view of the explicit aim of the 1998 Act and in keeping with the judicial recognition it has received, the substance of the Northern Ireland constitution is here taken to reside in the legal provisions and political principles dually enshrined in the 1998 Act and the 1998 Agreement, including the commitments and affirmations made by the UK and Irish governments in the British-Irish Agreement of 1998.[5]

3.3 Analytical Framework

Based on an understanding of Brexit as a complex, multifaceted process that can be broken down into four constitutive elements, and of the Northern Ireland constitution as deriving from provisions of the 1998 Agreement, as implemented in the 1998 Act, the intersection of Brexit and the constitution of Northern Ireland is visualised in Figure 3.1.

Each 'point of analysis' in Figure 3.1 represents one of the sub-questions of this research. In answering the overarching research question—what is the impact of Brexit on the constitution of Northern Ireland?—the particular

---

[4] A similar perspective on the 1998 Act was taken in case of *McComb* wherein Kerr J. held that the 1998 Agreement is important when interpreting and applying statutory provisions made under its aegis, such as the 1998 Act (*McComb* (2003: 31).

[5] The series of successor political agreements that have been signed since 1998 (see 2.1.4) resulted in changes to the 1998 Act to reflect new provisions as a result of the given successor agreement. Therefore, although not explicitly stated, the definition of the Northern Ireland constitution used here incorporates amendments made as a result of successor agreements including: the Weston Park Agreement (Northern Ireland Office and Department of Foreign Affairs, 2001), the St Andrew's Agreement (Northern Ireland Office, 2006), the Hillsborough Agreement (Northern Ireland Office, 2010), the Stormont House Agreement (Northern Ireland Office, 2014), and Fresh Start Agreement (Northern Ireland Office, 2015).

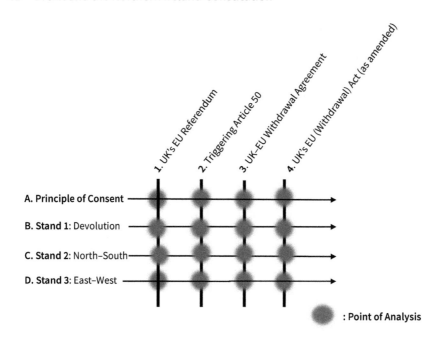

Figure 3.1 Analytical Framework

effect of political events and legal changes that occur in each of the constitutive elements (1) to (4) of Brexit, on each component of the constitution of Northern Ireland (reflected in the three strands of the 1998 Agreement and the principle of consent (A) to (D)) can be considered individually.

The structure of the empirical chapters of this book (5–8) corresponds to this analytical framework and the sub-questions it generates. Each of the four empirical chapters provides an account of the impact of the relevant constituent element of the Brexit process (1) to (4) on the Northern Ireland constitution; the internal structure of the empirical chapters follows that of the 1998 Agreement and 1998 Act with (A) to (D) being considered in turn. Content analysis of legal and political texts (including legislation, parliamentary debates, court judgments, and policy documents), produced by UK and EU institutions in each phase of Brexit, is the primary method used. Throughout the time period covered by each point of analysis (see Table 3.1), documents relating to the Brexit process, published by the UK Government and/or EU institutions have been systematically gathered. These key texts include UK Government command papers; UK primary and secondary legislation; UK parliamentary debates; European Commission notices/guidelines; European Council statements/decisions; European Parliament resolutions/debates. In addition, any relevant emerging case law relating to the process of UK withdrawal from the EU heard in domestic and/or European courts have been included in the bank of key documents gathered for time periods (1) to (4). Once gathered, the documents were closely analysed for direct references to the Northern Ireland constitution—the 1998 Agreement and 1998 Act—and/or its component parts (A) to (D), as well as indirect implications of the contents on the Northern Ireland constitution, as defined.

While analysis of 'black letter' legal change is a key aspect, the research also involved holistic analysis of the political context and political effect of the four constitutive elements of the Brexit process on the components of the Northern Ireland constitution (A) to (D). Therefore, alongside the systematic gathering and analysis of official UK/EU documents, the research findings incorporate analysis of the political rhetoric and statements of UK and EU politicians involved in the Brexit process. To achieve this, the texts of political speeches, press statements, and media reports of UK (including NI) and EU (including Irish) politicians directly involved in the Brexit process were systematically gathered during time periods (1) to (4) and analysed in the same manner as official 'black letter' texts. To aid this holistic analysis of legal change and political context, the data collection also involved a small number (four) of anonymous interviews carried out with officials directly involved in UK–EU negotiations—two from the UK side (with officials from the Department for Exiting the European Union) and two from the EU side (with officials from the European Commission). Where evidence from research interviews is included here, this is indicated explicitly.

Grounded on an understanding of Northern Ireland's history and its place in relevant literatures together with the theoretical assumptions and analytical framework just noted, Chapter 4 enters the Brexit-related fray with analysis of the impact of the first element of the process—the UK's EU referendum—on the components of the unique Northern Ireland constitution.

4
UK's EU Referendum

> 'We have the character of an island nation—independent, forthright, passionate in defence of our sovereignty. We can no more change this British sensibility than we can drain the English Channel.'
>
> **UK Prime Minister, David Cameron, 23 January 2013**[1]

In the 'Bloomberg Speech', Prime Minister David Cameron first committed to holding an 'in/out' referendum on the UK's EU membership. In that speech, the Prime Minister described the UK as 'an island nation' possessive of a 'British sensibility' that was limited only by the English Channel (2013). It was a depiction from which Northern Ireland was excluded. Using the singular definite article and referring only to the sea border that surrounds Great Britain, Cameron's language was indicative of how little consideration would be given Northern Ireland in the first element of the Brexit process—the UK's EU referendum.

Focusing on the first element of the complex and multifaceted Brexit process, this chapter sets out the impact of the UK's EU referendum on the constitution of Northern Ireland. There are three sections: the first gives an account of the process that led to the UK's EU referendum, the substance of the campaign and the result; the second sets out the impact of the UK's EU referendum on each component of the Northern Ireland constitution (see 3.3); and the third summarises the findings and their significance in the overall process of Brexit. Without giving too many spoilers, the key findings of this chapter can be summarised as follows: (1) the potential relevance of the principle of consent was not widely considered; (2) Northern Ireland was 'placed apart' in constructions of British identity and 'a place apart' in the politics of the referendum campaign; and (3) while Strand Two and Strand Three institutions were not engaged by the referendum, the campaign marked the beginning of a shift away from an established consensus-based approach on the part of the UK government and Irish government on issues pertaining to Northern Ireland.

---

[1] Cameron, D. (2013) 'EU Speech at Bloomberg' *gov.uk* Available: https://www.gov.uk/government/speeches/eu-speech-at-bloomberg (Accessed 4 February 2018).

4.1 UK's *EU (Referendum) Act 2015* and the Referendum Campaign

The pre-history of the UK's EU referendum can be told in two ways. For some, the vote was an unsuccessful attempt by Cameron to placate the Eurosceptic wing of his Conservative party and to mitigate against a growing electoral threat from UKIP (Craig, 2016; Rodgers, 2017; Bale, 2018). For others, the UK's EU referendum was the culmination of a longer tale of British exceptionalism in Europe and the majority Leave vote was the inevitable end of the 'awkward partner' role (George, 1996) the UK had played in the European integration project (see Nedergaard and Henriksen, 2018; Loughlin, 2018). The two kinds of explanation are not mutually exclusive, but they are both premised on events in Great British politics and history, and do not therefore give much credence to the position of Northern Ireland.

This first section of the chapter gives an account of the UK's EU referendum paying particular attention to the position of Northern Ireland in relation to UK-wide developments. What follows is not an exhaustive account but rather one that acts as a foundation for analysis of the impact of this element of Brexit on the Northern Ireland constitution.

4.1.1 The Story of the Referendum

The legislative path that led to the UK's EU referendum began with the *European Union Act 2011* (EUA 2011) An initiative of the Conservative–Liberal Democrat coalition government, the EUA 2011 prevented future UK governments from agreeing to any expansion of EU powers without first securing popular consent by referendum. At the 2010 general election, both the Conservatives and Liberal Democrats had committed to hold a referendum prior to any fundamental change in the relationship with the EU while Labour pledged to hold a vote before consenting to join the Eurozone (Conservative Party, 2010: 113; Liberal Democrats, 2010: 67; The Labour Party, 2010: 10:4). In Northern Ireland, only the UUP, who ran on a joint ticket with the Conservatives, mentioned a referendum in any circumstance (see UUP, 2010: 99).[2] That most Northern Irish parties did not set out a position on

---

[2] Like the Conservatives, the UUP manifesto committed to amending the 1972 ECA to include a 'referendum lock' to prevent the transfer of greater power to the EU without a referendum (2010: 99). The DUP manifesto stated their belief that 'too many powers have been ceded by our national Government to the European Union' and referenced a DUP attempt to secure a referendum on the Lisbon Treaty. However, the party did not make a clear statement or commitment to pursue a referendum on EU issues in future (2010: 65). Manifestos of the Alliance Party, Sinn Féin, and the SDLP did not make any reference to future

the prospect of a vote on EU membership in 2010 reflects the low political salience of Europe as an issue in Northern Irish politics as compared to [Great] British politics (see Murphy, 2014). Three months after the EUA 2011 became law, Cameron faced down a rebellion of 81 Tory MPs who defied a three-line whip to support a motion tabled by Tory MP David Nuttall that called for a referendum on the UK's EU membership by the end of May 2013 (see Sparrow, 2011). Although narrowly defeated, the extent of rebellion on the motion laid bare the enduring importance of the EU issue in Conservative party politics, notwithstanding the EUA 2011 'referendum lock'. Among the total of 111 MPs who voted for the motion and against the government, were eight sitting DUP MPs and Independent Unionist Lady Sylvia Hermon; however, the issue did not garner much attention in Northern Ireland politics at the time.

In July 2012, fulfilling another collective commitment, the coalition government launched a Balance of Competences Review (the Review) to audit the division of powers between the UK and EU (see HM Government, 2010: 19). The Review was intended to provide 'far better understanding' of UK–EU relations as a basis for future UK policies (Foreign and Commonwealth Office, 2012: 12). Ending in December 2014, the Review found that the balance of powers between the EU and the UK government was generally appropriate (see HL EU Committee, 2015; Stephens, 2013; Helm, 2015). Eurosceptics had hoped the Review's findings would provide 'ammunition' in a subsequent renegotiation of EU Treaties, but its conclusions were disappointing in this respect (see Craig, 2016: 8). This is likely why, despite praise for the 'ambitious' nature of the Review, there is little evidence its findings had any meaningful influence on government policy (HL EU Committee, 2015: 11; Craig, 2016). As a precursor to the UK's EU referendum, the Review is pertinent here because of what it did, or rather did not, say about Northern Ireland.

The significance of EU membership for Northern Ireland was noted in some Review reports (HM Government, 2014a)[3] but was not explored in any detail. A lack of interest from within Northern Ireland was a major contributing factor to the broad omission of the centrality of EU membership for Northern Ireland's post-1998 development in Review reports. In several key areas, the NI Executive had not contributed to the consultation and where

plebiscites on EU membership or the extent of EU powers and were all broadly pro-EU (see Alliance, 2010; Sinn Féin, 2010; SDLP, 2010).

[3] For example, the report on *Cohesion Policy* noted the importance of European Regional Development Funding, PEACE funding, and INTERREG funding for post-conflict development in Northern Ireland and the border counties of the Republic of Ireland (HM Government, 2014b: 28; 31; 42); the report on *Single Market: Free Movement of Goods* noted that the 'ability to move goods freely within the Single Market is "vital" to Northern Ireland' (HM Government, 2014c: 32) but did not elaborate any further.

submissions were made these tended to be short, narrow, and guided by immediate economic interest. The tone of contributions by Northern Ireland Ministers tended to be pro-EU, advocating for a continuation of the status quo or refinement of existing practices (see Hayward and Murphy, 2018). In hindsight, failure to recognise the importance of EU membership for Northern Ireland and, particularly, the extent of North–South cooperation on the island of Ireland in areas such as animal health and welfare, healthcare, fisheries, police and judicial cooperation and fundamental rights[4], paved the way for prolonged disagreements between the UK and EU27 in withdrawal negotiations.

As the Review continued, increasing pressure from Eurosceptics led Cameron to commit to holding an in/out referendum if his party won a majority at the next election (Cameron, 2013). After an unexpected Conservative victory in the 2015 general election, the reinstated Prime Minister wrote to the European Council outlining his government's request to renegotiate the UK's position in the EU in four areas or 'baskets': economic governance, competitiveness, sovereignty, and migration (The Prime Minister, 2015; European Council, 2015). At the same time, the UK Parliament approved the *European Union (Referendum) Act 2015* thus legislating for an in/out referendum before the end of 2016. After weeks of talks, mostly between the UK government and European Council President,[5] the European Council signed a legally binding agreement in February 2016 on a new settlement for the UK in the EU. The new settlement accommodated UK Government asks regarding protections for non-Eurozone member states (as a safeguard for the City of London and British business); an emergency break procedure authorising the UK to suspend freedom of movement when inward migration passed a critical threshold;[6] and an exemption from the EU's 'ever closer union' founding pledge (see European Council, 2016). The

---

[4] For example, the report on *Animal Health and Welfare and Food Safety* states the UK could take advantage of its 'island status' to operate higher health standards (HM Government, 2014d: 47), citing a previous example whereby the UK was granted a temporary derogation to continue to apply more stringent rabies vaccination requirements under the EU Pet Travel Scheme in 2003 'on the grounds of its rabies-free and island status' (*ibid.*: 24). In this example, the derogation was also granted to Ireland, alongside Malta and Sweden, see Article 6(1) of EC 998/2003 (*Official Journal* L146, 2003: 1), thereby allowing one standard to be applied in both jurisdictions on the island of Ireland. Cooperation on the island of Ireland, facilitated by EU law and regulation, is significant in the other areas mentioned—health, fisheries, police and judicial cooperation, and fundamental rights—but this was not reflected in the Review reports.

[5] The UK did attempt to negotiate directly with some Member States, Germany, and France in particular; however, discussions were primarily between the UK Government and the European Council President acting on behalf of the EU27. For a detailed account, see 'We Quit' by *BBC Two* (2019).

[6] There is no evidence that consideration was given in the renegotiation talks as to how the 'emergency brake' commitment to restrict EU citizens coming to the UK could or would be implemented on the island of Ireland. While, under the CTA, Irish citizens would not have been counted as EU migrants for the purposes of the 'emergency brake', how the entry of non-Irish EU citizens to the UK in respect of or via Northern Ireland would be monitored does not seem to have been considered.

terms of the new settlement were conditional on the UK deciding to remain in the EU and went quite far in sacrificing—in respect to the UK—some foundational EU principles to appease British requests (see Poptcheva and Eatcock, 2016). The deal was finalised, and 23 June set for the UK's EU referendum. The terms of the renegotiated new settlement were widely derided in the British press and hardly featured in the campaign that followed.

The referendum campaign was fractious and ill-tempered. Characterised by an unusually high level of public engagement in England, Scotland, and Wales, the campaign became a contest of competing narratives: vote Leave to 'Take Back Control' of British law-making, borders, and immigration, or vote Remain to avoid the economic harm of 'A Leap in the Dark' Brexit. In British politics, Labour, the Liberal Democrats, the SNP, the Green Party, and Plaid Cymru all supported Remain while UKIP supported Leave and the Conservative Party remained neutral. Labour and the Conservatives allowed MPs to campaign on either side of the issue, respective party positions notwithstanding; these decisions led to very public displays of intraparty divisions, particularly for the Conservatives. 'Britain Stronger in Europe', the official campaign for Remain, was fronted by Prime Minister Cameron and Chancellor George Osbourne while the official 'Vote Leave' campaign was led by Conservative former London Mayor (and future Prime Minister) Boris Johnson alongside party colleague Michael Gove and Labour MP Gisela Stuart. On both sides, the key messages were predominantly negative with Remain focusing on the likelihood of economic disaster in the event of UK withdrawal (see HM Government, 2016a; 2016b; Cameron, 2016; Hague in Elgot, 2016), while advocates for Leave mobilised voters' fears about immigration (see Gove and Raab, 2016; *BBC News*, 2016a; Ker-Lindsay, 2016). The result was an acrimonious, divisive campaign with the Remain—or IN—campaign dubbed 'Project Fear' and the Leave—or OUT—campaign regarded as 'Project Hate' (see Buckledee, 2018).

After weeks of political rancour, the UK public went to the polls. Defying most expectations, Leave received 51.9% and 17,410742 votes to the 48.1% and 16,141,241 votes received by Remain. The results revealed a divided nation. Scotland and Northern Ireland voted in favour of Remain by 62% and 55.8% respectively while England (including Gibraltar)[7] and Wales voted in favour of Leave by 53.4% and 52.5% respectively. Subsequent analysis of the vote in Great Britain also showed strong demographic divides with older

---

[7] The provisions of the *EU (Referendum) Act (EURA) 2015* extended to Gibraltar (s12) which, for the purpose of counting votes, was included in the 'South West' region of England (Sch 3 (5)(1)). Gibraltar voted overwhelmingly in favour of staying in the EU with 95.9% voting for Remain, 4.1% for Leave based on a turnout of 83.5%.

individuals on lower incomes, fewer educational qualifications, and who express concerns about immigration being more likely to vote leave than younger voters with higher incomes and educational qualifications (see Hobolt, 2016; Swales, 2016). As the value of sterling fell to a 31-year low against the dollar, Cameron announced his resignation on 24 June having lost the argument of his premiership. A fierce battle to become the new Conservative leader and next Prime Minister was triggered, from which former Home Secretary Theresa May emerged victorious, leading to events and consequences covered in subsequent chapters.

4.1.2 The Referendum Result in Northern Ireland

In Great Britain, the UK's EU referendum exposed political and social divisions that had received little previous attention; in Northern Ireland, it revealed and reaffirmed political divisions that had long defined the place and its politics.

Largely, voters in Northern Ireland heeded the cues of their respective political leaders on the referendum issue. Subsequent research found 89% of those who described themselves as Nationalist supported Remain, while only 35% of those who described themselves as Unionist had done the same; among those who identify as 'neither', 70% had supported Remain (Coakley and Garry, 2016; see also Garry, 2016).[8] A similar pattern was evident in overlapping areas of traditional division with 88% of those who consider themselves Irish supporting Remain, but only 38% of those who consider themselves British doing the same; while 85% of Catholics had supported Remain but just 41% of Protestants had done so (Garry and Coakley, 2016; Garry, 2016). The UK's EU referendum result, therefore, had a strong ethnonationalist quality and the campaign had reinforced traditional political fractures in Northern Ireland's 'deeply divided' society (Gormley-Heenan et al., 2017; Murphy, 2018).

Traditional divisions notwithstanding, a simplistic Nationalist–Unionist reading of the referendum result in Northern Ireland is unconvincing. Voting patterns showed splits among Unionist voters and some evidence

---

[8] According to the NILT survey, people who identify as *neither* Unionists *nor* Nationalists have formed the largest portion of the society since 2006 (see NILT, 2020). This demographic trend is significant given the constitutional weight granted cross-community, power-sharing governance premised on a binary understanding of a society divided between Unionist and Nationalist blocs, which, increasingly, does not reflect reality (see Hayward and McManus, 2018; Hayward and Rosher, 2020). From this point forward, 'Neither' is used to refer to those who do not identify as Unionists or Nationalists when asked to indicate political identity.

of the same divisions as were apparent in Great Britain, with those 'left behind' by globalisation being more likely to support Leave.[9] Individuals with higher levels of education and household income in Northern Ireland were more likely to vote Remain than those on lower incomes and with fewer educational qualifications (Garry and Coakley, 2016). There was also a strong geographic divide to the result in Northern Ireland as the seven constituencies with Leave majorities were clustered in the north-east of the region, all of which were represented by Unionist MPs, six DUP and one UUP (EONI, 2021). More significantly, five of the eleven constituencies with Remain majorities were represented by Unionist MPs in 2016 including three DUP, one UUP, and one Independent Unionist. This indicated that Unionist voters, in line with their political representatives, were more divided than Nationalist voters on the referendum question. The geographic clustering of the Leave–Remain divide in Northern Ireland also meant that no border constituency voted in favour of Leave, a fact which would become significant later in the Brexit process.

Overall, the UK's EU referendum result in Northern Ireland predominantly reflected its traditional ethno-nationalist political divide; however, the campaign and question had also had a cross-cutting effect in Northern Ireland politics. This matters for the constitution in Northern Ireland because the provisions of the 1998 Agreement and the 1998 Act are premised on the assumption of a 'deeply divided' society split on a Nationalist vs Unionist political binary. *If* the cross-cutting effect evident in the referendum result endured, a new political axis of Leave vs Remain could have emerged in Northern Ireland; this would have in turn raised questions about the longevity of the cross-community dimension of the post-1998 constitution; this hypothetical is considered again in later chapters. For now, we turn to the more immediate impacts of the referendum on the four components of the Northern Ireland constitution.

4.2 UK's EU Referendum and the Northern Ireland Constitution

The UK's EU referendum outcome was not legally binding. Prior to the vote, Cameron had made a strong commitment to implement the outcome which

---

[9] Proponents of the 'left behind' thesis argued that individuals who supported Leave were more likely to be in low socioeconomic groups and to have little or no educational qualifications (see McKenzie, 2017; Watson, 2017; Goodwin and Heath, 2016). Assessment of the intergenerational differences in voting behaviour also quickly emerged in analyses of the referendum result which indicated older voters were more likely to vote Leave than younger voters (See *Ipsos MORI*, 2016; Swales, 2016; Dorling et al., 2016). As stated at the beginning of the chapter, data from Northern Ireland was not included in much of this analysis.

led many to judge the result to be politically binding. The non-*legally* binding nature of the referendum did however mean that, notwithstanding legislation required to facilitate it, this first element of the Brexit process was ostensibly political. Its immediate impacts, therefore, were also political rather than legal. That said, although the UK's EU referendum did not change the legal substance of Northern Ireland's constitution, as defined, it did spark several changes in the politics of the region and highlighted its unique position within the UK.

4.2.1 Principle of Consent

The principle of consent was barely mentioned during the UK's EU referendum campaign. An attempt in March 2016 on the part of then Sinn Féin leader and deputy First Minister, Martin McGuinness to secure a referendum on Irish unity in the event of a Leave vote went largely unnoticed and was not pursued (*Irish Times*, 2016). In regard to constitutional implications of the vote, campaigners for 'Britain Stronger In Europe' tended to focus on the possible separatist threat of Scottish Nationalists without mentioning their Northern Irish equivalents.

No official response was given to the deputy First Minister's request that the UK Government commit to a referendum on a united Ireland in the event of a Leave majority (*Irish Times*, 2015).[10] UUP leader Mike Nesbitt rejected, however, McGuinness's position by arguing that the Secretary of State for Northern Ireland would have 'no basis' to call an Irish unity referendum under the 1998 Agreement or 1998 Act (*ibid.*). The deputy First Minister's public call was not repeated in Sinn Féin's Assembly election manifesto wherein the party pledged to campaign against Brexit but made no explicit link to an Irish Unity referendum (Sinn Féin, 2016: 17). In the aftermath of the UK's EU referendum, and in view of the majority Remain vote in Northern Ireland, McGuinness restated his argument that there was now a 'democratic imperative for a border poll' to avoid 'the North [being] dragged out [of the EU] on the tails of a vote in England' (*Belfast Telegraph*, 2016a). Again, no official UK Government response was given.

The requirement for cross-community consent on contentious issues under the terms of the 1998 Agreement (MPA, S1: 5(d)(i) and 1998 Act

---

[10] Full statement of the deputy First Minister: 'If Britain votes to leave the European Union, then that could have huge implications for the entire island of Ireland and given all the predictions, would run counter to the democratic wishes of the Irish people. If there was a vote to leave the EU, there is a democratic imperative to provide Irish citizens with the right to vote in a border poll to end partition and retain a role in the EU. I have proposed to Theresa Villiers that, given the enormous significance of these issues, the British government now give a firm commitment to an immediate border poll in the event Britain votes to leave the European Union' (in *Irish Times*, 2015).

s4(5)(a)–(b)) was not raised by any party during the campaign. Only in Scotland did the question of legislative consent receive any substantial attention prior to the referendum. In 2015, the SNP pledged to amend any legislation to hold a referendum on EU membership to 'ensure that no constituent part of the UK can be taken out of the EU against its will' (SNP, 2015: 9). An unsuccessful attempt was duly made during the committee stage of the *European Union Referendum Bill* in 2015 to add a 'double majority' clause that would have required a total majority across the UK and a majority in each of its four constituent parts before an overall majority could be declared (see HC, 2015a, clause 1). Eight SNP MPs and one Plaid Cymru MP tabled the amendment which was rejected without division (HC, 2015b; *BBC News*, 2015). Throughout the passage of the Bill, the government made clear that it did not require the legislative consent of devolved administrations under the Sewel Convention (see HC, 2015c: 2).[11] At their first meeting following the 2015 general election, the Prime Minister had rejected the request of Scottish First Minister Nicola Sturgeon to include a 'double majority' threshold in the 2015 Act by emphasising the reserved nature of foreign policy issues (see *Scottish Legal News*, 2015). Questioned afterward about the Conservative Party policy to repeal the Human Rights Act (HRA), the Prime Minister remarked that there would 'have to be talks between Westminster and the Scottish and Welsh assemblies about how this would work', apparently forgetting to mention the Northern Irish equivalent (cited in Bussey and Stone, 2015). This omission was particularly notable given the rights-based nature of the 1998 Agreement and the fact the 1998 Act is underpinned by UK rights law, including the HRA (1998 Agreement, MPA, S1: 1; 1998 Act, Sch. 7(1)(b); McCrudden, 2017).

Overall, the constitutional principle of consent played an exceptionally minor part in the first stage of the Brexit drama. Notwithstanding the efforts of the SNP and McGuinness's remarks, the language of the UK Government at the time made clear that little or no consideration was given to the potential constitutional implications in regard to consent of a majority Leave vote for Northern Ireland. Moreover, in a reversal of the norm, the campaign in Northern Ireland focused more on policy impacts of EU membership than on matters of a constitutional or nationally existential nature. As a consequence, the principle of consent did not feature prominently in referendum-related political or public debate, even in Northern Ireland.

---

[11] Paragraph 6 of the Explanatory Notes for *EU (Referendum) Bill* as introduced on 28 May 2015 stated: 'The Bill does not contain any provision which gives rise to the need for a legislative consent motion in the Scottish Parliament, the National Assembly for Wales or the Northern Ireland Assembly' (HC, 2015c: 2).

4.2.2 Devolved Government

The UK's EU referendum revealed the extent to which Northern Ireland differed from Great Britain on the political issue of the day. This distinctiveness of Northern Ireland had an internal and external aspect: on one hand, Northern Ireland was 'placed apart' in narratives of Britishness and British history promoted during campaign and in the conduct of the referendum which was managed separately in Northern Ireland; and, on the other, Northern Ireland was 'a place apart' in regard to the nature of the campaign and the result. Although relatively short-lived, Northern Ireland's distinctiveness in the UK's EU referendum campaign set a trajectory for the rest of the Brexit process.

4.2.2.1 Northern Ireland: Placed Apart

Northern Ireland was often excluded in the language of the referendum campaign. Leading campaigners on both sides of the Leave–Remain divide pitched the vote in nationally existential terms with appeals to various ideas of Britishness being used across the spectrum. However, the rhetorical construction of British identity and British exceptionalism tended not to include the particular position or history of Northern Ireland. For example, Vote Leave campaigner and then Secretary of State for Justice Michael Gove MP described how 'we established trial by jury in the modern world, we set up the first free parliament, we ensured no-one could be arbitrarily detained at the behest of the Government' (Gove, 2016). While not discounting the veracity of the sentiment, the narrative projected by Gove does not allow for the Northern Ireland experience of internment without trial during the 'Troubles' or the continued use of the 'Diplock Court' procedure in certain legal cases. In an example of exclusion by omission, during a televised debate on the referendum, the Prime Minister warned that a majority Leave vote would strengthen the cause of Scottish Nationalists, leading to the 'break-up' of the country; Cameron made no mention of Northern Ireland or Irish Nationalists during his remarks (in Carrell, 2016). Similarly, after quoting Leave campaign slogan 'give us our country back', previous Prime Minister and Remain campaigner John Major asked the rhetorical question: '… what country, exactly will we "get back"? Will Scotland remain part of the UK?'. Continuing, Major outlined the 'threat' posed by a Leave vote as Scotland could demand another independence referendum: 'The UK out of the EU and Scotland out of the UK would be a truly awful outcome' (Major, 2016). Here again, the possibility that a Leave vote may also strengthen Northern Irish Nationalists' calls for constitutional change did not feature. Although Major was among the few UK politicians to highlight the precarity of Northern

Ireland facing Brexit, in concluding one of his Remain campaign speeches Major presented the UK's EU referendum as a 'fateful choice' between 'Great Britain or Little Britain' (*ibid.*), explicitly, whether intentional or otherwise, excluding Northern Ireland.

In government literature prior to the campaign, Northern Ireland tended to be characterised as a place apart. A UK Government paper published in February 2016 on the process for withdrawal stated that in the event of a Leave majority, 'Northern Ireland would be confronted with difficult issues about the relationship with Ireland' (HM Government, 2016a: 19). The anticipated difficulties in North–South relations on the island of Ireland that would arise from the UK leaving the EU were framed here as an issue for Northern Ireland, not the UK. The paper went on to say it would 'be necessary to impose customs checks on the movement of goods' across the land border and 'questions would also need to be answered' about the Common Travel Area (CTA) 'which covers the movement of people' (HM Government, 2016a: 19). Leaving aside the sparse description of the CTA, the government's framing of the issue creates some ambiguity in the language about whose responsibility it would be to impose customs checks or answer the questions raised. The issue of customs was raised again in a report on alternatives to EU membership wherein the government recognised that 'there are no customs controls on the border between Ireland and Northern Ireland' (HM Government, 2016b: 101) as a consequence of joint EU membership; again this paper implied the issue was one 'for Northern Ireland' to confront and overcome (*ibid.*: 100). In general, efforts by the UK Government to highlight the vulnerability of Northern Ireland during the referendum campaign were infrequent, lacked detail, and tended to portray Northern Ireland as a place apart. By framing Northern Ireland in this way government literature (perhaps inadvertently) implied that problems raised by a Leave majority for Northern Ireland would need to be solved within the region.

Towards the end of the referendum campaign, 'Britain Stronger in Europe' did attempt to underline the unique political, economic, and constitutional exposure of Northern Ireland to the prospect of the UK leaving the EU. These endeavours occurred late and received little attention. A joint speech delivered by Major and his Labour successor as Prime Minister, Tony Blair, during a visit to Northern Ireland warned that a vote to leave would 'jeopardise the unity' of the UK and risk 'destabilising the complicated and multi-layered constitutional settlement' in Northern Ireland (*BBC News*, 2016b). A similar intervention from former United States President Bill Clinton stated his concern that Northern Ireland 'will really get whacked' if 'Britain' [*sic*] withdraws from the EU (in *Belfast Telegraph*, 2016b). Speaking during a visit to the Irish border in the final weeks of the referendum campaign, Chancellor George Osbourne warned there 'would have to be a hardening of the border imposed' in the event of a Leave majority (*BBC News*, 2016c). These efforts were contested by vocally pro-Leave Secretary of State for Northern Ireland Theresa Villiers and her predecessor Owen Paterson as well as by the pro-Leave DUP (see Villiers, 2016a; 2016b; Paterson in Crace, 2016). In the context of the broader political drama, any attempt to raise the issue of Northern Ireland received scant attention or media coverage. Indeed, subsequent accounts from insiders and close observers of the various Leave and Remain campaigns made clear that Northern Ireland was an 'afterthought' when considered at all by architects on either side of the national UK debate (O'Toole, 2017; also, Oliver, 2016; Banks, 2016). The veracity of insider testimonies is arguably evident in the exclusive language and literature of the campaign, and the lateness of attempts to highlight Northern Ireland's multifaceted vulnerability.

Northern Ireland was treated differently in the implementation of the referendum. Under the terms of the EURA 2015 Act, it was a single voting area, distinct from the eleven electoral regions of Great Britain and Gibraltar (included in the South West). The referendum in Northern Ireland was therefore overseen by the Chief Electoral Officer for Northern Ireland and run separately to that conducted by the Chief Counting Officer for the UK Electoral Commission (Electoral Commission, 2016; see also the European Union Referendum Act 2015 Act s11(2)(h)). While this differentiation is not unusual—the Chief Electoral Officer for Northern Ireland normally oversees elections in Northern Ireland—in their report on the implementation of the referendum, the Electoral Commission recommended that Northern Ireland be included as a UK electoral region in any future national referendum as, they argued, this would provide 'greater clarity' and 'better alignment with arrangements in the rest of the UK' (2016: 8; 12). Responding to the Electoral Commission's recommendations at the time, the government said they would 'consider whether any changes should be made to the framework for delivering referendums in Northern Ireland' after noting it had been 'considered unnecessary' to appoint the Chief Electoral Officer of Northern Ireland as a Regional Counting Officer to facilitate inclusion in the GB/Gibraltar-wide operation run by the Chief Counting Officer of the UK Electoral Commission (Cabinet Office, 2017: 4.1, 4.2). Although a technical point, different treatment in the administration of the UK's EU referendum serves to underline the point that Northern Ireland is often excluded, overlooked, and 'placed apart' in central government initiatives.

4.2.2.2 Northern Ireland: A Place Apart

Europe has never been as salient an issue in Northern Ireland as it has been in Great Britain. Prior to the 2016 referendum, political debates on the issue were muted and lacklustre in Northern Ireland compared to those in the rest of the UK (Houston in NIAC, 2016a; McGowa in NIAC, 2016b). A traditional lack of engagement with Europe as a political issue was also exacerbated by political distraction. Held in the aftermath of UK regional elections, including to the Northern Ireland Assembly,[12] the UK's EU referendum took place as a recently formed Executive were still in the process of confirming a Programme for Government (PfG). In contrast to the Scottish Parliament and Welsh Assembly, the requirements of devolution in Northern Ireland under the 1998 Agreement—power-sharing government by a cross-community, cross-party consociational executive—mean that it takes longer for a new cohort to establish normal government functions post-election or to reach agreement on divisive issues; the UK's EU referendum was one such issue. Following the 2016 Assembly elections, for the first time, eligible parties in Northern Ireland could opt not to enter government and to instead form an official opposition.[13] In what ought to be understood as a sign of the 'normalisation' of politics in post-conflict Northern Ireland, three parties—the UUP, SDLP, and Alliance—choose to take the pioneering step of not entering the power-sharing Executive. The Assembly election campaign had, moreover, been 'relatively good natured' (*BBCMarkSimpson*, 2016), unusually focused on 'non-traditional' issues regarding the economy and social policies, and also featured some convergence between the pledges of the DUP and Sinn Féin, the two parties expected to led the Executive, notwithstanding their longstanding divergence on 'traditional' issues of national identity and constitutional futures.[14] Although often overshadowed in analyses of subsequent events related to the Brexit process, it is important to underline the seemingly progressive political trajectory Northern Ireland was on prior to the referendum in 2016 (see Pow and Matthews, 2017). The 2016 Assembly campaign and result suggested that Northern Ireland was moving away from

---

[12] Elections to the Scottish Parliament, Welsh Assembly, Northern Ireland Assembly, 124 local councils, and four mayoral elections in England were held in May 2016.

[13] The provision for the formation of a potential opposition followed from the Fresh Start Agreement (2015: 59) and was implemented via the *Assembly and Executive Reform (Assembly Opposition) Act (Northern Ireland) 2016*.

[14] By way of illustration, both the DUP and Sinn Féin pledged to create 50,000 new jobs and invest and extra £1billion in healthcare in their respective party manifestos (see DUP, 2016; Sinn Féin, 2016); meanwhile the UUP campaign centred on educational reforms (UUP, 2016); the SDLP's flagship policy was to give £500 to newborn children in an effort to mitigate high levels of childhood poverty (SDLP, 2016), and the Alliance campaign focused on redirecting public money from policies that maintain sectarian divisions and towards (shared) frontline services (Alliance, 2016). For more comprehensive analysis of the Assembly 2016 election and its significance, see Pow and Matthews (2017).

a politics *necessarily* dominated by its conflicted past, and institutions orientated *entirely* towards safeguarding against divisions between Nationalists and Unionists. Any such progress, however, proved too fragile to withstand Brexit-related challenges to come.

The new Northern Ireland Executive did not take a position on the referendum and appeared unwilling to do so. In their draft PfG document, the First and deputy First Ministers explicitly noted their parties' 'different positions' on the referendum (Northern Ireland Executive, 2016b: 4). The content of the PfG appeared blind to the possibility of a majority Leave vote with reference to the pursuit and use of EU funding, EU legislation, and the European Commission's Trans-European Transport Network for Northern Ireland; it included no specific policy on the referendum. When asked about the upcoming referendum, deputy First Minister Martin McGuinness responded: 'I do not know what the outcome will be … there are so many unknowns about what will happen on the other side of the referendum … we will have to deal with them, whatever they are' (*Northern Ireland Assembly*, 2016a). Similar evasive responses emanated from the other side of the Executive table; DUP Minister for Finance and Personnel Mervyn Storey responded to a question regarding the future of EU peace funding in the event of a majority Leave vote by stating '… that is a debate, I believe, for when we know the outcome of the referendum' (*Northern Ireland Assembly*, 2016b). Indeed, there is no formal record to suggest that the Executive discussed the referendum at all in the lead-up to the vote; it was, however, a different story in party politics. Northern Ireland parties made their views on the referendum clear and campaigned accordingly but did so in a comparatively dispassionate manner vis-à-vis parties in Great Britain.

Northern Ireland parties' perspectives on the UK's EU referendum occurred on a spectrum from the vehemently pro-Leave TUV and UKIP positions to the 'considered' pro-Leave DUP stance, to the qualified pro-Remain of the UUP and Sinn Féin, through to the 'unashamedly' pro-Remain stances of the SDLP, Alliance, and Green Party (TUV, 2016; Foster, 2016a; DUP, 2016a; Sinn Féin, 2016; SDLP, 2016; Alliance, 2016; Green Party, 2016). Internal party tensions in the two largest Unionist parties, the DUP and UUP, were apparent in the run-up to the referendum. In the DUP, longstanding Eurosceptic MP Sammy Wilson publicly and controversially supported the pro-Leave campaign run by Nigel Farage's 'Leave.EU' prior to the conclusion of Prime Minister Cameron's negotiations on a new settlement for the UK in the EU (Cromie, 2015; *Belfast Telegraph*, 2015a); Wilson's support went against his party's official stance to await the outcome of negotiations. After the new settlement was published, Foster announced her party would 'on balance recommend a vote to leave the EU' (in *News Letter*, 2016). Qualifying this, Foster said the decision was 'fundamentally not one for parties' but for individuals to decide and stated her expectation that 'DUP members and voters will hold a range of differing personal views' on the issue (*ibid.*). Notwithstanding the DUP's pro-Leave position, some policies in their 2016 Assembly manifesto assumed access to EU funds. The party noted, for example, its ongoing discussions 'about leveraging in [*sic*] further finance from the European Investment Fund' (DUP, 2016a: 17) and its intention to look at the possibility of securing 'finance from the European Investment Bank' for Northern Irish farmers (*ibid.*: 25); as such, the DUP's position was arguably more nuanced than its official pro-Leave policy suggested.

In contrast to their Unionist rivals, the UUP presented a caveated pro-Remain position on the UK's EU referendum stating that 'on balance Northern Ireland is better remaining in the EU' (UUP, 2016a). In their 2016 Assembly election manifesto, the UUP highlighted aspects of Northern Ireland's unique vulnerability in the event of UK withdrawal as the basis for their seemingly reluctant decision (UUP, 2016b: 5). The UUP's pro-Remain position was sharply criticised by pro-Leave Unionists including some party members. A group of (ex-)senior UUP politicians (that included former party leader David Trimble and former MEP John Taylor) issued a statement in favour of the UK leaving the EU; it argued that the 'European Union has got out of control … We should not fear an exit from being governed and dictated to from Brussels' (*News Letter*, 2016b). Following the DUP's lead, the TUV, UKIP, and the PUP all adopted pro-Leave positions, leaving the UUP as the only pro-Remain Unionist party. In their 2016 Assembly manifesto, the TUV set out a vociferously Eurosceptic understanding of the 'tentacles of Brussels bureaucracy and diktats' and their hope to 'see our nation liberated' by voting for Leave (TUV, 2016: 3). In line with the party's *raison d'être*, UKIP outlined their belief that 'Northern Ireland will be better off outside the European Union' (UKIP, 2016: 20) in their manifesto. While also pro-Leave, the referendum was not a focus for the PUP at the election and the party did not campaign heavily in the run-up to the vote (PUP, 2016).

Although persistently opposed to the idea of a referendum on EU membership, Sinn Féin were dispassionately pro-Remain (*Belfast Telegraph*, 2015b). The party caveated their commitment to 'campaigning against Brexit' (2016: 4) with an otherwise euro-critical manifesto including policies to: 'continue to resist the dilution of national sovereignty'; campaign for 'greater democratisation' of the EU and oppose TTIP (Sinn Féin, 2016: 4; 17). Less equivocal pro-Remain positions were taken by Alliance, SDLP, and the Green Party. The Alliance Party manifesto stated their 'whole-heartedly pro-European' stance and belief in the 'ambitious and positive' role for the EU in Northern Ireland (2016). More than any other party, the UK's EU referendum was central to the SDLP's Assembly election campaign with the party pledging to 'lead the fight in convincing Northern Ireland to stay IN Europe' (2016: 9). Joining counterparts across the UK, the NI Green Party also campaigned to support the UK remaining in the EU (2016: 11).

Overall, the devolved government's engagement with the UK's EU referendum campaign was limited. The Executive and Assembly appeared to have little interest in related policy and legislative initiatives that preceded the EURA Act 2015 or in the substance of UK renegotiation talks in early 2016. During the referendum campaign, the Strand One institutions were preoccupied by the Assembly elections of March 2016 and related efforts to agree a programme for power-sharing government. Consequently, the campaign in Northern Ireland was lacklustre and characterised by limited public debate compared to the rest of the UK. A comparative lack of engagement in the lead-up to the referendum vote was in keeping with the low political salience of European issues in Northern Ireland politics and a strict reading of the devolution mandate whereby EU membership is excepted under international relations (1998 Act, Sch. 3). However, it is also the case that disagreement on the issue between the two largest parties of power-sharing government—DUP and Sinn Féin—meant that the UK's EU referendum was a source of additional tension in the already difficult political relationship underpinning Strand One of the Northern Ireland constitution; this latter impact would prove important in later stages of the Brexit process.

4.2.3 North–South Dimension

The impact of the UK's EU referendum on Strand Two was minimal. Although the result of the vote threatened to trigger fundamental change in relations between the two jurisdictions on the island of Ireland, the holding of referendum did not have significant immediate effect. The lack of impact is notable in itself. The fact that explanations of the importance of North–South relations and institutions for the governance and stability of Northern Ireland hardly featured during the referendum campaign underlines the limited engagement with the possible implications of a Leave vote in general and for Northern Ireland in particular.

Meetings of North–South Implementation Bodies in the lead-up to the referendum did not entertain the possibility of the UK voting to withdraw from the EU. There is no record, for example, that the UK's EU referendum was discussed in the December 2015 plenary session of the North South Ministerial Council (NSMC) in advance of the vote. A joint communiqué from the 21st meeting of the NSMC suggests Ministers present assumed the UK would vote Remain with minutes discussing ongoing 'collaboration to drawdown EU funding' and welcoming developments in the EU funded Horizon 2020, INTERREG V, and PEACE IV programmes (NSMC, 2015: 6–9). Sectoral meetings of the North South Language Body and the Inland Waterways held in the shadow of the referendum result on 24 June 2016 made clear a shared intention to continue to 'maximise the benefit of EU funding' and 'continue to seek new opportunities for potential projects which can attract such EU funding' (see NSMC 2016a: 4; 2016b: 9). Based on official records, then, there was no substantive impact of this first phase of Brexit on Strand Two institutions.

The UK's EU referendum did, however, put some strain on North–South political relations. Soon after Cameron announced his intention to hold an in/out referendum, the Irish Government had begun to map the likely implications of a UK withdrawal on the island of Ireland (see Connelly, 2018). From 2013 to 2016, the Taoiseach met with the Prime Minister six times and underlined Ireland's concerns about the 'strategic risk' posed by potential UK withdrawal (Department of the Taoiseach, 2016). In an address on 7 September 2015 in London, the Irish Minister for Foreign Affairs and Trade spoke of the 'difficult position' of Ireland who, on the one hand, '[had] more at stake than anyone else' yet could not 'interfere in the affairs of our friend and neighbour' (Department of Foreign Affairs and Trade, 2015). Once the campaign began, the Irish Government publicly supported Remain. Benefiting from domestic cross-party consensus on the issue (McGee, 2016), senior Irish politicians visited the UK during the campaign to speak about risks to the peace process in Northern Ireland and the likely economic damage to Ireland that would arise from UK withdrawal from the EU (Wintour, 2016), while, at the same time, seeking to mobilise Irish citizens eligible to vote (*Belfast Telegraph*, 2016c).[15] Such interventions from Irish politicians were not welcomed by pro-Leave Unionists in Northern Ireland. First Minister Foster refuted the view of Irish politicians describing 'purported threats to

---

[15] Under the *European Union Referendum Act 2015* ('EURA'), citizens of Ireland resident in the UK were entitled to vote in the UK's EU referendum. Irish citizens were the only foreign nationals granted eligibility to vote in the referendum who did not also belong to a British Commonwealth country (EURA, 2015 s2(2)(b)). Speaking in the Oireachtas prior to the referendum, the Taoiseach made clear his administrations intention to mobilise the Irish vote: 'Let nobody underestimate the scale of the challenge here. Irish citizens living in the UK will have a vote. Voters in Northern Ireland are estimated to be about 1.2 million. Around 120,000 UK citizens living here are also entitled to vote. The British embassy in Ireland is targeting them with a view to ensuring that they are registered to vote. While fully recognising that the outcome of the referendum is entirely a matter for the UK electorate, we will continue to ensure that the Irish perspective is presented to all interested parties' (Department of the Taoiseach, 2016).

our peace' as 'scare stories' (in Canning, 2016; Cunningham, 2016), while her party colleague and DUP deputy leader Nigel Dodds criticised Taoiseach Enda Kenny for being 'disrespectful' by '[lecturing] us as to what is best for Northern Ireland', which he said would prove 'counterproductive' to the Taoiseach's intent (Moriarty, 2016). In the wider referendum campaign, the apparent strain on North–South political relations between a pro-Remain administration in Ireland and pro-Leave Unionists in Northern Ireland was relatively low-profile. Nonetheless, it was, in retrospect, an important indicator of how the politics of Brexit would continue to play out on the island of Ireland.

4.2.4 East–West Dimension

Prima facie, the impact of the UK's EU referendum on East–West relations was similar to that on North–South relations. Some political tensions were evident between the position of the Irish administration and prominent Leave campaigners, but the intergovernmental relationship was not substantively affected given the Prime Minister and the Taoiseach both supported Remain, and East–West institutions were not engaged. However, such a surface-level reading belies the paradigmatic significance of the divergence between the Irish government and the UK Secretary of State for Northern Ireland, Theresa Villiers, on the implications of the referendum for Northern Ireland.

Throughout the campaign, Villiers insisted that Brexit would not require the imposition of a hard border on the island of Ireland and refuted the claims of the Irish Government that a vote to Leave could have a destabilising effect on the peace process (see Villiers, 2016a; 2016b). The position adopted by the Secretary of State at the time, and her predecessor, amounted to a little recognised shift in the established British-Irish bilateral approach to Northern Ireland affairs (Murphy, 2018: 39). Since the 1990s, British-Irish relations regarding Northern Ireland had developed to allow for a bilateral consensus to emerge on resolving the conflict; this shift was instrumental in the peace process (see Tannam, 2011; Coakley and Todd, 2020). Lack of unity between the Irish Government and the Secretary of State during the referendum campaign was the first occasion since the Anglo-Irish Agreement in 1985 that bi-national consensus on a key Northern Ireland issue did not prevail. A divergence of Irish and British perspectives on a sensitive constitutional question thus disrupted the *modus operandi* of British-Irish relations when dealing with Northern Ireland. This subtle shift was a signal of tensions yet to come in the Brexit process.

In addition to moving away from consensus-based bilateralism, the language of the UK Government about the nature of UK-Irish relations was consistently unclear throughout the referendum campaign. In its *Best of Both Worlds* White Paper, the government stated that in 1997 '[the] EU agreed that the UK and Ireland have the right to choose whether we want to take part in any new EU legislation concerning immigration, asylum, and civil law' (HM Government, 2016c: 28). Although likely incidental, the language here subsumes 'the UK and Ireland' into the 'we' granted the choice to opt in or out of Justice and Home Affairs matters at EU level (*ibid*.). Later, in a UK Government information leaflet distributed to all households prior to the UK's EU referendum, subtle reference was made to the unique immigration arrangements between the UK and Ireland. After stating the 'UK is not part of the EU's border-free zone', the claim was made that 'we control our own borders which gives us the right to check everyone, including EU nationals, *arriving from Continental Europe*' (HM Government, 2016d: 10, *added*). By specifying Continental Europe, the government implicitly acknowledged the unique reciprocal provisions under the CTA that allowed free movement between the UK and Ireland. The implications of the CTA for border control were not, however, explored; this raises the question as to who exactly the government envisaged as 'we'—did this include the whole of the Republic of Ireland as implied, and was the land border in Ireland to be considered 'our own'? The language indicates that the government at the time either did not consider, did not understand, or did not want to mention the particularities of border control, or its absence, on the island of Ireland.

Overall, then, Strand Three institutions were not engaged by the UK's EU referendum; however, the campaign did reveal a lack of understanding on the part of the UK Government as to the legal, political, and societal complexities on the island of Ireland and the implications these would have for any process of UK withdrawal from the EU. At the same time, the political position of Secretary of State Villiers resulted in a new divergence between the British Government's representative and the Irish Government's position on a key matter of pertinence to Northern Ireland.

4.3 Impact Assessment: UK's EU Referendum and the Northern Ireland Constitution

The first key finding arising from analysis of the UK's EU referendum is that the principle of consent underpinning the 1998 Agreement (and the 1998 Act) was not comprehensively considered in the context of the referendum campaign. An attempt was made by Sinn Féin to flag their view of the relevance of the principle of consent, broadly understood, as a possible constraint on UK withdrawal from the EU in the event of a majority Leave vote. Sinn Féin's position did not, however, garner much attention in the national referendum campaign and the party made no visible effort to move the issue forward in legislative or policy terms. Although the SNP attempted to introduce a requirement for devolved legislative consent in the early stages of the legislative process, the proposal was comprehensively dismissed by the UK Government. A failure to consider the *possible* implications of a broad understanding of the consent principle on a vote in favour of the UK leaving the EU could be seen as an affirmation of the tendency to 'blindspot' Northern Ireland particularities. This finding would, however, have to be caveated by noting that, in the aftermath of the referendum, it became clear that there had been a general failure on the part of the UK Government to consider the possible implications of a Leave majority.

The existence of a Northern Ireland blindspot at this stage of the Brexit process was more clearly evident in respect to the 'placing apart' of Northern Ireland in constructions of British identity. The campaign rhetoric of both Leave and Remain drew heavily on constructions of British identity and British history that either explicitly or implicitly excluded Northern Ireland. In this way, Northern Ireland and its particular constitutional history and structure were 'placed apart' by leading UK politicians. At the same time, Northern Ireland was 'a place apart' due to the way the UK's EU referendum played out practically and politically. The campaign in Northern Ireland was lacklustre compared to the rest of the UK and politicians in Northern Ireland tended to frame their positions in less existential terms. Turnout in Northern Ireland was lower than in the rest of the UK and the results showed ethno-nationalist identity to be the most significant factor effecting voting behaviour. Analysis of the Remain vote in Northern Ireland did, however, suggest that the referendum had cut across traditional political divides to a small but significant degree. This latter point is important because it suggested the potential for new political identities or groupings to be formed in Northern Ireland as a consequence of Brexit on an axis of Leave vs Remain; this possibility is picked up in later chapters.

The UK's EU referendum had a limited impact on Strand Two institutions and North–South relations. Some political tensions were evident during the campaign as the Irish Government took an active role advocating for Remain, which aggravated pro-Leave Unionists in Northern Ireland, most notably the DUP. Taking a broader view, however, the implications of UK withdrawal on North–South relations hardly featured in the campaign and the work of

North–South institutions continued under the assumption of ongoing EU membership. While perhaps unsurprising given the general failure to prepare for a Leave majority, the evident lack of consideration of the implications of a pro-Leave vote on Northern Ireland's unique constitutional provisions for North–South cooperation is notable.

In respect to the Strand Three East–West dimension, divisions in the Conservative Party on the referendum question led to a subtle but significant shift in British-Irish politics. The Secretary of State for Northern Ireland, Villiers, campaigned as a leading Brexiteer and thereby contradicted the Irish Government's position on the negative implications of a majority Leave vote for Northern Ireland. Although this did not receive much attention at the time, divergence between the British Government representative in Northern Ireland and the official Irish Government position constituted a step change in the consensus-based bilateral approach to Northern Ireland policy that had progressively developed since the Anglo-Irish Agreement of 1985.

Based on the findings of this chapter, the Northern Ireland constitution can be said to have been impacted by the UK's EU referendum in three ways. Firstly, the referendum revealed the extent to which Northern Ireland is overlooked in UK politics and, when considered, treated as a place apart. In view of the tendency identified in Chapter 2 (see 2.2.1) to overlook or under-analyse Northern Ireland in literature on the UK constitution and the comparatively low political salience of the European issue in Northern Ireland (see 2.2.2), this finding is arguably unsurprising but also important in view of the subsequently central position of Northern Ireland in UK–EU negotiations (see 6.1). Secondly, within Northern Ireland, the referendum reinforced ethno-nationalist divisions but simultaneously created at least a possibility for new political identities to be forged on the basis of positions adopted on a Leave–Remain axis. Third, and finally, the UK's EU referendum catalysed a shift in British-Irish approaches to Northern Ireland issues, away from consensus-based bilateralism and towards dissensus-based unilateralism. Although subtle in this first component of Brexit, this change in British-Irish approaches would become more pronounced as the process unfolded.

The significance of the findings detailed here and their relationship to the impacts of subsequent phases of the Brexit process are considered further in the concluding chapters of the book. Chapter 5 picks up the analysis from the UK's EU referendum result to the formal start of negotiations after the UK Government triggered Article 50.

5
Triggering Article 50

'… with the Labour Party tearing itself to pieces, and divisive nationalists in Scotland and Wales, it is nothing less than the patriotic duty of our Party to unite and govern in the best interests of the whole country … I favoured staying inside the EU because of … the threat to the Union between England and Scotland.'

Theresa May, June 2016[1]

'There are of course some issues on which the parties in the Executive do not share a single view—our different positions, for example, on the referendum on EU membership are well understood.'

Arlene Foster and Martin McGuinness, May 2016[2]

Article 50 of the Treaty on the European Union was not meant to be 'triggered'.[3] According to one of its authors, it was intended as a 'safety valve' inserted to placate the British Government during the drafting of the Lisbon Treaty; few thought it would ever be used (Hooton and Stone, 2016). Article 50 provides that 'any Member State may decide to withdraw from the

---

[1] May, T. (2016a) 'Theresa May's launch statement: full text' 30 June 2016. *Conservative Home* Available: https://www.conservativehome.com/parliament/2016/06/theresa-mays-launch-statement-full-text.html (Accessed 3 March 2018).

[2] Foster, A. and McGuinness, M. in Northern Ireland Executive (2016c) 'Programme for Government Consultation Document' northernireland.gov.uk Available: https://www.northernireland.gov.uk/sites/default/files/consultations/newnigov/pfg-consulation-document.PDF (Accessed 20 May 2019) and reproduced with permissions from https://www.northernireland.gov.uk/crown-copyright.

[3] The metaphorical adjective of 'triggering' was used almost unanimously in political, media, and academic discussions about initiating the Article 50 process. The imagery was employed by lead counsel for claimants in *Miller* at the Divisional Court, Lord Pannick QC, who likened notification under Article 50(2) to the firing of a bullet from a gun: the trigger being pulled by the act of notification, and the bullet eventually hits the target, causing the EU Treaties to cease to apply in the UK (see: *R (Miller) v Secretary of State for Exiting the European Union* 2016: 74). The line of reasoning underlying the metaphor, namely that the default consequence of 'triggering' notification would be vast changes in UK law including the removal of legal rights, was central in determining the outcome of the Divisional Court and later the Supreme Court judgments. In the *Agnew and McCord* cases, Maguire J. took a different view, characterising serving notice under Article 50 as 'the *beginning* of a process which ultimate will *probably* lead to changes in UK law' (2016: 105, *added*) but stating 'it remains to be seen what actual effect the process of change subsequent to notification will produce' (*ibid*.: 107). Notwithstanding the different reasoning used in the London litigation vis-à-vis the Belfast litigation, the language of 'triggering' became predominant; the dominance of the 'triggering' imagery arguably therefore underlines the supremacy of the reasoning used by the Supreme Court on the so-called 'main issue' (*Miller*, 2017: 5).

[European] Union in accordance with its own constitutional requirements' (*Official Journal*, 2016: C202/1). The months following the unexpected vote in favour of the UK leaving the EU, via Article 50, revealed the extent of disagreement over what the 'constitutional requirements' of the UK's uncodified and unsettled constitution were in the unprecedented legal scenario of a Member State withdrawing from the European Union. At the time, Northern Ireland did not feature prominently in domestic political and constitutional debates; however, as this chapter sets out, decisions made by the UK Government and the Supreme Court in the period between the referendum on 23 June 2016 and the triggering of Article 50 on 29 March 2017 set the trajectory for some of the impacts of the Brexit process overall in Northern Ireland.

This chapter has three sections: the first provides an account of key political and legal events in the period between the referendum in June 2016 and the triggering of Article 50 in March 2017 with a focus on those relevant to the Northern Ireland constitution; the second details the impact of this phase of the Brexit process on the components of the Northern Ireland constitution; the third provides a summary of findings and notes their significance in the overall picture of Brexit's effect.

The key findings of the chapter are as follows: (1) the orthodox position of the Supreme Court in *Miller* regarding the territorial constitution failed to account for *sui generis* aspects of the Northern Ireland constitution, including its basis in international law; (2) the aftermath of the UK's EU referendum exposed the fragility of the Strand One institutions which, catalysed by existing policy failures, led to the breakdown of devolved government in Northern Ireland; (3) an initial strengthening of North–South and East–West relations ended with the collapse of power-sharing government, paving the way for a deterioration in political and diplomatic relations in the next phase of the process.

5.1 The EU (Notification of Withdrawal) Act 2017 and Triggering Article 50

On one level, not much changed in respect to the formal process of UK withdrawal from the EU between June 2016 and March 2017. However, decisions made in the nine months between Brexit's political catalyst—the UK's EU referendum—and its official legal beginning—the triggering of Article 50—set the trajectory for the process that followed and are therefore crucial determinants of its impact. For the purpose of this analysis, three aspects of what happened in this period are important: (1) the decision of newly elected Prime Minister Theresa May to pursue a so-called 'hard Brexit'; (2) the collapse of the Northern Ireland Executive and the results of the Assembly election that followed; and (3) the Supreme Court's judgment in *Miller*, more specifically, its (mis)handling of the Northern Ireland references. Before analysing the impact of events during this period on the Northern Ireland constitution, a description of their substance is set out to contextualise what follows. In keeping with the approach taken in the previous chapter, particular attention is given to the position of Northern Ireland in UK-wide developments; this account is therefore not exhaustive; instead it provides the basis for considering the impact of this phase of Brexit on the Northern Ireland constitution.

5.1.1 Conservative Leadership Election and UK Negotiating Position

On the morning of the 24 June 2016, David Cameron announced his resignation as Prime Minister (see *Reuters* 2016a). This catalysed a dramatic Conservative Party leadership election from which dispassionate Remain supporter and previous Home Secretary Theresa May emerged victorious, having received the largest ever parliamentary mandate from her colleagues in the second ballot (see Heppell, 2008: 186). Following the withdrawal of pro-Leave contender Andrea Leadsom amid a series of controversies (see *BBC News*, 2016d; *BBC News*, 2016e), Theresa May was elected on 11 July 2016 and took up the post three days later (see *BBC News*, 2016f). Accepting the new position, May reiterated her campaign refrain 'Brexit means Brexit' (May, 2016b). This tautology would become familiar during her premiership, but it cloaked substantive uncertainty about the kind of Brexit the new government would pursue. Related debates centred around 'hard Brexit' vs 'soft Brexit': the former associated with leaving the EU single market, customs union, and the jurisdiction of the Court of Justice of the European Union (CJEU); and the latter with agreeing some sort of alignment with (or access to) the EU single market and customs union that would be short of membership but likely require continued CJEU competence and close alignment with the legal *acquis*.

Prime Minister May's speech to the Conservative Party conference on 5 October 2016 gave the first hint that her government would pursue a hard Brexit. A commitment to end free movement and ensure the authority of EU law was 'ended forever' was interpreted to mean that the UK would not seek membership of the EU single market or customs union; however, May also said the UK would seek an agreement involving 'free trade, in goods and services', thus leaving room for doubt (May, 2016c). From a Northern Ireland perspective, the language of the speech was notable; the Prime Minister referred to 'the United Kingdom' just once and to 'Britain' 40 times. In what was primarily an ideological speech to conference, the political philosophy May articulated centred on the 'spirit of [British] citizenship' which she characterised as the bedrock of 'the social contract' (*ibid.*). Given how politically divisive citizenship is in Northern Ireland and the unique provisions of the 1998 Agreement whereby individuals can choose British citizenship, Irish citizenship, or both, the applicability of the Prime Minister's political philosophy to Northern Ireland is questionable.

The government's approach to Brexit negotiations was *somewhat* clarified by the Lancaster House speech on 17 January 2017 in which the Prime Minister gave the first public airing of her government's twelve negotiating priorities which, taken together, suggested a hard Brexit. Among the priorities outlined, two had specific relevance to Northern Ireland: first, maintaining the CTA with Ireland; and second, strengthening the 'precious union' of the UK's 'four nations'[4] by ensuring devolved administrations are 'fully engaged' in the process through the work of a newly established sub-committee of the Joint Ministerial Council (JMC) (May, 2017). Neither of these, however, recognised the difficulties for Northern Ireland and its land border with Ireland created by the government's other priorities of leaving the single market, customs union, and ending the authority of EU law. Slightly clearer acknowledgement of the 'unique economic, social and political context' of the land border between Northern Ireland and Ireland came from the White Paper published after the speech (HM Government, 2017a: 4.10). The White Paper outlined the government's '*aim* to have as seamless and frictionless a border *as possible* between Northern Ireland and Ireland' (*ibid.*: 4.4, *added*) and made clear its 'explicit objective' to ensure '*full account* is taken for [sic] the particular circumstances of Northern Ireland' (*ibid.*: 4.10, *added*). Notably, in respect to Northern Ireland, the language of the government's negotiating priorities was aspirational, falling short of any policy commitments. By contrast, statement of its negotiating objectives regarding leaving the jurisdiction of the CJEU, ending free movement, and leaving the EU single market was unequivocal.[5]

---

[4] From the perspective of Northern Ireland, the 'four nations' narrative is problematic because to call Northern Ireland 'a nation' is to misunderstand or overlook its history and its politics; see Whitten (2021b).

[5] Echoing 'Vote Leave' campaign rhetoric, the Prime Minister stated, in respect to the CJEU, that 'we will take back control of our laws and bring an end to the jurisdiction of the European Court of Justice in Britain'; on free movement, it was made clear that 'Brexit must mean control of the number of people who

By 29 March 2017, the government's articulation of their position in respect to Northern Ireland had developed to include the importance of the peace process. The Prime Minister's letter to European Council President, triggering Article 50, underlined the 'important responsibility' the UK Government had to make sure 'nothing is done to jeopardise the peace process' in Northern Ireland, with an accompanying pledge to 'continue to uphold the Belfast Agreement' (The Prime Minister, 2017). While this development of language is significant, it is worth noting the immediate political context in Northern Ireland with the collapse of power-sharing government and decline of relations between the DUP and Sinn Féin in the aftermath of an Assembly election on 2 March 2017. Conceivably, this was at least part of the reason why protecting the peace process and upholding the 1998 Agreement came to the fore in UK Government Brexit rhetoric, rather than the change indicating a new substantive policy position or new understanding of Northern Ireland particularities in the face of UK withdrawal from the EU.

5.1.2 Collapse of the Northern Ireland Executive and the Assembly Election

In the nine months between the result of the UK's EU referendum on 24 June 2016 and the triggering of Article 50 on 29 March 2017, Northern Ireland did not feature prominently in the (extensive) political debates regarding UK withdrawal from the EU and its implications. Announcing her ultimately successful bid to become the new Conservative Party leader, Theresa May's portrayal of 'divisive Nationalists in Scotland and Wales' and of 'the threat to the Union between England and Scotland' posed by Brexit was indicative of the extent to which Northern Ireland was overlooked in the immediate aftermath of the referendum (2017). Just as in the campaign, the vulnerability of Northern Ireland received little attention throughout the second phase of the Brexit process. The result of the UK's EU referendum was, however, having a divisive effect in Northern Ireland politics due to stark differences in the positions of its two governing parties—the DUP and Sinn Féin—who acknowledged as much in their Programme for Government Consultation (Northern Ireland Executive, 2016c: 4). In the Executive and across Northern

---

come to Britain from Europe' excluding Ireland; and May said her government 'do not seek membership of the [EU] single market' but did seek 'the greatest possible access to it' through a free trade agreement (May, 2017). None of these statements were ambiguous or aspirational as was the case in respect to the land border on the island of Ireland on which the Prime Minister pledged to '*work* to deliver a practical solution' for maintaining the CTA 'as soon as we can' while the commitment in respect to devolved administrations was that they '*should* be fully engaged' (*ibid.*, added).

Ireland, different perspectives on the UK's EU referendum mapped onto existing political divisions (see 4.1.2), which added strain to an already difficult period in Northern Ireland politics with the two-party Executive in turmoil over mishandling of a (supposedly) green-energy Renewable Heat Incentive (RHI) scheme. Allegations of DUP complicity in the mishandling of the RHI scheme led to calls for DUP leader Arlene Foster to step aside; her refusal to do so led to the protest resignation of Sinn Féin leader Martin McGuinness and the consequent collapse of power-sharing institutions in Northern Ireland on 16 January 2017 (see *BBC News*, 2017a; McDonald, 2017; Donnelly, 2016; Coghlin, O'Brien, and MacLean, 2020; McBride, 2019). As the Prime Minister set out her government's negotiating strategy in Lancaster House on 17 January—the content of which raised serious questions for the future of governance in Northern Ireland—the Assembly passed a motion to recognize 'the continuing failure of the Executive to safeguard the interests of the people of Northern Ireland following the result of the EU referendum' in what proved to be the Assembly's last session before a three year hiatus (*Northern Ireland Assembly*, 2017: 69).[6]

Collapse of the Executive triggered an Assembly election on 2 March 2017.[7] After a brief but (this time) tense campaign featuring particularly harsh exchanges between DUP and Sinn Féin candidates, Northern Ireland went to the polls. Implementing previously agreed changes, the number of contested seats dropped from 108 to 90, rendering competition for seats more intense. The results showed support for the DUP dropping slightly to 28.1% of first preference votes (compared to 29.2% in 2016) and support for Sinn Féin increasing to 27.9% of first preference votes (compared to 24.0% in 2016), meaning that the DUP returned 28 seats and Sinn Féin 27 seats. This was the closest ever margin of electoral difference between the two largest parties and saw both drop below the 30-seat threshold required to trigger the 'petition of concern' mechanism, frequently used to block contentious legislation (see 1998 Act s42). Inter-party talks to form a power-sharing executive began in an atmosphere of growing tension as Sinn Féin leadership called for a referendum on Irish unity 'as soon as possible' (O'Neill in *BBC News*, 2017b) and

---

[6] The full text of the motion read '[t]hat this Assembly recognises the grave consequences for the people of Northern Ireland of the failure of the Executive to agree a Budget and Estimates for the financial year 2017–18, the failure of the Executive to set a regional rate for 2017–18, the failure of the Executive to endorse a Programme for Government and the continuing failure of the Executive to safeguard the interest of the people of Northern Ireland following the result of the EU referendum'; the motion had been proposed by Mike Nesbitt (UUP member for Strangford) and passed (as amended) by 34 in favour to 29 opposed (see Northern Ireland Assembly, 2017).

[7] In the interim, McGuinness announced his retirement from professional politics due to a decline in health. Former Agriculture Minister Michelle O'Neill was named as the new leader of Sinn Féin in Northern Ireland.

the DUP leader urged Northern Irish Unionists to 'wake up' (Foster, 2017a). The date set for reaching agreement passed on 26 March 2017. The Secretary of State for Northern Ireland, James Brokenshire, set a later deadline and so began a pattern of Northern Irish parties attempting and failing to reach agreement facilitated by repeated extensions granted by a UK Government distracted by the (all-encompassing) Brexit process.

5.1.3 United Kingdom 'Constitutional Requirements' and the Miller Case

In constitutional terms, *Miller* (2017)[8] was the most significant case the Supreme Court had heard since it was established in 2009. At issue was whether or not Article 50 could be triggered by royal prerogative without parliamentary approval, and/or the consent of devolved legislatures, and/or without recourse to the particular constitutional status and structure of Northern Ireland (*Miller*: 5; 6). In substance the judgment touched on the two constitutional fault lines exposed by the unexpected referendum result, namely the balance of parliamentary vs executive power and the balance of central government vs devolved governments' powers (see 1.1). On both issues, specific questions were put to the Supreme Court, through applications for judicial review referred from Northern Ireland courts in *Agnew* and *McCord*,[9] about the unique constitution of Northern Ireland and its implications for triggering Article 50.

In their judgment, the Supreme Court concluded, by a majority of eight Justices to three, that the government could only trigger Article 50 after first securing the approval of Parliament by primary legislation; all eleven Justices also concluded that the legislative consent of devolved administrations was not legally required nor did any of the 'arguments of a constitutional nature' raised in respect to Northern Ireland prevent the government from triggering Article 50 provided primary legislation to that effect had been passed in Westminster (*Miller*: 6). Parliamentary approval was duly granted

---

[8] Another case was brought by the applicants of *Miller* (2017) during the course of the Brexit process and was heard by the Supreme Court in October 2019; as such, the case regarding the triggering of Article 50 is sometimes referred to as *Miller I* and the 2019 case concerning the (un)lawful prorogation of Parliament as *Miller II*; this terminology is not adopted here.

[9] The references from Northern Ireland derived from separate applications for judicial review *Re McCord* (reference by the Court of Appeal for Northern Ireland) and *Re Agnew* (reference by the High Court on application of the Attorney General for Northern Ireland); both were heard between 4 and 6 October 2016 by Maguire J. who provided one ruling on the basis that the two cases 'substantially relate to the same subject matter', namely 'the intention of the Government … to use the Royal Prerogative to invoke Article 50 TEU to trigger the process by which withdrawal from the EU is effected' *Re McCord and Agnew* (2016: 1).

via the *European Union (Notification of Withdrawal) Act 2017* which received royal assent on 16 March 2017. The new legislation paved the way for the UK Government to trigger Article 50, via letter to European Council president Donald Tusk on 29 March 2017; this, in turn, set the metaphorical clock ticking on the (in theory) two-year timeframe for EU–UK withdrawal negotiations, the substance and consequences of which are considered in Chapter 6.

5.2 Triggering Article 50 and the Northern Ireland Constitution

This section considers the impact of events between the UK's EU referendum and the triggering of Article 50 on the constituent parts of the Northern Ireland constitution.

5.2.1 Principle of Consent

In the nine-month period between the UK's EU referendum and the triggering of Article 50, the process towards and the outcome of the *Miller* case was the most important event for the Northern Ireland constitutional principle of consent, and indeed one of the most significant of the whole Brexit process. This section details the relevant facts of the case, the problematic approach of the Supreme Court to the Northern Ireland dimension, and its significance for the constitution.

The first point to make is procedural. Although not always acknowledged, in *Miller* the Supreme Court heard a combination of two sets of cases. One set of cases focused primarily on whether the ECA 1972 and UK common law required that parliamentary legislation be passed before Article 50 could legitimately be triggered; these cases arrived on a leapfrog appeal from the Divisional Court of the High Court of England and Wales in London (*R Miller*, 2016, the 'London litigation'). A second set of cases arrived from the Northern Ireland courts and focused on a series of arguments from a specifically Northern Ireland constitutional perspective (the 'Belfast litigation'). The Belfast litigation derived from separate applications for judicial review *Re McCord* (referred by NI Court of Appeal) and *Re Agnew* (referred by NI High Court). These cases were heard together on 4 to 6 October by Maguire J. who provided one ruling for both. To the extent that issues raised in the Belfast litigation duplicated those being considered in the London litigation, Maguire J. stayed consideration of them, concentrating instead on 'the impact of Northern Ireland constitutional provisions in respect of notice under Article 50' (*McCord and Agnew*, 2016: 9). Maguire J. ruled in favour of the government having been unpersuaded that any 'constitutional bulwark … would be breached' by the *triggering* of Article 50 (*ibid.*: 106). In reaching this conclusion, Maguire J. placed considerable store by what he did—and did not—consider to be the consequences of the government serving notice under Article 50; Maguire J. characterised this step as 'the beginning of a process which ultimately will *probably* lead to changes in UK law' (*ibid.*: 105, added) but emphasised that, '[o]n the day after the notice has been given, the law will in fact be the same as it was the day before it was given' (*ibid.*: 105), concluding then that 'it remains to be seen what actual effect the process of change subsequent to notification will produce' (*ibid.*: 107). Maguire J.'s assessment of the relative insignificance of triggering Article 50 differed fundamentally from that of the Court in the London litigation, and later the Supreme Court, both of which focused not on the uncertainty as to the ultimate end of the process of UK withdrawal from the EU but rather on the fact that the default consequence of initiating the exit process was wholesale departure from the EU by dint of the EU Treaties ceasing to apply after two years. Such a distinction is crucial as the handling of the substance of the issues in the Belfast litigation turned on an understanding of the relative lack of legal and constitutional significance of triggering Article 50 which was, in effect, overruled by the Supreme Court. The higher court did not, however, seem motivated to review the facts of the Belfast litigation in any great detail, notwithstanding their fundamentally different view of the constitutional importance of the proposed 'triggering'.

Both the London litigation and the Belfast litigation were of formally equal status, but this was not reflected in the judgment or approach of the Supreme Court. From the outset, the Supreme Court treated the references from Northern Ireland courts as subordinate to those referred from English courts. The *Miller* (2016) reference was treated as the 'main issue' and *McCord* (2016) approached on the premise that '*most*' of the so-called 'devolution issues' arose from a contention regarding 'the terms on which powers have been statutorily devolved to the administrations of Scotland, Wales and Northern Ireland', with reference here made to the operation of the Sewel Convention (*Miller*, 2017: 5–6). This premise was substantively inaccurate. Not only was there no legal basis for granting the arguments raised in the London litigation more weight than those raised in the Belfast litigation, only one of the five questions referred in the Belfast litigation was directly related to the operation of the Sewel Convention, making the Court's use of the term 'most' a curious one. According to one of the junior counsels for *Agnew*, the majority of the time allocated for oral presentations before the Supreme Court was given to those instructed in the London litigation; this fact reflected an 'unarticulated, yet dominant, consensus' among those not directly involved in the Belfast litigation that 'the only real issue was parliamentary sovereignty versus the royal prerogative, and that everything else was a side-show' (McCrudden and Halberstam, 2017: 30).[10] The Supreme Court's subordination of the Belfast litigation was in keeping with an already evidenced tendency for Northern Ireland to be excluded from dominant political narratives of Brexit, but the *Miller* judgment was the first time this tendency had manifested itself legally.

Applicants in the Belfast litigation advanced five arguments, all of which were referred to the Supreme Court.[11] The Court in *Miller* (2017: 126) summarised the five questions referred from *McCord and Agnew* (2016) as follows:

(i) Does any provision of the NI Act, read together with the Belfast Agreement and the British-Irish Agreement, have the effect that primary legislation is required before Notice [to trigger Article 50] can be given?
(ii) If the answer is 'yes', is the consent of the Northern Ireland Assembly required before the relevant legislation is enacted?
(iii) If the answer to (i) is 'no', does any provision of the NI Act, read together with the Belfast Agreement and the British-Irish Agreement, operate as a restriction on the exercise of the prerogative power to give Notice?
(iv) Does section 75 of the NI Act [concerning equality law] prevent exercise of the power to give Notice in the absence of compliance by the Northern Ireland Office with its obligations under that section?
(v) Does the giving of Notice without the consent of the people of Northern Ireland impede the operation of section 1 [concerning popular consent to constitutional change] of the NI Act?

The Supreme Court's handling of the substance of the five questions referred from the Belfast litigation flowed from its assertion that these were not

---

[10] Professor Christopher McCrudden, Professor of Human Rights and Equality Law at Queen's University Belfast, who appeared as junior counsel for Mr Agnew and others in *Miller*, gives account of the allocation of time for oral presentations to the Supreme Court in McCrudden and Halberstam (2017).

[11] The first four issues raised in *Re McCord and Agnew* were particularly associated with the *Agnew* case, although several were also made by the applicant in the *McCord* case, and the fifth was unique to the *McCord* case. Maguire J. in his judgment to the Northern Ireland High Court referred the five arguments as issues 1 to 5 which were then translated into questions 1 to 5 in the Supreme Court and discussed collectively as 'devolution issues'.

main issue. While the Court recognised the 1998 Agreement as 'the product of the Belfast Agreement and the British-Irish Agreement' which had 'established institutions and arrangements which are intended to address the unique political history of the province and the island of Ireland' (*Miller*: 2017, 128), it proceeded to ignore the legal significance of these facts. Having just highlighted the particularity of governing arrangements in Northern Ireland, and their unique legal and historical origin, the Supreme Court went on to emphasise the 'relevant commonality in the devolution settlements in Northern Ireland, Scotland and Wales' (*ibid.*) and focused its analysis solely on relevant domestic statutes. Indeed, in its handling of all five questions referred, the Supreme Court failed to address the international legal dimension of the Northern Ireland constitution, deriving from the British-Irish Agreement; the Court thus provided no analysis of the extent to which the 1998 Agreement places any legal constraints on the UK Government.

The reductionist approach of the Supreme Court to issues raised by the Belfast litigation proved problematic in several respects. In their assessment of the London litigation, 'the *main* issue' (*ibid.*: 5), the Supreme Court concluded that the government would have to pass primary legislation before Article 50 could be legitimately triggered. As a consequence, the Court determined that question (i) was 'less significant than it otherwise might have been' (*ibid.*: 129) and therefore 'it [was] not necessary to reach a definitive view' in light of the preceding conclusion (*ibid.*: 132). Addressing question (i), the Court only referenced domestic statutory constraints posed by the 'devolution legislation' (*ibid.*: 129), reading the provisions of the 1998 [Northern Ireland] Act together with the Scotland Act 1998 and Government of Wales Act 2006 rather than, as question (i) had asked, reading the 1998 Act together with the 1998 Agreement. In doing so, the Court summarily failed to recognise the asymmetric nature of UK devolution and the relevance of the 'unique political history' of Northern Ireland it had just described (*ibid.*: 128).

A similar dynamic played out in the Court's dismissal of question (iii). Having already reasoned, on the basis of the London litigation, that primary legislation was required before Article 50 could be triggered, the Supreme Court determined that the third question, concerning whether or not provisions of the 1998 Act, together with the 1998 Agreement, operated as a restriction on the exercise of the royal prerogative to trigger Article 50, had been 'superseded' (*ibid.*: 129). Although it is unlikely that consideration of the facts posed by question (iii) would have changed the outcome of the judgment, by declining to answer the question the Supreme Court opted not to clarify the status of prerogative powers in the unique legal context of the Northern Ireland constitution and its history.

The Supreme Court also determined that question (iv) had been 'superseded' (*ibid.*: 133) by the aforementioned conclusion on the London litigation. On the substance of the question, the Court stated that 'in so far as the *Secretary of State* may have a role in the measures taken by the UK Parliament to give Notice [trigger Article 50], we are satisfied that section 75 [of the 1998 Act] imposes no obligation *on him* in that context' (*ibid.*: 133, added). As such, the Court did not address the actual question referred as to whether or not the *Northern Ireland Office* was obligated under section 75 to ensure the triggering of Article 50 did not breach equality law in Northern Ireland. By failing to distinguish between the functions of the Secretary of State for Northern Ireland and the functions of the Northern Ireland Office, the Supreme Court ruled, correctly, that the powers of the Secretary of State are not restricted by section 75 of the 1998 Act which places a statutory duty on 'public authorities' to comply with and promote equality of opportunity. Here the Court ignored the fact that the Northern Ireland Office *is* obliged, under the definition set out in section 75(3(a)) of the 1998 Act, to ensure compliance with equality law (see McCrudden and Halberstam, 2017: 34). Thus, in its approach to question (iv), the Supreme Court failed to consider the relevance or otherwise of that duty on the 'constitutional requirements' of the UK prior to triggering of Article 50.

The most detailed analysis in the handling of 'devolution issues' (*Miller*, 2017: 6) was granted to question (ii) which followed from question (i) and concerned the necessity or otherwise of achieving the consent of the Northern Ireland Assembly to any legislation passed by UK Parliament with the purpose of authorising the triggering of Article 50. The Supreme Court reasoned that this 'raises in substance the application of the Sewel Convention' which, it supposed, was 'adopted as a means of establishing cooperative relationships between the UK Parliament and the devolved institutions' in areas of overlapping legislative competence (*ibid.*: 136).[12] In like manner to its approach to question (i), the Court again responded to the question posed by reading the provisions of the 1998 Act together with those of the corresponding devolved legislation for Scotland and Wales and not in the context of the 1998 Agreement (as asked). Thus, the issue of legislative consent was detached from any more nuanced understanding of consent as 'a pervasive underlying principle' of constitutional arrangements in Northern Ireland

---

[12] The Supreme Court's description of the origin of the Sewel Convention here is incomplete. As was indicated by its namesake, Lord Sewell, in 1998 during the passage of the Scotland Bill, the contemporary Convention draws on practices established during the first era of government in Northern Ireland (HL, 1998: 791); arguably, it first arose from the failure of the UK Government to challenge the Northern Ireland Government over changes to the local government franchise in the 1920s (Evans, 2020).

(McCrudden and Halberstam, 2017: 32). The same reasoning was evident in relation to question (v) that concerned the 'operation of section 1 of NI Act' (*ibid.*: 126(i)). This the Court described as 'an important provision' arising 'out of the Belfast Agreement' but one which was only relevant to whether or not Northern Ireland remained part of the UK or became part of a united Ireland; it therefore 'neither regulated any other change in the constitutional status of Northern Ireland nor required the consent of a majority of the people of Northern Ireland to the withdrawal of the United Kingdom from the European Union' (*ibid.*: 135). Although perhaps incidental, the language of the judgment is notable here in that the Supreme Court concluded that provisions of section 1 of the 1998 Act did not require consent of the majority of the people of Northern Ireland to UK withdrawal from the EU when question (v) as asked related only to the 'giving of Notice' to trigger Article 50 (*ibid.*: 126(v)).

The Supreme Court's framing of the Northern Ireland references as 'devolution issues' (*ibid.*: 6) was indicative of the reductionist lens with which the Belfast litigation was viewed overall. By characterising the five questions referred as relating to the UK devolution settlement, broadly understood, without recognising its asymmetric legal basis and history in Northern Ireland, the Court missed the basic premise of the appellants' case in *Re McCord and Agnew* (2016); namely, that constitutional law in Northern Ireland is *sui generis* in ways that merited particular consideration prior to UK withdrawal from the EU. Through the Northern Ireland references in *Miller*, the Supreme Court were not being asked to adjudicate on the nature of relations between the UK Government and its devolved administrations but rather to determine the nature of the constitutional requirements placed on the UK state as a result of the commitments it made when it signed the 1998 Agreement; this, the Court opted not to do.

5.2.2 Devolved Government

The period between the UK's EU referendum and the triggering of Article 50 revealed the fragility of political relations that are the bedrock of power-sharing government in Northern Ireland. Existing tensions between the governing parties—DUP and Sinn Féin—were exacerbated by policy disagreement over the best way to safeguard Northern Ireland interests in the unfolding process of UK withdrawal from the EU. Yet, as this subsection argues, while the second element of the Brexit process undoubtedly exposed weaknesses in the Strand One institutions, this was also a period of increasing political polarisation throughout the UK, meaning that the breakdown of political consensus in Northern Ireland was not wholly unique. However, as the only part of the UK that governs by mandatory coalition, the disintegration of political relations in Northern Ireland had more significance for the operation of government. Moreover, as subsequent subsections detail, the interdependence of the three-strand structure of the 1998 Agreement and 1998 Act meant that the collapse of Strand One institutions also had unwelcome repercussions for Strand Two and Strand Three. This subsection is structured chronologically because the effect of Brexit in this period resulted in progressive polarisation between political parties in Northern Ireland which, in turn, contributed to the collapse of the Executive and failure to form another power-sharing government.

The fact that 'parties in the Executive [did] not share a single view' on the UK's EU referendum was very clear in its immediate aftermath (Northern Ireland Executive, 2016c: 4). On 24 June, the deputy First Minister argued that the 56% Remain majority in Northern Ireland in the context of a 52% Leave majority in the UK provided a 'democratic imperative for a border poll' on Northern Ireland's position within the UK (*BBC News*, 2016h; *Belfast Telegraph*, 2016a). Speaking the same day, the First Minister described her governing partner's response as 'opportunistic' and the referendum outcome as a 'good result', signifying the UK's support for 'hope … aspiration' and 'future potential' (*ibid*). On the morning of 24 June, Northern Ireland's senior officials reflected on the 'critical event' of the referendum and committed to 'urgently consider' key issues (NICS Board, 2016e: 10); the strength of language from officials revealed their apprehension about the implications of the referendum for devolved government. The starkly different reactions of the DUP and Sinn Féin leaders to the referendum result and the officials' concern were a portent of what was to come; however, a consensus position did emerge between June and August 2016, albeit one that lacked detail and proved delicate.

The most substantive articulation of the tenuous consensus in the Executive following the referendum came in the form of a letter to the Prime Minister on 10 August 2016 which set out its position and priorities. Writing jointly, the First and deputy First Ministers stated their shared understanding that 'this region is unique' as 'the only part of the UK which has a land border with an EU member state' (Northern Ireland Executive, 2016a). The leaders acknowledged the 'difficult issues relating to the border throughout our history and the peace process' and noted Northern Ireland's multifaceted vulnerability due to its history, geography, and economic structure (*ibid.*). On this basis, the letter outlined priorities for upcoming UK–EU negotiations as follows: there should be no impediment to free movement of goods, people, or services across the border; no incentives for illegal activities related to the border; ease of access to the EU single market for purposes of trade and free movement of labour; protection of the single electricity market; access to EU funding, including PEACE funding, and safeguards for the uniquely exposed agri-food sector (*ibid.*). In hindsight, the degree of consensus between the DUP and Sinn Féin leaders here was remarkable; the language of the First Minister is particularly significant. In the Assembly on 13 September, Foster stated '… just because [she] campaigned for Brexit does not mean that there will not be short-term issues' and, while it was her belief that 'in the medium to long term' it would 'be right for the United Kingdom to be outside the European Union', this was not 'to say that we do not have to deal with short-term challenges' (*Northern Ireland Assembly*, 2016c: 6). In the same session, the deputy First Minister spoke of the 'duty' and 'responsibility' he felt to 'work with the First Minister and the other Ministers in the Executive to make the best fist of what we can' from UK–EU withdrawal negotiations (*ibid.*: 5). These displays of solidarity did not, of course, last long as the parties' positions and rhetoric changed radically during UK–EU negotiations.

Just days after she delivered her speech to Conservative Party conference (in which Northern Ireland was not mentioned), the Prime Minister replied to the Executive. In her letter, May pledged to account for the 'specific interests of the people of Northern Ireland' during the UK withdrawal process and acknowledged several aspects of the 'unique issues' relating to Northern Ireland (The Prime Minister, 2016). May's language was noticeably less robust than the Executive's in characterising the nature of Northern Ireland's vulnerabilities, and substantial commitments were only made regarding process, not policy. A commitment to 'full engagement' and 'working with' the Northern Ireland Executive, Joint Ministerial Committee, Irish Government, and EU to achieve the 'wish' of all involved that 'free movement of people and goods across the island of Ireland' would continue, and an earlier pledge that 'no one wants to see a return to the borders of the past' was repeated (*ibid.*).[13] This phrase, which became a refrain of May's premiership, is an interesting epithet but, given that 'returning to the past' is a practical and philosophical impossibility, it was arguably a flimsy policy commitment, albeit one that May appeared to find rhetorically useful. Stronger pledges

---

[13] On her first visit to Northern Ireland, the Prime Minister stated that 'no one wants a return to the border of the past'; at the time this was welcomed by both the First and deputy First Minister but to the party leaders struck notably different tones: Foster spoke of her delight at May's assurance that there 'must be no new internal borders within the United Kingdom' while McGuinness said there was 'no good news' for the people of Northern Ireland (in McDonald, 2016b).

were made to 'make sure' Northern Ireland energy supplies would not be adversely impacted but, even here, no actual policy commitment was made. In what, in retrospect, is a poignant statement, the Prime Minister agreed 'the future of the border with Ireland is of the *highest priority* for Northern Ireland, and indeed is [only] an *important priority* for the UK as a whole' (*ibid., emphasis added*). The fact that arrangements for the border on the island of Ireland would become the linchpin in UK–EU withdrawal negotiations, the stumbling block of May's attempts to ratify the (2017) UK–EU Withdrawal Agreement, and the indirect root of her resignation, was evidently not foreseen.

The relative convergence between Executive parties' positions on Brexit did not last. McGuinness resigned on 16 January, principally because of the RHI scandal, but colleagues and commentators cited divisions over Brexit as an exacerbating factor (see *Northern Ireland Assembly*, 2017: 66). Power-sharing government collapsed and, as according to the 1998 Act at the time,[14] an election was called. The 2017 Assembly election campaign was more divisive than its predecessor (see 5.1); that said, there was somewhat of a consensus in parties' positions on Brexit with the five largest parties all advocating for recognition of Northern Ireland's 'special', 'unique', or 'particular' circumstances (see Hayward and Whitten, 2018).

The idea of a 'special status' for Northern Ireland was much debated throughout this period. On 17 October, the SDLP brought a motion to the Assembly calling for 'legal recognition of the unique status of Northern Ireland' as part of the arrangements for the UK to leave the EU (*Northern Ireland Assembly*, 2016d).[15] The language of 'special status' was unpalatable to Unionist representatives who opposed the SDLP motion, which was defeated in a knife-edge vote of 47 against to 46 for. All parties did, however, seem to agree on the concept of 'special status' but they disagreed on how it ought to be realised and discussed. Sinn Féin sought special status for Northern Ireland '*within* the European Union' (2017: 2, *added*); the SDLP proposed special status within the European Economic Area (2017: 6) while Alliance

---

[14] At the time, under s16A and s32 of the 1998 Act, the Secretary of State was obliged to propose a date for an Assembly election if the offices of First Minister and deputy First Minister were not filled after fourteen days of vacancy.

[15] The full text of the original motion brought stated '[t]hat this Assembly notes the current public concern arising from the European Union referendum vote; endorses the proposal of the Irish Government and others that there should be legal recognition of the unique status of Northern Ireland and the circumstances on the island as part of arrangements to leave the European Union; believes that this is one mechanism that can safeguard the interests of the people of Northern Ireland, including future access to European Union funding opportunities; and calls on the British Government to fully endorse, and to negotiate for, this outcome in discussions on leaving the European Union' (see *Northern Ireland Assembly*, 2016d).

advocated for Northern Ireland to be 'recognised through *a* Special Status' (2017: 3, *emphasis added*), presumably of a bespoke nature. Unionist parties sought 'Northern Ireland-specific solutions' (DUP, 2017: 19; UUP, 2017a) to recognise its 'unique position' (UUP, 2017b: 6) and 'particular circumstances' (DUP, 2017: 19) *outside* the EU without detailing how this could or should be achieved. Notwithstanding varying opinions on what 'special' or 'particular' status ought to be granted, in the Assembly election campaign, all five of the parties supported: continuation of EU funding for Northern Ireland; maintenance of the CTA; ongoing access to the EU single market and customs union for Northern Ireland; a frictionless border on the island of Ireland; arrangements to continue free movement of people, goods, and services with Ireland *and* the rest of the EU; all to be achieved by some sort of Northern Ireland-specific arrangement (again, see Hayward and Whitten, 2018).

The Assembly election was polarising. With the narrowest possible margin between the two largest parties, and both parties below the 30-seat petition of concern threshold, the result did little to incentivise the DUP or Sinn Féin to compromise at inter-party talks. Notwithstanding a display of cross-community solidarity at the funeral of Martin McGuinness, the political atmosphere proved too toxic for parties to reach agreement for power-sharing government.[16] So began a period of sustained political stagnation in Northern Ireland and a (nearly) record-breaking three years without a fully functioning government.[17]

Overall, the nine months between the UK's EU referendum and the triggering of Article 50 exposed the fragility of political consensus in the Executive and the tenuous nature of policy convergence in the Northern Ireland context. While a consensus did emerge, it lacked detail and was more a statement of shared principles than an actual policy framework. Northern Ireland party manifestos in the run-up to the March Assembly elections suggest that a collective position *may* have developed under the banner of some form of Northern Ireland exceptionalism *if* political relations had been such that

---

[16] Just weeks after his retirement from professional politics, former deputy First Minister and leader of Sinn Féin in Northern Ireland, Martin McGuinness, died at age 66 after suffering from a heart condition. In a rare show of unity, representatives from all communities in Northern Ireland, including DUP leader Arlene Foster, attended an inter-faith funeral for the former politician on 23 March 2017. Delivering McGuinness's eulogy, Sinn Féin President Gerry Adams called for tolerance and respect from Catholics towards Protestants. Such a display of intercommunal solidarity did not translate into compromise across the table at ongoing talks to form an executive (see McDowell, 2017; *Irish News*, 2017; *The Guardian*, 2017).

[17] In total, Northern Ireland was without government for 1,089 days (17 January 2017 until 11 January 2020). Although far surpassing a previous record of 589 days without government held by Belgium, the new Northern Irish record was not formally recognised due to its position as a sub-state, devolved region (see Whitten, 2018).

another power-sharing government was formed. Any (actual or potential) consensus that existed in the Executive and Assembly was rendered irrelevant as the attempts to reach agreement between parties repeatedly failed amid an increasingly arid political atmosphere.

Undoubtedly the second phase of the Brexit process exposed and exacerbated existing institutional weaknesses in Strand One. That said, a breakdown of political consensus in Northern Ireland was not wholly unique as this was a period of widespread political polarisation in the UK; however, the unique constitutional arrangements of Northern Ireland which, under Strand One, require government by cross-community coalition rendered the effect of that polarisation all the more damaging.

5.2.3 North–South Dimension

In the six months following the UK's EU referendum, North–South relations were strengthened as politicians and officials on both sides of the land border worked together, via Strand Two institutions, to map the likely implications of UK withdrawal from the EU on the island of Ireland. Following the collapse of Strand One institutions in January 2017, this period of collaboration between Belfast and Dublin ended due to the absence of Northern Ireland Ministers. The impact of the second phase of Brexit on Strand Two was therefore a tale of two halves: initially, the prospect of UK withdrawal from the EU incentivised North–South cooperation and led to effective cross-border working; this collaboration was, however, short-lived and the contingency of the Strand Two institutions on the, often unreliable, politics of power-sharing was underlined after the January 2017 Executive collapse.

On 4 July 2016, at the first plenary session of the NSMC since the referendum result, Ministers of the Northern Ireland Executive and Irish Government had a 'detailed discussion' on implications of the referendum outcome and agreed a work programme to 'optimise joint planning and engagement on key issues' (NSMC, 2016c: 8). Notwithstanding some tension between the Taoiseach and the First Minister over the necessity, or otherwise, of an all-island civic form on Brexit (see Connelly, 2018: 35), the agreed programme was comprehensive and significant. The NSMC agreed to 'ensure that Northern Ireland's interests are protected and advanced' while seeking to make sure the 'benefits of North/South cooperation are fully recognised' in any new UK–EU future relationship. Four priority areas were identified: the economy and trade; Northern Ireland and British-Irish relations; the CTA and the EU; alongside a 'full audit' in 'all sectors' (*ibid.*). It was further agreed that meetings between the Irish Government and senior Northern Ireland officials should increase in frequency and include consideration of 'issues arising from the referendum decisions' (*ibid.*). Although some political tensions between Leave-supporting First Minister and the Remain-supporting Irish administration were evident in the coverage of the NSMC plenary, its outcome demonstrated the willingness and intent of all parties to pursue an extensive collaborative work programme at official level with political backing.

Agreements made at the 4 July plenary were carried forward. From July 2016 to March 2017, minutes from NICS Board meetings indicate the Irish Government and Northern Ireland Executive engaged on Brexit-related issues regularly. Indeed, the language used by the NICS to record ongoing engagement with 'Whitehall and Irish Government officials' suggests cooperation between Belfast and Dublin was more effective than cooperation between Belfast and London. A NICS Board meeting on 26 August 'noted the ongoing engagement with Whitehall and Irish Government officials' then states that Permanent Secretaries present were invited to 'advise [Head of NICS] Sir Malcolm of any specific issues relating to dissatisfaction with information sharing which he would raise with the Cabinet Office and NIO'; this suggests that communication challenges only or primarily arose between officials in Belfast and in London (NICS Board, 2016d: 2). At a NSMC plenary session on 18 November, those present noted that 'full sectoral audits' had been carried out by departments in both jurisdictions to identify the 'possible impacts, risks, opportunities and contingencies'. It was further noted that discussions between Ministers and officials North and South would continue and senior officials from the Executive Office, the Department of the Taoiseach, and the Department of Foreign Affairs and Trade would continue 'to meet regularly on a Northern Ireland Executive to Irish Government bilateral basis … serving as a high-level working group on Brexit issues' (NSMC, 2016d: 3). The language of 'bilateralism' is normally used to describe collaboration between two states. Leaving aside the applicability or otherwise of the term as a description of North–South cooperation, it is demonstrable of the exceptional nature of Strand Two provisions and of what was ongoing at the time. Ministers of the sub-state region of Northern Ireland were working together with Ministers of neighbouring state, Ireland, to prepare for the impact of a change in the UK's international status as an EU Member State.

It is worth noting that, during this time, the posture of the UK Government towards North–South cooperation was contradictory. On one hand, the government supported independent cross-border working on post-Brexit solutions, via Strand Two institutions; thus, reflecting the unique provision in the 1998 Act (Sch2(3)(b)) for Northern Ireland Ministers to exercise legislative powers in excepted areas 'so far as required for giving effect to any agreement or arrangement' entered into at an NSMC meeting or for the purpose of implementing policies developed on a North–South basis. On the other hand, in *Miller* (2017), the government argued *against* any role for devolved administrations in the formal process of UK withdrawal. In response to a letter from SDLP MLA, Mark Durkan, then Secretary of State for Exiting the EU, David Davis, explicitly addressed the operation of Strand Two institutions in the context of Brexit. Writing on March 20, Davis stated: 'Strand 2 of the [1998] Agreement concerns co-operation between the Northern Ireland Executive and the Irish Government, rather than the UK Government' and stated that the NSMC 'remains an important forum for the Northern Ireland Executive and the Irish Government to continue to address the implications for future relations with the EU' (2017). The perspective articulated here by Davis contradicts the position in respect to the role of devolved administrations argued in *Miller* (2017). Speaking in the House of Commons weeks earlier, the DExEU Secretary had cited the summary judgment in *Miller* (2017) to underline his and the government's position whereby 'relations with the EU and other foreign affairs matters are reserved to the UK Government and parliament, not to the devolved institutions' (*Hansard*, 2017). Taking the DExEU Secretary's two positions together, Northern Ireland's relations with the Republic of Ireland did not seem to qualify as 'foreign affairs' nor was North–South cooperation to address the implications of Brexit for 'future relations with the EU' included as 'relations with the EU'. Arguably, this seeming contradiction is the outworking of the 1998 Schedule 2(3) exception; at the same time, however, it also demonstrates the propensity of the UK Government to overlook the uniqueness of the Northern Ireland constitution and its significance.

After the collapse of the Northern Ireland Executive and dissolution of the Assembly in advance of the March 2017 election, North–South meetings at the political and ministerial level ended. Work begun to map the impact of UK withdrawal from the EU on the island of Ireland could no longer continue on a 'bilateral' North–South basis. Instead, this was taken forward in the context of UK–EU negotiations.

5.2.4 East–West Dimension

In the period between the UK's EU referendum and the triggering of Article 50, the operation of Strand Three of the Northern Ireland constitution was impacted in two ways. The first is similar to the effect on Strand Two whereby the prospect of UK withdrawal from the EU incentivised collaboration between the UK's devolved administrations, Crown Dependencies, and the Irish Government via the British-Irish Council (BIC) but, after the collapse of Strand One institutions, there was a pause in the meetings of Strand Three institutions. The second is less tangible and relates to the posture of the UK Government whose language and approach indicated that it considered the implications of Brexit for Northern Ireland and Ireland as two facets of the same problem; this constituted another shift away from the previous norm of consensus-based intergovernmentalism between the UK and Ireland on problems pertaining to Northern Ireland.

In regard to preparing for Brexit, coordination between the UK's devolved administrations, Crown Dependencies, and the Irish Government, via the BIC, was initially substantive. An extraordinary summit of the BIC was convened on 22 July to 'consider the outcome' of the UK's EU referendum and '[reflect] on the implications for each individual British-Irish member administration' (BIC, 2016b: 1). Attendees included the First Minister of Scotland, First Minister of Wales, the First and deputy First Ministers of Northern Ireland, the Taoiseach, and Irish Minister for Foreign Affairs and Trade and, for the UK Government, the Secretary of State for Wales, the Secretary of State for Northern Ireland, and a junior minister from DExEU (BIC, 2016b: 4). Presenting a similar list to the one developed at the NSMC plenary on 4 July, the BIC identified broad 'priority areas' in the context of Brexit: 'the economy and trade, the CTA, relations with the EU and the status of all citizens affected' by the UK's EU withdrawal (*ibid.*). Those present 'reaffirmed the importance' of the BIC and agreed it 'should be fully utilised' in light of Brexit (*ibid.*). At the next BIC Summit on November 25, Ministers provided updates on their activities regarding the UK's exit from the EU with particular reference to relations between the Member Administrations. It was noted that arrangements to 'strengthen engagement' had been put in place with a more extensive list of priority sectors noted as 'agriculture, agri-food and fisheries industries, economy and trade, free movement of goods and people, the CTA and relations with the EU' (2016c: 1). Participants reiterated their commitment to 'facilitating harmonious and mutually beneficial relationships among the people of these islands as set out in the 1998 Agreement' (BIC, 2016c: 2). After the collapse of Strand One institutions in Northern Ireland, there was a pause in the meetings of the BIC; however, the 29th Summit meeting was held in Jersey in November 2017, without a Ministerial delegation from Northern Ireland (BIC, 2017: 3). The ongoing work of the BIC, minus Northern Ireland, is discussed in more detail in Chapter 6; for the purpose of this discussion, the break in BIC meetings serves to again underline the interdependence of the three-stranded structure of the Northern Ireland constitution.

Also, during this second phase of the Brexit process, the UK Government had some engagement with the Irish Government on the implications of the referendum result but there is no evidence these endeavours were supported by substantive UK policy proposals for British-Irish relations post-Brexit (Connelly, 2018). In the initial aftermath of the referendum, the UK Government framed the impact of Brexit on Northern Ireland and the Republic of Ireland as the same issue; one that would be dealt with bilaterally and not in the context of UK–EU negotiations. When delivering a statement in parliament on the outcome of the referendum on 27 June, Prime Minister Cameron spoke of meetings with the Irish Government beginning immediately 'to work through challenges relating to the *common border area*' (in *Hansard*, 2016, *emphasis added*). Likely, the Prime Minister meant to refer to the CTA, but the language is unconventional and arguably indicates a limited understanding of the nature of the issues. In the same statement, Cameron, likely inadvertently, seemed to refer to Ireland as a devolved administration stating: 'I have spoken to the First Ministers of Scotland and Wales, as well as the First and deputy First Ministers in Northern Ireland and the Taoiseach, and *our* officials will be working intensively together over the coming months to bring *our* devolved administrations into the process for determining the decisions that need to be taken' (*ibid.*). This phrasing suggests the Prime Minister included the Taoiseach in the collective 'officials' and 'devolved administrations' mentioned. No doubt a rhetorical slippage, the language here could be said to reflect a tendency in the UK Government to consider 'Irish issues' as domestic.[18]

5.3 Impact Assessment: Triggering Article 50 and the Northern Ireland Constitution

The most significant event for the Northern Ireland constitution in this second phase of the Brexit process was the Supreme Court judgment in *Miller* (2017) for two reasons. First, because the Supreme Court's handling of the

---

[18] In a similar example, on 1 September, the DExEU Secretary used almost identical phrasing in an article in the *Belfast Telegraph* as he used a week later in an *Irish Times* article: in the first, Davis stated that the 'United Kingdom is a great and strong country with a bright future and Northern Ireland plays a huge part in its success …' (Davis, 2016a); and in the second, 'the United Kingdom is a great and strong country with a bright future and its links with Ireland play an enormous part in its success …' (Davis, 2016b). No doubt unintended, the similarity of the language used in the two articles suggests they were written from the same template on the basis of an [Island of] Ireland policy.

'devolved' questions embraced a 'power-hoarding' (King, 2001; see 1.1) logic that would make it more difficult to accommodate the constitutional particularity of Northern Ireland in the context of Brexit. Second, because the Court's handling of 'questions of a constitutional nature' related to Northern Ireland demonstrated a willingness on the part of the judiciary to marginalise these. By inaccurately framing the Belfast litigation as subordinate to the London litigation, the Supreme Court in *Miller* (2017) was able to decline to take a definitive view on the former because it had already ruled on the latter. In particular, this meant that on the specific question referred in the Belfast litigation as regards the status of the 1998 Agreement in UK law and any consequential constraints on the prerogative power of the UK Government to trigger Article 50 was unanswered. In its approach to the other questions referred by the Belfast litigation, the Court failed to recognise the international legal dimension of the Northern Ireland constitution deriving from the British-Irish Agreement element of the 1998 Agreement. Instead, the Northern Ireland questions were subsumed into a 'devolutionary straight-jacket' (Campbell et al., 2003: 319) and answered accordingly.

This phase of the Brexit process also demonstrated the inherent fragility of Strand One institutions. Divergent perspectives of the Executive parties—DUP and Sinn Féin—on the UK's withdrawal from the EU exacerbated an already strained relationship. Thus, after a brief period of fragile consensus, the Executive and Assembly collapsed amid the fallout from the internal policy failures of the RHI scheme. The Assembly election that followed resulted in the narrowest possible margin between the DUP and Sinn Féin—gaining 28 seats and 27 seats respectively—an outcome that did little to incentivise compromise at inter-party talks and paved the way for a three-year hiatus in devolved government. While this breakdown in the devolved institutions cannot be directly attributed to Brexit, progressive polarisation between parties in Northern Ireland in the months following the referendum was exacerbated by divisions over UK withdrawal and its implications. Importantly, this was a period of political polarisation across the whole of the UK; however, the unique constitutional requirement for power-sharing devolution in Northern Ireland made it much more vulnerable to institutional breakdown as a consequence of divided politics.

In respect to the North–South dimension, the work of Strand Two initially increased in the wake of the UK's EU referendum as Belfast and Dublin worked together via the NSMC and on an *ad hoc* basis to map the possible repercussions of UK withdrawal from the EU on both jurisdictions. However, following the collapse of devolved government, cross-border cooperation at an official level diminished as Strand Two institutions could no longer meet.

As a consequence, work begun to map the implications for the island of Ireland was carried forward in the international context of UK–EU withdrawal negotiations. Similarly, in the immediate aftermath of the UK's EU referendum result, Strand Three institutions were used as a forum for collaboration between the UK's devolved administrations, Crown Dependencies, and the Irish Government regarding the likely implications of Brexit. After the collapse of the devolved institutions, there was a hiatus in the functioning of the East–West institutions; the BIC did, however, begin meeting again in the summer of 2018, absent Northern Ireland representation. Overall then the impact of this second phase of Brexit on Strand Two and Strand Three served to underline the interdependence of the three-stranded structure of the Northern Ireland constitution.

Chapters 8 and 9 discuss these findings in more detail and in the context of the overall research. The substance of UK–EU withdrawal negotiations and the Withdrawal Agreement they produced is where the focus of analysis now turns in Chapter 6.

6
UK–EU Withdrawal Agreement

> 'This is a wonderful thing for Northern Ireland because it allows the whole of the UK to leave while making sure there isn't any border at all between Northern Ireland and the south. But also, and this has been a very, very important point to get across, there are no frictions at all west–east or east–west.'
>
> **Prime Minister, Boris Johnson, November 2019**[1]

> '… of course, there will be checks between Northern Ireland and Great Britain as it is written down in the Withdrawal Agreement. The checks will be done by the Brits under the supervision of the European Union and the European Court of Justice.'
>
> **European Commission President, Ursula von der Leyen, January 2020**[2]

Northern Ireland was a stumbling block to consensus in UK–EU withdrawal negotiations. Attempts to reach an agreement repeatedly fell down because of the two sides' different perspectives on the 'problem' of Northern Ireland and how to 'solve' it. The disagreement derived primarily from the irreconcilability of UK Government negotiating objectives that proposed to leave the EU single market and customs union, avoid a hard border on the island of Ireland and/or any new trade barriers within the UK internal market, while also respecting the EU's 'red line' of protecting the legal integrity of its single market and customs union; these objectives could not all be achieved.

The 'solution' of Prime Minister May was to compromise on the nature of the UK's departure from the single market and customs union. Under the unratified UK–EU Withdrawal Agreement (2019)[3] negotiated by May,

---

[1] Johnson, B. (2019) 'Boris Johnson says single market access after Brexit is "great deal" for Northern Ireland' *The Independent*. 2019, 8 November. Available: https://www.independent.co.uk/news/uk/politics/brexit-deal-boris-johnson-northern-ireland-speech-general-election-single-market-a9194476.html (Accessed 20 September 2020).

[2] Von der Leyen, U. in Connelly, T. (2020) 'Von der Leyen contradicts Johnson on Brexit checks' *RTÉ*. 2020, 31 January. Available: https://www.rte.ie/news/2020/0131/1112284-brexit-europe/ (Accessed 28 January 2021).

[3] Reference here and throughout is to the official version of the draft UK–EU Withdrawal Agreement published in the EU *Official Journal* on 19 February 2019 (C66I: 1–184).

in the absence of a future UK–EU relationship that avoided any need to harden the border on the island of Ireland, Northern Ireland would remain aligned to EU single market regulations necessary to allow the continuation of North–South cooperation and frictionless trade in goods between Ireland and Northern Ireland. Following from this, and to mitigate the need for new checks or controls on goods moving 'East–West' between Great Britain and Northern Ireland, the whole of the UK would, under May's Withdrawal Agreement, remain in a customs union with the EU *unless and until* the 'red line' negotiating objective of avoiding a hard land border could be met by alternative arrangements. This 'backstop' approach was premised on the pursuit of a 'deep and special' future UK–EU trading partnership which would, in theory, minimise the legal significance of any UK-wide alignment deriving from the 'unique circumstances' of Northern Ireland (HM Government, 2017b: 43). The 'backstop' solution was unpopular among parliamentarians who three times rejected May's Withdrawal Agreement. The Prime Minister's inability to get this agreement passed in the UK Parliament, eventually forced her to resign. May's successor, Prime Minister Boris Johnson, agreed to a different 'solution', this time foregoing the previous commitment to avoid any new barriers to trade within the UK single market. The revised *Protocol on Ireland/Northern Ireland* (hereafter 'Protocol') in the UK–EU Withdrawal Agreement (2020)[4] (hereafter 'Withdrawal Agreement') avoided a hard border on the island of Ireland by applying the EU customs code and EU single market regulations necessary for the free movement of goods between Northern Ireland and Ireland (and so the EU). With the UK outside a customs union with the EU and Great Britain eschewing regulatory alignment with the EU single market *acquis*, new customs procedures and regulatory checks and controls on goods moving between Great Britain and Northern Ireland would be necessary, alongside the possibility of tariffs needing to be collected. Despite opposition in Northern Ireland to the Prime Minister's 'great' new deal (Johnson, 2019), the Withdrawal Agreement was supported by a majority of MPs following a landslide Conservative victory for Johnson in the December 2019 general election. Notwithstanding Johnson's assertion that the revised Withdrawal Agreement required 'no frictions at all' on trade between Great Britain and Northern Ireland, as this chapter sets out, implementing the Protocol would necessitate 'checks' (Von der Leyen, 2020) or 'additional process[es]' (Cabinet Office, 2020b: para. 17(3)) between Northern Ireland and Great Britain, the implementation of which, alongside

---

[4] Reference here and throughout is to the official version of the UK–EU Withdrawal Agreement published in the *Official Journal* of the EU on 31 January 2020 following ratification and signature (L29: 7–187).

other novel provisions in the Protocol, would further differentiate Northern Ireland as a constitutional 'place apart' in a post-Brexit UK.

In assessing the impact of this phase of Brexit on the Northern Ireland constitution, this chapter focuses more on the implications of the legal text—the Withdrawal Agreement and specifically the Protocol—than on the political process that led to it. Such an approach is justified as, more than in the two preceding chapters on the UK's EU referendum and triggering Article 50, the legal outcome of this phase has had and will have a significantly greater impact on the Northern Ireland constitution than the political events leading to it; this notwithstanding, those political events are still relevant and are considered.

This chapter has three parts: the first provides an overview of key political events between the triggering of Article 50 in March 2017 and the ratification of the Withdrawal Agreement in January 2020; the second sets out the impact of the Withdrawal Agreement on the Northern Ireland constitution; and the third reviews the findings and their significance in the broader story of Brexit. By way of summary, the key findings are as follows: (1) the Protocol establishes the EU as a 'protector' of the 1998 Agreement; (2) the 'democratic consent mechanism' contained in the Protocol represents a new formulation of the principle of consent that moves away from the popular, cross-community consent enshrined in the 1998 Agreement and towards majoritarian, parliamentary consent; (3) by not requiring oversight from Strand One institutions the arrangements for implementing the Protocol strengthen UK Government executive powers vis-à-vis devolved government powers in a manner beyond the balance envisaged in the 1998 Agreement; (4) the Protocol privileges Strand Two by creating new legal protections for North–South cooperation in respect to cross-border trade in goods while also incentivising deeper North–South cooperation in areas not covered in the Protocol text; (5) there is no explicit provision for Strand Three institutions' involvement in the operation of the Protocol, yet the process of UK withdrawal has motivated renewed engagement with Strand Three institutions and resulted in some legal clarification as to the nature of bilateral UK–Ireland relations post-Brexit.

6.1 The UK–EU Withdrawal Negotiations and UK–EU Withdrawal Agreement

The period between the triggering of Article 50 in March 2017 and the ratification of the Withdrawal Agreement in January 2020 was one of profound political instability caused, directly and indirectly, by disagreement over the meaning of Brexit and the UK Government's handling of the process. It is not necessary for our purposes to account for every political development during this third phase of the Brexit process, nor would this be possible in the space available. However, to properly contextualise an analysis of the impact of the Withdrawal Agreement on the Northern Ireland constitution it is necessary to account for events as they related to Northern Ireland. This is best achieved with reference to three phases in the withdrawal negotiations, each associated with alternative approaches to the 'problem' of Northern Ireland—from 'flexible and imaginative' solutions in phase one to the unpopular 'backstop' Protocol in phase two to the eventually ratified 'front-stop' Protocol in phase three.

6.1.1 Phase One of Withdrawal Negotiations: 'Flexibility and Imagination'

A search for 'flexible and imaginative' solutions to address the 'unique circumstances' of Northern Ireland became a shared aim of UK and EU negotiators in the first phase of withdrawal negotiations (European Council, 2017: 11; HM Government, 2017b: 1). The focus on arrangements for Northern Ireland and its border with Ireland arose, primarily, from the prominence granted this issue in European Council guidelines for Article 50 negotiations, wherein the EU[5] underlined its view of the 'paramount importance' of ensuring the 'achievements, benefits, and commitments' of the peace process and the 1998 Agreement 'in all its parts' were protected in the withdrawal process (2017: 11). To this end, the EU called for 'flexible and imaginative solutions' to be found in the first phase of UK–EU negotiations to address the 'unique circumstances' on the island of Ireland (*ibid.*). In her letter to European Council President Donald Tusk to trigger Article 50, Prime Minister May underlined the UK's 'important responsibility' to 'make sure nothing is done to jeopardise the peace process in Northern Ireland and to continue to uphold the Belfast Agreement' but did so in language that was more muted and equivocal than that of the EU (The Prime Minister, 2017). Initially, the UK resisted an EU proposal to prioritise 'sufficient progress' on the shared aim of protecting

---

[5] Although the UK remained a member of the EU until 31 January 2020, from this point onwards reference to 'the EU' should not be understood to include the UK. On 29 June 2016, leaders of the 27 remaining heads of state or government of the EU met for the first time to discuss the UK decision to withdraw from the EU. With the launch of the Article 50 process, EU27 leaders met formally as 'European Council (Art. 50). In the Council, the EU(27) discussed UK withdrawal in meetings of the 'General Affairs Council (Art. 50)'. In this discussion, 'the EU' and 'the EU27' are used interchangeably.

the peace process and avoiding a hard border on the island of Ireland as one of three 'separation issues' to be addressed in the first phase of negotiations before any discussion of UK–EU future relations in the second phase (European Commission, 2017a: 19). Instead, the UK Government proposed the two sides 'establish working principles' and 'high-level … criteria' to address issues related to Northern Ireland, including North–South cooperation and the movement of goods, but argued that practical, 'technical solutions' could only be addressed in the context of UK–EU future relationship negotiations (HM Government, 2017b: 5). The EU position on the scheduling of negotiations prevailed, meaning 'sufficient progress' in the search for 'flexible and imaginative' solutions to preserve the peace process, avoid a hard border, and maintain North–South cooperation became a condition of progress in withdrawal negotiations.

Before negotiations began, Prime Minister May called an early general election in the hope of securing a larger majority to strengthen her hand in UK–EU negotiations but failed to do so. Conservatives were returned as the largest party with 318 seats but were short of the number required for majority government (326 seats). So, controversially,[6] Prime Minister May choose to enter minority government backed by a confidence-and-supply agreement with the DUP and their ten Northern Ireland MPs. In view of the ongoing absence of devolved government in Northern Ireland, this governing arrangement gave the pro-Brexit, hard-line Unionist DUP a disproportionate influence over the handling of issues pertaining to Northern Ireland in UK–EU negotiations. Six rounds of talks took place in the first phase of negotiations between 19 June and 8 December 2017, wherein arrangements for Northern Ireland and its border with Ireland emerged as the most complex and contentious issue. Constrained by the UK's negotiating 'red lines'—leaving the EU single market and customs union while avoiding a hard border on the island of Ireland—Prime Minister May sought a withdrawal agreement that would be acceptable to pro-Brexit and anti-Brexit factions of the Conservative party as well as her DUP partners who insisted: 'Northern Ireland must leave the European Union on the same terms as the rest of the United Kingdom' (Foster, 2017b). This would prove an impossible task.[7]

---

[6] Those who warned against the Tory–DUP confidence and supply arrangement included previous Conservative Prime Minister John Major who said it risked disrupting Northern Ireland's 'fragile peace' by jeopardising the UK Government's crucial role as an 'honest broker' (Syal and Walker, 2017). After it was signed, Wales' First Minister, Labour's Carwyn Jones, described the deal as 'unacceptable' saying it 'further weakens the UK' (in Anushka et al., 2017); while the Liberal Democrat leader, Tim Farron, described it as 'a grubby attempt' by Theresa May to 'keep her Cabinet squatting in Number 10' (ibid.).

[7] The logical incompatibility of the UK governments' three 'red lines'—avoiding a hard border on the island of Ireland, leaving the single market and customs union and avoiding new checks or

Agreement in principle was reached in this phase on arrangements necessary for continuing the CTA and preserving the rights of Irish citizens under the 1998 Agreement. However, the two sides remained far apart on issues pertaining to the land border (including free movement of goods), and on arrangements necessary to maintain North–South cooperation. The UK Government continued to emphasise their view that these issues could 'only properly be finalised in the context of the new, deep and special [UK–EU] partnership' (HM Government, 2017b: 43); UK proposals relied on 'innovative and untested' approaches that would use not-yet-developed 'technology-based solutions' (*ibid.*: 51) combined with 'cross-border trade exemption[s]' (*ibid.*: 48). From an EU perspective, these aspirational proposals and future solutions provided insufficient legal certainty. There was a *partial* reconciliation of these two perspectives in the *Joint report from the negotiators of the European Union and the United Kingdom Government on progress during phase 1 of negotiations under Article 50 TEU on the United Kingdom's orderly withdrawal from the European Union* (the 'Joint Report') that provided a basis for European Council decision to move to the next phase of negotiations and in which the concept of a 'backstop' was born. The Joint Report outlined three solutions to achieve the shared aims of avoiding a hard border and protecting North–South cooperation: the first reflected the UK ideal of achieving said aims through the UK–EU future relationship; but, if this was not possible, the UK secondly committed to proposing 'specific solutions' (including those reliant on technological innovation) to address the unique circumstances on the island of Ireland; and, if this was also not possible, the UK thirdly committed to 'maintain full alignment with those rules of the Internal Market and the Customs Union which now or in future, support North–South cooperation, the all-island economy and the protection of the 1998 Agreement' (Joint Report, 2017: 49).[8] This was the origin of what

---

controls between Great Britain and Northern Ireland—was often referred to as 'the Brexit Trilemma' (see @rdanielkelemen, 2020; Papazian, 2018).

[8] The Joint Report contained the most important demonstration of the DUP ability to exert influence in UK–EU talks. A draft text was agreed by UK and EU negotiators but rejected by the DUP; this forced the May Government to seek amendments to make it more agreeable to the DUP. Paragraphs 49 and 50 of the final text of the Joint Report are the result of those amendments. In paragraph 49 the UK Government committed to 'maintain full alignment' with the EU single market and customs union necessary to 'support North–South cooperation, the all-island economy and the protection of the 1998 Agreement'—this was the origin of the UK-wide 'backstop' solution developed by the May Government (2017: 49). In paragraph 50, the UK Government committed to ensure 'no new regulatory barriers' between Northern Ireland and the rest of the UK developed 'unless, consistent with the 1998 Agreement, the Northern Ireland Executive and Assembly agree that distinct arrangements are appropriate for Northern Ireland' (2017: 50)—while this commitment does not wholly align with the eventually agreed Withdrawal Agreement, the genesis of the Johnson Government's emphasis on democratic consent as a means to legitimate 'new regulatory barriers' between Northern Ireland and the rest of the UK is evident in the language of paragraph 50. Thus, the final version of the Joint Report demonstrates that the Tory–DUP confidence and supply arrangement

became the 'Backstop' Protocol in the unratified Withdrawal Agreement, agreed by Prime Minister May but rejected by the UK Parliament.

6.1.2 Phase Two of Withdrawal Negotiations: The 'Backstop' Protocol

Provisions in the Joint Report reflected an agreement on a 'framework' for addressing the unique circumstances on the island of Ireland, but discussions continued as to the 'detailed arrangements required' to implement that framework in the second phase of negotiations (2017: 2). Based on the Joint Report, the EU published a draft legal text of an agreement in February 2018 that included its interpretation of the requirements necessary to give effect to the third 'backstop' scenario in the first iteration of an Ireland/Northern Ireland Protocol (hereafter 'draft EU Protocol'). The draft EU Protocol text proposed a common regulatory area comprising of the Union and the United Kingdom in respect of Northern Ireland (European Commission, 2018: 100, Article 3); under this arrangement, Northern Ireland would be fully included in the EU customs territory, meaning duties and quantitative restrictions on imports and exports on trade between Northern Ireland and the EU would be prohibited and customs duties and quantitative restrictions would therefore be applied on trade between Great Britain and Northern Ireland (*ibid.*: 100, Article 4). The proposed text received strong pushback from the UK Government. Speaking in the House of Commons, the Prime Minister said, if implemented, the draft EU Protocol would 'undermine the UK common market and threaten [the] constitutional integrity of the UK by creating a customs and regulatory border down the Irish Sea' and, therefore, 'no UK Prime Minister could ever agree to it' (2018). The Prime Minister had the full support of her DUP partners in government but a more politically agreeable alternative, still within the framework of the Joint Report, was not forthcoming. Between February and November 2018, UK–EU negotiations sought a mutually acceptable interpretation of the Joint Report commitment by the UK to 'maintain full alignment' to the extent necessary to protect North–South cooperation, the 1998 Agreement, and avoid a hard border (Joint Report, 2017: 49). Finding a compromise that was legally operable from an EU27 perspective yet politically acceptable from a UK perspective was not easy.

After months of talks during which May was effectively in parallel negotiations with the EU27, pro-Brexit and anti-Brexit factions within her party,

enabled the DUP to influence the UK position in negotiations, albeit not to the extent that the party wanted.

and her DUP partners in confidence and supply, the UK and EU reached agreement on the terms of the UK's withdrawal. An agreed UK–EU Withdrawal Agreement text (hereafter the 'unratified Withdrawal Agreement') was published on 14 November 2018.

Although also based on the third scenario set out in the Joint Report, the unratified Withdrawal Agreement provisions for Northern Ireland had developed considerably from those envisaged in the February 2018 EU draft legal text. Unlike earlier drafts, the 'Backstop' Protocol in the unratified Withdrawal Agreement had both Northern Ireland-specific provisions and UK-wide provisions. Under its terms, Northern Ireland would be treated as part of the EU customs territory and stay aligned with EU regulations necessary for continued free movement of goods with the rest of the EU, including Ireland—thus avoiding the need for a hard border on the island of Ireland. At the same time, the whole of the UK would form a 'single customs territory' for the purposes of trade in goods—meaning that new checks on goods moving from Great Britain to Northern Ireland (GB–NI), necessary under the Northern Ireland-specific elements, would be kept at a minimum also, because of a guarantee of 'unfettered access' for goods moving from Northern Ireland to Great Britain (NI–GB); there would be no new checks required on NI–GB trade. In addition to its provisions regarding trade, the 'Backstop' Protocol set out arrangements for the rights of individuals, the CTA, the maintenance of North–South cooperation, the single electricity market, and state aid, while also setting out institutional arrangements for oversight and implementation via a UK–EU Joint Committee, a Specialised Committee, and a Joint Consultative Working Group; its provisions on these latter issues were carried forward into the revised, later ratified, Protocol with minimal alteration.

Among UK parliamentarians, the 'Backstop' Protocol was not popular: the DUP rejected it because it differentiated Northern Ireland; Conservative Brexiteers rejected it because the UK would have to accept aspects of the EU legal *acquis*; and opposition parties rejected the unratified Withdrawal Agreement in its entirety because they did not want the kind of 'hard Brexit' it would achieve. In this context, attempts to get an *EU (Withdrawal Agreement) Bill* approved in Westminster were unsuccessful. Notwithstanding UK Government and EU efforts to guarantee the temporary nature of the 'Backstop' Protocol and to underline their shared intention to disapply its provisions as soon as 'alternative arrangements' were found,[9] the May deal was rejected

---

[9] Following talks with President Tusk and President Juncker and still facing significant opposition to the agreed text, Prime Minister May announced she had secured 'legally binding changes' to ensure the backstop could not apply indefinitely (The Prime Minister, 2019a); these included a joint instrument and

three times.[10] Facing a political impasse, the Prime Minister had to request extensions to the Article 50 process and was eventually forced to resign on 24 May 2019 expressing, as she did, her 'deep regret' at not delivering Brexit (in *BBC News*, 2019a).

6.1.3 Phase Three of Withdrawal Negotiations: The 'Front-Stop' Protocol

A Conservative Party leadership contest to replace Theresa May was triggered, from which former Foreign Secretary and former London Mayor Boris Johnson emerged victorious, having promised to deliver Brexit 'do or die, come what may' before the new deadline for the end of the Article 50 process on 31 October (in Honeycomb-Foster, 2019). Prime Minister Johnson immediately sought to re-open negotiations on the unratified Withdrawal Agreement to remove what he described as the 'unviable' and 'anti-democratic' backstop which, he argued, would undermine the 'delicate balance' of the 1998 Agreement because it afforded 'the people of Northern Ireland no influence over legislation which applies to them' (The Prime Minister, 2019b). The EU27 had consistently said that the Withdrawal Agreement was 'not open for renegotiation' but that they would be open to discussions 'if the position of the United Kingdom were to evolve' (European Council, 2019). Talks with the new UK administration thus began with Johnson accepting that the 'onus' was on the UK to come up with mutually acceptable alternatives to the 'backstop' Protocol (see *BBC News*, 2019b).

As preparations for a potential 'No Deal' exit on 31 October ratcheted up (see *Hansard*, 2019b; HM Government, 2019c), the two sides remained far apart on arrangements for Northern Ireland, particularly on issues regarding customs and consent (see Varadkar in Wall, 2019). A breakthrough came from a meeting of Taoiseach Leo Varadkar and Prime Minister Johnson after which the two premiers could 'see a pathway to a deal' (*BBC News*, 2019c). Several days later, on 17 October 2019, a revised Withdrawal Agreement was published. The only substantial difference between the new deal and its predecessor was in respect to the provisions for Northern Ireland.

---

a unilateral declaration that followed an earlier exchange of letters. May's efforts were subsequently undermined by Attorney General Geoffrey Cox in a legal opinion and his statement in the House of Commons to the effect that 'there is no ultimate unilateral right out of [the backstop] arrangement' (*Hansard*, 2019a).

[10] The UK Government lost the first 'Meaningful Vote' by a majority of 230 (with 202 MPs voting 'for' and 432 'against') on 15 January 2019; the government lost 'Meaningful Vote 2' by a majority of 149 (with 242 MPs voting 'for' and 391 'against') on 12 March 2019; the government lost 'Meaning Vote 3' by a majority of 58 (with 286 MPs voting 'for' and 344 'against').

While arrangements for post-Brexit Northern Ireland in the unratified Withdrawal Agreement were designed as an insurance policy, arrangements set out in the Protocol in the revised Withdrawal Agreement would automatically apply at the end of the transition period after the UK left the EU, scheduled for 31 December 2020. Whereas the 'backstop' in the unratified Withdrawal Agreement contained measures specific to Northern Ireland and UK-wide aspects, provisions of the revised Protocol would only apply in Northern Ireland. Prime Minister May's UK-wide backstop had transformed into Prime Minister Johnson's NI-specific front-stop.

Under the terms of the new Protocol, Northern Ireland would remain *de jure* inside the UK customs territory but *de facto* in the EU customs union; and would continue to apply EU rules and regulations relevant to the free movement of goods, as necessary, to allow frictionless trade on the island of Ireland to continue—in substance, the provisions bore very strong resemblance to the draft EU Protocol with those on regulatory alignment being identical. Therefore, similar to the draft EU Protocol, as a consequence of the provisions on cross-border trade and in order to ensure compliance with EU law, GB–NI and NI–GB trade would be subject to additional checks and controls. In contrast to the draft EU Protocol, however, the Protocol addressed concerns about consent that had come to the fore during parliamentary debates on the 'Backstop' Protocol and which Prime Minister Johnson had emphasised in renegotiations. A new 'democratic consent mechanism' in the Protocol provided that an opportunity be granted to the Northern Ireland Assembly to vote on whether or not to retain core aspects of the Protocol regarding customs, trade, and regulatory alignment in 2024 and again every four or eight years thereafter, contingent on the type of consent achieved.

Prime Minister Johnson hailed the revised Withdrawal Agreement as an 'excellent deal', but it was not warmly welcomed in Northern Ireland (*BBC News*, 2019d). DUP deputy leader Nigel Dodds said the Prime Minister had been 'too eager by far to get a deal at any cost'; a DUP statement later made clear the party would not support the agreement as it 'undermine[d] the integrity of the Union' and was not economically beneficial for Northern Ireland (in *BBC News*, 2019d). The UUP and TUV were more vehement in their language respectively describing the Protocol as an 'absolute disgrace' and an agreement that 'puts [NI] in a waiting room for Irish unity' (in Carroll and O'Carroll, 2019). Northern Ireland's non-Unionist parties' reactions were more muted but not positive. Sinn Féin described the new deal as the 'least-worst option' in the circumstance while the SDLP and Alliance took the view that the new deal was worse than Prime Minister May's but better than 'No Deal' (in Bell, 2019). Facing the same parliamentary arithmetic that had plagued May's attempts to ratify her deal, and unable to rely on his DUP partners, Johnson began pursuing a general election.

A few weeks of parliamentary acrobatics later, UK voters went to the polls for the first December general election in nearly a century and the third general election in five years. During the campaign, the UK Government gave mixed messages regarding the implications of the Withdrawal Agreement for Northern Ireland. On October 21, Secretary of State for Exiting the EU, Steven Barclay, said exit summary declarations would be needed for trade in goods moving NI–GB (McCormack, 2019a). On October 23, at Prime Minister's Questions, Johnson said 'no checks' would be necessary for goods moving from NI–GB, a direct contradiction of the DExEU Secretary's testimony and his government's own impact assessment (Buchan, 2019). Lack of clarity over the implications of the Protocol for Northern Ireland caused serious concern among the businesses and politicians in Northern Ireland with Chief Constable of the PSNI also warning of Loyalist disorder if the Brexit deal threatens, or is perceived to threaten, the Union (in *BBC News*, 2019e). Johnson's Conservative Party won a landslide victory capturing the 'red wall' of traditionally Labour heartlands in the Midlands and North of England. The results were also historic in Northern Ireland where, for the first time since it was established, the electorate returned a minority of Unionist representatives to Westminster with the DUP losing two seats, the SDLP gaining two, and Alliance winning the previously independent Unionist seat of North Down (see Whitten, 2020). The Prime Minister returned to Downing Street with an 80 seat majority, comfortable enough to pass his Withdrawal Agreement through the Houses of Parliament in January, putting the UK on course to leave the EU on 31 January 2020 and to prepare to implement an untested set of arrangements in Northern Ireland at the end of the transition period on 1 January 2021.

6.2 The UK–EU Withdrawal Agreement and the Northern Ireland Constitution

An explicit objective of the Protocol in the revised, ratified Withdrawal Agreement is 'to protect the 1998 Agreement in all its parts' (Article 1(3)). By agreeing an international treaty with this aim, the UK and EU, in effect, strengthened the legal standing of the 1998 Agreement by setting the EU up as its protector. The EU's new role in respect of the 1998 Agreement is distinctive to that of the post-1998 co-guarantor roles of the UK and Ireland Governments. Unlike the 1998 Agreement, the Withdrawal Agreement includes a dispute resolution mechanism, means of redress for violations of applicable EU law via the CJEU, establishes bodies to oversee the implementation of the Protocol, and grants these bodies power to amend its terms in accordance with its efficacy. These arrangements for implementation, oversight, and enforcement of the Protocol are significantly different to their equivalent in the 1998 Agreement. Under Article 2 of the (British-Irish) 1998 Agreement, the two governments committed to 'support, and where appropriate implement the provisions of the Multi-Party Agreement', thus establishing them as guarantors. The 1998 Agreement did not, however, include any mechanism for dispute resolution or legal redress between the parties and has relied instead on the political and diplomatic relations of its guarantors as the *modus operandi* for its implementation.[11] In view of the mechanisms for implementing the Protocol, the EU's protector role in respect of the 1998 Agreement is therefore more legally robust than the guarantor roles of the UK and Ireland Governments, albeit of less political significance.

Notwithstanding the comprehensive language of the Protocol as regards the 1998 Agreement, in practice, its implementation is only likely to protect some aspects of it. This is because the Protocol text relies on a particular interpretation of what 'protecting the 1998 Agreement' means; that interpretation privileges some aspects—namely cross-border trade in goods and citizens' rights—and relies on the manifestation of these in EU law. As such, the Withdrawal Agreement's legal protection of the 1998 Agreement in 'all its dimensions' is, in practice, only likely to be enforced in areas that are specifically protected by the Protocol. Arguably, this is an unsurprising outcome of efforts to protect an intentionally 'constructively ambiguous' bilateral treaty that has been variously implemented for over 20 years. That said, the Protocol's emphasis on certain aspects is also more a consequence of UK and EU negotiating objectives and the politics of the process than reflective of the provisions and principles enshrined in the 1998 Agreement. By agreeing 'arrangements necessary' to address the unique circumstances on the island of Ireland, maintain North–South cooperation, avoid a hard border, and protect the 1998 Agreement 'in all its dimensions' (Article 1(3)) in the specific political context of UK withdrawal from the EU, the Protocol necessarily reflects a particular contemporaneous interpretation of the 1998 Agreement, Northern Ireland's constitutional status, and North–South cooperation. As a

---

[11] The process of implementing the 1998 Agreement has had a staccato and iterative quality; lengthy periods of institutional stagnation, most notably between 2002 and 2007 and 2017 and 2020, have been resolved through inter-party talks mediated by the UK and Irish Governments in a similar manner to the process that led to the initial agreement. For an account of the evolution of the 1998 Agreement, see Humphreys (2018: 21–56) or Coakley and Todd (2020: chapter 6).

consequence, the effect of the Protocol is to rebalance the 1998 Agreement and Northern Ireland constitution by providing greater legal protections for some aspects, reformulating others, and excluding still others. This fact and its implications for the components of the constitution in Northern Ireland are explored in detail here, beginning with the principle of consent.

6.2.1 The Principle of Consent

The impact of the Protocol on the 1998 Agreement principle of consent is paradoxical. On one hand, it reaffirms a conventional understanding of the principle of consent to constitutional change as set out in the 1998 Agreement while, on the other, it creates a new form of consent via the 'democratic consent mechanism' whereby the Northern Ireland Assembly will have opportunity to vote on aspects of the Protocol in 2024 and, depending on the outcome, at regular intervals thereafter. There is, therefore, an incongruity in the effect of the Protocol's consent-related provisions: the reaffirmation of the consent principle provides a legal reassurance of the constitutional status quo, while the new 'democratic consent mechanism' introduces a degree of perpetual legal uncertainty as to the implementation of the Protocol and provides for a political process that will likely be destabilising and which breaks domestic constitutional convention. In addition, this latter novel provision for consent in the Protocol prioritises parliamentary consent within the Assembly and majoritarian decision-making, and therefore moves away from provisions for consent in the 1998 Agreement which prioritised popular consent and cross-community decision-making.

6.2.1.1 Constitutional Status Reaffirmed

In Article 1, 'Objectives', the Protocol states that its terms are 'without prejudice to the provisions of the 1998 Agreement in respect of the constitutional status of Northern Ireland and the principle of consent' which provides that 'any change in that status can only be made with the consent of a majority of its people' (Article 1(1)). In reaffirming the constitutional status quo, this statement provides a legal reassurance for the UK and, more particularly, for Northern Ireland Unionists who perceive the provisions of the Protocol as a threat to Northern Ireland's place in the UK. Similar confirmatory language regarding the constitutional status of Northern Ireland first appeared in the Joint Report wherein both parties recognised 'the need to respect the provisions of the 1998 Agreement regarding the constitutional status of Northern Ireland and the principle of consent' (2017: 44). Exactly the same recognition appeared in the preamble of the draft EU Protocol (European Commission, 2018: recital 13). In the unratified Withdrawal Agreement signed by Prime Minister May, the reaffirmation had been moved to Article 1 and stated in the same language as is used in the ratified Withdrawal Agreement and Protocol delivered by Prime Minister Johnson. The timing of this development—from preamble to objective—suggests that the reaffirmation of constitutional consent came as a result of a UK Government ask during May's premiership to reassure her DUP governing partners.

In light of its origin and apparent political purpose, the phrasing used to affirm the principle of consent in Article 1 of Protocol is noteworthy; it reflects that used in Article 1(iii) of the 1998 (British-Irish) Agreement which states that 'the present wish of a majority of the people of Northern Ireland, freely exercised and legitimate, is to maintain the Union and ... that it would be wrong to make *any change in the status* of Northern Ireland save with the consent of the majority of its people' (*added*) (also in MPA *Constitutional Issues*: s1(iii)). This is the only time that the 1998 Agreement text refers to '*any* change in the status of Northern Ireland' in discussing the consent principle.[12] By using this language to characterise the principle of consent, Article 1 of the Protocol therefore reflects what could be termed the 'maximalist' version of the principle of constitutional consent described in the 1998 Agreement.

A 'maximalist' version of the constitutional consent principle is important because, in UK domestic law, the phrasing is more specific, the 1998 Act states that 'Northern Ireland in its entirety remains part of the United Kingdom and shall not cease to be so without the consent of a majority of the people of Northern Ireland' (s1(1)); here, the 'majority consent' requirement is explicitly linked to Northern Ireland's current status within the UK.[13] Although perhaps incidental, the discrepancy between the articulation of the principle of constitutional consent in the Protocol, and its articulation in UK domestic law, highlights a general inherent tension between international treaties and their domestic implementation in the UK's dualistic legal order. Further, this linguistic discrepancy underlines the more specific challenge of seeking to protect the 1998 Agreement 'in all its dimensions' (Article 1(3)) when,

---

[12] In para. 1(vi) of *Constitutional Issues* in the Multi-Party Agreement, the right to hold British or Irish citizenship is said to 'not be affected by *any future change* in the status of Northern Ireland' (*added*) thereby also using the 'maximalist' version of the consent principle, but as the phrasing is different, and (iv) is referencing 1(iii), the point stands.

[13] As noted in 5.2.1., the Supreme Court in *Miller* only ruled on the principle of consent provision in the 1998 Act, affirming this 'neither regulated any other change in the constitutional status of Northern Ireland nor required the consent of a majority of the people of Northern Ireland to the withdrawal of the United Kingdom from the European Union' (2017: 135).

since 1998, the operation of that agreement has been almost entirely contingent upon its interpretation and implementation in UK law which has not always matched the original text (see, for example, Mac Síthigh, 2018; *Secretary of State for the Home Department v De Souza* 2019; Harvey, A. 2020). The interpretation of the Protocol in domestic law is explored more fully in the next chapter. For the purpose of this discussion, the phrasing used in Article 1 and the timing of its inclusion in the various versions of the Withdrawal Agreement suggest, first, that it was a UK Government ask to include it in the main body of the Protocol and, second, that the 'maximalist' characterisation of the principle of consent differs from that used in UK law and is thus more likely to derive from an Irish Government characterisation of the 1998 Agreement. This latter point suggests a lack of familiarity among UK negotiators as to the details of the 1998 Act and 1998 Agreement—this finding was confirmed by interviews carried out as part of the research for this book. An official from the EU Task Force 50 team confirmed the predominance of Irish Government understandings of the 1998 Agreement and Northern Ireland issues more generally in the context of UK–EU negotiations (Task Force 50 Interviewee, 2019); an interview with a civil servant in the DExEU Protocol team stated a lack of prior knowledge about Northern Ireland and reliance on the expertise of NICS colleagues who were not directly involved in the negotiations (DExEU Interviewee, 2020).

6.2.1.2 Self-Determination of National Identity and Citizenship Rights

The principle of consent is reaffirmed in Article 2 of the Protocol regarding 'Rights of Individuals', albeit less explicitly than in the preceding Article 1 provision. Under Article 2, the UK have committed to ensure 'no diminution' of rights, safeguards, or equality of opportunity—'as set out in [the] part of the 1998 Agreement' with the same title—resulting from UK withdrawal from the EU, 'including' those rights that derive from the provisions of EU law listed in Annex 1 of the Protocol (Article 2(1)). This creates an indirect link between Article 2 of the Protocol and the 1998 Agreement provision for people born in Northern Ireland to be able to 'identify themselves and be accepted as Irish or British, or both' (CI: 1(vi)). The named section of the 1998 Agreement (RSE) introduced a requirement for 'parity of esteem' in respect to rights available to individuals from 'both communities' in (RSE: 4) Northern Ireland and an obligation on the Irish Government to ensure 'an equivalent level' (RSE: 9) of rights protections would pertain for citizens south of the border.

Although excluded from a narrow definition of the principle of constitutional consent, provisions for self-determination of British or Irish national identities and citizenship are integral to the multifaceted principle of consent set out in the first section—Constitutional Issues—of the 1998 Agreement and are reinforced later in the RSE section mentioned in Article 2 of the Protocol. By putting the onus on the UK to uphold rights-based guarantees set out in the 1998 Agreement, as well as in Article 2(2), requiring the UK to 'continue to facilitate' the 'related work' of institutions and bodies set up 'pursuant to the 1998 Agreement including' the Northern Ireland Human Rights Commission (NIHRC), Equality Commission for Northern Ireland (ECNI), and the Joint Committee of representatives of the Human Rights Commissions of Northern Ireland and Ireland (JCHRC), Article 2 represents a strong legal reaffirmation of rights-based guarantees that underpin the principle of consent, broadly understood.

While reaffirming the consent principle by enabling 'parity of esteem' (1998 Agreement, S2: 4) in Northern Ireland regardless of national or religious identity, Article 2 also demonstrates the paradoxical impact of the Protocol on consent because, by linking 'parity of esteem' to specific existing EU laws, Article 2 may, in effect, reformulate the broad and normative commitments made in relevant section of the 1998 Agreement. In 'Rights, Safeguards and Equality of Opportunity' signatories to the 1998 Agreement affirm a comprehensive set of rights that is broader than the six EU directives listed in Annex 1. Whereas rights specifically protected under Article 2 and Annex 1 of the Protocol are related to gender equality, protection against racial or ethnic discrimination and employment rights, the rights guarantees in the 1998 Agreement are more expansive;[14] these include, for example, freedom of political thought, freedom of expression, freedom to choose one's place of residence as well as socioeconomic, linguistic, and cultural rights alongside mandating the full incorporation of the ECHR in UK law.[15] Comparison between Article 2 and Annex 1 of the Protocol and

---

[14] 1998 Agreement 'Rights, Safeguards and Equality of Opportunity' has two sections, one on human rights and the other on economic, social, and cultural issues. Those human rights explicitly affirmed include: the right of free political thought; the right to freedom and expression of religion; the right to pursue democratically national and political aspirations; the right to seek constitutional change by peaceful and legitimate means; the right to freely choose one's place of residence; the right to equal opportunity in all social and economic activity, regardless of class, creed, disability, gender, or ethnicity; the right to freedom from sectarian harassment; and the right of women to full and equal political participation. Those economic, social, and cultural rights set out in the relevant section are more diffuse but include: pursuit of broad policies for sustained economic growth and stability; the promotion of social inclusion and community development; the advancement of women in public life; a new regional development strategy; respect and tolerance for linguistic diversity, particularly the Irish language; recognition of the sensitivity of symbols and emblems and imperative to promote mutual respect in use of symbols for public purposes.

[15] Annex 1 of the Protocol includes: directive 2004/113/EC on equal treatment between men and women in access to goods and services, directive 2006/54/EC on equal treatment of men and women

the 'Rights, Safeguards and Equality of Opportunity' section of the 1998 Agreement underlines the importance of implementation in determining the Protocol's impact. The commitment to 'no diminution', in theory, relates to the whole spectrum of rights affirmed in the relevant section of the 1998 Agreement; however, in practice, some rights have more specific protection, under the Protocol, than others because they have been newly linked to particular EU directives. For example, the 'right to equal opportunity in all social and economic activity regardless of … gender' (1998 Agreement, RSE(HR): 1) is arguably likely, in practice, to have greater protection under the Protocol than 'the right of free political thought' (*ibid.*) because the former is specifically protected under directive 2006/54/EC on the principle of equal opportunities and equal treatment of men and women in matters of employment and occupation, listed in Annex 1. Overall, then, Article 2 indirectly reaffirms the principle of consent in respect to self-determination of national identity but at the same time rebalances the spectrum of rights-based guarantees that underpin the 1998 Agreement by only specifically reinforcing those realised in EU law, including in the instruments listed in Annex 1.

6.2.1.3 Territorial Integrity and Territorial Waters

According to Article 1(2), the Protocol 'respects the essential State functions and *territorial integrity* of the United Kingdom' (*added*); the phrasing and necessity of its inclusion are a reflection of, and response to, Unionist fears that new checks and controls required under the Protocol on GB–NI trade would pose a threat to the constitutional integrity of the UK. Concerns about the constitutional and therefore territorial integrity came to the fore during withdrawal negotiations after the publication of the EU draft Withdrawal Agreement text was said to 'undermine the UK common market and threaten [the] constitutional integrity of the UK by creating a customs and regulatory border down the Irish Sea' (May in *BBC News*, 2018). From this point forward in negotiations, constitutional and territorial integrity were explicitly linked, in UK political discourse, to customs and regulatory procedures; this explains an emphasis on 'territory' in the Protocol. The Article 1(2) statement therefore offers an important endorsement of the constitutional status quo in Northern Ireland whereby 'the present wish of a majority of the people of Northern Ireland … is to maintain the Union [of the UK]' (1998 Agreement, CI: 1(iii)). While Article 1(2) is a clear legal affirmation of the territorial

---

in matters of employment, directive 2000/43/EC on equal treatment of persons irrespective of race or ethnicity, directive 2000/78/EC establishing a framework for equal treatment and occupation, directive 2010/41/EU on the equal treatment of men and women engaged in self-employment, and directive 79/7/EC on equal treatment of men and women in matters of social security (*Official Journal*, 1979; 2000a; 2000b; 2004; 20006; 2010).

integrity of the UK, and therefore Northern Ireland's place within it, there is a contradiction between the provisions of the Protocol in respect to territory and the 'territorial integrity' of Northern Ireland when read in the context of UK law.

The only current definition for Northern Ireland that exists in domestic law is in section 98 of the 1998 Act which states: '"Northern Ireland" includes so much of the internal waters and territorial sea of the United Kingdom as are adjacent to Northern Ireland.'[16] Leaving aside that it may have been useful to know what Northern Ireland 'is' rather than just what it 'includes', for this analysis the definition's importance lies in how it conflicts with the definition of [the territory of] 'Northern Ireland' in the Protocol.[17] Under Article 5(3) of the Protocol, the EU customs code applies 'to and in the United Kingdom in respect of Northern Ireland (*not including the territorial waters* of the United Kingdom)' (*emphasis added*). So, under UK law, the territory of 'Northern Ireland' includes adjacent territorial waters but, under the Protocol, the territory of 'Northern Ireland' excludes adjacent territorial waters. The territorial application of the Protocol in respect to Northern Ireland is, therefore, novel.

The definition of 'Northern Ireland' under the Protocol is also *sui generis* from an EU law perspective. Under Article 13(1), 'any reference to the territory defined in Article 4 of Regulation (EU) No 952/2013' in applicable provisions of either EU law or the Withdrawal Agreement (including the Protocol) that are applicable 'to and in the United Kingdom in respect of Northern Ireland' because of the Protocol are to be read as including 'the part of the territory of the United Kingdom to which [the EU Customs Code] applies by virtue of Article 5(3)'. The 'territory defined' in Article 4 of Regulation (EU) No 952/2013 is the 'customs territory of the Union' (*Official Journal*, 2013); it comprises 'the following territories, *including their territorial waters*, internal waters and airspace', followed by a comprehensive list of EU Member States, that includes 'the territory of the United Kingdom of Great Britain and Northern Ireland and of the Channel Islands and the Isle of Man' and also 'the territory of Ireland' (*ibid.*, *added*). As such, the definition of the territory of Northern Ireland set out in Article 5(3) not only differs from its definition in UK law under section 98 of the 1998 Act but also from the pre-existing definition of the EU customs territory as it applied to

---

[16] Northern Ireland was statutorily defined in the *Government of Ireland Act 1920* as consisting of the Parliamentary counties of Antrim, Armagh, Down, Fermanagh, Londonderry, and Tyrone and the Parliamentary boroughs of Belfast and Londonderry (s1(2)); this definition was reiterated in the *Northern Ireland Constitution Act 1973* (s43(2)) but these two Acts, and the definitions they contained, were repealed under the 1998 Act (s2; 100 and Sch15).

[17] A similar point was made by previous Attorney General for Northern Ireland, John Larkin QC in his analysis of *Miller* (2017) and the Northern Ireland constitution; see Larkin (2018).

and in the United Kingdom in respect of Northern Ireland which, before the Protocol, included territorial waters.

In view of the discrepancy between the UK definition of 'Northern Ireland' and the Protocol definition of 'Northern Ireland', the Article 1(2) affirmation of 'territorial integrity' is problematic when viewed from Northern Ireland. This is not to say that the discrepancy undermines the territorial integrity of the UK; it does not, nor does it invalidate the Protocol's 'respect' for it. However, in view of the political origin of the Article 2(1) affirmation as primarily a reassurance to Unionists in Northern Ireland, read alongside affirmation of constitutional status (see 6.2.1.2), the fact that the Protocol offers a new legal definition of 'Northern Ireland'—one which excludes adjacent territorial waters—is somewhat ironic. Moreover, the discrepancy creates the possibility of contradictions as regards the territorial application of domestic legislation to implement the Protocol; this issue is covered in more detail in Chapter 7. For now, the discrepancy between domestic law and the Protocol definitions can be said to, first, create a new legal definition for 'Northern Ireland' and, second, reveal a lack of familiarity among UK negotiators as to the particularities of UK law as it applies to and concerns Northern Ireland.

6.2.1.4 Democratic Consent Mechanism

Article 18 of the Protocol is to be read alongside a unilateral UK declaration on the operation of the 'Democratic consent [mechanism] in Northern Ireland'. In both texts the UK Government commit to 'provide the opportunity' (Article 18(1); Unilateral Declaration, 2019: *preamble*) for a vote in the Northern Ireland Assembly on the continued application of Articles 5 to 10 of the Protocol in 2024, four years after the end of the transition period and at regular intervals thereafter depending on the nature of the result. Under Article 18, three possible scenarios arise from future consent votes: (1) if there is a 'cross-community' majority (understood here as either a majority of MLAs including a majority of Nationalist and Unionist representatives or a 60% majority of MLAs including 40% of Unionist and 40% of Nationalist representatives) in favour, the relevant provisions continue to apply, until another vote is held eight years later; (2) alternatively, if there is a 'simple' majority vote in favour, the provisions continue to apply, the UK Government commission an independent review on the functioning of the Protocol, and another vote is held four years later; finally, (3) if a majority vote against the continued application, Articles 5 to 10 cease to apply two years after the vote and, in the interim period, the Joint Committee make recommendations to the UK and EU on the 'necessary measures' to deal with disapplication of the articles, taking account of the 'obligations of the parties to the 1998

Agreement'. In formulating their recommendations, the Joint Committee may also 'seek an opinion from institutions created by the 1998 Agreement' (Article 18(4)). What this means is that the procedure for the expression of Northern Ireland legislative consent via the Protocol democratic consent mechanism is to be repeated indefinitely unless and until there is a majority of MLAs in favour of disapplication. If at any point a majority do vote in favour of disapplication, there is very little clarity as to what would happen next. It is not unreasonable to assume the Joint Committee would struggle to reach consensus on the 'necessary measures' required to achieve the objectives that Articles 5 to 10 are designed to meet, namely, avoiding a hard border on the island of Ireland. Articles 5 and 6 concerning customs and trade in goods were the most contentious in UK–EU withdrawal negotiations and their implementation, alongside Article 10 on state aid, remain the most politically contentious in UK–EU relations—it is not unlikely that this would still be the case in the event of a vote in favour of disapplication under the democratic consent mechanism.

Taking the provisions of the Protocol and Unilateral Declaration[18] together, the 'democratic consent mechanism' breaks new ground on the matter of executive vs devolved power in UK constitutional arrangements. On one hand, the 'democratic consent mechanism' upholds a conventional view of the UK constitution in that the power to notify the EU of the outcome of the vote is retained by the UK Government in accordance with Schedule 2(3) of the 1998 Act under which international relations, including those with the EU, are an excepted matter in Northern Ireland—the Unilateral Declaration underlines this specifically (2019 *preamble*). Notwithstanding a nod to the existing division of power between the UK Government and the devolved Northern Ireland legislature, the democratic consent mechanism is, in practice, unconventional. Fundamentally, the purpose of the consent mechanism is to give the Northern Ireland legislature the option to disapply aspects of an international legal treaty—this power clearly falls in the remit of 'international relations' as defined in the 1998 Act (Sch2(3)). Furthermore, most of the areas of policy covered by Articles 5 to 10 of the Protocol are among those 'reserved' powers listed in Schedule 3 of the 1998 Act that are not yet—but could in future be—devolved to the Northern Ireland Executive. For example, import and export controls and trade with any place outside the UK (such as NI–EU trade as per Article 5) are reserved under Schedule 3(20) of the 1998 Act. To take another example, under Schedule 3(26) of the 1998 Act, the

---

[18] The Unilateral Declaration sets out the procedural requirements for the operation of the democratic consent mechanism in more detail than Article 18. As such, the content of the Unilateral Declaration is more relevant to the implementation of Article 18 in UK law, which is analysed in detail in 7.2.1.4.

'regulation of anti-competitive practices and agreements; abuse of dominant position; monopolies and mergers' are powers reserved by the UK Government and are within the remit of EU state aid law, applicable under Article 10 of the Protocol. The impact of the 'democratic consent mechanism' on the constitution of Northern Ireland can therefore be said to establish a new convention whereby a devolved UK legislature is given regular opportunity to vote, definitively, on measures over which the UK's central institutions retain powers. In this way, the democratic consent mechanism essentially reverses the UK's legislative consent mechanism: rather than a devolved administration granting or withholding its consent to changes in policy areas enacted by the UK Government, the democratic consent mechanism allows the Northern Ireland legislature to grant or withhold its consent on matters technically retained by the UK Government but which in practice are decided bilaterally between the UK and EU.

The provisions of the democratic consent mechanism are also, in effect, a new formulation of the (broadly understood) multifaceted principle of consent provided for in the 1998 Agreement. Although the Article 18 provision, for votes every four years or every eight years, recognises the importance of 'cross-community' consent in the Northern Ireland context, achieving cross-community consensus is not a requirement (see 7.2.1.4). Consent can be granted on the basis of a simple majority of MLAs. This sits awkwardly with the 1998 Agreement 'safeguard' whereby 'key decisions' in the Northern Ireland Assembly are to be taken on a cross-community basis (S1: 5). In this way, the democratic consent mechanism marks a partial departure from the principle of mandatory power-sharing decision-making on controversial issues by instead prioritising majoritarian decision-making of the kind practised in Westminster.[19] Further, by providing for the exercise of legislative consent, the provisions of Article 18 and the Unilateral Declaration move away from the 1998 Agreement emphasis on popular consent. In the 1998 Agreement, the language of consent is used to describe the exercise of consent by 'the people' (CI: 1(ii); (iv)) voting in referenda and to describe the safeguard requirement for 'parallel' cross-community consent in the Assembly on 'key decisions' (S1 5(i); 11); the term 'democratic consent' is not used. Yet, under Article 18(2), the UK is required to seek '*democratic* consent in Northern Ireland in a manner *consistent with* the 1998 Agreement' (*emphasis added*).

---

[19] A wider historical point could also be made here. In preferring majoritarian parliamentary consent, the Article 18 mechanism echoes arrangements for government in Northern Ireland between 1920 and 1972: the *Northern Ireland Constitution Act 1973* was the first time a UK statute provided that a vote of 'the people of Northern Ireland' rather than the Parliament of Northern Ireland to determine any future poll on its constitutional status (s1).

The nomenclature here is significant. While 'democratic consent' is not used in the 1998 Agreement, the institutions established by Strand One are characterised as the 'Democratic Institutions' (S1) of Northern Ireland. In language and procedure, therefore, the democratic consent mechanism provided for in Article 18 of the Protocol, read alongside the Unilateral Declaration, offers a novel formulation of the principle of consent set out in the 1998 Agreement by using the concept of 'consent' to describe a 'democratic' exercise in the Northern Ireland Assembly; for the Northern Ireland constitution, this is novel.[20] In an interview with a DExEU official involved in the renegotiation of the Protocol under the Johnson government, the addition of the 'democratic consent mechanism' was described as the UK's 'biggest win' (DExEU Interviewee, 2020). Given the high likelihood that future democratic consent votes further polarise politics in Northern Ireland, the framing of Article 18 as a UK victory is, at least, questionable.

6.2.2 Devolved Government

Strand One institutions are referred to once in the preamble of the Protocol which recalls the 'roles, functions and safeguards of the Northern Ireland Executive, [and] the Northern Ireland Assembly' (recital 5);[21] and again in Article 18 which, as just discussed, provides for the expression of 'democratic consent' in Northern Ireland in accordance with the 'unilateral declaration concerning the operation of "Democratic consent in Northern Ireland" … including with respect to the roles of the Northern Ireland Executive and

---

[20] On this issue, the language of the UK Government has been notable and misleading. Speaking to the House of Commons, Cabinet Office Minister Michael Gove stated: 'we must all remember if the Protocol is to work, it must work for the whole community in Northern Ireland. And whether it is to be maintained in the future, as the Protocol itself sets out, is for the people of Northern Ireland to decide through the democratic consent mechanism' (*Hansard*, 2020b). Mr Gove conflates 'the people' with a mechanism that only allows for legislative consent and erroneously suggests the Protocol in its entirety is contingent on the outcome of the democratic consent mechanism when it only applies to Articles 5 to 10.

[21] The phrasing of this sole reference to the Strand One institutions is curious. In recital 5, the Parties recognise that: 'cooperation between Northern Ireland and Ireland is a central part of the 1998 Agreement and is essential for achieving reconciliation and the normalisation of relations on the island of Ireland, and recalling the roles, functions and safeguards of the Northern Ireland Executive, the Northern Ireland Assembly and the *North-South Ministerial Council (including cross-community provisions)*, as set out in the 1998 Agreement' (2021: recital 5, *added*). The omission of the Strand Three British-Irish Council that also enables cooperation between Northern Ireland and Ireland albeit in a wider context is notable. Furthermore, the reference to 'cross-community provisions' in parenthesis after the NSMC seems to suggest that cross-community decision-making is required here but this is not exactly the case; at the NSMC, any decision must be unanimously agreed (1998 Agreement, S2 3(iii)(iv)); arguably, the presence of the First and deputy First Minister makes this 'cross-community' but this is more a by-product of the mandatory cross-community provisions in the Strand One institutions than a particular provision of Strand Two, all of which renders the use of parentheses curious. The language first appeared in the draft EU legal text of February 2018 (also recital 5) and could therefore be assumed to reflect an Irish Government emphasis.

Assembly' (Article 18(2)). Of these two mentions, only the Article 18 reference directly affects the operation of devolved government. Yet, here, the text only provides the Northern Ireland Assembly with an intermittent 'yes/no' vote on some aspects of the Protocol. There is therefore no provision in the Withdrawal Agreement that necessitates Northern Ireland Assembly or Executive input to, or oversight of, the implementation of the Protocol.

Compared to the Protocol's provisions concerning the principle of consent and Strand Two relations and institutions, Strand One gets very little attention. It may then appear that the impact of the Withdrawal Agreement and Protocol on Strand One is not significant; the relative silence of the legal text in respect to Strand One is, however, the reason for its *potentially* transformative effect. According to Article 12 the Protocol, the CJEU retains its jurisdiction in the UK for the purposes of applying and interpreting those aspects of Union law made applicable under Article 12(2), Article 5, and Articles 7 to 10 of the Protocol. Under Article 13, all aspects of EU law applicable under the Protocol are to be read 'as amended or replaced' and any new EU legislation falling within the scope of the Protocol can be added to a relevant Annex via Joint Committee decision (Article 13(3) and (4)). In this way, post-Brexit Northern Ireland is in a relationship of dynamic alignment with the EU in those areas of Union law covered by the Protocol. This dynamic alignment of post-Brexit Northern Ireland sets it apart within the UK and creates a new legal procedure for the development of laws in respect to Northern Ireland. While the domestic implications of these facts are discussed further in Chapter 7, as this subsection sets out, the unique relationship of Northern Ireland to applicable EU law and the CJEU under the Protocol is why the lack of requirement for Strand One input into the institutional framework set up to oversee the Protocol's implementation is of potential constitutional significance. The effects are twofold: first, the UK executive powers vis-à-vis devolved government in Northern Ireland are strengthened and, second, the implementation of the Protocol risks creating a perpetual democratic deficit in areas of devolved competence due to a lack of transparency and/or scrutiny regarding the amendment or addition of laws by the Joint Committee.

Whether or not this latter democratic deficit scenario is realised depends in part on UK Government decisions about the make-up of UK delegations to implementation bodies, established under the Withdrawal Agreement, as well as on any domestic provision for Strand One institutions to input into development of the UK position in relevant policy areas. While the extent of the material impact of the Protocol on the legislative competence and democratic accountability of Strand One institutions will only start to become evident after the end of the transition period (not covered here), its immediate legal impact is to change the default primary decision-making body in some areas of devolved competence. The Protocol thereby introduces a new external contingency to the democratic process in Northern Ireland.

6.2.2.1 Applicable Union Law and CJEU Jurisdiction

Under Article 12(1) of the Protocol, authorities in the UK are responsible for 'implementing and applying' those provisions of EU law it makes applicable in Northern Ireland. Notwithstanding a UK commitment to facilitate EU representatives 'to be present during any activities' related to the implementation and application of the EU law aspects of the Protocol (Article 12(2)),[22] this arrangement whereby a Third Country has primary responsibility for the application of Union law is unorthodox from an EU perspective (see Gstöhl and Phinnemore, 2019). According to Article 12(4), the CJEU retains jurisdiction in the UK over Union law provisions that now or in future are included in the scope of Articles 5, 7–10, and 12(2) of the Protocol (and relevant Annexes). In addition, Article 13(2) provides that all applicable EU law will be interpreted in conformity with CJEU case law and, unless otherwise provided, any EU legislation listed will be read 'as amended or replaced' with an additional provision for the Joint Committee to agree by mutual consent to, in future, add any new legislation that falls within the scope of the Protocol. Notably, Articles 12 and 13 apply in perpetuity and regardless of the outcome of any future Article 18 democratic consent mechanism vote; it is, however, also the case that, if such a vote was to end the effect of Articles 5–10, it would denude Articles 12 and 13 of much of their effect.

Taking the provisions of Article 12 and 13 together, applicable EU law will continue to have direct effect in post-Brexit Northern Ireland but, importantly, without any access to the normal means of representation in EU institutions throughout the legislative process. This fact of continued direct effect of aspects of the EU *acquis* in Northern Ireland elevates the significance of arrangements for oversight and implementation established by the Withdrawal Agreement. Before accounting for these and their implications for Strand One it is first worth noting the *sui generis* nature of the selection of EU law that applies as a consequence of the Protocol and why it matters.

At the time of ratification, there were 333 instruments of EU law listed in the Annexes of the Protocol which would continue to apply in post-Brexit

---

[22] Based on correspondence with the UK Government under May, the EU presumed Article 12 amounted to agreement to establish a permanent EU office in Northern Ireland, but this was rejected by the UK Government under Johnson who characterised this as a violation of UK sovereignty. The matter was resolved along with other outstanding matters by Joint Committee decisions announced on 8 December and accepted on 17 December 2020.

Northern Ireland at the end of the transition period.[23] In addition, under the Protocol, thirteen Articles of the TFEU would also continue to apply: seven of these apply to the UK in respect of Northern Ireland and six to the UK as a whole, in accordance with conditions set out therein.[24] In addition, 37 European Council guidelines or European Commission notices regarding EU State Aid law apply under Annex 5 of the Protocol. Taken together, the Protocol therefore requires a substantial amount of EU law to be applied in Northern Ireland only, or in the UK, as the case may be. It is worth noting that, in doing so, the Protocol effectively splits the EU legal *acquis*, particularly as it pertains to its single market. EU Treaty internal market rules on the free movement of persons and services, applicable under Article 26 of the TFEU, clearly do not apply under the Protocol; nor do EU laws on consumer and environmental protection which are, under Article 114 of the TFEU, ordinarily internal market rules as a matter of EU constitutional law.[25] While the selection of EU law applicable under the Protocol calls into question its fidelity to the 'indivisibility' of the four freedoms, its importance for Strand One of the Northern Ireland constitution lies in the implications of its novelty.

The selection of EU law that applies under the Protocol, and the arrangements for its implementation, are designed to address the 'unique circumstances on the island of Ireland' (Article 1(3)) and are, therefore, untested. While this is perhaps an obvious point to make, it is important because the fact of the novel combination of directly applicable EU legislation increases the probability that further clarifications regarding implementation, including CJEU rulings, will be necessary. To take an example, under Article 5(4) and Annex 2 of the Protocol, '*obligations stemming from* the international agreements concluded by the Union, or by Member States acting on its

---

[23] These instruments of EU law are listed in five of the nine Protocol Annexes; the (original) 333 total breaks down as follows: 6 EU instruments apply under Article 2(1) and Annex 1; 287 EU instruments apply under Article 5(4) and Annex 2; 19 EU instruments apply under Article 8 and Annex 3; 7 EU instruments apply under Article 9 and Annex 4, and 14 EU instruments apply under Article 10(1) and Annex 5.

[24] Those aspects of the TFEU that apply only in Northern Ireland are as follows: Articles 30 and 110 of the TFEU apply to the UK in respect of Northern Ireland under Article 5(5) of the Protocol; Articles 34 and 36 of the TFEU apply to the UK in respect of Northern Ireland under Article 7(1) of the Protocol; Articles 346 and 347 of the TFEU apply to the UK in respect of Northern Ireland under Article 13(7) of the Protocol; and any restrictive measures enacted by Article 215 of the TFEU apply in the UK in respect to Northern Ireland insofar as they relate to goods between the EU and Third Countries under Article 5(4) and Annex 2 of the Protocol. Under Article 10(1) and Annex 5 of the Protocol, Articles 107 to 109, Article 93, and Article 106 (insofar as it concerns State Aid) apply to the whole of the UK but only 'in respect of measures which affect that trade between Northern Ireland and the Union which is subject' to the Protocol. Under Article 12(4) of the Protocol, the second and third paragraphs of Article 267 of the TFEU, which grant CJEU primacy on interpretation of EU law, shall apply in the UK.

[25] Article 26 of the TFEU defines the internal market as 'an area without internal frontiers in which the free movement of goods, persons, services and capital is ensured'; Article 114 provides for 'harmonisation' of national measures relevant to the 'establishment and functioning of the internal market' including in areas related to environmental and consumer protection (see Weatherill, 2020).

behalf, or by the Union and its Member States acting jointly, *insofar as they relate* to trade in goods between the Union and third countries' (*added*); this provision stops short of applying Article 216 of the TFEU which would see Northern Ireland included in the scope of EU international agreements yet requires any 'obligations stemming from' those agreements to apply 'insofar as they relate' to EU–Third Country trade. From the text, it is not clear what criteria will be used to judge whether or not an obligation can be said to 'stem from' an EU international agreement or 'relate to' trade in goods; in the event of a dispute, a CJEU ruling on the matter may be necessary. In a similar way, any 'restrictive measures' in force under Article 215 of the TFEU apply under Article 5 and Annex 2 'insofar' as these relate to EU–Third Country trade in goods, *prima facie*; there is scope here for different interpretations regarding the extent of application of Article 215 TFEU measures. A further example can be found in Article 10 and Annex 5 of the Protocol whereby Article 106 of the TFEU (that concerns the application of competition law to 'public undertakings' TFEU Article 106(1)) applies 'insofar as it concerns State Aid' (Protocol Annex 5) to the UK 'in respect of measures which affect that trade between Northern Ireland and the [European] Union' that are subject to the Protocol (Protocol Article 10(1)). Already, during the Transition Period, the UK and EU disagreed over their respective interpretations of the State Aid requirements set out in Article 10 of the Protocol; the disagreement was resolved in principle at the Joint Committee with the EU and UK issuing corresponding unilateral declarations (see 7.1.2). Notably, however, the EU declaration, of which the UK 'took note', only concerned the application of Article 107 of the TFEU, not Article 106 (or, indeed, Articles 93, 108, 109 that also apply under Article 10 and Annex 5). Although the practical impacts of the application of these aspects of the EU legal *aquis* will only be clear as the Protocol provisions take practical effect and any disputes are only likely to arise in time, the novelty of the selection and the unique circumstances of application elevate their importance for devolved government in Northern Ireland.

As a result of the continued direct effect of *some* EU law, the continued supremacy of the CJEU—as provided for by Article 12 of the Protocol and Article 267 of the TFEU—will likely be more significant in the governance of post-Brexit Northern Ireland than it was in the governance of pre-Brexit Northern Ireland, because the novel selection of applicable law is more likely to be contested and require judicial interpretation. A significant role for the CJEU as a determinant of the legal implications of the Protocol affects the powers of the Northern Ireland Executive and Assembly because, on relevant matters, CJEU rulings will be binding yet without any prior Strand One input to the development of a given policy. As discussed in the next subsection, any democratic deficit created by the elevated role of the CJEU in post-Brexit Northern Ireland could be mitigated by arrangements for oversight and implementation of the Protocol on a UK–EU and intra-UK level.

6.2.2.2 Arrangements for Implementation and Representation

The Withdrawal Agreement introduced a new and exclusive level of governance to Northern Ireland's already multileveled governing landscape. Implementation of the Protocol is to be overseen by three new bodies established by the Withdrawal Agreement: the Joint Committee, the Specialised Committee, and the Joint Consultative Working Group. The Protocol puts Northern Ireland in a unique position as a place within and between both the UK and the EU internal legal orders by requiring the application of the EU customs code inside the UK customs territory and putting it in a relationship of dynamic alignment to applicable EU rules, under CJEU jurisdiction, despite Northern Ireland having left the EU along with the rest of the UK (see Phinnemore, 2020). In view of this unique status, the Withdrawal Agreement establishes three new bodies to implement the untested Protocol framework and grants them powers to determine its efficacy and impact in Northern Ireland. Notwithstanding the extent of their potential influence, the three implementation bodies are not required to receive input from or consult with the Northern Ireland Executive or Assembly. Such a scenario risks creating an indefinite democratic deficit in post-Brexit Northern Ireland.

Given the importance of the oversight bodies for the operation of the Protocol, it is worth setting out their respective structures and responsibilities in some detail. Overall responsibility for managing the implementation of the Withdrawal Agreement, including the Protocol, is given to the Joint Committee (Article 164 WA, Annex VIII). The Joint Committee is co-chaired by the EU and UK and comprises representatives of both; its decisions are binding on both parties and taken by mutual consent; the Joint Committee are required to meet at least once a year and to produce an annual report on the functioning of the Withdrawal Agreement (Article 166 WA). The role of the Joint Committee is: to supervise and facilitate the implementation and application of the Withdrawal Agreement; to decide the tasks of the various Specialised Committees also established under the Agreement and supervise their work on an ongoing basis; to seek appropriate ways of preventing problems that arise in areas covered by the Agreement and/or resolving disputes regarding the interpretation and application of the Agreement; to consider any matter of interest relating to any area covered by the Agreement; to adopt decisions and make recommendations to the EU and the UK; and to adopt amendments to the Withdrawal Agreement (*ibid.*). The scope of the Joint Committee's responsibilities grants it considerable power to affect the impact of implementing the Withdrawal Agreement and Protocol; the requirement for decisions to be made by mutual consent mean however that the exercise of Joint Committee powers is contingent on UK–EU diplomatic relations.

The work of the Joint Committee is supported by six specialised committees including a committee on issues related to the implementation of the Protocol (Article 165(1)(c) WA). Like the Joint Committee, Specialised Committees are comprised of EU and UK representatives but, unlike the Joint Committee, Specialised Committees can only make recommendations and/or draw up draft decisions and refer these to the Joint Committee (Article 165(2) WA). The responsibilities of the Specialised Committee on issues related to the implementation of the Protocol are: to facilitate its implementation and application; to examine proposals from Strand Two institutions concerning its implementation and application; to consider matters relating to Article 2 of the Protocol regarding rights and equality, referred by the NIHRC, the NIEC, or the JCHRC; to discuss any point raised by the EU or UK of relevance to the Protocol; and to make recommendations to the Joint Committee as regards the Protocol (Protocol Article 14). In addition, and unique to the Protocol on Ireland and Northern Ireland, a Joint Consultative Working Group (JCWG) is established under Article 15 of the Protocol to 'serve as a forum for the exchange of information and mutual consultation' on matters pertaining to implementation (Article 15(1)); the JCWG will also be comprised of and co-chaired by EU and UK representatives, hold meetings (at least) every month, and be supervised by the Specialised Committee. The JCWG also has no power to take binding decisions other than to adopt its own rules of procedure. These latter two bodies—the Specialised Committee and JCWG—are less significant as regards Strand One of the constitution given that they have no decision-making power; that said, particularly after the full entry into force of the Protocol at the end of the transition period, the Specialised Committee and JCWG could prove important fora for Northern Ireland Executive or Assembly input to the Joint Committee if the UK and EU were to agree to it.

Prior to the end of the transition period, the Withdrawal Agreement required and recommended the Joint Committee take several important decisions on the operation of the Protocol; examining these helps elucidate the actual and potential impacts of the Protocol on Strand One. The tasks set for the Joint Committee by the Protocol fit into three categories: those that *should* be taken before the end of transition; those that *ought* to be taken before the end of transition; and those ongoing after transition ends. In the first category, the Protocol specifies the Joint Committee 'shall', before the end of the transition period, decide the criteria under which a good travelling into Northern Ireland from Great Britain is classified as 'at risk' of onward movement into the EU and therefore subject to tariffs (Article 5(2)). In the second 'ought' category, the Protocol specifies the Joint Committee shall decide: the maximum level of subsidy that can be paid to Northern Ireland agriculture and fisheries industry (Article 10(2) and Annex 6); the working arrangements to facilitate EU oversight of the implementation of the Protocol in Northern Ireland, including the presence of European Commission officials in Northern Ireland (Article 12(2)); and customs exemptions for fishery and aquaculture products landed in Northern Ireland by UK vessels registered in Northern Ireland (Article 5(3)), ideally, but not necessarily, before the end of the transition period. In the final category, the Joint Committee shall, after the Protocol enters into force on 1 January 2021: keep under review the parties' 'best endeavours' to facilitate trade between NI and GB (Article 6); 'regularly discuss' the implementation of VAT and excise rules in Northern Ireland (Article 8); keep under constant review the extent to which the Protocol maintains the necessary conditions for North–South cooperation (Article 11); determine whether new EU acts that are within the scope of the Protocol should be included in a relevant Annex (Article 13(4)); and have consultations with the aim of finding a solution if/when the EU or UK are considering taking unilateral safeguard measures to address 'serious economic, societal, or environmental difficulties' arising under the Protocol (Article 16 and Annex 7).[26] Joint Committee decisions in all of these areas will affect the extent of the economic and administrative impact of the Protocol in the short and long term. In view of the scope of these outstanding issues and the untested nature of the Protocol arrangements, the lack of a requirement for input from the Northern Ireland Executive or Assembly on the making of decisions in Joint Committee dilutes the level of executive and legislative authority envisaged in the 1998 Agreement. However, the extent to which these new legal provisions are realised depends on decisions on the part of the UK Government. This point is best demonstrated through a specific example.

Under Article 5(2), the Joint Committee are to agree the criteria by which goods brought into Northern Ireland ports and airports shall be considered 'not at risk' of onward movement into the EU market and which therefore can be exempted form applicable customs duties. The *default* requirement of Article 5 is that the EU customs code would apply to goods travelling

---

[26] The Joint Committee also has a role in the event that the NI Assembly withholds consent to the continued operation of Article 5 to 10 of the Protocol under Article 18, but as this task is not ongoing and could only apply in the event of the relevant outcome, it is distinguished from the above list.

GB–NI after the end of the transition period, meaning duties would need to be paid (see European Commission, 2020b: FN45; European Commission, 2020c: 37). If applied, the economic impact of the default arrangement could be devastating as Northern Ireland is reliant on imports from Great Britain, particularly in the retail and wholesale sectors wherein, if applied, UK and EU tariff differentials on some goods would be significant.[27] Crucially, the extent of the economic impact of Article 5(2) depends on the 'not at risk' criteria determined by the Joint Committee. If the agreed criteria were narrow, applicable duties would have to be paid on the majority of goods travelling GB–NI but wider criteria would mean a smaller number of goods liable for duties and the economic impact would be reduced accordingly. The Joint Committee decision therefore shapes the economic trajectory of post-Brexit Northern Ireland as it has the potential to make some pre-existing GB–NI trade unviable in the short, medium, and long term. What is most striking for the purpose of this discussion is that such a decision is made without direct input from Strand One institutions.

On a literal reading, the relationship between the powers conferred on the Joint Committee under Article 5(2) and the powers conferred on Strand One institutions under the 1998 Agreement and 1998 Act is ambiguous. The 1998 Agreement provides that the Northern Ireland Assembly 'will be the prime source of authority in respect of all devolved responsibilities' (S1(4)). Under the 1998 Act, those matters which are neither 'excepted' (Sch2) nor 'reserved' (Sch3) are 'transferred' and, therefore, fall within the 'devolved responsibilities' of the Northern Ireland Assembly (s4(1)). As noted in the previous subsection, under Schedule 3 of the 1998 Act, trade with any place outside the United Kingdom is a reserved power (s20) but 'the furtherance of the trade of Northern Ireland' is not (s20(a)). Taking these together, the decision of the Joint Committee under Article 5(2) Protocol regarding what goods are 'not at risk' of onward movement from Northern Ireland into the EU internal market relates to UK external trade and is, under Schedule 3(20), clearly a reserved power. At the same time, the decision of the Joint Committee regarding which goods are 'at risk' also relates to 'the furtherance of the trade of Northern Ireland' *within* the UK which is, under Schedule 3(s20(a)), a transferred power

---

[27] Statistics on NI trade are not always collected or published by HMRC; however, according to available analysis, in 2018, NI had a £3.9bn trade deficit with Great Britain (importing £10.4bn in goods and services; exporting £6.5bn in goods and services). Purchases from GB accounted for 29% of NI total purchases—17.8% of which were goods and 11.2% services—this compares to imports from the Republic of Ireland, Northern Ireland's largest external trading partner, accounting for 6% to NI total purchases/imports. Of the £10.4bn NI goods purchased from GB, £6.5bn or 63% were in the retail and wholesale sector (NISRA, 2020). The extent of NI reliance on trade from GB underlines the significance of the criteria for determining which goods are 'at risk' of onward travel and therefore subject to tariffs.

and therefore in the 'devolved responsibilities' of the Strand One institutions for which, the 1998 Agreement asserts, the Northern Ireland Assembly is 'the prime source of authority' (S1(4)). In this way, the Protocol could be said to change the default primary decision-making body on a matter concerning an area previously within the devolved competence of Northern Ireland—arrangements for moving goods GB–NI—away from Strand One institutions towards the Joint Committee.

On 8 December 2020, the UK and EU co-chairs of the Joint Committee announced that 'agreement in principle' had been reached on 'all issues' outstanding, including on the criteria to determine 'at risk' goods. A draft version of the relevant decision was published on 10 December and a final version—decision 4/2020—was adopted on 17 December 2020. Decision 4/2020 sets out that goods entering Northern Ireland shall not be considered subject to commercial processing if the legal person declaring the good has an annual turnover of less than £500,000; the processing is for sale of food to UK-based consumers; processing is for construction at UK site; processing is for health or care services in Northern Ireland; processing is for non-profit activity in Northern Ireland; or the end use of processing is for animal feed in Northern Ireland (*Official Journal* 2020e: Article 2). Alongside this, the decision establishes that: goods shall not be considered 'at risk' of onward movement into the EU when brought directly GB–NI by an authorised or 'trusted trader' according to criteria for authorisation set out in Articles 5 to 7 of the Joint Committee decision and/or when brought directly and the duty payable is equal to zero under the EU customs code; for goods entering Northern Ireland not from elsewhere in the EU or UK, these goods shall not be considered 'at risk' if the EU duty is equal to or less than the UK duty, or they are brought by a trusted trader for the purpose of sale to or final use by consumers in Northern Ireland and the tariff differential is less than 3% of the customs value of the good (*ibid.* Article 3; see also 7.2.3). Neither the Article 2 criteria on determining commercial processing nor the Article 3 criteria on determining at risk goods shall apply to any goods subject to EU trade defence measures. These provisions regarding goods not at risk of onward movement are not permanent. Under Article 9 of the decision, either party can inform the Joint Committee in the event there is 'significant diversion of trade, or fraud or other illegal activities' by 1 August 2023; if no 'mutually satisfaction resolution' can be found, the provisions will cease to apply from 1 August 2024 unless the Joint Committee decides otherwise by the 1 April 2024; in the former scenario the Joint Committee must decide an 'appropriate alternative' approach, meaning, in short, the provisions of decision 4/2020 avoid the potentially damaging default scenario of all GB–NI goods being presumed 'at risk' of entering the EU market and thereby subject to tariffs. For the purpose of this analysis, the relevance of decision 4/2020 to Strand One of the Northern Ireland constitution lies in the process involved in reaching it. Speaking in the Northern Ireland Assembly on 14 December 2020, First Minister Arlene Foster acknowledged that she and the deputy First Minister were informed by Chancellor of the Duchy of Lancaster, Michael Gove, of the 'agreements in principle' reached by the Joint Committee *after* these had been announced and that the Northern Ireland Executive would be 'analysing the text' of the draft decisions (Northern Ireland Assembly, 2020d). Notwithstanding that the substance of decision 4/2020 relates to the furtherance of Northern Ireland trade, a transferred power under 1998 Act (Sch3 s20(a)), it is clear from the First Minister's statement that the Northern Ireland Executive were not directly involved in Joint Committee discussions prior to agreement.

It is important to distinguish here between the formal and informal means available to the Northern Ireland Executive and Assembly to influence decisions of the Joint Committee. On 5 November, the First and deputy First Minister wrote a joint letter to Vice-President Šefčovič asking for the 'unique context' of Northern Ireland to be considered in the matter of SPS controls on goods arriving in Northern Ireland (The Executive Office, 2020d). The two Ministers welcomed the 'constructive work' ongoing between UK and EU negotiators to seek 'a pragmatic application of the principles and purposes of the SPS controls' and committed 'our own officials to play as full and positive a part in this process as may be possible' (*ibid.*). This joint letter highlights the potential for Strand One institutions to influence actions of the Joint Committee by informal or political means. Yet, at the same time, the text also underlines the observer or outsider status of the Northern Ireland Executive leaders in relation to the Joint Committee—that the letter was written underlines the fact that the First and deputy First Minister could not articulate the same message in the negotiating room.

There is nothing in the Protocol to *prevent* the UK Government from providing Strand One institutions a much more influential role in the domestic processes for oversight and implementation of the Protocol. Based on the legal text, however, it stands that the institutional framework established to oversee the implementation of the Protocol does not *require* input from the Northern Ireland Executive or Assembly on explicitly devolved matters. From a constitutional perspective, the overall effect here is to strengthen the powers of the UK Government vis-à-vis the Northern Ireland devolved government and to bolster the power of the executive vis-à-vis parliamentary powers in view of the lack of requirement for transparency regarding Joint Committee, Specialised Committee, or JCWG meetings.

6.2.3 North–South Dimension

It is an explicit objective of the Protocol to set out arrangements needed 'to maintain the necessary conditions for continued North–South cooperation' and 'to avoid a hard border' on the island of Ireland in the context of UK withdrawal from the EU (Article 1(3)). As a consequence, the provisions of the Protocol address Strand Two of the 1998 Agreement more than any of the other three components of the Northern Ireland constitution.[28] By way of simple demonstration, the term 'North–South cooperation' is used more times (eleven) in the Protocol than 'principle of consent', 'Northern Ireland Executive and Assembly' and 'East–West cooperation' (four in total) combined. Notwithstanding the stated aim of the Protocol in respect to maintaining North–South cooperation generally, its provisions are nonetheless focused in particular on those areas of cooperation required to facilitate the continuation of frictionless cross-border trade in goods and therefore avoid a physical hardening of the border on the island of Ireland. In respect to other areas of North–South cooperation—excluding the single electricity market—the Protocol still reflects the logic of the 'Backstop' Protocol which sought a minimal framework for maintaining North–South cooperation 'unless and until' (Article 1(4)) these could be superseded in the context of a 'deep and special' UK–EU future relationship agreement (HM Government, 2017b: 43). The impact of the Protocol on Strand Two of the 1998 Agreement is therefore uneven: it reaffirms the importance of North–South cooperation, provides strong legal guarantees for some specific areas, but provides only limited legal guarantees for others.

Rather than arising directly from the 1998 Agreement, the prioritisation of preserving cross-border trade in goods in the Protocol arose from a political compromise between UK and EU negotiating objectives and the shared objective of avoiding a hard border on the island of Ireland—narrowly defined as avoiding physical infrastructure at the border. As a consequence, the legal protections granted to North–South trade under the Protocol arguably have the effect of rebalancing the 1998 Agreement by adding new legal weight to Strand Two as a facilitator of cross-border trade in goods. An additional indirect effect of gaps in the Protocol in respect to other

---

[28] 'North–South cooperation' is mentioned eleven times in the Protocol text and the NSMC and North–South implementation bodies are mentioned three times; this compares to two mentions of the Northern Ireland Executive and Assembly, one mention of the principle of consent, and one mention of East–West cooperation. In the Preamble, nine of the 24 recitals address North–South cooperation or the need to avoid a hard border, which compares to three recitals that indirectly refer to each of the other three constitutional components. Articles 5, 7, 8, 9, 10, and 11 of the Protocol set out arrangements directly linked to North–South cooperation.

areas of existing North–South cooperation is to introduce new incentives for a deepening of cross-border cooperation via Strand Two institutions to make up for areas not directly covered; the provisions in respect to the potential role of the NSMC and Implementation Bodies arguably makes this scenario more probable. As this subsection sets out, the Protocol's rebalancing of the 1998 Agreement towards Strand Two in general and cross-border trade in goods in particular have significant implications for Northern Ireland's place in the UK internal market (see 6.2.4) as well as for 'East–West' economic, political, and diplomatic relations.

6.2.3.1 Defining the Border and Mapping Cross-Border Cooperation

The Protocol's provisions in relation to Strand Two fall into two categories: those that facilitate cross-border trade in goods and thereby avoid any need for physical infrastructure at the land border and those that aim to maintain the necessary conditions for North–South cooperation, broadly understood. Provisions in the first category (Article 5–8; 10) are more comprehensive and more legally enforceable than those in the second category (Article 9; 11). To understand the difference and its significance for Strand Two of the Northern Ireland constitution it is necessary to briefly revise the origin in UK–EU negotiations of these two kinds of provisions.

From early on in UK–EU negotiations, the 'problem' of the border on the island of Ireland was defined differently by the two parties. On the UK side, the problem to be addressed in withdrawal negotiations was narrowly understood as mitigating a need for any physical checks or controls on goods crossing the winding 500km borderline demarcating the boundary of the UK nation. This framing of the problem was in keeping with an ideal of national sovereignty and narratives of border control that had underpinned the Leave campaign; its result was a UK Government negotiating position that sought 'technical solutions' to achieve a 'goods border' on the island of Ireland 'that is as seamless and frictionless as possible' (HM Government, 2017b: 5; 34). This narrow UK Government understanding of the border problem sits uncomfortably with the 1998 Agreement which had required the removal of physical border infrastructure (SEC (2)(ii)) but, more importantly, had envisaged a holistic transformation of 'the totality of relationships' (S2(1)) North–South and East–West through the interdependent multi-levelled government framework it established, and which diminished the significance of physical borderlines. The UK's proposal to address 'the full spectrum of North–South and East–West cooperation' in a 'bold and ambitious Free Trade Agreement' in future relationship negotiations (HM Government, 2017b: 65) relied on splitting the task of protecting the 1998 Agreement across two sets of negotiations and agreements (see Davis in Mance, 2017). On the EU side, by contrast, avoiding physical checks or controls on the land border was understood as just one aspect presented by the 'unique circumstances' on the island of Ireland that would require 'flexible and imaginative solutions … *including* with the aim of avoiding a hard border' (European Council, 2017: 11, *added*). While underlining a need to avoid a physical hardening of the land border, the EU also emphasised 'the very specific and interwoven political, economic, security, societal and agricultural frameworks on the island of Ireland' (European Commission, 2017b: 1) and the need to protect North–South cooperation 'across all the relevant sectors' (*ibid.*: 3) in the withdrawal negotiations.[29]

In the first phase of negotiations, the EU position in respect to protecting the 1998 Agreement 'in all its parts' *in the withdrawal agreement* prevailed. An apparent change in the UK position on the matter can be traced to the findings of a joint exercise to map existing North–South cooperation and determine the extent to which it relied on EU legal or policy frameworks or the 1998 Agreement. Completed in 2017, the UK Government refused to publish the full details of the mapping exercise until, in 2019, these were obtained by the House of Commons European Union Select Committee following a freedom of information request (see O'Carroll and Rankin, 2019). In total, 142 areas of North–South cooperation had been identified, 54 of which were classified as 'directly underpinned by or linked' to EU legal or policy frameworks, 42 as 'partially underpinned by or linked', and 46 as 'not underpinned or linked to' EU legal or policy frameworks. No detail was given as to the criteria or thresholds used to determine which category any given area of North–South cooperation fell into in any of the documents published. The mapping exercise had nonetheless revealed, first, that North–South cooperation on the island of Ireland had expanded significantly from the twelve areas of possible cooperation specified in the 1998 Agreement (S2, Annex) and, second, that this expansion had been facilitated by joint UK and Irish EU membership; it has thus underlined the vulnerability of a majority of areas of existing North–South cooperation to the consequences of UK withdrawal from the EU.

---

[29] Different UK and EU conceptualisations of the border problem reflect different approaches to and understandings of sovereignty in international relations. The traditional, state-centric UK ideal conceives of sovereignty as indivisible and nationally bound by clearly demarcated boundaries of inclusion and exclusion (see Whittaker, 2017). By contrast, the EU ideal conceives of sovereignty as more diffuse, shared across national boundaries that are less sharp lines division and more sites of integration and cooperation (see Hayward and Komorova, 2019). The multi-levelled governing framework provided for in the 1998 Agreement aligns much more closely with the latter EU perspective on sovereignty, borders, and interdependence (see Campbell et al., 2003)

Findings from the North–South mapping exercise were reflected in the Joint Report. In the text, the UK, under May's premiership, held to its preference to address the 'substantial challenges' (Joint Report, 2017: 47) posed to the maintenance and development of North–South cooperation 'through the overall EU–UK relationship' (*ibid.*: 49) but committed in the interim to 'maintain full alignment with those rules of the Internal Market and Customs Union which, *now or in future*, support North–South cooperation, *the all-island economy* and the protection of the 1998 Agreement' (*ibid.*: 43; 49, added). The inclusive language regarding future cooperation and the all-island economy amounted to a UK commitment in principle to dynamic alignment of the kind required to facilitate ongoing cooperation on the island of Ireland. If implemented, this would have allowed for the continuation of post-1998 all-island integration, as envisaged by the EU, rather than simply mitigating the need for physical checks on goods at the border, as originally envisaged by the UK Government.

The 'Backstop' Protocol upheld the UK commitment to dynamic alignment, in accordance with paragraph 49 of the Joint Report necessary to achieve its objective. Importantly, however, the provisions in the 'Backstop' Protocol were designed as a minimal framework to operate alongside the 'bold and ambitious' FTA that the May Government were intending to negotiate (HM Government, 2017b: 65). In this way, the 'Backstop' Protocol amounted to a compromise between the respective UK and EU starting positions in regard to the nature of the border problem—it reflected an EU understanding of a need to protect North–South cooperation broadly understood yet provided for the UK's preferred strategy of doing so *primarily* through the future relationship agreement. Notwithstanding the fact that the 'Backstop' Protocol was designed to 'maintain the necessary conditions for continued North–South cooperation' (Article 1(3)), it was only meant to do so 'unless and until' (Article 1(4)) the UK and EU concluded an agreement to supersede it 'in whole or in part' using 'best endeavours' (Article 2(1)).

This context is important because, as the following subsections set out, those provisions that related directly to maintaining conditions for North–South cooperation in the 'Backstop' Protocol (Articles 6(2); 7–13) on an insurance policy basis are almost identical to those set out in the Protocol (Articles 5–11) despite the latter being agreed on a fundamentally different premise regarding its longevity and comprehensiveness. While it is possible for any subsequent UK–EU (free trade) agreement to supersede the Protocol in whole or in part (under Article 13(8)), there is no 'best endeavour' requirement for the parties to do so and, more importantly, this was not the intention of the Johnson Government. Therefore, although an objective of the Protocol is to maintain the necessary conditions for maintaining North–South cooperation (Article 1(3)), in reality, it still reflects the logic of a minimal framework insurance policy to avoid a physical hardening of the border on the island of Ireland by facilitating cross-border trade in goods while allowing the full spectrum of current and future North–South cooperation to be more comprehensively addressed through a 'deep and special' UK–EU future relationship agreement of a kind that was not agreed.

6.2.3.2 Cross-Border Trade in Goods

As already noted, the prioritisation of cross-border trade in goods in the Protocol arose from the shared UK–EU objective of avoiding physical infrastructure on the border on the island of Ireland. This shared objective had to be balanced with the EU's objective of securing its single market and customs union and the UK's objective of leaving the EU single market and customs union without dividing the UK's internal market. To reconcile these three seemingly incompatible aims, the Protocol sets out a 'constructively ambiguous' balance between the *de jure* position of Northern Ireland remaining within the UK customs territory (Article 4) and internal market (Article 6) and the *de facto* position of Northern Ireland remaining within the EU customs union and single market for the purpose of trade in goods (Article 5) with related provisions for: the recognition of technical regulations, assessments, certifications, and authorisations (Article 7); the payment of VAT and excise in respect to goods (Article 8); and the application of EU state aid rules to any trade subject to the Protocol (Article 10). This balance between the *de jure* and *de facto* status of Northern Ireland met the negotiating objectives of both sides: it avoids the need for a hard border by ensuring continued cross-border trade in goods yet allows Northern Ireland to be legally within the UK internal market while at the same time securing the EU Single Market by necessitating new checks and controls on goods moving GB–NI *as if* Northern Ireland was part of the EU single market for goods. Northern Ireland's *de jure* status as part of the UK customs territory (Article 6(1)) also safeguarded the legal integrity of the UK customs territory and thereby avoided any conflict with a domestic law provision in the *Taxation (Cross-border Trade) Act 2018* which made it 'unlawful for Her Majesty's Government to enter into arrangements under which Northern Ireland forms part of a separate customs territory to Great Britain' (s55(1)).[30] Simultaneously, however, the *de*

---

[30] A domestic legal principle regarding the indivisibility of the UK customs union dates from the 1707 'Articles of Union' that provided 'all parts of the United Kingdom for ever and after' shall be 'under the same Prohibitions Restrictions and Regulations of Trade and lyable [sic] to the same Customs and Duties on Import and Export' (Article VI). Some argued during the course of UK–EU withdrawal negotiations

facto requirement for the application of the EU customs code and EU derived regulations on goods entering Northern Ireland from the rest of the UK *could* be said to undermine that same domestic law provision in Taxation (CBT) Act 2018 because it defines a 'customs territory' as 'any territory with respect to which separate tariffs or other regulations of commerce are maintained for a substantial part of the trade of such territory with other territories' (Taxation (CBT) Act, 2018 s55(2); GATT, 1947 Article XXIV(2)). Under the Protocol, as already set out, goods entering Northern Ireland from the rest of the UK are subject, by default, to 'separate tariff' requirements and 'regulations of commerce' notwithstanding its legal position in the UK customs territory (Protocol Article 6(1) and Taxation (CBT) Act, 2018 s55(1) respectively). As such, the Protocol provisions for cross-border trade in goods have significant implications for Northern Ireland's position in the UK internal market because they create, in effect, a GB–NI trade border in respect to goods as the default arrangement.

Articles 5-8 and 10 of the Protocol are those that set out detailed provisions for the 'constructively ambiguous' compromise to avoid a hard border by maintaining cross-border trade in goods. The language used in these Articles reflect the political demands of the contentious negotiating process that led to the development of the Protocol's 'solution' in that the drafting presumes detailed knowledge of the EU legal *acquis*; the phrasing is opaque and, in some respects, arguably misleading. For example, Article 5(1) states that 'no customs duties shall be payable for a good brought into Northern Ireland' from another part of the UK 'notwithstanding paragraph 3'—which applies the EU customs code to and in Northern Ireland—'*unless* that good is at risk of subsequently being moved into the Union' (Article 5(1), *added*). Article 5(2) supplements this by providing that a good entering Northern Ireland from outside the EU '*shall be considered* to be at risk of subsequently being moved into the [European] Union *unless* it is established' that (a) the good will not be subject to commercial processing in Northern Ireland and (b) the good fulfils the criteria established by the Joint Committee regarding which goods are considered 'at risk' and which are not (Article 5(2),

---

that this provision ought to prevent the UK Government from agreeing to any proposal that would involve differentiating Northern Ireland in terms of trade and customs. In respect to this argument, it is important to note that the island of Ireland was not, in 1707, part of the United Kingdom; further, that the 1800 Acts of Union under which 'Great Britain and Ireland' were 'united into one kingdom' (1800 c.67 Article First) did similarly provide that 'all prohibitions and bounties on the export of articles the produce or manufacture of either country to the other shall cease' and imports from one country to the other shall be 'duty free'; however, the later 1800 Acts also provided for 'bounties, prohibitions or duties' to 'hereafter be imposed by the united Parliament' (*ibid*. Article Sixth) if so agreed. The relevance or otherwise of this latter provision in Article 6 of the 1800 Acts of Union featured prominently in the case of *Allister and others v Northern Ireland Secretary* [2022]; for discussion and analysis, see Chapter 9.

added). So, under Article 5(1) and 5(2), the collection of customs duties on goods travelling GB–NI is the default scenario despite the wording of Article 5(1) suggesting the opposite. Under Article 5, only if goods moving GB–NI can be proven to be '*not* at risk' (*added*) of onward travel into the EU single market, either by themselves or as part of another good after processing, will customs duties not be required. The 'not at risk' criteria, agreed by the Joint Committee during the transition period, therefore does much of the heavy legislative lifting as regards the economic impact of Article 5 in Northern Ireland.

As set out in 6.2.2.2, on 17 December 2020, the UK–EU Joint Committee adopted a decision (*Official Journal*, 2020c) setting out criteria to determine 'at risk' goods. Article 5(2) of the Protocol requires goods entering Northern Ireland to be considered at risk of entering the EU if they are (a) subject to commercial processing or (b) align with the 'at risk' criteria determined by the Joint Committee. On the former, decision 4/2020 states that goods entering Northern Ireland will *not* be considered subject to commercial processing if declarations are made by a legal person with an annual turnover below £500,000, or any processing is for the purpose of the sale of food to UK customers, construction at UK construction sites, use in Northern Ireland health or social care services, for non-profit activities, or for use as animal feed (*ibid*.: Article 2). In substance, these criteria provide a comprehensive set of exemptions to facilitate Northern Ireland-based commercial processing. Addressing the latter requirement in Article 5(2)(b), decision 4/2020 states that goods shall not be considered 'at risk' of onward movement into the EU when brought directly GB–NI by a 'trusted trader' (as defined in Articles 5–7 of the decision); and/or when brought directly GB–NI and the duty payable is equal to zero under the EU customs code; further, goods coming from outside the EU or UK, are not 'at risk' if the EU duty is equal to or less than the UK duty, or they are brought by a trusted trader to be sold in Northern Ireland, and the tariff differential is less than 3% of the customs value of the good (*ibid*.: Article 3). Again, these criteria are comprehensive and represent a significant shift away from the potentially very damaging default scenario of all GB–NI goods being presumed 'at risk' of entering the EU and thereby subject to tariffs. That said, and notwithstanding the relatively broad nature of the criteria agreed, this does not mitigate 'non-tariff barrier' requirements for new checks and controls on GB–NI trade under the Protocol, not least to determine which goods and which traders fulfil the demands of decision 4/2020.

In summary, as a consequence of UK and EU negotiating objectives—to avoid a hard border on the island of Ireland, preserve the EU single Market and customs Union and for the UK to leave the EU single market and customs union—the Protocol introduces new barriers to trade between Northern Ireland and the rest of the UK. The arrangements agreed have the effect of rebalancing the 1998 Agreement to prioritise Strand Two in general and cross-border trade in goods in particular.

6.2.3.3 Current and Future North–South Cooperation

In view of the findings of the North–South mapping exercise, and echoing previous 'Protocol' iterations, the Protocol states that it is needed so as 'to maintain the necessary conditions for continued North–South cooperation' (Article 1(3); *Preamble*, Recital 16). Using its own measure, the provisions of the Protocol presumably ought to ensure those 'necessary conditions'; however, close reading of Article 11—the provision most explicitly related to the ongoing development of North–South cooperation—reveals that this is not so. Article 11 states:

> Consistent with the arrangements set out in Articles 5 to 10, and in full respect of Union law, *this Protocol* shall be implemented and applied so as to maintain the necessary conditions for continued North–South cooperation, including in the areas of environment, health, agriculture, transport, education, and tourism, as well as in the areas of energy, telecommunications, broadcasting, inland fisheries, justice and security, higher education, and sport. (Protocol Article 11(1), *added*)

By requiring the implementation and application of the Protocol in a manner conducive to ongoing North–South cooperation, Article 11 appears to be a broad and dynamic safeguard for the kind of 'consultation, cooperation and action within the island of Ireland' (1998 Agreement S2(1)) envisaged in the 1998 Agreement. *Prima facie*, this could be seen to achieve the Article 1 objective to 'maintain the necessary conditions for continued North–South cooperation'. However, Article 11 only requires the provisions *of the Protocol* to be implemented and applied in a manner consistent with continued cross-border cooperation, its implicit premise being that there are no 'necessary conditions' for North–South cooperation extraneous to those provisions; this is not the case. Indeed, the mapping exercise identified EU legal and policy frameworks relevant to all of the areas listed in Article 11 that are *not* guaranteed elsewhere in the Protocol. Extrapolating from this, one of the impacts of the Withdrawal Agreement on the Northern Ireland constitution is, arguably, to provide a renewed momentum for North–South cooperation via its Strand Two institutions, including the NSMC and cross-border implementation bodies, in areas that are highlighted by Article 11 but for which the Protocol alone does not provide the necessary conditions.

North–South cooperation in respect to the generation, transmission, and distribution of electricity is granted specific protection under Article 9 of the Protocol. Ensuring the preservation of the single electricity market was an objective shared by the UK and EU and one of the few that had cross-party support in Northern Ireland (see The Executive Office, 2016a; Hayward and Whitten, 2018). Under Article 9 and Annex 4, the seven listed EU acts are to apply in Northern Ireland '*insofar* as they apply to the generation, transmission, distribution, and supply of electricity, trading in wholesale electricity or cross-border exchanges in electricity' (Annex 4, *added*); those provisions relating to retail markets and consumer protection 'shall not apply' and any other acts referenced in provisions listed do not otherwise apply 'unless it is a provision governing wholesale electricity markets which applies in Ireland *and is necessary* for the joint operation of the single wholesale electricity market on the island of Ireland' (*ibid.*). Article 9 therefore provides a strong legal foundation for North–South cooperation in respect to electricity markets and allows for discretionary and dynamic alignment in the area. Included in the seven acts listed in Annex 4 are two that relate to environmental controls on energy supply—directive 2010/75/EU on industrial emissions (integrated pollution prevention and control) and directive 2003/87/EC establishing a system for greenhouse gas emission allowance trading—notwithstanding the requirement that these acts are only to be applied 'insofar as' they apply to the operation of the single electricity market; their inclusion underlines the potential 'spillover' effects of safeguarding cooperation in one area (electricity) on other areas (environment) (see Gravey and Whitten, 2021).

Arrangements for oversight of the implementation of the Protocol create a new role for Strand Two institutions. Under Article 14(b) of the Protocol, the Specialised Committee '*shall* ... examine proposals concerning the implementation and application' (*added*) of the Protocol from the NSMC and North–South Implementation Bodies. This grants an imperative for the consideration of Strand Two concerns in respect to implementing the Protocol that is not granted to Strand One or Strand Three institutions. Read in the context of the Article 11 affirmation of the principle that cooperation in areas not specifically covered by the Protocol ought to continue post-Brexit, the role of Strand Two institutions could provide a new process for developing North–South cooperation. To demonstrate: the North–South mapping exercise found that the EU Water Framework Directive (*Official Journal* 2000c) directly underpinned the work of the NSMC in respect to ensuring water quality and mitigating water pollution on the island of Ireland (UK Government, 2017: 22; 23; 24); the Water Framework Directive is not among the articles of EU legislation included in the Annexes of the Protocol which continue to apply in Northern Ireland under its terms. However, *if* Waterways Ireland, the cross-border implementation body responsible for the maintenance of inland water systems, decided that the post-Brexit absence of the Water Framework Directive in Northern Ireland hinders its work, a proposal *could* be made to the Specialised Committee to add this directive to those listed in Annex 2. Under Article 14 of the Protocol, the Specialised Committee *could* forward this proposal regarding the 'functioning of the Protocol' to the Joint Committee wherein it *could* be adopted as a necessary 'amendment' to the Protocol within the scope of the Article 11 commitment to ensure North–South cooperation, including in respect to the 'environment' (Article 11(1)). Such an example is, of course, hypothetical; its realisation would be contingent on political relations both within the implementation body and between UK and EU representatives on the Joint Committee. The Water Framework Directive example does, however, demonstrate the rebalancing effect of the Protocol on the 1998 Agreement through the provision of a uniquely influential role for Strand Two bodies.

An additional route for developing North–South cooperation is laid down in Article 2 of the Protocol. As already discussed (see 6.2.1.2), in Article 2 the UK commits to ensuring that 'no diminution' of rights, safeguards, or equality of opportunity results from its withdrawal from the EU (Article 2(1)). Alongside this, the UK commits to 'continue to facilitate the related work' of the rights bodies established under the 1998 Agreement, including the NIHRC, ECNI, and JCHRC. According to the 1998 Agreement, the purpose of the NIHRC and ECNI is to ensure 'equality of treatment' and 'equality of opportunity' in Northern Ireland regardless of religion, identity, or ethnicity (RSE: 4). Following commitments made in the rights section of the 1998 Agreement, the Irish Government established the Irish Human Rights Commission to 'ensure at least an equivalent level of protection of human rights as will pertain in Northern Ireland' (*ibid.*: 9). What this means is that, in view of the 1998 Agreement, the effect of Article 2 is not only to hold the UK to existing arrangements enshrined in EU law but, read together with the commitment to facilitate the work of 1998 Agreement rights bodies, Article 2 suggests dynamic alignment with rights available to Irish citizens in Northern Ireland *and* Ireland. In this respect, the Article 14(c) requirement on the Specialised Committee to consider 'any matter of relevance to Article 2' that is 'brought to its attention' by the NIHRC, ECNI, or JCHRC affords the three rights and equality bodies a new role in post-Brexit Northern Ireland; one that is like unto that established for Strand Two bodies under the Protocol, albeit narrower in scope. As in other areas, the extent of significance of the Article 2 requirement for North–South equivalence in regard to rights will depend on the nature of the Protocol's implementation.

The European Council decision regarding the Withdrawal Agreement provides a further possible route by which areas of North–South cooperation not already guaranteed under the Protocol, or new areas, could develop post-Brexit. According to the Council decision, the European Council could authorise Ireland, Cyprus, or Spain to negotiate bilateral agreements with the UK in areas of exclusive EU competence on the basis of a 'duly justified request' (*Official Journal*, 2020a Article 4(1)). The criteria for 'due justification' requires the Member State to show that the proposed bilateral agreement is 'necessary for the proper functioning' of arrangements set out in, respectively, the Protocol, the Protocol on Sovereign Base Areas of the UK in Cyprus, or the Protocol on Gibraltar; it appears the agreement would be 'compatible with Union law'; and would not risk an external action objective in the given area or be 'otherwise prejudicial to the Union's interests' (*ibid.*: 1(a)(b)(c)). The language of 'proper functioning' echoes Article 14 of the Protocol and Article 164 of the Withdrawal Agreement setting out the respective mandates of the Joint and Specialised Committee; again, this adds *potential* significance to the Article 11 affirmation of comprehensive North–South cooperation in principle. Notably, Article 4 of the Council decision also provides for European Commission oversight of related negotiations and states that authorisation from the European Council may be conditional on the 'inclusion in or removal from the [bilateral] agreement in question of any provision … where necessary' to ensure consistency with the criteria outlined (*ibid.*: 2). What this means is that, if the UK and Ireland want, in future, to sign any new bilateral agreements in areas of exclusive EU competence, this would be conditional on EU authorisation which would only be forthcoming if deemed 'duly justified' to achieve the 'proper functioning' of the Protocol. This again has the indirect effect of rebalancing the three strands of the 1998 Agreement in that it reorientates aspects of bilateral Strand Three cooperation as a facilitator of all-Island Strand Two cooperation.

6.2.3.4 North–South as a Challenge to Northern Ireland in the UK Internal Market

By prioritising the 'necessary conditions' for continued cross-border trade in goods, the Protocol has implications for Northern Ireland's place in the UK internal market. The Protocol necessitates the application of the EU customs code and relevant aspects of the EU legal *acquis* to be applied to goods entering Northern Ireland. In practice, this means that the default arrangement will require EU checks and controls to be applied on goods travelling GB–NI and export summary declarations to be completed for goods travelling NI–GB. The legal and political implications of new checks and controls on goods travelling across the Irish Sea will depend on arrangements for, and the nature of, their implementation, both of which are contingent on domestic legislation, Joint Committee decisions, and a UK–EU future relationship agreement. Contingency notwithstanding, close analysis of the Protocol's provisions to 'protect' the UK internal market reveal the extent to which the prioritisation of EU–NI trade raises challenges for GB–NI trade.

Article 6 of the Protocol specifically concerns the 'Protection of the UK Internal Market' but its title arguably belies its effect; Article 6(1) states:

> *Nothing in this Protocol* shall prevent *the United Kingdom* from ensuring unfettered market access for goods moving from Northern Ireland to other parts of the United Kingdom's internal market. Provisions of Union law made applicable by this Protocol which prohibit or restrict the exportation of goods shall only be applied to trade between Northern Ireland and other parts of the United Kingdom to the extent strictly required by any international obligations of the Union … (Protocol, *added*)

Notably, the reference to 'unfettered access' in the first sentence of Article 6 is more descriptive than committal; it is a statement about the scope of the Protocol which does not *necessitate* the regulation of goods moving from NI to the rest of the UK. The extent of 'fettering' required on goods moving NI–GB depends to a large degree on the terms of the future UK–EU trading relationship, which is, of course, outside the scope of the Protocol. The second sentence underlines the way in which 'unfettered access' for NI–GB goods may be conditional on UK domestic legislation which is extraneous but subordinate to the Protocol. Under Article 5 and Annex 2 of the Protocol, EU Regulation 2015/479 (regarding EU common rules for exports) is to apply in Northern Ireland. However, the Article 6(1) provision suggests that any restrictions on exports, under Regulation 2015/476, would only effect NI–GB trade in areas governed by international *and* EU law. This is an innovation in EU law terms as it involves splitting single market rules governing imports and those governing exports. According to Article 7(1) of the Protocol, the placing of goods on the Northern Ireland market will be governed by applicable UK law and 'as regards goods imported from the Union' by Articles 34 and 36 TFEU. Article 34 TFEU prohibits quantitative restrictions on *imports* between Member States; Article 36 TFEU allows prohibitions or restrictions on imports, exports, or transit goods between Member States only in specific, exceptional circumstances. Notably, and in accordance with Article 6(1), Article 7(1) does not apply Article 35 TFEU, which prohibits quantitative restrictions on *exports* between Member States. Rules governing trade to and from Northern Ireland under the Protocol are therefore not only highly complex but they also break new legislative ground in both the EU and UK legal orders.

Article 6(2) underlines Northern Ireland's new status as a place within and between the two markets it straddles and also highlights the challenges this raises for its place in the UK internal market, albeit implicitly:

> Having regard to Northern Ireland's integral place in the United Kingdom's internal market, the Union and the United Kingdom shall use their best endeavours to facilitate the trade between Northern Ireland and other parts of the United Kingdom, *in accordance with applicable legislation* and taking into account their respective regulatory regimes as well as the implementation thereof. (*added*)

Alone, Article 6(2) appears to reaffirm the 'integral place' of Northern Ireland in the UK internal market.[31] However, read in the broader context of the Protocol, Article 6 underlines the new contingency of the stated 'regard'. The 'applicable legislation' referenced includes legislation that applies by virtue of Article 5 and Annex 2 of the Protocol and thereby includes EU Regulation 2015/476 regarding common rules on exports. Therefore, notwithstanding the Article 6 commitment to apply export restrictions only to the extent 'strictly required' under EU law, and the onus on both parties to use 'best endeavours' to facilitate NI–GB trade, by prioritising NI–EU trade so as to avoid a hard physical border on the island of Ireland, the Protocol creates new barriers for trade flows to and from Northern Ireland. The impact of the domestic implementation of these provisions for the Northern Ireland constitution is considered in more detail in the next chapter.

6.2.4 East–West Dimension

One of the repercussions of the (necessary) attention on Strand Two of the Northern Ireland constitution in UK–EU withdrawal negotiations was

---

[31] The 'internal market' is a relatively new term and concept in UK political and legal discourse. In the context of the Brexit process, discussion of the UK internal market arose only after the publication of the EU draft legal text which the Prime Minister May suggested 'undermined the UK 'common market' (in *BBC News*, 2018). The language and concept clearly echo that used for the EU common or 'single market'.

comparative inattention on Strand Three cooperation; this is reflected in the text of the Protocol. 'East–West' relations are only mentioned once in the Protocol and Strand Three institutions—the British-Irish Council (BIC) and British Irish Intergovernmental Conference (BIIC)—are not mentioned explicitly. Such comparative absence of 'East–West' relations and Strand Three institutions suggests that as a consequence of the Withdrawal Agreement, Protocol, and their enforcement mechanisms, Strand Two of the 1998 Agreement now enjoys greater legal protection than Strand Three. That said, and while none of the Protocol Articles specifically provide for or are designed to facilitate East–West cooperation via Strand Three institutions, these are covered by overarching commitments in the text to set out 'arrangements necessary … to protect the 1998 Agreement *in all its dimensions*' (Article 1(3)). Further, the 'enduring nature' of the bilateral relationship between the UK and Ireland is recognised in several provisions of the Protocol, most specifically in Article 3 regarding the continuation of the CTA (*Preamble*, Recital 1). Taken together then, although the provisions of the Protocol in respect to Strand Three relations and institutions provide less legal certainty than is the case for Strand Two, or indeed Strand One and the principle of consent, they also do not undermine or weaken the legal status of Strand Three of the Northern Ireland constitution; in this way, the *direct* impact of the Protocol on Strand Three is comparatively small.

Given the lack of Protocol provisions dedicated to preserving Strand Three, its impact on this component of the Northern Ireland constitution will depend on the way in which general commitments to the 1998 Agreement are interpreted and applied. In this respect, it is notable that throughout UK–EU withdrawal negotiations, Strand Three institutions were used as fora for bilateral and multilateral engagement in such a way as to suggest that they could become more politically significant post-Brexit than pre-Brexit. In particular, intergovernmental engagement, via the BIIC, resulted in greater clarity as to the legal status and substance of 'East–West' relations and commitments. An apparent renewed momentum for East–West cooperation via Strand Three institutions may therefore prove to be an *indirect* impact of the Protocol on this aspect of the Northern Ireland constitution.

This subsection details those aspects of the Protocol that recognise or enable the continuation of East–West relations before going on to set out the activities of Strand Three institutions during this phase of the Brexit process and the significance of these activities in light of the Withdrawal Agreement and Protocol.

6.2.4.1 'East–West' Provisions in the Withdrawal Agreement and Protocol

In the Protocol, 'the United Kingdom' recalls its enduring commitment 'to protecting and supporting continued North–South and East–West cooperation across the full range of political, economic, security, societal and agricultural contexts' (*Preamble*, Recital 15); as the sole explicit reference to 'East–West cooperation' in the Protocol text, it is notable that this is a unilateral UK commitment. On three occasions, the Protocol refers to the 1998 Agreement in an inclusive manner. The first is in the already noted statement of the Protocol's objective to protect the 1998 Agreement 'in all its dimensions' (Article 1(3)). The second inclusive reference is in Article 2(2) which, also already noted, commits the UK to 'continue to facilitate the *related* work of the institutions and bodies set up pursuant to the 1998 Agreement' (*added*); the qualifier 'related' is important in respect to Strand Three as Article 2 concerns the preservation of rights-based legal protections that underpin the 1998 Agreement. In this area, the work of Strand Three institutions is not as significant as other institutions established by the 1998 Agreement (namely the NIHRC, ECNI, and JCHRC); it is therefore not likely that this provision could be used judicially to protect an area of East–West cooperation which is not very specifically related to the 'Rights, Safeguards and Equality of Opportunity' section of the 1998 Agreement named under Article 2. The final inclusive reference to bodies established under the 1998 Agreement is in Article 18(4) which states the Joint Committee '*may* seek an opinion from institutions created by the 1998 Agreement' regarding the necessary measures in the event of the Northern Ireland Assembly voting to disapply Articles 5 to 10 of the Protocol via the 'democratic consent mechanism' (*added*). Notably, this provision does not necessitate the Joint Committee to seek an opinion from any or all of the 1998 Agreement institutions. In view of the membership of Strand Three institutions which includes the Irish Government, other UK devolved administrations, and Crown Dependencies, it is unlikely that Article 18(4) would be used to give primacy to an opinion of Strand Three institutions. Based on the whole text of the Protocol, while Strand Three institutions are clearly incorporated into the broad (Article 1(3)) commitment to protect all dimensions of the 1998 Agreement and are implicitly referred to by inclusive references to 1998 Agreement institutions, it is also the case that the context in which those references are made suggests that the perspectives of Strand Three institutions are, or would be, less influential than Strand One, Strand Two, or rights bodies on matters concerning the implementation of the Protocol.

Notwithstanding the lack of explicit mention, the provisions of the Protocol do recognise and allow for the intergovernmental 'East–West' relationship of the UK and Ireland in several ways. The most explicit example is Article 3 which allows the UK and Ireland to 'continue to make arrangements between themselves relating to the movement of persons between their territories (the "Common Travel Area")' subject to such arrangements 'fully respecting' the rights of natural persons conferred by EU law. Importantly, this provision allows for bilateral arrangements regarding the CTA *narrowly* defined as relating to the movement of persons rather than enabling new arrangements as regards the reciprocal rights and privileges associated with the CTA, *broadly* defined (including the right to work, reside, access healthcare, access social security, access education, and vote). Article 3(2) addresses a broader definition of the CTA by acknowledging 'rights and privileges associated' with it (without recording their substance) and commits that *the UK* 'ensure' these rights 'can continue to apply without affecting the obligations of Ireland under Union law'. Under Article 3 therefore, onus is placed on post-Brexit UK Governments to make sure the UK does not diverge from EU law in such a way as to undermine the CTA broadly understood as including the full array of reciprocal rights and privileges afforded UK and Irish citizens in one another's states.

6.2.4.2 Intergovernmental Relations: British-Irish Intergovernmental Conference

In July 2018, the British-Irish Intergovernmental Conference (the Conference) met for the first time since February 2007. At the Conference, the UK and Irish Governments 'reiterated their strong support for the Belfast/Good Friday Agreement and subsequent agreements' and 're-affirmed their shared commitment to all of the political institutions' it established and to 'securing the effective operation of power-sharing devolved government in Northern Ireland', the resumption of the NSMC, and the participation of Northern Ireland in the British-Irish Council 'at the earliest opportunity' (Cabinet Office, 2018a). The Conference also 'considered the strength' of the bilateral relationship and agreed that the 'high levels' of existing cooperation 'needed to be maintained and, where possible, strengthened following the departure of the United Kingdom from the European Union' (*ibid.*); to this end, officials were asked to come forward with proposals for future East–West cooperation for consideration at a future meeting of the Conference. At the next meeting of the Conference in November 2018, 'a number of possible models' for maintaining and strengthening bilateral cooperation after Brexit were discussed (Cabinet Office, 2018b). The Conference agreed new structures should provide Ministers and officials 'to continue to engage both formally and informally' and maintain 'the spirit of cooperation that has been engendered … in an EU context'; officials were again asked to take forward work in this area with a view to presenting 'ambitious' proposals at a future meeting (*ibid.*). At each meeting of the Conference, the two governments reaffirmed their shared intent 'to continue working closely together in full accordance with the three-stranded approach' of the 1998 Agreement (Cabinet Office, 2018a; 2018b; DFA, 2019).

In May 2019, the Conference met again. Further commitments were made to ensure 'the current high level of bilateral cooperation' is maintained and strengthened after UK withdrawal from the EU. Ministers reviewed the progress made by officials on this matter and 'requested further proposals for new, reinvigorated and regular opportunities for future co-operation' (DFA, 2019). At the May 2019 Conference, the two governments agreed a Memorandum of Understanding (hereafter 'MOU') on the operation of the CTA in which they reaffirmed a 'shared commitment' to protect the CTA and associated reciprocal rights and privileges, agreeing to 'reinforce the excellent and highly valued cooperation that already exists' (Cabinet Office, 2019 (2)). The MOU set out shared commitments and understandings regarding arrangements for the CTA and reciprocal rights of British and Irish citizens in regard to free movement, right to reside, right to work, access to healthcare, social security rights, access to social housing, access to education, and voting rights (*ibid.* paras 3–14). The MOU also provided for greater oversight of the CTA by establishing a group of senior officials dedicated to monitoring its operations (*ibid.* (16)). While the MOU was not legally binding, in it the two governments committed to taking 'any necessary legislative steps' to give effect to CTA rights and privileges, including any relevant 'bilateral agreements that may be entered into now or in the future' to this end (*ibid.* (14)). The prospect of future new bilateral agreements facilitated by Strand Three institutions elucidates an additional dynamic of the EU's new role as protector of the 1998 Agreement: if any future UK–Ireland bilateral agreement concerned areas of exclusive EU competence (such as customs, level playing field issues, or fisheries), under Article 4 of the European Council decision on the Withdrawal Agreement, the Irish Government would first need authorisation from the European Council and the EU would have oversight powers on the process (see 6.2.3.3). While this is another merely hypothetical scenario, given the legal novelty of the process and the likely political sensitivities involved, it is nonetheless an important one to note.

6.2.4.3 Intra-UK and East–West Relations: British Irish Council

As described in the previous chapter, the functioning of Strand Two and Strand Three institutions was hindered by the collapse of the Executive and Assembly in January 2017. Without Northern Ireland Ministers, the NSMC could not meet; however, the work of the British-Irish Council (the Council) did continue after a brief hiatus. Under the 1998 Agreement, the Council ought to hold two summits annually and meet regularly at sectoral level (S3(3)). Only one summit meeting was held in 2017 due to the collapse of the Executive, but, after this, the regular bi-annual scheduling resumed. This means that in the period between the triggering of Article 50 in March 2017 and the ratification of the Withdrawal Agreement in January 2020, there were five meetings of the Council and Northern Ireland was not fully represented at any of them.[32] There is some precedent for the Council continuing to operate without Northern Ireland representatives. Between 2002 and 2007, the Council met at summit level once annually before resuming normal bi-annual meetings after Strand One institutions were restored following the St Andrews Agreement (see 2.1.4).

At the five meetings held during UK–EU withdrawal negotiations, the Council received an update on political developments in Northern Ireland and Member Administration delegates consistently noted that they 'looked forward to the restoration of the devolved institutions in Northern Ireland' (BIC, 2017; 2018a; 2018b; 2019a; 2019b: 1).[33] Summit communiqués note that Ministers present updated one another on activities relating to the UK's exit from the EU, with particular reference to the themes identified in the extraordinary meeting of the Council in July 2016 and the 28th Summit in November 2016 (BIC, 2016a; 2016b). These priority themes included: agriculture, agri-food and fisheries, economy and trade, free movement of goods and people, the CTA, relations with the EU, transition, and implementation (BIC, 2017: 2). Under the Protocol, arrangements for Northern Ireland across all of these priority areas are distinct. It is significant, therefore, that throughout the period of UK–EU withdrawal negotiations, discussions on

---

[32] The UK Government delegation throughout the period included the Secretary of State for Northern Ireland. However, in the BIC format, UK devolved institutions are normally represented by elected First and, in the Northern Ireland case, also deputy First Ministers so it is true to say that Northern Ireland was not represented (see 1998 Agreement S3(2)).

[33] There is an interesting change in the phrasing of BIC communiqués on the restoration of Strand One institutions as the period of absence went on. In the Nov. 2017, June 2018, and Nov. 2018 communiqués, the Council records that members 'looked forward to the restoration of the devolved institutions in Northern Ireland *as soon as possible*' (1); in the June 2019 and Nov. 2019 communiqués, the same sentiment is expressed with less urgency as members state they 'looked forward to the restoration of the devolved institutions' (1). Dropping of the 'asap' clause was perhaps an incidental change in language, but ist also seems to suggest a lack of urgency and optimism among delegates as to the possibility of restoring Strand One.

these issues at the Council were missing full Northern Ireland representation. Further, under the 1998 Agreement rules of procedure, the Council '*normally* will operate by consensus' (S3(7), *added*); individual members can, however, opt not to participate in common policies or actions, and these can be agreed just between 'all members participating' (*ibid.*). This *modus operandi* allows for flexibility and for differentiated levels of cooperation and integration of Member Administrations; however, it also, arguably, places Northern Ireland at a disadvantage. As the only Member Administration that operates mandatory power-sharing coalition government, it is the most likely to experience periods of political instability and the only Member Administration required to reach internal consensus prior to participating in any bilateral or multilateral agreements with other members of the Council.

At the two 2019 Summits, the Council reflected on the 20th anniversary of the establishment of the BIC and 'agreed that twenty years on, the Council remained a valued strand of the Belfast –Good Friday Agreement' (BIC, 2019a: 2), describing its function as a forum that offered 'ministers and officials regular opportunities to exchange information, discuss, consult and co-operate on matters of mutual interest within the respective competencies of the eight Member Administrations', and which therefore 'continued to positively strengthen the links and relationships between the people of these islands' (BIC, 2019b: 1). The emphasis of the Council on the importance of its work despite a Northern Ireland absence could perhaps be said to reflect its renewed significance as a forum for cross-jurisdictional coordination in the post-Brexit era wherein divergence between its Member Administrations in relevant areas is guaranteed.

6.3 Impact Assessment: UK–EU Withdrawal Agreement and the Northern Ireland Constitution

For this research, the most significant impact of the UK–EU Withdrawal Agreement is the new legal relationship it creates between the EU and the Northern Ireland constitution. The explicit purpose of the Protocol is to 'protect the 1998 Agreement in all its parts' and 'maintain the necessary conditions for continued North–South cooperation' in the context of Brexit (Article 1(3)). By its own terms, therefore, this international treaty establishes the EU, alongside the UK, as a 'protector' of the 1998 Agreement in the specific circumstance of UK withdrawal from the EU and its consequences. It should be stated that this new role for the EU is short of the UK and Irish Governments' responsibility in respect to the 1998 Agreement as co-guarantors of the Multi-Party Agreement and signatories of the British-Irish Agreement. Instead, the EU's 'protector' role is limited to the scope of the Protocol as it relates to the 1998 Agreement. That said, the specificity of the EU's new relationship to the 1998 Agreement should be read against mechanisms for enforcement. Under the Withdrawal Agreement and Protocol, the EU and UK 'protector' roles are linked to a dispute resolution mechanism and bodies established to oversee its implementation with legal powers to amend its terms. These arrangements are very different to those made for implementation and oversight of guarantors in the 1998 Agreement which contains no mechanisms for legal redress or formal monitoring, relying instead on political and diplomatic relations between its signatories as the *modus operandi* of implementation. In the long term, therefore, the impact of the UK–EU Withdrawal Agreement is to introduce an indefinite EU dimension to Northern Ireland governance, albeit one that is constrained by its specificity, contingency on relations with the UK more broadly, and the possibility of being denuded of the majority of its substance via consent votes in the Northern Ireland Assembly.

The impact of the Withdrawal Agreement and Protocol on consent in the Northern Ireland context is profound. While a narrow understanding of the principle of consent is affirmed in the Protocol (Article 1(1)), the novel 'democratic consent mechanism' amounts to a reformulation of the principle of consent broadly understood. In the 1998 Agreement, the requirement for consent to constitutional change is underpinned by a preference for popular consent, and the requirement for consent to 'key' legislative decisions at the devolved level is underpinned by a preference for cross-community consent. By contrast, the Protocol consent mechanism is underpinned by a preference for parliamentary (over popular) consent and majoritarian (over cross-community) consent; it therefore constitutes a reformulation of, and addition to, the broad principle of consent set out in the 1998 Agreement. Of the changes identified in this chapter, the addition of this novel form of consent is likely to have the greatest political impact on Northern Ireland in the medium to long term. By providing for recurring votes concerned with the degree of alignment with either Great Britain or Ireland, the 'democratic consent mechanism' will likely prove a source of perpetual destabilisation in Northern Ireland politics as it is very likely to act as a proxy for traditional Unionist vs Nationalist political discourses.

For devolution in Northern Ireland, the lack of a requirement for Strand One institutions to input on key decisions regarding the implementation of the Protocol risks creating a democratic deficit in Northern Ireland and/or the perception of one. The three bodies established to oversee the implementation of the Protocol—UK–EU Joint Committee, Specialised Committee, and Joint Consultative Working Group—are not *required* to consult with the Northern Ireland Executive or Assembly or Northern Ireland stakeholders more broadly. The nature of the Protocol's implementation will, however, have profound economic, social, and political implications for areas within the competence of the devolved administration. On a black-letter analysis, therefore, the Protocol creates a democratic deficit that departs from the level of competency envisaged for the devolved institutions in the 1998 Agreement. However, there is the possibility, even probability, that any such deficit will be mitigated by UK Government decisions to include Northern Ireland officials or politicians in UK delegations to and representations on the oversight bodies. This issue is considered further in Chapter 7 and returned to in Chapter 9.

The impact of the Withdrawal Agreement and Protocol on the North–South dimension is twofold: it provides new legal protections for North–South cooperation in respect to trade in goods and incentivises deeper North–South cooperation in areas not explicitly covered in the text. Although a stated aim of the Protocol is to enable the continuation of North–South cooperation, its provisions prioritise *some* areas of cooperation over others and provide greater overall protection for Strand Two of the 1998 Agreement over and above Strand One and Strand Three. A particular focus in the Protocol on facilitating continued cross-border trade in goods is more a reflection of UK and EU negotiating 'red lines' than it is a derivative of the 1998 Agreement. The Protocol will apply in Northern Ireland indefinitely (notwithstanding Articles 5 to 10 being subject to regular consent votes), yet its provisions retain the 'backstop' logic of its earlier iteration. As such, its provisions for continuation of North–South cooperation were intended to be accompanied by a 'deep and comprehensive' UK–EU future relationship agreement which did not arise from UK–EU future relationship negotiations led by Prime Minister Johnson on the UK side. While the comparatively 'thin' nature of the UK–EU future relationship agreement secured by Johnson has important knock-on effects on Northern Ireland's place in the UK internal market, it also has the indirect effect of making the Protocol provisions for North–South cooperation more significant in political and policy terms.

Finally, in respect to the East–West dimension of the Northern Ireland constitution, the process of UK–EU withdrawal negotiations catalysed greater legal clarification of Strand Three intergovernmental relations. Strand Three institutions are not specifically mentioned in the Protocol text, yet the negotiation process motivated intergovernmental engagement via the BIIC which led to a Memorandum of Understanding between the two guarantor governments of the 1998 Agreement and commitments to secure areas of bilateral cooperation in forthcoming legislation and bilateral agreements. This suggests an indirect impact of the Brexit process could be a formalisation of existing British-Irish intergovernmental cooperation in the medium to long term.

Chapters 8 and 9 consider the key findings from this chapter in light of the impacts of domestic implementation of the UK–EU Withdrawal Agreement and Protocol, to which the next chapter now turns.

7
Implementing the UK–EU Withdrawal Agreement in UK Law

> 'We must all remember that, if the protocol is to work, it must work for the whole community in Northern Ireland. Whether it is to be maintained in the future, as the protocol itself sets out, is for the people of Northern Ireland to decide …'
>
> **Chancellor of the Duchy, Michael Gove, December 2020**[1]

> 'The Assembly notes the request from the Secretary of State for Exiting the European Union for the consent of the Assembly for the provisions of the European Union (Withdrawal Agreement) Bill which affect its competence; and affirms that the Assembly does not agree to give its consent'.
>
> **Northern Ireland Assembly, January 2020a**[2]

To address the 'unique circumstances' of Northern Ireland, provisions of the Ireland/Northern Protocol in the UK–EU Withdrawal Agreement[3] require that aspects of European Union law continued to apply in Northern Ireland after the end of a transition period on 1 January 2021 when they ceased to apply in the rest of the United Kingdom (Protocol Article 1(3)). Operationalising this new arrangement, under the Withdrawal Agreement and Protocol, for the legal relationships between the EU, the UK as a whole, and the UK in respect of Northern Ireland, necessitated significant legislative and practical steps to be taken before the beginning of 2021. These preparations to ensure 'the protocol is to work' (Gove, 2020) were, however, made more

---

[1] Gove, M. (2020) 'EU Withdrawal Agreement Volume 685: debated on Wednesday 9 December 2020' *hansard.parliament.uk* Available: https://hansard.parliament.uk/Commons/2020-12-09/debates/F5A28792-DDD8-4D10-A254-FE777E6703FC/EUWithdrawalAgreement 12.54pm

[2] Northern Ireland Assembly (2020a) 'Official Report (Hansard) Monday 20 January 2020 Volume 125, No 3' *niassembly.gov.uk* Available: http://data.niassembly.gov.uk/HansardXml/plenary-20-01-2020.pdf page 27 and reproduced with permissions from https://www.northernireland.gov.uk/crown-copyright.

[3] In-parenthesis references to the Withdrawal Agreement further abbreviate to 'WA'; this is for the purpose of brevity.

difficult by UK–EU disagreement over what its provisions required, or ought to require, and by the unpalatability of its terms to political parties in the restored Northern Ireland Assembly who did 'not agree to give ... consent' to its implementation in UK law (NI Assembly, 2020a). Recognising this context, this chapter examines the impact of actions taken during the transition period to implement and operationalise the Withdrawal Agreement and Protocol on the constitution of Northern Ireland.

The majority of preparations for implementing the Protocol were domestic. Under the UK's dualist legal system, international treaties are given legal force when corresponding domestic legislation is passed to implement the substance of the international text. In the case of the Withdrawal Agreement, the international treaty could only be ratified after the UK Parliament approved its substance via the *European Union (Withdrawal Agreement) Act 2020* (hereafter EU(WA) Act or 2020 Act). The EU(WA) Act 2020 received Royal Assent on 23 January, paving the way for the Withdrawal Agreement, following approval by the European Parliament on the EU side, to be ratified on 30 January and for the UK to formally leave the EU on 31 January. The Withdrawal Agreement, and thereby the EU(WA) Act 2020, provided for an eleven-month transition period during which EU law would continue to apply in the UK.[4] In that transition period, the UK and EU would attempt to negotiate the terms of their future relationship while also making arrangements necessary to implement what had been agreed in the Withdrawal Agreement, particularly in respect of the Protocol. To achieve the latter task, several significant decisions would, ideally, need to be taken by the UK–EU Joint Committee and these also given legal effect in domestic legislation. The Withdrawal Agreement and Protocol were given direct effect in UK law by way of (new) section 7A of the *European Union (Withdrawal) Act* 2018 (hereafter 'EUWA 2018' or 2018 Act) that was added by section 5 of the 2020 Act. Under section 7A of the 2018 Act, UK Ministers and devolved authorities were granted sweeping powers to implement the terms of the Withdrawal Agreement and Protocol by regulations, thereby enabling any loose ends or future obligations to be addressed via secondary legislation. Additional primary legislation as well as secondary legislation made under the EU(WA) Act 2020 and EUWA 2018 would also be required to

---

[4] The Withdrawal Agreement provided for a transition or implementation period to start on the day the Agreement entered into force and end on 31 December 2020 (WA Article 126), during which time EU law would continue to apply in the UK unless specifically provided for in the Agreement (WA Article, 127(1)); the Joint Committee had opportunity in July 2020 to extend the transition period for one to two years (WA Article, 132(1)) but decided not to do so.

deal with the extent of legal changes needed to operationalise the Withdrawal Agreement and Protocol. Among other things, domestic legislation passed during the transition period would need to incorporate any Joint Committee decisions on the Protocol and adopt measures necessary in view of a future UK–EU relationship agreement, or lack thereof. These features of the transition period—an imperative to ensure the Protocol would be operational by 2021, notwithstanding UK–EU disagreement over its implementation, and ongoing UK–EU future trade negotiations—are the backdrop for this final empirical chapter of the book. It considers the impact of UK legislation to implement the Withdrawal Agreement and Protocol on the Northern Ireland constitution.[5]

This chapter has three parts: the first provides an overview of the relevant legislative context and an account of key political events between the Withdrawal Agreement coming into force on 31 January 2020 and end of the transition period on 31 December 2020; the second section sets out the impact of domestic implementing legislation on the components of the Northern Ireland constitution; the third section provides a summary of findings.

Looking ahead, the key findings from this phase of the Brexit process are as follows: (1) there are discrepancies between existing UK legal definitions of the 1998 Agreement and territory of Northern Ireland and the definitions and provisions of the Protocol introduced onto the UK statute book by implementing legislation; (2) the implementation of the 'democratic consent mechanism' offers a new formulation of the principle of consent enshrined in the 1998 Agreement; (3) the lack of any legislative requirement for Northern Ireland Executive or Assembly input to or oversight of the implementation of the Protocol strengthens UK Government executive powers vis-à-vis the devolved government in Northern Ireland; (4) discrepancies between the provisions for North–South cooperation in the Protocol, in UK implementing legislation, and in the Northern Ireland constitution create some uncertainty regarding the development of North–South cooperation and the role of Strand Two bodies post-Brexit; (5) the 'power-hoarding' effect of implementing legislation in respect to the UK internal market poses a challenge to the operation of the British-Irish Council by centralising policymaking powers in its priority work sectors; (6) UK and EU disagreements

---

[5] The global coronavirus pandemic declared in March 2020 affected the logistics involved in Joint Committee discussions, UK–EU future relationship negotiations, and the legislative procedures in the UK during the transition period as well as the political and societal environment in which they were carried out. The pandemic did not, however, change the substance or outcome of discussions, negotiations, or legislation in any significant way and as such its effects are not directly addressed in this analysis.

during the transition period suggest implementing Brexit in general and the Protocol in particular will strain British-Irish relations for the foreseeable future.

7.1 The UK's EU Withdrawal Act(s) and the Transition Period

The EU(WA) Act 2020 supplemented, amended, and repealed parts of its sister Act, the EUWA 2018. The primary purpose of the EUWA 2018 was to prepare the statute book for the legal effects of UK withdrawal from the EU by: repealing the *European Communities Act* 1972 (ECA 1972), thereby ending the 'direct effect' of EU law in the UK; converting existing EU law into 'retained EU law' and providing for the amendment of this new type of law at devolved and central levels; as well as making provision for Parliament to approve a future UK–EU Withdrawal Agreement (for detailed analysis of the 2018 Act see Elliot and Tierney 2019; HL Constitution Committee, 2018; Craig, 2019). In this latter purpose, providing for parliamentary approval of a future agreement, the EUWA 2018 had prepared the way for the EU(WA) Act 2020 by which the revised Withdrawal Agreement was approved, and arrangements made for its implementation. Both of these Acts were therefore central to the legal process of implementing UK withdrawal from the EU in domestic law and ought to be read together. Notwithstanding the comprehensive legislative scope of the EUWA 2018 and the EU(WA) Act 2020, and the sweeping executive powers they granted, these Acts were not on their own sufficient to enact the vast array of legal changes associated with UK withdrawal from the EU or to address the changes required to implement the Withdrawal Agreement in domestic law. As such, while this chapter is primarily focused on the EU(WA) Act 2020 and the EUWA 2018 it amends, it also incorporates analysis of other relevant primary and secondary implementing legislation including, in particular, the *Taxation (Cross-Border Trade) Act 2018*, the *United Kingdom Internal Market Act 2020*, and the *Taxation (Post-Transition Period) Act 2020*.

Before considering the impact of implementing legislation on the components of the Northern Ireland constitution, it is necessary to contextualise the analysis by detailing the political and legal circumstances in which the provisions were made. To do so, this section outlines relevant political and legislative developments that preceded the transition period followed by a brief account of political events and legislation initiated during the eleven months from 1 February to 31 December 2020.

7.1.1 Key Political and Legislative Developments Prior to Transition Period

The EUWA 2018, which received royal assent on 26 June 2018, sought to provide 'legal certainty' in the UK by repealing the ECA 1972 but allowing any existing EU law as it applied in the UK on 'exit day' to be converted into domestic law (HM Government, 2017a: 1.1). Under section 2 of the EU Withdrawal Act 2018, the estimated 20,000 UK laws that were 'EU-derived' immediately before 31 January 2020 ('exit day') were given domestic legal effect. This substantial body of new domestic law, 'retained EU law', could then be assessed and a decision taken to either repeal, revoke, or retain the given legislation as appropriate and according to the powers and processes granted under the EUWA 2018 (s7). This was a 'gargantuan' legal undertaking (Elliott and Tierney, 2019: 1) and one of 'a type and scale that is unique and unprecedented' (HL Constitution Committee, 2018: 3). While a landmark piece of legislation overall, it is the EUWA 2018 provisions in respect of devolved powers in general and Northern Ireland in particular that are most relevant here.

The EUWA 2018 granted devolved authorities two new categories of powers 'corresponding' to those granted UK Ministers: first, to make regulations to 'prevent, remedy, or mitigate' any failures or deficiencies arising in the operation of retained EU law (Sch2 s1(1)); and second, to make such provision as 'the devolved authority considers appropriate for the purposes of implementing the withdrawal agreement' (Sch2 s2(12)). These otherwise broad powers of amendment and implementation granted devolved authorities were constrained in accordance with their respective existing competencies. Acting alone, devolved authorities could not make regulations under the Act in any area outside their competence (*ibid.* s2(1)); and the consent of, or consultation with, central UK Government Ministers would be required for regulations made under Schedule 2 if the same consent or consultation would have been required in an act of the devolved legislature (*ibid.* s2(5)). Arguably, as set out in detail in later subsections (see 7.2.3 and 7.2.4), a failure to fully account for the particularity of devolved competence in Northern Ireland in respect to the Strand Two North–South dimension and Strand Three East–West dimension of its constitution, created some uncertainties, or at least complexities, in the exercise of devolved authorities' powers granted under the EUWA 2018.

The EUWA 2018 contained specific provisions regarding the continuation of North–South cooperation and prevention of 'new border arrangements' between Northern Ireland and Ireland (*ibid.* s10). Under section 10, any

Minister of the Crown or a devolved authority exercising 'any of the powers under [the] Act' would be required to do so 'in a way that is compatible with the terms of the Northern Ireland Act 1998' (*ibid.* s10(1)(a)) and to have 'due regard' to the Joint Report of UK and EU Negotiators agreed in December 2017 to conclude phase one of withdrawal negotiations (*ibid.* s10(1)(b); see also 6.1.1). While both of these provisions are significant, the required 'compatibility' with the 1998 Act is notably more substantive than the 'due regard' required for the Joint Report. Section 10 also constrained the regulation-making powers of Ministers (central and devolved) granted under the Act, by preventing them from authorising any measure that would: 'diminish any form of North–South cooperation provided for by the Belfast Agreement (as defined by section 98 of the Northern Ireland Act 1998)' (*ibid.* (2)(a)); or to create or facilitate 'border arrangements' between Northern Ireland and the Ireland 'which feature physical infrastructure … that did not exist before exit day and are not in accordance with an agreement between the United Kingdom and the EU' (*ibid.* para. 2(b)). The EUWA 2018 therefore distinguished between the 1998 Act and the 1998 Agreement, requiring broad 'compatibility' with the former but only protecting one aspect of the latter from 'diminution' by regulation. By restricting the exercise of powers in this way, the EUWA 2018 recognised the particular vulnerability of the Northern Ireland constitution to the legal consequences of Brexit and reflected the strategy of the May Government to ensure this was 'protected in all its parts' (Joint Report, 2017: 42). However, as set out in section 7.2 below, the 'compatibility' requirement, although retained in the EU(WA) Act 2020, creates areas of contradiction and uncertainty when read alongside the Protocol, agreed by Johnson, and given direct effect by the later Act.

Under the EU Withdrawal Act 2018, corresponding devolved authorities' powers were given to 'Scottish Ministers', 'Welsh Ministers', and to 'Northern Ireland department[s]' (s11; Sch2(8) to (10); (17) to (19)). The different language in respect to Northern Ireland reflects a longstanding particularity of its devolution arrangement whereby powers are delegated to 'departments' rather than 'Ministers'. According to Section 17(3) of the 1998 Act, Ministers in Northern Ireland are 'in charge' of their departments, meaning *ordinarily* the different terminology did not substantively affect the nature of any powers devolved.[6] However, this delegation of powers to departments in Northern Ireland was more significant given the continued lack of devolved government following the collapse of the Executive in January 2017, and

---

[6] See section 4(1) of the *Departments (Northern Ireland) Order 1999* which provides that '[t]he functions of a department shall at all times be exercised subject to the direction and control of the Minister'.

without direct rule from Westminster. After a decision to grant planning permission for a waste incinerator on the outskirts of Belfast—taken without ministerial oversight by the most senior civil servant in the Department of Infrastructure—was ruled unlawful in the Court of Appeal (see *Re Buick*, 2018: 56) on a matter of procedure, primary legislation was introduced at Westminster that in effect consolidated the previously quixotic delegation of powers to Northern Ireland 'departments'.[7] The *Northern Ireland (Executive Formation and Execution of Functions)* (hereafter 'NI (EFEF)') Bill was introduced to the House of Commons on 18 October 2018 and received royal assent just thirteen days later. The purpose of the NI(EFEF) Act 2018 was to suspend the statutory duty on the Secretary of State to call another Northern Ireland Assembly election and, again, extend the period during which ministerial appointments could be made following such an election.[8] In addition, the NI(EFEF) Act provided for 'the exercise of governmental functions' (*Long Title*) by giving civil servants powers to administer government departments subject to a 'public interest' test. Under Section 3 of the NI(EFEF) Act, 'senior officers' in the NICS[9] were granted general discretionary powers to exercise the functions of their respective departments 'if the officer is satisfied that it is in the public interest' to do so. Alongside the Act, the UK Government published guidance for Northern Ireland Departments exercising powers granted

---

[7] The *Buick* case centred on whether or not a decision by the Permanent Secretary in the Department of Infrastructure to grant planning permission under section 26 of the *Planning Act (Northern Ireland) 2011* which states that 'developments of regional significance' are within the 'Department's jurisdiction' (s26 heading). The planning application had been made before the collapse of the Executive but by the time the decision was made there had been no ministerial oversight for eight months. In a judicial review case at the NI High Court, the civil servants' decision, which was taken after consultation with officials in the Department of Agriculture, Environment and Rural Affairs, was initially deemed unlawful by Keegan J. on the basis that the 'natural and ordinary' meaning of Article 4(1) of the *Departments (Northern Ireland) Order 1999* rendered the decision *ultra vires* (*Buick*, 2018a: 42). Later at the Court of Appeal, the majority likewise held that the decision was unlawful but on different reasoning; the higher court stated that Article 4(1) was ambiguous when considered in its wider statutory setting but that the illegality of the decision derived from the fact that it was a 'cross-cutting' decision within the meaning of the ministerial code and would therefore normally have required specific ministerial approval at the Executive Committee (as according to 1998 Agreement S1: 19–20 and 1998 Act s20(3)) which was beyond the competence of a civil servant (*Buick*, 2018b 56). The Court of Appeal ruling therefore left a broader question as to whether or not civil servants could lawfully take decisions that would not otherwise require ministerial approval due to their 'cross-cutting' nature. The NI(EFEF) Act 2018 addressed this issue directly. For further analysis of *Buick*, see Anthony (2021).

[8] Following failure to form an executive in the wake of the 2 March 2017 election, the statutory limit on the period of time during which a First and deputy First Minister can be appointed (under s16A(3) of the 1998 Act which allows 'fourteen days') was extended to 108 days in April 2017 under the *Northern Ireland (Ministerial Appointments and Regional Rates) Act* 2017.

[9] As defined by section 2(3) of The *Departments (Northern Ireland) Order 1999* (N.I. 1999/283) wherein a 'senior officer' is a member of the 'Northern Ireland senior civil service' or a member of the NICS 'designated by the department as a senior officer for the purpose of this Order' (s2(3)(a)(b)). The definition of 'senior officer' therefore effectively broadened the scope of the discretionary power granted under the NI(EFEF) Act 2018 as the definition allowed non-senior officers to be designated 'senior officers' for the purpose of exercising powers granted by virtue of the later Act.

under the NI(EFEF) 2018 wherein seven principles for NICS senior officers were set out; the guidance instructed civil servants to follow the 'priorities and commitments of the former Executive' but enabled them to deviate from these in 'an exceptional circumstance such as a significant emerging challenge, new strong objective evidence or significant changing circumstance' (HM Government, 2018: 11(b)).[10] A 'significant emerging challenge' could include, for example, the need to address the 'unique and unprecedented' legal task of revoking, repealing, or amending 'retained EU law' under the EUWA 2018 (HL Constitution Committee, 2018: 3). As such, the broad powers to amend legislation by regulation granted under the EUWA 2018 was, uniquely in Northern Ireland, being given to civil servants.

A successor NI(EFEF) Bill was introduced to the House of Commons on 4 July 2019 and (again) fast-tracked through both Houses, receiving royal assent on 24 July 2019. The NI(EFEF) Act 2019 once more extended the period during which an Executive is required to be formed following an election. This was the fourth such extension creating a new deadline of 21 October 2019 alongside a provision for the Secretary of State to extend the period to 13 January 2020, by regulations.[11] Reports of NICS decisions made under the NI(EFEF) Act(s) reveal that powers granted under the EU Withdrawal 2018 Act in respect to EU retained law were used by civil servants to address the legal consequences of UK withdrawal prior to the restoration of the Executive in January 2020 (see 7.2.2). The NI(EFEF) Acts are therefore relevant because for a period of time they changed the default process for the exercise of powers granted under the EUWA 2018 and EU(WA) Act 2020 in respect to Northern Ireland. The potential constitutional impact of the NI(EFEF) Acts in the context of implementing legislation was, however, constrained by the changed political situation in Northern Ireland following the return of devolved government.

On 9 January 2020, the Secretary of State for Northern Ireland, Julian Smith, and Tánaiste, Simon Coveney, published the text of a deal to

---

[10] The HL Constitution Committee report of the NI(EFEF) Act 2018 concluded that 'in any other circumstances provisions such as these, which challenge established constitutional principles would not be acceptable and that no part of this Bill—nor the fast-track procedure by which it is being taken through both Houses—should be taken as a precedent for future legislation' (24).

[11] The fourteen-day period was extended to 29 June 2017 under the *Northern Ireland (Ministerial Appointments and Regional Rates) Act 2017*, then to 26 March 2019 by the NI(EFEF) Act 2018, then to 25 August 2019 by statutory instrument (see *Northern Ireland (Extension of Period for Executive Formation) Regulations 2019* (SI 2019/616)) under the 2018 Act. On 21 October 2019, the Secretary of State extended the period a fifth time to 13 January 2020 under the NI(EFEF) 2019 (see *Northern Ireland (Extension of Period for Executive Formation (No. 2) Regulations 2019* (SI 2019/1364)). Further changes have subsequently been made—including by the *Northern Ireland (Ministers, Elections and Petitions of Concern) Act 2022*—to the requirements placed on the Secretary of State for NI, under the 1998 Act, regarding the calling of elections in the event that a NI Executive cannot be formed; for discussion, see Murray 2022.

restore devolved government in Northern Ireland. Entitled, *New Decade, New Approach* (hereafter 'NDNA'), the deal included measures to reform public services, ensure institutional stability, improve transparency and accountability of governance, address longstanding divisions over minority languages and reform the petition of concern (see Haughey, 2020; Hayward and Phinnemore, 2020). In respect to Brexit, the NDNA included an Executive commitment to establish a Brexit sub-committee to 'consider Brexit-related issues' and carry out an impact assessment as a matter of urgency (2020, part 2: 3.5). Alongside this, the UK Government committed to ensure Executive representative would be invited to be part of the UK delegation in any meetings of the Joint Committee or Specialised Committees at which 'Northern Ireland specific matters' would be discussed and 'which are also being attended by the Irish Government' as part of the EU delegation (New Decade New Approach, 2020, Annex, A: 9). In addition, the UK Government also committed to 'ensuring that Northern Ireland remains an integral part of the UK internal market' and to bring forward legislation to 'guarantee unfettered access for Northern Ireland's businesses to the whole of the UK internal market' before the end of the transition period (*ibid.*: 10). In the event, the realisation of this commitment to legislate for unfettered access prior to the full entry into force of the Protocol proved controversial because, as set out in the next subsection, the legislation as it was introduced included powers to disapply aspects of the Withdrawal Agreement relating to Protocol requirements on NI–GB trade.

Further to the regulation-making powers conferred by the EUWA 2018, the *Taxation (Cross Border Trade) Act 2018* (hereafter 'Taxation (CBT) Act 2018') granted more specific but similar powers to the Chancellor and HM Treasury to, by regulations, make 'provision in relation to any duty of customs in connection with the withdrawal of the United Kingdom from the EU' and to 'amend the law relating to value added tax, and the law relating to any excise duty on goods, in connection with that withdrawal' (*Long Title*). The Taxation (CBT) Act 2018, which received royal assent on 13 September, also gave 'the Treasury' a general power to make provisions for the purposes of import duty 'by regulations' (s30(1)); granted 'HMRC Commissioners' a general power to make regulations 'for excise duty purposes' (s45(1)); and gave the 'appropriate Minister' a time-limited power to make any such provision relating to VAT, customs duties or excise duties as they consider appropriate 'in consequence of, or otherwise in connection with, the withdrawal of the United Kingdom from the EU' and to do so by statutory instrument (s51(1)). As set out in 7.2, these section 51 powers, which expired on 1 April 2022, were used during transition to enact legislative changes required to implement the Protocol in domestic law.

The relationship between these political and legislative developments—the EUWA 2018, The NI(EFEF) Act(s), the Taxation (CBT) Act 2018, and restoration of devolution under the NDNA—with Brexit-implementing legislation and their combined impact on the Northern Ireland constitution are considered in detail in section 7.2, but first an account of political events and legislative developments during the transition period is necessary.

7.1.2 Key Political and Legislative Developments During the Transition Period

Although intended to be 21 months, had the UK left the EU as scheduled on 29 March 2019, the transition period which began on 1 February 2020 was not extended as a result of the multiple '[flex]tensions' granted to the Article 50 timeframe. Originally 24 months, actually 33 months, the elongated withdrawal negotiation timetable left just 11 months for the UK and EU to negotiate a future relationship agreement and to agree arrangements for the full implementation of the Withdrawal Agreement on 31 December 2020. For Northern Ireland, this left less than a year to operationalise an unprecedented new status under the Protocol as a region that straddles the two markets of the UK and the EU—a task that would have to happen in parallel with UK–EU future relationship negotiations, the outcome of which would determine, to a large degree, the nature and impact of Northern Ireland's new status.

The EU(WA) Act 2020 became law one week prior to the beginning of the transition period. Compared to its predecessors, the EU(WA) Act 2020 passed through the Houses of Parliament with relative ease on the back of the landslide Conservative victory in the 2019 general election;[12] it received Royal Assent on 23 January 2020 just over a month after it was introduced. Amending the EUWA Act 2018, the EU(WA) Act 2020 gave direct effect to 'all such rights, powers, liabilities, obligations and restrictions' created by or arising under the Withdrawal Agreement in domestic law (s5(1)(a)). Sections

---

[12] The three failed 'Meaning Votes' on the unratified Withdrawal Agreement of Prime Minister May as well as the failed European Union (Withdrawal Agreement) Bill introduced by the government under Prime Minister Johnson in October 2019 that passed second reading (with 329 votes to 299 votes) but was rejected on the Programme Motion (by 322 votes to 308) which had sought an accelerated passage through the parliamentary stages; the defeat led to a further extension of the Article 50 timeframe (from 31 October to 31 January) and ultimately to the general election on 12 December (via a 'one line bill', the *Early Parliamentary General Election Act 2019*).

8 and 9 of the EU(WA) 2020 granted UK Ministers broad discretionary powers to make such provisions as they 'consider appropriate' for the purposes of implementing the Withdrawal Agreement (s9(1)) and/or to deal with any deficiencies arising from that implementation (s8(1)) by regulations. Under section 4 of the EU(WA) Act 2020, the EUWA 2018 was amended to grant devolved authorities corresponding powers to implement and/or to deal with deficiencies arising from the implementation of the Withdrawal Agreement (EUWA 2018, Sch2 (11)A), provided these would otherwise be within their respective competencies (*ibid.* (11)B(1)). Alongside powers to implement the Withdrawal Agreement, the 2020 Act gave similar but more specific powers to Ministers of the Crown and devolved authorities to implement the Protocol. Section 21 of the EU(WA) Act 2020 amended section 8 of the EUWA 2018 to enable central government Ministers to make such provisions by regulations as they considered appropriate to implement the Protocol; this was followed by section 22, that amended Schedule 2 of the EUWA 2018 to give devolved authorities corresponding powers in relation to implementing the Protocol within their respective competencies (EUWA 2018 Sch2 (11)N). The nature and impact of these powers are considered in detail in the next section.

In preparation for the full entry into force of the Protocol, the UK, and the EU published papers during the transition period regarding arrangements for its implementation;[13] the content revealed differences in the approach of both parties. On 30 April 2020, an EU Technical Note on the *Implementation of the Protocol on Ireland/Northern Ireland* (hereafter 'EU Technical Note') recalled that the Protocol 'cannot be renegotiated' and made clear that 'faithful and effective' implementation of its terms would be a condition of any new UK–EU partnership agreement. The EU's Technical Note, further set out the 'urgent need' for the UK to take forward specific preparations to implement the Protocol across a range of areas corresponding to its provisions (European Commission, 2020f: 2). By contrast, a UK Government Command Paper on *The UK's Approach to the Northern Ireland Protocol* (hereafter 'UK Command Paper'), published on 20 May 2020, underlined its view that the Protocol 'is not codified as a permanent solution' and ought to therefore 'reflect the reality that the alignment provisions [Articles 5 to 10] may not be in place

---

[13] The Withdrawal Agreement provided that some aspects of the Protocol entered into force on 31 January 2020 when the UK formally left the EU and entered an eleven-month transition period; others only entered into force after transition on 1 January 2021. Under Article 185 of the WA, the following applied from the beginning of the transition period: Article 1; the third, fourth, and sixth subparagraphs of Article 5(2); the second sentence of Article 5(3); the last sentence of Article 10(2); Article 12(3); Article 13(8); Article 14; Article 15(1) to (4) and (6); Article 19 and the first paragraph of Annex 6. These provisions which applied from the date of formal UK departure relate, primarily, to decisions to be made by the Joint Committee before the end of the transition period. All other provisions of the Protocol only entered into force on 1 January 2020.

for ever' given their contingency on the outcome of the democratic consent mechanism provided for in Article 18 of the Protocol (Cabinet Office, 2020b: 4). While there was broad agreement between the EU Technical Note and UK Command Paper as regards the need for SPS checks for products of animal origin moving GB–NI and the importance of dedicated mechanisms to uphold Article 2 commitments on rights of individuals and implement Article 3 commitments regarding the CTA, the two texts underlined the different interpretations of the two parties as regards the requirements of Article 5 to 10. The two texts differed in particular on the necessity, or otherwise, for exit summary declarations on goods moving NI–GB, arrangements for the collection of tariffs on goods moving GB–NI, the scope of EU state aid rules applicable under the Protocol, the nature of EU presence in Northern Ireland, and the need or lack thereof for further negotiations at the Joint Committee.[14]

Similar differences in the two sides' view of the Protocol were apparent in their respective approaches to UK–EU future relationship negotiations and related texts. Northern Ireland's new status under the Protocol was more explicitly reflected in EU documents than those of the UK. European Council directives for UK–EU future relationship negotiations stated that any agreement should be 'without prejudice to the Protocol on Ireland/Northern Ireland' (European Council, 2020: 166), premised on its effective implementation and should ensure the 1998 Agreement is protected 'in all its parts' (*ibid.*: 5). Additionally, of the 87 'readiness notices' issued by the European Commission in preparation for the end of the transition period, 51 provided that 'references to the EU' in the document 'have to be understood as including Northern Ireland' by virtue of the Protocol, whereas 'references to the UK have to be understood as referring only to GB' (see, for example, European Commission, 2020c). By contrast, the UK Government White Paper on future relationship negotiations made no specific reference to Northern Ireland or its unique new status under the Protocol. Statements such as 'the UK will no longer be a part of the EU single market or the EU customs union' or 'we will not agree to any obligations for our laws to be aligned with the EU's, or for the EU's institutions, including the Court of Justice, to have any jurisdiction in the UK' (HM Government, 2020: 2; 5) failed to mention that the UK Government had already committed to continue to apply the EU

---

[14] On exit declarations for NI–GB trade, for example, according to the EU Technical Note '*all* goods leaving Northern Ireland' to enter Great Britain or a third country would be 'subject to prohibitions and restrictions applicable to exports' under relevant EU law; goods moving NI–GB would therefore require export summary declarations (European Commission, 2020f: (b)(iv)) but, according to the UK Command Paper, 'it makes no sense for Northern Ireland businesses to be required to complete an export or exit summary declaration as they send goods directly to the rest of the UK' (Cabinet Office, 2020b: 20).

customs code and aspects of the legal *acquis* to goods entering Northern Ireland, or that Northern Ireland remained in dynamic alignment with EU laws within the scope of the Protocol over which the CJEU retained jurisdiction (see 6.2.1). While the text of the EU negotiating mandate referred directly to the Protocol, the UK Government White Paper reflected a view of the Protocol as 'not … a permanent solution' (Cabinet Office, 2020b: 4) and one that was not therefore integrated into the planning of UK–EU relations in the long term. The content of UK preparatory documents therefore *appeared* to indicate a shift away from the language of the Protocol and commitments therein. Any slight or implicit move away from the Protocol text apparent in the UK Command Paper and White Paper on UK–EU future relations was, however, explicitly realised with the introduction of domestic legislation concerning the internal market of the UK.

On 9 September 2020, the UK Government introduced the *United Kingdom Internal Market* Bill (hereafter 'UKIM') to the House of Commons. The stated purpose of the UKIM Bill was to make provisions in connection with 'the internal market for goods and services in the United Kingdom' and 'the provisions of the Northern Ireland Protocol relating to trade and state aid' (2020: *Long Title*). If passed unamended, Part 5 of the UKIM Bill concerning the 'Northern Ireland Protocol' would require authorities to have 'special regard' for Northern Ireland's integral place in the UK internal market, customs territory, and the need to facilitate the free flow of goods between Great Britain and Northern Ireland when implementing the Protocol (*ibid.*, Part 5, c40(1)).[15] In making provisions for the Protocol, under the UKIM Bill, authorities would be prevented from introducing any new check, control, or administrative process for goods moving NI–GB (*ibid.* c41(1)(a)(b)); and UK Ministers would have powers to disapply any exit procedures for goods moving NI–GB, including those applicable by virtue of the Protocol (*ibid.* c42(1)(2)). Addressing State Aid requirements under Article 10 of the Protocol, the UKIM Bill sought to give discretionary power to the Secretary of State for Northern Ireland who, by regulation, would be able to make provisions to disapply, modify, or [re]interpret Article 10 provisions (*ibid.* c43(1)(2)(3)); relatedly, under the UKIM Bill, the NI Secretary would be the only public authority authorised to comply with any provision of EU law applicable in the UK under Article 10 of the Protocol (*ibid.* c44(1)). Alone, clauses 41 to 43 directly contradicted requirements of the Protocol; the most controversial provision of the UKIM Bill, however, was clause 45 which would have

---

[15] All clause numbers cited reflect the UKIM Bill as introduced; the UKIM Act as passed differs in numbering and substance.

provided that clauses 42 and 43—regarding the power to disapply exit procedures for goods moving NI–GB and to modify or disapply Article 10 of the Protocol—would have effect 'notwithstanding any relevant international or domestic law with which they may be incompatible or inconsistent' (*ibid.* c45(1)). These provisions in respect to the Protocol would therefore enable UK Ministers to break the Article 4 provision of the Withdrawal Agreement whereby any applicable EU laws ought to produce 'the same legal effects' in the UK as in EU Member States (WA, Article 4(1)). The UK Government's legal position acknowledged that the UKIM Bill 'partially disapplies Article 4' but claimed this to be necessary to 'protect peace in Northern Ireland and the Belfast/Good Friday Agreement' and legally possible given that the 'legislation which implements the Withdrawal Agreement including the Northern Ireland Protocol is expressly subject to the principle of parliamentary sovereignty' (HM Government, 2020b; see also Finnis and Larkin, 2020). Elaborating in the House of Commons, NI Secretary Brandon Lewis stated that the UKIM Bill would 'break international law' but only 'in a very specific and limited way' (in Hansard 2020a: 509).

In response to the UK proposal in the UKIM Bill to breach the Withdrawal Agreement, the EU initiated an extraordinary Joint Committee meeting.[16] Speaking after the extraordinary meeting, European Commission Vice President Maroš Šefčovič stated that the 'EU does not accept the argument that the aim of the draft Bill is to protect the Good Friday (Belfast) Agreement' and set out the EU27's perspective that, if adopted, the UKIM Bill 'would constitute an extremely serious violation of the Withdrawal Agreement and international law' (European Commission, 2020e). The European Parliament 'UK Coordination Group' and the leaders of political groups in the European Parliament stated their response that, should the UK breach or threaten to breach the Withdrawal Agreement through the UKIM Bill or in any other way, the European Parliament would not ratify any UK–EU agreement on future relations (2020).[17] In view of the UKIM Bill 'law-breaking' clauses, the European Commission sent a letter of formal notice to the UK on 1 October

---

[16] Unusually, representatives of all 27 EU Member States sat in to observe the emergency Joint Committee meeting in London after the UK Government stated its willingness to break international law via the UKIM Bill (O'Leary, Staunton, and Leahy, 2020). This indicates the seriousness with which the EU27 viewed the UK Government proposal to break the terms of the WA and arguably signals a consequential breakdown of trust.

[17] The European Parliament UK Coordination Group (UKCG) served as its primary point of contact with the 'UK Task Force' the group of European Commission officials, led initially by Michel Barnier, who negotiated directly with the UK Government. The purpose of the UKCG is to monitor UK–EU future relationship negotiations and the implementation of the Withdrawal Agreement as well as to liaise with European Parliamentary political groups and committees regarding relevant developments. The UKCG is a successor group to the European Parliament Brexit Steering Group which operated throughout UK–EU withdrawal negotiations, and which ended in January 2020.

regarding the UK's intentions to breach the terms of the Withdrawal Agreement (European Commission 2020). Notwithstanding diplomatic pressure and calls from prominent figures in his party to remove 'law-breaking clauses' in the UKIM Bill, Prime Minister Johnson initially reiterated his determination to ensure they remained in the final version of the text. Further, the UK Government stated its intention to include provisions that would have enabled UK Ministers to disapply aspects of the Protocol relating to checks on GB–NI trade in an upcoming *Finance Bill* and then a *Taxation (Post-Transition Period) Bill* ('Taxation Bill'); in the end, this threat did not materialise.

On 8 December, the Joint Committee issued a joint statement announcing that 'agreement in principle on all issues' regarding the implementation of the Protocol had been reached (European Commission, 2020). Following the announcement, four decisions for the Joint Committee and five sets of Unilateral Declarations were published which set out the details of the 'in principle' agreements. The four decisions addressed: the maximum level of subsidies for agricultural, fisheries, and aquaculture products in Northern Ireland; a determination regarding those goods 'not at risk' of onward movement to the EU; errors and omissions in Annex 2 of the Protocol; and the practical working arrangements for EU officials to monitor the implementation of the Protocol in Northern Ireland.

The five unilateral declarations contained three UK declarations, of which the EU 'took note' and two EU declarations, of which the UK 'took note'. The unilateral declarations on the part of the UK concerned: their approach to requirements for export declarations on goods moving NI–GB; a six-month delay on requirements for the movement of certain meat products GB–NI; and a three-month delay on requirements for certain food suppliers of supermarkets to move goods GB–NI without a full Export Health Certificate ultimately required under the Protocol. The unilateral declarations on the part of the EU concerned: a twelve-month adaptation period for suppliers of medicinal products to Northern Ireland so as to allow stakeholders to establish new routes 'where necessary'; and a declaration regarding the approach to the application of EU State Aid laws under Article 10 of the Protocol. In view of these 'mutually agreed solutions', the UK committed to withdraw the 'law-breaking' clauses in the UKIM Bill and not to introduce any similar provisions in the Taxation Bill (*ibid.*). The five Joint Committee decisions were adopted on 17 December 2020. On the same day, the UKIM Bill passed the final stage of its parliamentary passage, without any provisions that would enable UK Ministers to override the Withdrawal Agreement or Protocol. Part 1 of the UKIM Act 2020 established market access principles for the sale of goods in the UK internal market—a mutual recognition principle (s2–4) and a non-discrimination principle (s5–9)—but provided that these would not apply to the sale of goods in Northern Ireland, which would instead be subject to provisions of 'the Northern Ireland Protocol and sections 7A, 7C, and 8C of the European Union (Withdrawal) Act 2018' which empowered Ministers to implement the Protocol (s11(1)). Furthermore, the principles of mutual recognition and non-discrimination would only apply to 'qualifying Northern Ireland goods' (s11(2); s11(5)) as defined by regulations made under section 8C of the EU Withdrawal Act 2018 (s8C(6); see 7.2.3) and in accordance with the Joint Committee decision on the criteria for those goods that qualified as 'not at risk'. Provisions concerning 'unfettered access' for NI–GB goods that had previously (in clause 42 of the UKIM Bill) allowed disapplication of aspects of the Protocol were now restricted by 'any international obligation or arrangement to which the United Kingdom is a party' (s47(2)(b)) and, in particular, 'the exercise of a function in relation to a check, control or administrative process … necessary to secure compliance with … the Northern Ireland Protocol' (s47(3)). In addition, provisions in the UKIM Act 2020 in respect to implementing Article 10 of the Protocol on state aid now required this to be read in light of decisions or recommendations of the Joint Committee (s48(2)) and contained no 'law-breaking' enabling power (as in c43 of the UKIM Bill).

With one week to go until the end of the transition period, the UK and EU announced that negotiations had concluded, and a UK–EU Trade and Cooperation Agreement (hereafter 'TCA') had been reached. Key features of the TCA included: a no tariff, no quota agreement for trade in goods between the UK and EU, subject to rules of origin conditions; the creation of a UK–EU Partnership Council to oversee the governance of the TCA, supported by a range of specific sectoral committees; binding dispute settlement mechanisms involving an independent arbitration tribunal, leaving no direct role for the CJEU and allowing for either party to take retributory action in the event of non-compliance; both parties committing to an effective system for subsidy control with independent oversight and provision for remedial measures in the event of unresolved disputes; an arrangement for 25% of EU fisheries quota in UK waters to be transferred over a five-year period and annual discussions thereafter; a security partnership providing for data sharing, police and judicial cooperation, but with reduced access for UK to EU databases, and a new surrender agreement to replace the European Arrest Warrant; provision for security cooperation, to be suspended if either side diverges from the ECHR; continuation of UK participation in some EU research programmes; provision for the TCA to be reviewed every five years with possibility for either side to terminate it on any occasion with twelve months' notice unless on rule of law or human rights grounds (for more detail, see Fella et al., 2020). On 29 December, the UK Government published the *European Union (Future Relationship) Bill 2020*, the purpose of which was to implement the TCA in domestic law and address 'connected purposes' (c.29: *Long Title*); the Bill received royal assent on 31 December 2020, becoming the *EU (Future Relationship) Act 2020*.

7.2 UK Implementing Legislation and the Northern Ireland Constitution

In seeking to 'protect the 1998 Agreement in all its parts' (Protocol Article 1(3)), the provisions of the Withdrawal Agreement and Protocol reflect a particular interpretation of what protection involves and requires in the specific context of UK withdrawal from the EU. As set out in the previous chapter, notwithstanding the stated purpose of the Protocol, its provisions privilege some aspects of the 1998 Agreement (namely cross-border trade in goods, North–South cooperation, and citizens' rights), reformulate others (namely the principle of consent), and connect all those specifically protected aspects of the 1998 Agreement to their contemporaneous manifestation in EU law. Building on the analysis of Chapter 6, this section sets out the impact of the implementation of the Protocol's interpretation of the 'arrangements necessary' to protect the 1998 Agreement 'in all its parts' (*ibid.*) in domestic legislation.

By setting out the impact of UK implementing legislation on the components of the Northern Ireland constitution, the following analysis highlights the discrepancies between the Withdrawal Agreement and Protocol, their enforcement in UK law, and the pre-existing legal basis of the Northern Ireland constitution as set out in the 1998 Agreement and 1998 Act. It is argued that discrepancies between the Withdrawal Agreement, implementing legislation, and pre-existing Northern Ireland constitution are a consequence of the untested nature of the Protocol's provisions, diverging UK and EU interpretations about what is required, and a lack of awareness of or accommodation for the particularities of the Northern Ireland constitution in the domestic legislative process. As a consequence, the analysis suggests that UK implementing legislation effectively *reinterpreted* parts of the mutually agreed Protocol interpretation of what 'protecting the 1998 Agreement in all its parts' (*ibid.*) means and requires in the context of Brexit.

7.2.1 Principle of Consent

7.2.1.1 New and Existing Legal Definitions of the '1998 Agreement'

Under the EUWA 2018 and EU(WA) Act 2020, the provisions of the Withdrawal Agreement and Protocol have direct effect in UK law. Included in the 'general implementation' provision (2018 Act, s7A as inserted by the 2020 Act s5) is an affirmation of the principle of consent set out in Article 1 of the Protocol which states that it is 'without prejudice to the provisions of *the 1998 Agreement* in respect of the constitutional status of Northern Ireland and the principle of consent' ((1), *added*). In this, UK implementing legislation appears to unequivocally reaffirm the principle of constitutional consent enshrined in the 1998 Agreement and provided for in the 1998 Act, but this is not quite so.

The definition of 'the 1998 Agreement' used in Protocol differs from its definition in UK law in general and in the EUWA 2018 in particular. To elucidate the matter, some additional context about UK law provisions for the 1998 Agreement is necessary. There are two versions of the same 1998 Agreement on the UK statute book; in substance, the texts are identical, but they differ in structure, status, and (arguably) in their relationship to the consent principle. The first version was laid before Parliament on 20 April 1998 in Command Paper 3883; in substance, it is a copy of the Multi-Party Agreement signed by political parties in Northern Ireland with a draft British-Irish Agreement attached as an Annex. This Cm3883 version had not received the consent of the 'people of the island of Ireland' (1998 Agreement CI 1(iii)), nor had 'such legislation as may be necessary to give effect to all aspects of [the] agreement' (*ibid.* VIR: 3) been passed. Following concurrent referenda and the passing of domestic and bilateral implementation legislation, the text signed on Good Friday in 1998 was again laid before Parliament in March 1999, this time as Command Paper 4292—in substance, a now ratified bilateral British-Irish Agreement treaty with a copy of the political Multi-Party Agreement between Northern Ireland parties attached as an Annex; this '1998 Agreement' entered into force in December 1999. The difference between these two versions of the 1998 Agreement is partly a consequence of the ordinary ratification procedure for international treaties in the UK's dualist system; however, given the unique (in UK constitutional terms) use of consultative referenda and the need for supplementary bilateral treaties to be agreed prior to 1998 Agreement's entry into force, the Cm4292 version *arguably* has greater legal standing and a different relationship to the consent principle. The more pertinent point for this analysis, however, is how the Cm3883 and Cm4292 versions relate to definitions used in the Protocol and UK implementing legislation respectively.

In UK law, the agreement signed on 10 April 1998 is referred to as the 'Belfast Agreement' and defined as the 'agreement reached at multi-party talks on Northern Ireland set out in Command Paper 3883' (1998 Act, s98); section 10 of the EU Withdrawal Act 2018 referenced this specifically when ensuring regulation-making powers could not 'diminish any form of North–South cooperation provided for by the Belfast Agreement (as defined by section 98 of the Northern Ireland Act 1998)' (s10(2)(a)). It is therefore the earlier unconfirmed Cm3883 version that has prominence in domestic law. By contrast, the definition used in the Withdrawal Agreement reflects the later confirmed Cm4292 version. The Protocol Preamble describes:

> AFFIRMING that the Good Friday or Belfast Agreement of 10 April 1998 between the Government of the United Kingdom, the Government of Ireland and the other participants in the multi-party negotiations (the '1998 Agreement'), which is annexed to the British-Irish Agreement of the same date (the 'British-Irish Agreement'), including its subsequent implementing agreements and arrangements, should be protected in all its parts.
>
> **(Protocol *Preamble*: Recital 4)**

The structure of this definition—multi-party agreement annexed to bilateral treaty—reflects the later confirmed and ratified version that has legal force in international law and is represented in Cm4292 in domestic law. From a UK perspective, however, there is arguably some confusion in the description of the '1998 Agreement' as being between the two governments as well as 'other participants'. In the preamble of the Multi-Party Agreement, 'the participants' explicitly 'endorse the commitment made by the British and Irish Governments' set out in the British-Irish Agreement (CI (1)). The two governments were therefore not 'participants' in the Multi-Party Agreement, and neither were the political parties 'participants' in the British-Irish Agreement. Such a semblance of confusion could be explained with reference to an Irish law version of the text. In parallel with the laying of Cm4292 before the Houses of Parliament, the Agreement entered into force in Ireland on 2 December 1999 as Treaty Series 2000 N°18, which differed from the Cm4292 UK version in only one respect: whereas the UK version had the British-Irish Agreement with the Multi-Party Agreement as an annex, the Irish version had the British-Irish Agreement with the Multi-Party Agreement *and* British-Irish Agreement (repeated) as an annex (Government of Ireland, 2000). This being so, the definition of 'the 1998 Agreement' used in the Protocol only makes sense from the perspective of Irish law.

Given that the UK Government ratified the 1998 Agreement, following consultative referenda, via Cm4292, and implemented its terms via the 1998 Act alongside supplementary bilateral treaties, the definitional discrepancy between the Protocol and domestic legislation in respect to the 1998 Agreement is mostly academic. An area of dispute could conceivably arise in relation to 'subsequent implementation agreements and arrangements' (*Preamble*: Recital 4). The scope of this reference to 'subsequent' agreements is not wholly clear: it could be interpreted broadly to include all subsequent political agreements between Northern Ireland political parties, brokered by the British and Irish Governments as well as related implementing bilateral treaties; or it could be interpreted more narrowly to include only implementing bilateral treaties or a certain number of these.[18] Regardless of the intended scope of the definition in the Protocol in respect to later agreements, it is clear that, in UK law, the definition of the 'Belfast Agreement' does not include any subsequent or successor agreements. If then there was any disagreement between the UK and EU concerning the relationship between the Protocol and one of, for example, the implementation bodies established by the four bilateral treaties signed in 1999, the diverging definitions could *perhaps* be relevant, but this is not likely. A more significant implication arising from the definition of the 1998 Agreement used in the Protocol is what it suggests about the level of familiarity among UK negotiators with the constitutional arrangements of Northern Ireland in general and their realisation in the 1998 Act in particular. The fact that the definition of the 1998 Agreement in the Protocol only makes sense with reference to Irish law, and that UK negotiators do not appear to have realised any discrepancy with the 'Belfast Agreement' definition in UK law, suggests a lack of detailed knowledge about Northern Ireland among those negotiating on its behalf.[19]

---

[18] This definition appears to have originated from a European Commission 'Guiding Principles' paper transmitted to the EU27 for the Dialogue on Ireland/Northern Ireland in September 2017 (see European Commission, 2017b: 2).

[19] To reiterate this point of analysis, it is worth noting that, on several occasions throughout UK–EU withdrawal negotiations, several UK Ministers demonstrated a lack of in-depth understanding about the political and constitutional context in Northern Ireland. During questioning from the Northern Ireland Affairs Committee in 2019, previous DExEU Secretary Dominic Raab admitted to never having read the 1998 Agreement (see Kelly, 2019); and, in 2018, the then NI Secretary Karen Bradley said that she 'didn't understand things like when elections are fought for example in Northern Ireland—people who are nationalists don't vote for unionist parties and vice-versa' before taking up the office (see Embury-Denis, 2018).

7.2.1.2 Self-Determination of National Identity and Citizenship Rights

Under Article 2(1) of the Protocol, the UK committed to ensure 'no diminution' of those provisions set out in the 'Rights, Safeguards and Equality of Opportunity' section of the 1998 Agreement and to implement this 'through dedicated mechanisms'. These commitments were realised in section 23 and Schedule 3 of the EU(WA) Act 2020 which set out the 'dedicated mechanisms' in the form of amendments to the 1998 Act to introduce a requirement for devolved legislation to be compatible with Article 2(1) of the Protocol and to confer new powers on the NIHRC and ECNI to monitor, report, and advise on the implementation of the Article 2(1) commitment, and to work collaboratively to that end (see 1998 Act s6(2)(ca); s78A to s78E). As set out in 6.2.1.2, the Article 2 requirement for 'no diminution' of rights in the context of UK withdrawal from the EU effectively ensures people born in Northern Ireland continue to be able to identify 'as Irish or British, or both' after Brexit without a rights-based trade-off (1998 Agreement, CI: 1(vi)). This, therefore, upholds the principle of self-determination of national identity and citizenship that is integral to a broad definition of the multifaceted principle of consent which underpins the 1998 Agreement.

By directly implementing the Article 2 commitment in domestic law, the EU(WA) Act 2020 amends the 1998 Act in such a way as could be said to expand the scope of rights-based safeguards available in Northern Ireland. Under the 1998 Act, the primary function of the NIHRC is to 'keep under review the adequacy and effectiveness in Northern Ireland of law and practice relating to the protection of human rights' (s69(1)); any references to the 'Belfast Agreement' in the relevant sections of the 1998 Act are to specific paragraphs regarding the provision of advice to the Secretary of State and an endeavour to establish an all-Island Joint Committee on Human Rights (s69(7)(10)). Prior to the EU(WA) Act 2020, there was therefore no requirement or provision, under the 1998 Act, for the NIHRC to monitor, report, advise, or legally defend all of those rights laid out in the Rights, Safeguards and Equality of Opportunity section of the 1998 Agreement— its functions were rather defined with reference to domestic human rights law and practice. Similarly, the mandate and scope of the ECNI principal functions derived primarily from section 75 of the 1998 Act that requires public authorities in Northern Ireland to carry out their functions with 'due regard to the need to promote equality of opportunity' (s75(1)). So, although arising from the 1998 Agreement, the mandates specifically given to the NIHRC and the ECNI under the 1998 Act prior to the EU(WA) Act 2020 were narrower in scope than those laid out in the 'Rights, Safeguards and

Equality of Opportunity' section of the 1998 Agreement, which the UK Government committed to uphold in Article 2 of the Protocol. In this matter, it should be noted that there is little substantive difference between those rights referred to in the relevant section of the 1998 Agreement and those already enshrined in UK law primarily through a requirement under the *Human Rights Act 1998* for domestic legislation to be compatible with the ECHR, also reflected in the 1998 Act (s6(2)(c)). This upholds a UK commitment in the 1998 Agreement to 'completely incorporate' the ECHR in Northern Ireland law (RSE: 4).[20] There is, however, an additional guarantee in the 'Rights, Safeguards and Equality of Opportunity' section of the 1998 Agreement for 'rights supplementary' to the ECHR in respect to 'principles of mutual respect for the identity of both communities and parity of esteem' (*ibid.*) to be upheld. In light of the Article 2 'no diminution' requirement, reflected in the amendments to the 1998 Act, the 'parity of esteem' requirement could prove problematic in post-Brexit Northern Ireland as the rights available to Irish citizens, as EU citizens, diverge from those of British citizens, as non-EU citizens. Conceivably the NIHRC or ECNI could take a case under new powers granted by the EU(WA) Act 2020 (s23; Sch3) on behalf of a Northern Ireland-born British citizen on the grounds of a violation of Article 2(1) of the Protocol requirement for 'right not to be discriminated against and to equality of opportunity' regardless of national or ethnic identity (1998 Agreement, RSE: 4). By preventing any diminution of those rights set out in the 1998 Agreement, the EU(WA) Act 2020 could therefore *in theory* protect non-Irish Northern Ireland citizens from a loss of rights that normally derive from EU citizenship; the extent to which this has effect in practice will depend on action taken by the NIHRC and ECNI.

To summarise, for the purpose of this analysis, the importance of the 'dedicated mechanism' to implement Article 2 of the Protocol has two aspects:

---

[20] It is worth noting that the UK Government proposed to disapply the HRA 1998 requirement for public authorities to only act in ways compatible with the ECHR (s6(1)); while this clause 47 proposal in the UKIM Bill was removed following agreement reached at the Joint Committee, the apparent willingness of the UK Government to move away from a domestic requirement for ECHR compliance is concerning from the perspective of the 1998 Agreement. On the issue of UK ongoing commitment to the ECHR, it is also important to note that Part 3 of the TCA on law enforcement and criminal justice cooperation is 'based on' the 'long-standing respect for democracy, the rule of law and the protection of fundamental rights and freedoms of individuals, including as set out in the Universal Declaration of Human Rights and in the European Convention on Human Rights, and on the importance of giving effect to the rights and freedoms in that Convention domestically' of both the UK and the EU (Article LAW.GEN.3(1)). Furthermore, cooperation provided for under Part 3 of the TCA can be terminated at any point if on account of 'the United Kingdom or a Member State having denounced the European Convention on Human Rights' (Article LAW.OTHER.136). Together draft clause 47 in the UKIM Bill and the condition for ECHR compliance in Part 3 of the TCA demonstrate that the UK Government are *currently* committed to the ECHR, but that commitment is not sacrosanct.

it strengthens the powers of the NIHRC and ECNI vis-à-vis the Northern Ireland Executive and Assembly, and it creates some ambiguities as to the future practice of the constitutional principle of self-determination of national identity and citizenship without a rights-based trade-off.

7.2.1.3 New and Existing Definitions of 'Northern Ireland'

As set out in 6.2.1.3, the territorial application of aspects of the Protocol relies on a novel definition of Northern Ireland. Under Article 5 and Article 13 of the Protocol, the customs code of the EU applies 'to and in the United Kingdom in respect of Northern Ireland (*not including the territorial waters of the United Kingdom*)' (Article 5(3), *added*). This conflicts with the UK law definition of Northern Ireland which is said to 'includ[e] so much of *the internal waters and territorial sea* of the United Kingdom as are adjacent to Northern Ireland' (1998 Act, s98, *added*). So, in domestic law, the territory of Northern Ireland includes adjacent waters but under the Protocol the territory of Northern Ireland excludes adjacent waters.

Leaving aside that the *de jure* separation of the land territory of Northern Ireland from its territorial waters appears to violate the concept of a 'territorial sea' in international law,[21] for the purpose of this discussion the importance of the territorial definition lies in how it relates to powers granted under UK implementing legislation. Under the EUWA 2018, 'all such rights, powers, liabilities, obligations and restrictions from time to time created or arising by or under the withdrawal agreement' have direct 'legal effect' without further enactment (2018 Act, s7A(1)(a) as inserted by the 2020 Act s5). Provisions of the Withdrawal Agreement thereby have direct effect under the status of 'separation agreement law' (see 2018 Act s7C). What this means is that, in effect, the territorial definition in the Protocol now exists as a new category in the territorial scope of laws applicable to 'Northern Ireland', one that excludes its territorial waters.

The new legal definition for the territory of Northern Ireland creates some discrepancies in implementing legislation. For example, *The Definition of Qualifying Northern Ireland Goods (EU Exit) Regulations* made under powers granted by section 8C of the EUWA 2018 states that 'in these Regulations, "Northern Ireland" does not include any part of the territorial waters of the United Kingdom' (2020/1454 s2). According to SI 2020/1454, goods are considered 'qualifying Northern Ireland goods' only if they are either 'present in Northern Ireland [excluding territorial waters]' and not subject to customs

---

[21] Article 1 of the Geneva Convention on the Territorial Sea and the Contiguous Zone states that the 'sovereignty of a State extends, beyond its land territory and its internal waters, to a belt of sea adjacent to its coast, described as the territorial sea' (1958: Article 1(1)).

supervision, restriction, or control 'which does not arise from the goods being taken out of the territory of Northern Ireland [excluding territorial waters] or the European Union' (SI 2020/1454 s3) or if they are 'NI processed products' as defined by criteria set out in the instrument. While SI 2020/1454 therefore recognises the new territorial scope of laws deriving from the direct effect of the Protocol, it also conflicts with provisions in regulations made elsewhere in connection with UK withdrawal from the EU. *The Travellers' Allowances and Miscellaneous Provisions (Northern Ireland) (EU Exit) Regulations 2020* was made by HM Treasury under regulation-making powers conferred by section 51 of the Taxation (CBT) Act 2018; this instrument allows for the continued application of EU laws on the importation of goods intended for sale that previously applied in 'the territorial sea of the United Kingdom' (under *The Excise Goods (Sales on Board Ships and Aircraft) Regulations 1999* (SI 1999/1565)) to now only apply in 'the territorial sea adjacent to Northern Ireland' (SI 2020/1619 s10–18) notwithstanding that the Protocol and EUWA 2018 (as amended) does *not* provide for this.

Other examples of legislative discrepancies created by the new legal definition of 'Northern Ireland' could be cited; however, for the purpose of this discussion, arguably the most important implication of this novel definition is its relationship to consent. Introducing a new definitive category for the application of laws to 'Northern Ireland' is significant for the principle of consent for two reasons; firstly, as territorial scope is conventionally understood to be a definitive feature of any polity, any new legal definition of the term 'Northern Ireland' is of *prima facie* constitutional significance; and secondly, in the specific historical context of a polity characterised by territorial conflict, any jurisdictional reformulation of Northern Ireland is of even more political and symbolic import than would otherwise be expected.

7.2.1.4 Legislating for a Democratic Consent Mechanism

Under Article 18 of the Protocol, the UK committed to 'seek democratic consent in Northern Ireland' to the continued application of Articles 5 to 10 of the Protocol—primarily concerned with cross-border trade in goods—in 2024 and every four or eight years thereafter depending on the outcome of the vote (Article 18(1)). According to the Protocol, the operation of this 'democratic consent mechanism' is to be carried out 'strictly in accordance' with terms laid out in a Unilateral Declaration by UK Government published alongside the Protocol (Article 18(2)). In the Unilateral Declaration, the UK undertook to 'reflect as necessary in … legislation … the commitments in respect of the democratic consent mechanism' (HM Government, 2020: para. 1). Exercising powers conferred by section 8C and pursuant to paragraph 21 of Schedule 7 of the EUWA 2018 (as inserted by 2020 Act s21), the NI Secretary laid *The Protocol on Ireland/Northern Ireland (Democratic Consent Process) (EU Exit) Regulations* (2020/1500) which gave effect to the Unilateral Declaration commitment by adding new Schedule 6A 'EU Withdrawal: Democratic Consent Process' to the 1998 Act. The *Democratic Consent Process* statutory instrument (2020/1500) was approved by affirmative procedure and thus made on 9 December 2020.

The provisions of new Schedule 6A implementing the democratic consent process departs from normal requirements for cross-community consent under the 1998 Act in two ways: one substantive, the other procedural. In accordance with Article 18 and the Unilateral Declaration requirement for (only) 50%+1 majority consent for the continuation of Articles 5 to 10 for a subsequent four years, new Schedule 6A disapplies the petition of concern procedure in relation to the democratic consent mechanism (1998 Act Sch6A (18)(5)). Under the petition of concern, if 30 MLAs lodge a petition expressing concern on any matter to be voted on by the Assembly, that matter shall require cross-community support to pass (*ibid.* s42(1)); this procedure was introduced as a 'safeguard' to ensure inclusive decision-making in Northern Ireland under Strand One of the 1998 Agreement. Although initially intended to be used only for 'key decisions' on cross-community issues (1998 Agreement S1: 5(d)), petitions of concern have, since 1998, been used with increasing liberality by Northern Ireland political parties to veto politically contentious legislation.[22] Additionally, new Schedule 6A departs from normal requirements for cross-community consent in more minor ways related to Assembly standing orders. Where the procedures for implementing the democratic consent process 'are inconsistent' with the standing orders of the Assembly, the provisions of new Schedule 6A take precedence (1998 Act Sch6A s1(6)); in effect, this circumvents a section 41 provision whereby standing orders 'shall not [normally] be made, amended or repealed without cross-community support' (*ibid.* s41(2)). The disapplication of the petition of concern procedure to the democratic consent mechanism and its precedence over standing orders reflects a compromise between UK and EU positions on the matter during the renegotiation of the 'Backstop' Protocol that resulted in the revised Protocol including the democratic consent mechanism (see 6.1.3). An initial UK Government proposal would have required the

---

[22] Concern over the increasing frequency of use of Petitions of Concern in the Assembly were addressed in the NDNA in which political parties committed to certain reforms including (see 2020, 9–13; Annex B); as part of the NDNA, the UK Government committed to 'keep under review' (*ibid.* Annex A: 2) the use of the Petition of Concern procedure and publish reports every six months; the first was issued in July 2020 and recorded no such petitions lodged (NIO, 2020: 4).

Northern Ireland Executive *and* Assembly to consent to the Protocol before it entered into force, thereby necessitating Unionist and Nationalist consent (The Prime Minister, 2019b; HM Government, 2019b),[23] whereas the EU position, reflecting that of the Irish Government, rejected proposals requiring the exercise of consent which would give any political party a potential veto on the outcome (European Parliament, 2019; Smyth, 2019; O'Halloran and Bray, 2019).

While cross-community consent is not *required* for the continued application of Articles 5 to 10 of the Protocol, the procedure for the exercise of democratic consent does recognise the significance of cross-community consent in the Northern Ireland context by incentivising its use in future votes. This is so because Article 18(5) requires, under new Schedule 6A, if a consent resolution is passed with cross-community consent—either parallel or weighted—then the 'continuation period' of Articles 5 to 10 will be eight years rather than four years (1998 Act, Sch6A s3(2)). In addition, if a consent resolution passes only by a simple majority, the NI Secretary must commission an independent review into the functioning of the Protocol which will conclude within two years and make recommendations to the government regarding any new measures which could command cross-community support (*ibid.* Sch6A s21; Unilateral Declaration 2019: 7–9). In this way, the democratic consent mechanism recognises the principle of the petition of concern 'safeguard' set out in the 1998 Agreement and provided for in the 1998 Act but does not mandate that it be fulfilled. In effect, provision for the 'democratic consent mechanism' in Article 18 of the Protocol and its implementation in UK law therefore offers a new formulation of the cross-community consent principle; deciding whether or not Articles 5 to 10 of the Protocol ought to continue to apply in Northern Ireland is self-evidently a 'key decision' which, as the Protocol and existing legislation indicate, would benefit from cross-community support yet progress is not contingent on achieving it—this is a new formulation.

---

[23] The DUP supported the terms of Johnson's initial proposals, describing these as 'entirely consistent' with the spirit and principles of the 1998 Agreement; by contrast, Sinn Féin voices strong opposition to any 'situation whatsoever when the DUP are going to be afforded a veto, a lock, a blocking mechanism of any form in which to thwart any progress that could potentially be made on Brexit between both the EU and the British government' (in *Belfast Telegraph*, 2019a).

The DUP strongly opposed the terms of the agreed democratic consent mechanism not requiring cross-community consent, with Arlene Foster stating the need for 'a sensible deal which unionists and nationalists can support' (@DUPleader, 2019, October 16; Belfast Telegraph, 2019b). There are notable echoes between the democratic consent mechanism and the UK Government's efforts under May to secure DUP support for the unratified Withdrawal Agreement by proposing a 'strong role' for NI Assembly in the event of the backstop coming into force (HM Government, 2019a); these were rejected as 'cosmetic and meaningless' by the DUP (O'Carroll, 2019).

7.2.1.5 Legislative Consent

The Northern Ireland Assembly did not give legislative consent to the EUWA 2018 or the EU(WA)Act 2020. In the first case, the Assembly was not sitting during the parliamentary passage of the 2018 Act; in the second, the 2020 Act was expressly rejected by the recently returned Northern Ireland legislature. Legislative consent to the EU(WA) Act 2020 was also withheld by the Scottish Parliament and Welsh Assembly. The UK Government's accelerated passing of the 2020 Act regardless of devolved authorities' rejection underlines the constitutional fault line, exposed by Brexit, between the executive and devolved government in the UK (see 1.1). However, in the particular Northern Ireland context, the cross-party nature of the rejection of the EU(WA) Act 2020 adds to the constitutional significance.

On 20 January 2020, the Northern Ireland Assembly rejected a legislative consent motion (LCM) for the provisions of what became the EU(WA) 2020.[24] The consent motion followed a request from the Secretary of State for Exiting the EU in accordance with the Sewel Convention because of the effect the 2020 Act on devolved competence. The LCM presented jointly by the First and deputy First Minister was unamendable as the EU Withdrawal Agreement Bill was due to have its third reading in the House of Lords on 21 January—this was thus the first and last time the Assembly would have opportunity to express a view. There was an unusual level of cross-party agreement during the LCM debate as representatives from all sides of the political spectrum recorded their concerns about the Withdrawal Agreement, Protocol, and the EU Withdrawal Agreement Bill, albeit for different reasons (NI Assembly, 2020a).[25] The decision to reject the DExEU Secretary's request for consent was made by the Assembly without division. Notably, the vote in the Assembly had been preceded by cross-party efforts by sitting Northern Ireland MPs in the House of Commons to amend the Bill so as to mitigate some of the potential effects implementing the Protocol would have on Northern Ireland's place in the UK internal market, none of which were successful.[26]

---

[24] The text of the LCM brought by the First and deputy First Minister read: 'That the Assembly notes the request from the Secretary of State for Exiting the European Union for the consent of the Assembly for the provisions of the European Union (Withdrawal Agreement) Bill which affect its competence; and affirms that the Assembly does not agree to give its consent' (NI Assembly 2020a: 26).

[25] During the LCM, the First Minister stated: 'the deputy First Minister and I agree that we should recommend that consent is not given, albeit for different reasons' (Foster in NI Assembly, 2020a: 5); the sentiment was reiterated by the deputy First Minister who commented: 'There is no doubt—the First Minister said this in her opening remarks—that it is for different reasons that we come to this position today; nonetheless, it is significant that we are in the space we are in' (O'Neill in *ibid.*: 25). Concluding the debate, the Speaker thanked Members for the 'conduct of the debate' which he described as 'very respectful' (Maskey in *ibid.*: 27).

[26] Prior to the rejection of the LCM on the EU(WA) Act 2020, attempts were made by Northern Ireland MPs to amend the Bill. Amendments which would have required the government and devolved authorities

The lack of Northern Ireland Assembly legislative consent to the EU(WA) Act 2020 (including its many amendments to the earlier EUWA 2018) could be seen to undermine a broad understanding of the principle of consent. In particular, the 1998 Agreement provision that the Assembly 'will be the prime source of authority in respect of all devolved responsibilities' (S1: 4) was not upheld. As stated, this rejection can be elided with that of the devolved legislatures in Scotland and Wales. Arguably, however, given the disproportionate impact of the Withdrawal Agreement on Northern Ireland, the (rare) cross-community consensus in the Assembly debate and the emphasis of the UK Government on consent as a legitimating principle for the Protocol, its withholding in Northern Ireland bore particular constitutional significance.

7.2.2 Devolved Government

Strand One institutions are impacted by UK implementing legislation in some ways that are general to the devolved administrations and in other ways that are particular to Northern Ireland. The extent of regulation-making powers granted to UK Ministers in domestic implementing legislation strengthen the powers of the UK executive vis-à-vis the devolved administrations. The kind of legal changes required to implement UK withdrawal from the EU in general, and to implement the Protocol specifically, give a particular potency to the sweeping regulation-making powers bestowed on UK Ministers by domestic implementing legislation. In addition, during the three-year hiatus of devolved government in Northern Ireland, secondary legislation was made by UK Ministers and Northern Ireland officials, under the EUWA 2018 and NI(EFEF) Acts respectively, in preparation for EU exit with almost no scrutiny. Since the restoration of power-sharing government, secondary legislation continued to be used at the devolved and national level to make the majority of legal changes necessary in advance of EU exit. As this section sets out, because of the Protocol, Northern Ireland is disproportionately affected by changes made under secondary legislation to implement UK withdrawal from the EU, without, or with very limited, opportunity for scrutiny. This notwithstanding, some exemptions in implementing legislation read alongside existing exemptions for Strand Two and Three of the 1998 Agreement could, in effect, protect some Northern Ireland competencies from what

to ensure unfettered access for goods moving NI–GB when exercising regulation-making powers under the EU(WA) Act 2020 were tabled by a cross-party group of all sitting Northern Ireland MPs including DUP, SDLP, and Alliance representatives (House of Commons, 2020: NC50; 51).

Scottish and Welsh Ministers characterise as a 'power grab' from Westminster.[27] Somewhat paradoxically then, Northern Ireland's position under the Protocol and its unique three-stranded constitutional structure mean that the power-hoarding effect of domestic implementing legislation is simultaneously concentrated and diluted in the context of post-Brexit Northern Ireland.

The extent to which the powers of Strand One institutions are, or are not, diminished by the domestic implementation of the Withdrawal Agreement and Protocol will depend on the level of oversight and representation they have in the process of operationalising its provisions in the short and long term. In this regard, the lack of any domestic legislative *requirement* on the UK Government to provide for Northern Ireland Executive or Assembly input into, or oversight of, the implementation of the Protocol risks diminishing the competency of Strand One institutions. The impact of this fact could, however, be mitigated if UK political commitments to allow Northern Ireland representation at relevant meetings of the Joint Committee and to facilitate input to the Specialised Committee and Joint Consultative Working Group (JCWG) are realised. This section sets out two categories of impact of domestic implementing legislation on Strand One of the Northern Ireland constitution: arrangements for implementation and arrangements for representation.

7.2.2.1 Arrangements for Implementation

In the eighteen-month period between the collapse of the Assembly in January 2017 and the enactment of the EUWA 2018, the UK Parliament made eighteen statutory instruments applicable in Northern Ireland. In the following eighteen-month period between the EUWA 2018 coming into effect and the restoration of devolved government in January 2020, the UK Parliament made 63 statutory instruments applicable in Northern Ireland; of which, 50 were made under EU Exit law (mostly the EUWA 2018 but also the Taxation (CBT) Act 2018). The significant increase in the use of secondary legislation demonstrates how regulation-making powers bestowed by, in particular, the EUWA 2018 served to strengthen executive government over devolved government. While this 'power-hoarding' effect of implementing legislation

---

[27] The extent to which domestic implementing legislation represents a 'power surge' (Sharma in *Hansard*, 2017) or 'power grab' (Sturgeon and Jones, 2017) regarding the balance between executive and devolved competencies was subject of extensive debate and source of disagreement between central UK Government and, in particular, the Scottish and Welsh Governments. For an account of relevant events, see Torrance (2020); for analysis, see Rawlings (2017).

applies for the whole of the UK, its impact was exacerbated in Northern Ireland initially because of a lack of devolved government and subsequently because of changes required to implement the Protocol.

In view of the hiatus in devolved government in Northern Ireland (as outlined in 7.1.1), the NI(EFEF) Acts provided civil servants with discretionary powers to make decisions without ministerial oversight, subject to a 'public interest' test. At the time of enactment, the NI(EFEF) provisions were said to 'challenge established constitutional principles' in a such a way as 'would not be acceptable' in any other circumstances and 'should [not] be taken as a precedent for future legislation' (HL Constitution Committee, 2018: 24; see also *Buick* 2019b: 58; 62). Notwithstanding such concerns, the discretionary powers granted to devolved authorities under the EUWA 2018 read together with those granted senior civil servants under the NI(EFEF) Acts, in effect, gave responsibility to address the 'gargantuan' legal undertaking (Elliott and Tierney, 2018: 1) of dealing with retained EU law and preparing for UK withdrawal in Northern Ireland, to officials with very little democratic accountability. In the fourteen months during which powers available under the NI(EFEF) Acts and EUWA 2018 were exercised by civil servants eighteen regulations were made and eighteen decisions were taken that either: incorporated 'direct EU legislation' as understood in section 3(2) of the EUWA 2018;[28] addressed 'deficiencies arising from withdrawal' as provided for under Schedule 2 of the same;[29] or introduced mitigations to deal with the consequences of EU Exit directly.[30] According to the NI(EFEF) Acts, civil servants exercised these functions in line with government guidance that established the Secretary of State as the primary source of statutory oversight in Northern Ireland. The exercise of NI(EFEF) Act powers therefore

---

[28] Some regulations made under the NI(EFEF) Acts updated UK law to reflect EU derived legislation to 'ensure the current regime is compliant' with changes introduced since the Executive collapsed in January 2017 and which 'also need to be made before subsequent EU Exit' (The Executive Office, 2018a) to ensure compliance with a requirement for direct EU legislation 'so far as operative immediately before exit day, forms part of domestic law on and after exit day' (EU(W) Act 2018 s3(1)). These included, for example: Water Environment (Floods Directive) (Amendment No. 2) Regulations (Northern Ireland) 2018; Carcase Classification and Price Reporting Regulations (Northern Ireland) 2018; the Sea Fish Licensing Order (Northern Ireland) 2019 and Sea Fishing (Licences and Notices) (Amendment) Regulations (Northern Ireland) 2019 (see The Executive Office, 2018a; 2018b; 2019b)

[29] For example: a decision to establish a £1m grant fund scheme for ports as part of preparations for EU exit (The Executive Office, 2019c); a decision to introduce an InterTrade Ireland Brexit 'Start to Plan Voucher Scheme' to assist SMEs plan for the UK's exit (*ibid.*: 2019a); a decision to agree the most appropriate option of delivery for Export Health Certificates (EHCs) in a no deal Brexit scenario (*ibid.*: 2019d).

[30] For example: The International Joint Investigation Teams (International Agreements) (EU Exit) Order (Northern Ireland) 2019 (SR 2019/40); The Allocation of Housing and Homelessness (Eligibility) (Amendment) (Northern Ireland) (EU Exit) Regulation 2019 (SR 2019/86); The Social Security (Income-related Benefits) (Updating and Amendment No. 2) (EU Exit) Regulations (Northern Ireland) 2019 (SR 2019/90); The Social Security (Amendment) (EU Exit) Regulations (Northern Ireland) 2019 (SR 2019/213).

amounted to a significant concentration of executive power. In this respect, UK implementing legislation arguably undermined the 1998 Agreement provision for the Assembly to be 'the prime source of authority in respect of all devolved responsibilities' (S1 (4)), albeit justified on the basis of 'necessary steps' to deliver public services (HM Government, 2018: 4).

The EUWA 2018, as amended by the EU(WA) Act 2020, grants UK Ministers discretionary powers to introduce regulations they 'consider appropriate' to implement the Protocol or to deal with 'matters arising' out of, or related to, the Protocol (2018 Act s8C as inserted by 2020 Act s21; see 7.1.2). Regulations made under these powers have the force and effect of primary legislation once approved by Parliament according to the affirmative procedure process which allows little time for parliamentary scrutiny; regulations made under this process are almost never rejected (see Kelly, 2016: 10). Concerns have been raised about the general scope of executive powers provided for by the EUWA 2018, as amended, with critics arguing that parliamentary scrutiny is diminished, and devolution undermined, by the Act. The potential 'power-hoarding' effect of these broad discretionary powers granted (in particular) under the EUWA 2018 are, however, more significant in Northern Ireland than elsewhere in the UK due, directly and indirectly, to the Protocol.

Some aspects of the Protocol require specific legislation to take effect. One such example is *The Protocol on Ireland/Northern Ireland (Democratic Consent Process) (EU Exit) Regulation* (SI 2020/1500) which makes provision for the democratic consent mechanism provided for in Article 18 of the Protocol. This regulation was debated and approved in Parliament in just sixteen minutes. A draft of SI 2020/1500 came before the Delegated Legislation Committee on 26 November 2020 and was passed in a meeting that lasted seventeen minutes in total. During the short debate, concerns were raised regarding the lack of Northern Ireland input to the development of the consent process, the contingency of the Protocol on the outcome of UK–EU future relationship negotiations ongoing at the time, and the potentially destabilising nature of consent votes in the politics of Northern Ireland. Notwithstanding concerns, and the constitutional significance of the regulation for Northern Ireland (see 7.2.1.4), the motion passed unopposed (*Parliament Live*, 2020). The mechanism provided for in statutory instrument 2020/1500 will apply unless and until a consent motion is rejected by the Northern Ireland Assembly: it is therefore a significant piece of new legislation but, under the EUWA 2018 and EU(WA) Act 2020, not one that Strand One institutions could influence.

To take another example, *The Definition of Qualifying Northern Ireland Goods (EU Exit) Regulations* (SI 2020/1454), made under section 8C(6) of the EUWA 2018 (as inserted by s21 of the 2020 Act), set out a definition for those 'qualifying Northern Ireland goods' which would be included in domestic legislative provisions for 'unfettered access' for goods moving NI–GB (under s8C and Sch2 part 1C of EUWA 2018 and s11 and s47 of the UKIM Act 2020). This regulation 2020/1454 makes provision in domestic law for Article 6 of the Protocol whereby nothing 'shall prevent' the UK ensuring 'unfettered market access for goods' moving NI–GB and any restrictions on exports will only be applied to NI–GB trade to the extent 'strictly required by any international obligations' of the EU (Article 6(1)). This is important because under Article 5(4) and Annex 2 of the Protocol, EU Regulation 2015/936 laying down common rules on exports applies to and in Northern Ireland; however, according to Article 6(1) and UK regulation 2020/1454, export restrictions will only apply to *non-qualifying* goods that move NI–GB to the extent *strictly required* by EU international commitments. Under the EUWA 2018, the power to define qualifying Northern Ireland goods is vested only in UK Ministers who can amend this at any time (s8C(6)). After regulation 2020/1454 was made, Secretary of State for Northern Ireland, Brandon Lewis, indicated that the broad definition it set out was an 'initial approach ... intended to be a bridge to a longer-lasting regime' (NIO, 2020b). For goods travelling GB–NI, *The Customs (Northern Ireland) (EU Exit) Regulations* (SI 2020/1605), made by the Treasury under the Taxation (CBT) Act 2018, gives effect to Joint Committee Decision 4/2020 regarding criteria for determining GB–NI goods deemed 'not at risk' of onward movement to the EU and therefore not subject to tariffs. The SI 2020/1605 establishes new rules to govern Northern Ireland imports and exports (chapter 3 and chapter 4 respectively) and amends a significant amount of existing legislation to reflect new rules governing GB–NI trade in goods. By way of demonstration, the regulation changed an existing need to charge import duties 'if goods are exported from the United Kingdom' (set out in *The Customs (Import Duty) (EU Exit) Regulations* (s41(1)(d)), to read '*or removed* from Great Britain to Northern Ireland' (part 6 s37(2), *added*). Similar changes are made to eleven pieces of customs and excise legislation to replace 'the United Kingdom' with 'Great Britain' or to append references like the above regarding new arrangements for the removal of goods from Great Britain to Northern Ireland.[31] For Strand One, SI 2020/1500 on the democratic consent mechanism, SI 2020/1454 on the

---

[31] The eleven amended acts and regulations are: the Customs and Excise Management Act 1979; Customs and Excise (Transit) Regulations 1993; Customs Traders (Accounts and Records) Regulations 1995; Customs (Contravention of a Relevant Rule) Regulations 2003; Customs (Import Duty) (EU Exit) Regulations 2018; Customs (Special Procedures and Outward Processing (EU Exit) Regulation 2018; Customs Transit Procedures (EU Exit) Regulations 2018; Customs (Managed Transition Procedure) (EU Exit) Regulations 2019; Taxation Cross-border Trade (Special Procedures and General Provision etc.) (EU Exit)

definition of qualifying Northern Ireland goods, and SI 2020/1605 on 'at risk goods', all underline the particular potency of regulation-making powers granted by UK implementing legislation in the Northern Ireland context because of the necessity to give effect to its unique post-Brexit position.

Alongside regulations to directly implement aspects of the Protocol, secondary legislation has been used extensively to amend existing EU-derived legislation so as to place Northern Ireland on a different legal footing to the rest of the UK in respect to parts of the EU legal *acquis* that continue to apply by dint of the Protocol. A majority of these changes involve textual amendments to replace previous references to 'the United Kingdom' with references to 'Northern Ireland' to reflect the continued applicability of certain EU laws in Northern Ireland only.[32] In the short term, changes of this order are less significant for Northern Ireland than for the rest of the UK as the former will simply maintain the (EU-derived) legal status quo in relevant areas; in this respect, one could therefore argue that Northern Ireland is protected from some of the 'power-hoarding' effects of implementing legislation. In the long term, however, by aligning Northern Ireland with parts of the legal *aquis* after the UK has left the EU, changes of this nature create the possibility (or probability) of GB–NI divergence without recourse for devolved government input. In this respect, one could also therefore argue that Northern Ireland is potentially more exposed to the 'power-hoarding' effect of implementing legislation than the rest of the UK; the specific impacts in policy and political terms will depend to a large degree on future decisions of the UK Government. For Strand One of the constitution, the most important point is that implementing legislation did not provide any opportunity for Executive or Assembly consultation or scrutiny of these changes brought forward by regulation.

An indirect consequence of implementing the Protocol in domestic law is to increase the power of the Secretary of State for Northern Ireland. Primarily, these new powers derive from the continuation of the direct effect of EU laws within the scope of the Protocol as the Secretary of State performs a gatekeeper role in some areas, particularly those that are reserved in the Northern Ireland context. Perhaps the most significant examples arise from Article 10 of the Protocol concerning State Aid. Under sections 48 and 49 of the UKIM Act 2020, the Secretary of State is required to publish

---

Regulations 2020; Customs (Crown Dependencies Customs Union) (EU Exit) Regulations 2019; and Customs (Reliefs from a Liability to Import Duty and Miscellaneous Amendments) (EU Exit) Regulations 2020.

[32] See, for example, new regulations on Value Added Tax (SI 2020/1545 and 2020/1546), export controls (SI 2020/1502) regulation of sea fishing (SI 2020/1599) regulation in respect to REACH (SI 2020/1577).

guidance on the application of EU State Aid laws in the UK under Article 10 and Annex 5 of the Protocol. The Secretary of State is to consider relevant decisions, recommendations, or declarations of the Joint Committee (s48(2)) but can 'revise or replace' the guidance or 'withdraw' it if 'satisfied it is no longer necessary' (s48(5)). Further, under section 49 of the UKIM Act, the Secretary of State is the only public authority permitted to 'comply with a requirement of a provision of EU law' to notify or to provide relevant information to the European Commission (s49(1)). Concentration of implementation powers in respect to Article 10 of the Protocol is in keeping with the division of competencies under the 1998 Act, according to which the 'regulation of anti-competitive practices and agreements' are reserved to the UK Government. This notwithstanding, the scope of laws applicable under Article 10 and Annex 5 is notable; it incorporates five Articles of the TFEU, sixteen EU Regulations, Directives, or Decisions, and 35 Commission guidelines, communications, or notices; the application of these 'in respect to measures which affect that trade between Northern Ireland and the Union', subject to the Protocol, will require discretion (Article 10(1)) which, on the UK side, is wholly invested in the Secretary of State without any requirement for consultation with the Northern Ireland Executive or Assembly. This is therefore an additional demonstration of the 'power-hoarding' implications of the domestic implementation of UK withdrawal from the EU in and for Northern Ireland.

7.2.2.2 Arrangements for Representation

As set out in detail in the preceding chapter (see 6.2.2.2), the Withdrawal Agreement establishes three bodies to oversee the implementation of the Protocol—the Joint Committee, the Specialised Committee, and the JCWG—and grants the Joint Committee power to make binding decisions on the operation of the Protocol. UK implementing legislation does not provide significant additional detail as to the status or operation of these three bodies outside of the general implementation provision and outlining some procedural matters in respect to the Joint Committee (see 2020 Act s34; s35l; Sch 2 and Sch5 part2 s44(d)). In view of the lack of new domestic provisions for oversight provided for in UK implementing legislation, the lack of requirement according to the Withdrawal Agreement and Protocol for the three oversight bodies to receive input from or consult with the Northern Ireland Executive or Assembly regarding implementation (see again 6.2.2.2) is reinforced under the EUWA 2018 and EU(WA) Act 2020. This notwithstanding, political commitments made by the UK Government during the transition period regarding Northern Ireland representation have the potential to mitigate the democratic deficit otherwise established in respect to post-Brexit devolution in Northern Ireland.

Under the NDNA agreement, political parties in Northern Ireland, supported by the UK Government and Irish Government, reaffirmed a 'commitment to greater transparency and improved governance arrangements' in Northern Ireland (NDNA, 2020: 3). Within the 'ambitious package of measures' (*ibid.*: 4) designed to achieve these aims, the NDNA created an Executive Sub-Committee on Brexit intended to 'improve collaboration and partnership and improve the sustainability of the institutions' (*ibid.*: 16). Established on 4 February 2020, the Brexit Sub-Committee was a non-decision-making body; it was subsequently replaced by 'an arrangement whereby certain specific meetings of the Executive Committee now have a single agenda focus on EU Exit Related Matters' (The Executive Office, 2020a: 2). This decision was taken by agreement of the five-party Executive in recognition of the fact that it 'needs to be able to respond in an agile manner to ensure that its view is appropriately reflected in [UK–EU future relationship] negotiations' (*ibid.*). Records from meetings of the Executive Committee on EU Exit underline the need for 'clarity on the implementation of the Protocol' as its top priority (The Executive Office, 2020a: 9). A meeting of the Executive Committee on EU Exit on 29 September 2020 focused on the operational readiness for a possible 'non-negotiated outcome' whereby the UK would leave the transition period without a UK–EU future relationship agreement; the Committee listed the various categories of issues affecting operational readiness in Northern Ireland; of the 21 categories identified only three were not contingent on either UK–EU future relationship negotiations, the Joint Committee, or central UK Government policy decisions (The Executive Office, 2020b: Annex A).[33] The categorisation of issues listed at the 29 September meeting underlines the extent to which the impact of the Protocol

---

[33] The 21 categories of issues affecting operational readiness were grouped as (1) those dependent on UK–EU future relationship negotiations (trade in goods, i.e. zero tariff zero quota FTA; trade in services; UK-wide state aid regime; data adequacy agreement; MRPQ; possible agreement on SPS standards; transport issues, passenger and road haulage; participation in EU programmes); (2) those subject to negotiations and decision in Joint Committee (mitigations on application of standard SPS controls on entry of relevant agri-food products; definition of goods moving GB–NI 'at risk' of entering EU single market; requirement for Exit Declarations on goods moving NI–GB; Interpretation of Protocol provisions for VAT and excise; movement of highly regulated goods GB–NI, e.g. chemical and medicines); (3) those subject to UKG policy decisions (definition of qualifying NI goods; how unfettered access for qualifying goods works in practice under proposed provisions in the UKIM; operation of the external border; interaction between the Protocol and state aid for GB; domestic future funding); and (4) those solely a matter of implementation of known obligations or matters which are solely the responsibility of the NI Executive and Assembly (devolved legislative programme; guidance to NI business on devolved issues; compliance with the regulations in the Protocol) (The Executive Office, 2020b: Annex A).

in Northern Ireland is, *by default*, outside the control or influence of Strand One institutions. In view of the 1998 Agreement assertion of the Northern Ireland legislatures' primacy in devolved matters and the NDNA commitment to improve transparency and governance, the lack of any legislative commitment for Executive or Assembly oversight of the implementation of the Protocol risks creating an indefinite democratic deficit in Northern Ireland. However, if implemented, the UK Government's commitments in the NDNA have the potential to mitigate the democratic risk posed by the current legislative framework; whether or not that potential is realised in the medium to long term remains to be seen.

7.2.3 North–South Dimension

UK implementing legislation provides some explicit protections and provisions for North–South cooperation; however, read in the context of the 1998 Agreement and 1998 Act, the EUWA 2018, as amended, also contains some contradictions and ambiguities in respect to North–South cooperation. The resultant discrepancies in the legislative framework for North–South cooperation are, it is here argued, a legacy of the 'Backstop' Protocol which was designed to be supplemented and/or superseded by a comprehensive UK–EU Free Trade Agreement of the kind *not* agreed by the Johnson Government. For Strand Two of the Northern Ireland constitution, the provisions of UK implementing legislation also raise some questions about the process for continued North–South cooperation post-Brexit.

7.2.3.1 Continued Development of North–South Cooperation

The EUWA 2018 provided for the '*continuation of* North–South cooperation and the prevention of new border arrangements' (s10); the title was amended by the EU(WA) Act 2020 to instead make provision for the '*protection for* North–South cooperation …' (Sch5 part2 s41). This seemingly small change is important because it underlines a difference of approach between the May and Johnson Governments.[34] Under the 'Backstop' Protocol, the

---

[34] The original EUWA 2018 section heading, 'Continuation of North–South cooperation and the prevent of new border arrangements' was raised in the *Re McCord* (2019) case as appellants 'placed considerable weight on the heading as indicating an intention to impose upon Ministers an obligation to secure the objectives stated in the heading in all circumstances' (106). On this issue, the Court distinguished between a 'black letter approach' and 'purposive approach', suggesting, on the basis of judicial precedent, that the latter should be adopted in regard to headings and thus the importance placed on the heading by appellants in the case was inappropriate (111). It is perhaps the case that the point made regarding the language of 'continuation' in *Re McCord* influenced the UK Government decision to change the term to 'maintenance'.

UK Government's intention was to address the 'substantial challenges' UK withdrawal posed to the 'maintenance *and continuation*' of North–South cooperation (Protocol *Preamble*: Recital 14) 'through the overall EU–UK relationship' (Joint Report, 2017: 49). While agreeing a minimal framework of arrangements for the island of Ireland as an insurance policy—the 'Backstop' Protocol—was designed to 'maintain the necessary conditions for continued North–South cooperation' (Article 1(3)) but, crucially, only 'temporarily' (Article 1(4)) albeit with the UK and EU using their 'best endeavours' to conclude an agreement to supersede it 'in whole or in part' (Article 2(1)). By contrast, the revised Protocol agreed by Johnson applies indefinitely, albeit with Articles 5 to 10 subject to the democratic consent mechanism. The Protocol's provisions in respect to North–South cooperation, however, retain the logic of a backstop in so much as they do not alone provide for the *continuation* of North–South cooperation but rather offer *protection* for just some aspects of existing North–South cooperation. The most developed protection is for cross-border trade in goods (see 6.2.3.2). The different approaches of the two UK administrations are thus reflected in the change in terms between the EUWA 2018 and EU(WA) Act 2020; the language change could also explain certain contradictions and discrepancies in UK implementing legislation in respect to the *continuation* of North–South cooperation, as described below.

Under Article 11 of the Protocol, the Joint Committee 'may make appropriate recommendations to the Union and the United Kingdom' regarding 'the extent to which the implementation and application of this Protocol maintains the necessary conditions for North–South cooperation' (2). As such, if realised, Article 11(2) would provide a new process by which to 'develop consultation, co-operation and action' in areas of 'mutual interest' to the two jurisdictions on the island of Ireland (1998 Agreement, S2(1)). UK implementing legislation, however, prevents this. Section 10 of the EUWA 2018 (as amended 2020 Act s24) prohibits any UK Minister from agreeing to 'the making of a recommendation by the Joint Committee under Article 11(2) of the Protocol' which would 'alter the arrangements for North–South cooperation as provided for by the Belfast Agreement', alter the functions of an existing implementation body, or establish a new implementation body (EUWA 2018 s10(3)). In this way, the 2018 and 2020 Acts appear to ensure that any expansion or alteration of North–South cooperation shall only occur via the NSMC and/or existing implementation bodies. The domestic prohibition on any 'alteration' of North–South cooperation via the Joint Committee raises a question about the significance of the Protocol provision for the NSMC and North–South implementation bodies to submit 'proposals' to the Specialised

Committee regarding the 'implementation and application' of the Protocol (Article 14(b)). If, for example, the NSMC were to make a proposal to the Specialised Committee concerning North–South cooperation in respect to the operation of the Single Electricity Market under Article 9 of the Protocol which would involve any alteration of existing arrangements, under amended section 10 of the EUWA 2018, a UK Minister could not agree to the proposal at the Joint Committee under current UK law; this situation seems to be contrary to the Article 14 provision for input from Strand Two institutions.

In addition to discrepancies regarding the development of North–South cooperation and the role of institutions, there is a more general contradiction in domestic implementing legislation in respect to Strand Two of the Northern Ireland constitution. As already discussed, the exercise of any powers under the EUWA 2018, as amended, must be compatible with the terms of the 1998 Act (s10(1)(a)); it is not, however, clear how this requirement is to be interpreted in light of provisions in that Act for the unique three-stranded structure of the Northern Ireland constitution. A particular question is raised regarding police and judicial cooperation. Under Schedule 2(3) to the 1998 Act, international relations are an excepted matter but with several relevant exceptions. With regard to cooperation between the PSNI and An Garda Síochána, these concern transfers, secondments, exchanges or training of officers (aa)(i); communications (including liaison and information technology) (aa)(ii); joint investigations (aa)(iii) and disaster planning (aa)(iv). The North–South Mapping Exercise carried out during UK–EU withdrawal negotiations found existing cross-border cooperation in policing, including joint investigations and information exchange, provided for in Schedule 2 to the 1998 Act, are underpinned by EU legal frameworks that are *not* referenced in the Protocol.[35] This presents a possible contradiction within the EUWA 2018 which, as amended, gives direct effect to a Withdrawal Agreement that removes, for example, UK entitlement to access the European Arrest Warrant database (WA Article 8). The domestic implementation of this fact, however, ought to be enacted in manner which is compatible with the 1998 Act

---

[35] Entry 94 in the comprehensive N-S Mapping document notes that cooperation between the PSNI and An Garda Síochána was facilitated by: Council Framework Decision 2002/465/JHA on joint investigation teams; Council Decision 2008/615/JHA on the stepping up of cross-border cooperation, particularly in combating terrorism and cross-border crime; Council Framework Decision of 13 June 2002 on the European arrest warrant and the surrender procedure between Member States; Council Act of 29 May 2000 establishing, in accordance with Article 34 of the Treaty on European Union, the Convention on Mutual Assistance in Criminal Matters between the Member States of the European Union (the Convention also provides a legal basis for Joint Investigation Teams); and Council Framework Decision 2006/960/JHA of 18 December 2006 on simplifying the exchange of information and intelligence between law enforcement authorities of the Member States of the European Union. None of these EU instruments are within the scope of the Protocol.

provision for police and judicial cooperation North–South, including in respect to communications and information technology sharing; this seems counterintuitive to the purpose and provisions of the Protocol, particularly Article 11.

A related, more specific contradiction is raised by the necessity for EUWA 2018 section 8 powers to make regulations to deal with deficiencies in EU retained law to ensure 'any form of North–South cooperation provided for by the Belfast Agreement' is undiminished (s10(2)(a)). The scope of provision for North–South cooperation in the 1998 Agreement is broad; twelve areas are listed but the provision is open-ended (S2: 8). Areas listed include relevant EU programmes, cross-border cooperation in healthcare, aquaculture and marine matters, education, and social security, all of which are likely to be diminished by UK withdrawal from the EU due to the consequential decoupling of legal and policy frameworks between the two jurisdictions on the island of Ireland. The EUWA 2018 section 10 requirement therefore raises questions regarding the exercise of regulation-making powers under section 8 of the Act. Conceivably, the 'no diminishment' provision could be read as a non-regression clause in respect to existing North–South cooperation but this does not seem to be compatible with the overall concept of Brexit or, more specifically, the type of UK withdrawal achieved under terms of the Withdrawal Agreement and TCA.

In addition to requiring compatibility with the 1998 Act, section 10 of the EUWA 2018 requires powers enacted under its terms to have 'due regard' to the Joint Report of UK–EU negotiators (s10(1)). When the Act became law, those powers did not include the general implementation power to enact 'all such rights, powers, liabilities, obligations and restrictions from time to time' created by or arising under the Withdrawal Agreement and Protocol (s7A(1) as inserted by 2020 Act s5).[36] Following the EU(WA) Act 2020, these section 10 obligations now apply to the implementation of the

---

[36] It is worth noting that in *Re McCord* the section 10 obligations were judged 'not [to] expressly or by necessary implication abrogate or constrain' (2019: 127(iii)) the UK Government's exercise of prerogative power in conducting UK–EU negotiations so as to prohibit any possible outcome, including a so-called 'no deal exit'. The decision arose from the Court's determination that the prerogative powers to negotiate were not 'under this Act' (s10(1)) so could not be constrained by the section 10 obligations (*ibid.*: 117) but that all such powers as the EUWA 2018 did grant were so constrained. At the time, this included a section 9 provision for Ministers to make such provisions considered appropriate 'for the purposes of implementing the withdrawal agreement' (s9(1)) before 'exit day'; on this matter, the Court in *McCord* determined that the prohibition on amending or repealing the 1998 Act in section 9 of the EUWA 2018 would 'largely secure compliance' in accordance with section 10(1)(a) but that the 'due regard duty on section 10(1)(b) would have to be considered in the context of whatever withdrawal agreement had been reached' (*ibid.*: 117). The EU(WA) Act 2020 repealed section 9 of the earlier Act (s36(a)) and amended it to include new section 7A power to implement 'all such rights, powers, liabilities, obligations and restrictions' created by or under the Withdrawal Agreement (2020 Act s5).

Protocol, but this creates discrepancies and possible conflicts in the amended EUWA 2018. The Protocol agreed by the Johnson Government departs from some commitments made by the May Government in the Joint Report. Primarily, discrepancies arise from paragraphs 49 and 50 of the Joint Report. In paragraph 50, the UK committed to 'ensure … no new regulatory barriers develop' between Northern Ireland and the rest of the UK 'unless, consistent with the 1998 Agreement, the Northern Ireland Executive and Assembly agree that distinct arrangements are appropriate for Northern Ireland' (2017). The requirements of Article 5(3) of the Protocol whereby the EU customs code and applicable EU laws listed in Annex 2 apply to 'non-qualifying' goods moving GB–NI clearly reach the paragraph 50 threshold of 'new regulatory barriers' yet neither the Northern Ireland Executive nor Assembly agreed to them (see 7.2.1.4). In paragraph 49 of the Joint Report, the UK committed to 'maintain full alignment' with rules of the EU single market and customs union which 'now or in the future, support North–South cooperation, the all-island economy and the protection of the 1998 Agreement' (*ibid.*). Again, it is unclear how implementation of the Protocol can be said to have 'due regard' for this paragraph 49 commitment when it enables divergence from the EU single market and customs union on the part of Great Britain and only provides for 'full alignment' with the single market in goods on the part of Northern Ireland.

7.2.4 East–West Dimension

Strand Three institutions are not mentioned in the EUWA 2018, the EU(WA) Act 2020, or the UKIM Act 2020. Outside of the requirement for compatibility with the 1998 Act, there are no provisions that are explicitly relevant to either the BIC or BIIC in any domestic implementing legislation. While it is therefore the case that the legislative implementation of the Withdrawal Agreement and Protocol has less direct effect on Strand Three than on the other components of the constitution, the lack of consideration does have an indirect effect as new legislation creates some contradictions and/or ambiguities about the operation and status of Strand Three institutions in a post-Brexit UK.

Further to the indirect legislative effects detailed in this subsection, the proposed 'law-breaking' clauses in the UKIM Bill, as introduced, and the manner in which they were brought by the UK Government also have an indirect but significant implication for bilateral East–West relations. The guarantor roles of the British and Irish Governments in respect to the 1998 Agreement have relied on intergovernmental cooperation as the *modus operandi* for facilitating the resolution of disputes between political parties in Northern Ireland. Bilateral diplomatic relations are thus essential for the continued development of the 'achievements, benefits and commitments of the peace process' in Northern Ireland (Protocol *Preamble*: Recital 2). Events of the transition period suggest, however, that the new UK and EU roles as co-chairs of the Joint Committee overseeing implementation of the Withdrawal Agreement, and in the context of the new UK–EU relationship under TCA, will put new strains on British-Irish relations which could undermine the management of Northern Ireland's still-in-process peace.

7.2.4.1 East–West Institutions in Implementing Legislation

UK implementing legislation contains some contradictions in respect to Strand Three institutions when read alongside existing legislative provisions. The EUWA 2018, as amended, restricts the powers given to UK Ministers and devolved authorities in respect to the second sentence of Article 11 paragraph 1 of the Protocol which reads:

> In full respect of Union law, the United Kingdom and Ireland may continue to make new arrangements that build on the provisions of the 1998 Agreement in other areas of North–South cooperation on the island of Ireland.

Under section 8C and Schedule 2 to the EUWA 2018, the power to 'by regulations make such provision', considered appropriate by Ministers or devolved authorities, respectively, to implement the Protocol or address related matters, 'does not include the second sentence of Article 11(1) of the Protocol' (s8C(7); Sch2 part1C(8)). This restriction suggests that the UK Government interpret the second sentence of Article 11(1) as designed to facilitate new areas of *intergovernmental* cooperation which is, conventionally, the sole purview of the UK Government. Yet, from the perspective of the 1998 Agreement, the phrasing of Article 11(1) and the related restriction in the EUWA 2018 are curious. Strand Two of the 1998 Agreement that concerns North–South cooperation was 'established to bring together those with executive responsibilities in Northern Ireland and the Irish Government' (S2: 1). There is no provision for intergovernmental cooperation under Strand Two as the mandate of the NSMC and implementation bodies are limited to 'the competence of the Administrations, North and South' (*ibid.*). By contrast, Strand Three of the 1998 Agreement does not mention 'North–South cooperation'; the intergovernmental dimension—the BIIC—is rather intended to address 'issues of mutual concern … with *non-devolved* Northern Ireland matters'

(S3: 5, *added*). There is a provision in the 1998 Agreement for intergovernmental cooperation on 'all-island and cross-border cooperation' but, under Strand Three, this only relates to 'non-devolved matters' (S3: 5–6). In view of the 1998 Agreement provisions, the second sentence of Article 11 para. 1 could be interpreted in two ways: one in which 'the United Kingdom' ought to be understood as a broad term but which, in practice, refers only to the Northern Ireland Executive as the 'provisions of the 1998 Agreement' that allow for North–South cooperation are only available to the Northern Ireland Government; or, less conventionally, the permission to 'make *new* arrangements that *build on* the provisions of the 1998 Agreement' could be taken as a new mechanism for the development of North–South cooperation via British-Irish intergovernmental cooperation. The EUWA 2018 restriction suggests that the UK Government prefer the latter interpretation. If this potential new procedure for the development of North–South cooperation via East–West cooperation were to be used it would introduce an important new dynamic to the operation of the 1998 Agreement institutions by rebalancing Strand Three as a facilitator of Strand Two and further undermining Strand One as the primary authority on devolved matters.

According to the 1998 Agreement, the mandate of the BIC is to 'exchange information, discuss, consult and use best endeavours to reach agreement on cooperation' on any matters of mutual interest that are within the competence of the relevant Administrations (S3: 5). Implementation of the Withdrawal Agreement and Protocol raises challenges for the BIC in fulfilling this mandate because one of the immediate effects of implementation is to enable divergence between BIC Member Administrations. At present, across the eleven priority work sectors of the BIC, the most common form of activity amounts to the sharing of best practice rather than taking any more formal agreed action. What this means is that, while any future divergence ought not to prevent the continued operation of the BIC, it does have the potential to undermine its usefulness by introducing the possibility that best practice identified in Member Administrations outside the EU (governments of the UK, Scotland, Wales, the Isle of Man, and the Channel Islands) or aligned with aspects of the EU *acquis* (Northern Ireland) cannot be replicated by those inside the EU (Ireland) or vice versa.

Provisions in the 1998 Agreement and 1998 Act for Northern Ireland participation in the BIC could become more significant post-Brexit in view of the new capacity for BIC Member Administrations to diverge from the EU and, therefore, each other. The 1998 Agreement provides BIC 'members to develop bilateral or multilateral arrangements between them' without prior approval from the Council as a whole (S3: 10); since 1998, this provision has not been widely used but it could become more significant for Northern Ireland post-Brexit. According to the 1998 Act, the exercise of legislative powers 'so far as required for giving effect to any agreement or arrangement entered into' by Ministers participating in a meeting of the BIC is an exception to the 'international relations' restriction on Northern Ireland devolved competence (Sch2(3)(b)(i)). There is no equivalent exception contained in the Scotland Act 1998 or Wales Act 2006 despite their participation in BIC meetings. Following this, the Northern Ireland Executive could *in theory* agree new areas of cooperation with, in particular, the Irish Government in one or more priority work sectors via the BIC whereas the Scottish or Welsh Ministers could not without prior domestic legislative approval. So, although UK implementing legislation has had no direct impact on existing provisions for UK devolved administrations participation in the BIC, by changing the legal environment in which that participation takes place, the fact of continued Northern Ireland alignment with EU rules and regulations increases the possibility that an existing legislative exception to 'give effect' to agreements or arrangements with BIC members materialises. Again, the indirect effect of the Protocol here is to potentially reorientate a Strand Three institution to serve as a facilitator of the development of Strand Two of the Northern Ireland constitution.

7.2.4.2 East–West Relations and Implementing Legislation

Since the 1998 Agreement was signed, its implementation has heavily relied on its co-guarantor governments to uphold their 'solemn commitment' to ensure its provisions are implemented (1998 Agreement: Article 2). British-Irish intergovernmental cooperation and diplomatic engagement has been the primary mechanism for resolving disputes between political parties in Northern Ireland that disrupt, or threaten to disrupt, the operation of the 1998 Agreement institutions in general and Strand One in particular. As noted in previous chapters, the process of UK withdrawal from the EU placed a new strain on British-Irish bilateral relations as the two governments' positions on the UK's Brexit policy overall, and more specifically its proposals for Northern Ireland, diverged sharply. Existing bilateral tensions were further exacerbated during the transition period following the UK Government proposal to break international law and renege on aspects of the Protocol via the UKIM Bill.

Notwithstanding the UK Government's removal of the proposed 'law-breaking' clauses before the UKIM Bill was enacted, damage to the level of trust between the British and Irish Governments could not, arguably, be mitigated. While the longevity, or otherwise, of any such damage to bilateral relations remains to be seen, the UKIM dispute demonstrates a much more fundamental shift in the means for the resolution of disputes concerning 'non-devolved Northern Ireland matters' (1998 Agreement S3: 5) of interest to Ireland which were, previously, the sole purview of the BIIC. The fact that an international disagreement over Northern Ireland was resolved not by British-Irish bilateral diplomacy but by the UK–EU Joint Committee underlines a significant indirect implication of the Protocol's implementation, namely that protection of 'the 1998 Agreement in all its dimensions' (Protocol Article 1(3)) is no longer only a 'solemn commitment' (1998 Agreement, Article 2) on the part of the British and Irish governments; the EU are now, in effect, a third guarantor of those aspects of the 1998 Agreement that fall within the scope of the Protocol.

7.2.4.3 Great Britain and Northern Ireland as 'East–West'

Neither the 1998 Agreement nor the 1998 Act use the term 'East–West'. Since 1998, however, 'East–West' has been used in academic, political, and public discussions about the 1998 Agreement to refer to institutions established under Strand Three and the 'totality of relationships' they reflect (S3: 1). Although a linguistic rather than legalistic point of analysis, it is worth underlining that, prior to UK–EU withdrawal negotiations, 'East–West' was used almost exclusively to refer to Strand Three institutions and the bilateral British-Irish relationship. The necessary negotiation of an arrangement to address the 'particular circumstances' of Northern Ireland in the context of UK withdrawal from the EU has led to more expansive use of the term and concept of 'East–West cooperation' to now include 'the internal links between Northern Ireland and Great Britain' (UKG, 2017: 61). By way of demonstration, the UK Command Paper described the need for 'a consensual and proportionate approach' to implementing the Protocol that recognised 'the important social and economic links *both East–West and North–South*' (2020: 3, *emphasis added*) yet, crucially, the Command Paper did not contain any measures relevant to the operation of Strand Three institutions or bilateral British-Irish relations but rather focused on arrangements between Great Britain and Northern Ireland in the post-Brexit context. Although an indirect impact of the domestic implementation of the Protocol, this discursive shift to understand GB–NI relations as 'East–West' amounts to an important reframing of the balance of relationships envisaged in the 1998 Agreement.

7.3 Impact Assessment: UK Implementing Legislation and the Northern Ireland Constitution

The first key finding arising from the impact of UK implementing legislation relates to discrepancies between international and domestic legal provisions for Northern Ireland. Existing UK law definitions of the 1998 Agreement and the territory of Northern Ireland conflict with definitions and provisions used in the Protocol introduced onto the UK statute by implementing legislation (EUWA 2018 s7A as amended by EU(WA) Act 2020 s5). In regard to the 1998 Agreement, the definition contained in the Protocol reflects Ireland law rather than UK law. Given that this discrepancy relates to versions of substantively the same 1998 Agreement text, it is unlikely to prove judicially significant; however, it suggests a politically significant lack of detailed awareness of the 1998 Agreement and 1998 Act among UK negotiators. This finding could be said to demonstrate a 'Northern Ireland blindspot' in action which is like unto that identified in academic literature on the UK constitution and wider historical narratives of the same (see 2.2.1). An additional discrepancy between the definition of the territory of Northern Ireland in the Protocol (which excludes territorial waters) and the territory of Northern Ireland in domestic law (which includes territorial waters) has more immediate legal significance. As a consequence of this disagreement in definitions of 'Northern Ireland', domestic implementing legislation has introduced a new territorial scope of domestic legislation as it applies to and in Northern Ireland.

Following the findings in respect to consent in Chapter 6 (see 6.3), the legislative implementation of the 'democratic consent mechanism' offers a new procedure for the exercise of consent in the Northern Ireland context. By establishing a process that prioritises parliamentary consent over popular consent and majoritarian consent over cross-community consent, the legislation made to implement Article 18 of the Protocol reformulates the consent principle as it appears in the 1998 Agreement and is provided for in the 1998 Act. In addition, the provision for this novel consent procedure in domestic law marks a departure from UK constitutional convention with regard to the balance between devolved and executive powers. By offering MLAs a definitive vote on the continued application of Articles 5 to 10 of the Protocol—a matter concerning UK international relations and therefore excepted under the 1998 Act—the democratic consent mechanism departs from UK constitutional orthodoxy with regard to the balance of competencies between devolved and executive powers.

In respect to Strand One, the most important finding arising from this chapter is that Northern Ireland Executive and Assembly input to the implementation of the Protocol depends on political rather than legislative commitments; democratic oversight is therefore weak. There is no provision in relevant implementing legislation for Northern Ireland devolved institutions input to or oversight of the Protocol's implementation. UK Government commitments to facilitate Northern Ireland representation at relevant Joint Committee and Specialised Committee meetings are politically significant but ultimately contingent. In respect to Strand Two, a discrepancy between provisions for North–South cooperation set out in the Protocol, and in the EUWA 2018 (as amended by 2020 Act), creates some uncertainty over the process for ongoing development of North–South cooperation. Article 11 of the Protocol allows the Joint Committee to agree new areas of North–South cooperation but UK implementing legislation prohibits this. Any deepening of North–South cooperation can therefore only occur through the established mechanism of the NSMC and cross-border implementation bodies and not via the Joint or Specialised Committee.

Although UK implementing legislation makes no direct provision for Strand Three institutions, it does indirectly impact the British-Irish Intergovernmental Conference by establishing a new procedure for resolving non-devolved Northern Ireland issues via the Joint Committee. Reflecting their absence in the Protocol, the BIC and BIIC are not mentioned in UK implementing legislation. The indirect effects of implementing the Protocol, however, impact the work of the BIIC by setting up a new mechanism for resolving issues pertaining to Northern Ireland in areas not devolved to Strand One or Strand Two bodies, via the Joint Committee. In addition, by enabling UK-wide and GB-specific divergence from EU law, the domestic implementation of UK withdrawal will make the post-Brexit operation of the BIC more difficult because of the overlap with BIC priority work sectors.

A final finding arising from this chapter relates to Strand Three and Strand One. Due to the implications of implementing the Protocol's provision on Northern Ireland's place in the UK internal market, there has been a discursive shift in the language and concept of 'East–West' cooperation as it pertains to the Northern Ireland constitution. As an indirect consequence of implementing the Protocol, the term 'East–West' now incorporates relations between Great Britain and Northern Ireland in a way that does not arise from the 1998 Agreement nor the 1998 Act. As set out in Chapter 9, this shift, and the changes from which it derives, have the potential to be extremely politically significant in the Northern Ireland context as the impact on Northern Ireland's place in the UK internal market is very likely to be perceived by Unionist/Loyalist communities as a threat to their national identity and constitutional preference.

The impacts of UK implementing legislation on each component of the Northern Ireland constitution can be expected to be of enduring significance given their (relatively) definitive origin in primary law. That said, in the short term, the legislative provision for the 'democratic consent mechanism' and the absence of legislative provision for Northern Ireland Executive or Assembly input to bodies established to oversee implementation of the Protocol are most notable from the perspective of Northern Ireland politics. Recurring votes on the degree of alignment with Great Britain and/or Ireland (EU) will be divisive in the already divided political context of Northern Ireland. Furthermore, the lack of requirement for Northern Ireland representation on the various oversight bodies could fuel a sense of disenfranchisement—perhaps most particularly within political Unionism—that may also prove a source of polarisation with consequential implications for the stability of devolved institutions.

In view of the findings from this chapter and the preceding three empirical chapters, the discussion in Chapter 8 sets out a summative analysis of the impact of Brexit on the Northern Ireland constitution.

8
Brexit and the Northern Ireland Constitution

> 'There is no "Irish Sea Border". As we have seen today, the important preparations the Govt and businesses have taken to prepare for the end of the Transition Period are keeping goods flowing freely around the country, including between GB and NI.'
>
> Brandon Lewis, Secretary of State for Northern Ireland,
> 1 January 2021[1]

> 'We have been seeking urgent progress with the EU on the outstanding issues in relation to the practical operation of the Protocol to ensure it has as little impact on the everyday lives of people and communities in Northern Ireland ... because stability, security, and prosperity are the very least that this integral part of our Union deserves.'
>
> Brandon Lewis, Secretary of State for Northern Ireland,
> 4 March 2021[2]

Brexit changed the constitution of Northern Ireland. When the Protocol, agreed as part of the Withdrawal Agreement, came into force on 1 January 2021, the legal relationship between the UK in respect of Northern Ireland and the EU entered a new and unprecedented era. Although in principle post-Brexit Northern Ireland remains inside the UK customs territory and internal market, in practice, under the Protocol, it is treated as part of the EU single market for goods and is in a position of dynamic alignment with those areas of the legal *aquis* necessary to avoid a physical hard border on the island of Ireland. This post-Brexit arrangement reinforces the

---

[1] Lewis, B. (2021a) 1 January. @*BrandonLewis*. Available: https://twitter.com/brandonlewis/status/1345057483887411200?lang=en (Accessed 9 March 2021).

[2] Lewis, B. (2021b) 4 March. 'Our lawful steps are consistent with a good faith implementation of the Northern Ireland Protocol' *The Telegraph*. Available: https://www.telegraph.co.uk/politics/2021/03/04/lawful-steps-consistent-good-faith-implementation-northern-ireland/ (Accessed 9 March 2021).

Brexit and the Northern Ireland Constitution. Lisa Claire Whitten, Oxford University Press.
© Lisa Claire Whitten (2023). DOI: 10.1093/oso/9780198881940.003.0008

constitutional uniqueness of post-1998 Northern Ireland within the UK, but also poses significant challenges for its place in the UK internal market, thus making its implementation politically very difficult. Disruptions to GB–NI trade during the first three months of 2021 were destabilising as Unionist and Loyalist communities in Northern Ireland perceived the new barriers to 'East–West' trade as an 'affront' (DUP, 2021a) to their national identity. For the UK Government, upholding the terms of the Protocol in the context of the wider UK–EU relationship (under the TCA and WA), and notwithstanding Unionist/Loyalist ire, presents ongoing domestic political and diplomatic challenges. A shift in the language of the Secretary of State for Northern Ireland, Brandon Lewis, reflects the strained UK Government position with Lewis asserting on the first day of implementation that goods were 'flowing freely' yet only ten weeks later was in 'urgent' pursuit of resolving 'outstanding issues' due to disruptions in GB–NI trade (Lewis, 2021a; 2021b). The long-term effects of implementing Northern Ireland's unique post-Brexit arrangements will continue to unfold years after this publication; however, by tracing the impact of the process on its constitution in real time, the four preceding chapters have provided an important initial mapping of the constitutional effects of Brexit on Northern Ireland and one that can inform ongoing discussions about 'constitutional futures' within the UK and on the island of Ireland.

Drawing on political constitutionalism and contributing to the still relatively under-developed literature on Northern Ireland and European integration (see 2.2.1; 2.2.2), the preceding chapters have presented an interdisciplinary analysis of the unprecedented process of UK withdrawal from the EU on the unique and 'constructively ambiguous' post-1998 constitution of Northern Ireland. Based on the understanding that the fundamental political principles and established legal precedents for government in Northern Ireland are largely codified in the 1998 Act which serves 'in effect' as its constitution when interpreted in line with principles laid down in the 1998 Agreement (*Robinson*, 2002: 11), the analytical framework used the components of the 1998 Agreement—the principle of consent, devolved government, the North–South dimension, and the East-West dimension—to structure an empirical analysis. Through four empirical chapters, each devoted to a specific element of the withdrawal process—the UK's EU referendum, the triggering of Article 50 TEU, the UK–EU Withdrawal Agreement, and domestic UK implementing legislation—this book has been able to track the progressive impact of Brexit on the Northern Ireland constitution. Echoing the structure of the preceding empirical chapters (4–7), this chapter provides a summative analysis of the nature and extent of the impact of Brexit on the Northern Ireland constitution as a whole, and on each of its four component parts; it argues that, overall, the impact of UK withdrawal from the EU—Brexit—on the unique constitution of Northern Ireland—dually enshrined in the 1998 Agreement and 1998 Act—has been profound.

8.1 Brexit and the Northern Ireland Constitution

Key Finding 1: Brexit has established the EU as 'protector' of the 1998 Agreement

Prior to the Brexit process, there was no direct legal relationship between the EU and the Northern Ireland constitution. The 1998 Agreement described the UK and Ireland as 'friendly neighbours and partners in the European Union' (BIA, *preamble*); however, the 'essential' facilitative role (Phinnemore and Hayward, 2017: 7) of joint EU membership, specific EU support for Northern Ireland's 'constitutional moment' of 1998 (Harvey, 2012) and its post-conflict development (Hayward and Murphy, 2018; Murphy, 2019) were not legally formalised. Brexit changed this. The EU's prioritisation of ensuring the 'achievements, benefits, and commitments' of the peace process and the 1998 Agreement 'in all its parts' were protected in the process of UK withdrawal (European Council, 2017a: 11) led to the signing of an international treaty that changes the relationship between the Northern Ireland constitution and the EU. As it is an explicit purpose of the Protocol to 'protect the 1998 Agreement in all its dimensions' (Article 1(3)), Brexit can be said to have established the EU as a 'protector' of the Agreement. As the analysis in Chapter 6 demonstrated (see 6.2), the EU's new role differs from that of the co-guarantor governments of the UK and Ireland in two respects: it provides stronger guarantees for some aspects (namely cross-border trade in goods and citizens' rights equivalence) of the 1998 Agreement than others (namely Strand One and Strand Three institutions); and it includes stronger procedures for enforcement and oversight via a dispute resolution mechanism and various new implementation bodies, one of which (the EU–UK Joint Committee) has power to amend the Protocol by agreement. These arrangements are a substantial departure from those that exist for oversight of the 1998 Agreement which do not include specific mechanisms for legal redress and have instead relied on political and diplomatic relations between its signatories as the *modus operandi* for its implementation. One of the key impacts of the Brexit process on the Northern Ireland constitution is, therefore, the establishment of the EU as a 'protector' of the 1998 Agreement.

The new legal relationship between the EU and Northern Ireland, established under the Protocol, has important implications for literature on the constitutional effects of membership. As set out in Chapter 3 (see 3.1), debates about the impact of EU membership on the domestic constitutions of Member States have coalesced around the concept of constitutional pluralism (see MacCormick, 1999; Walker, 2016). While one must be cautious about generalising on the basis of the unique case of Northern Ireland, *prima facie* the fact that what the 'constitutional requirements' (Article 50(1) TEU) of the UK were in respect to the 1998 Agreement was a point of disagreement in UK–EU withdrawal negotiations could be said to affirm constitutional pluralists' argument that EU membership introduces a plurality of potentially legitimate claims to constitutional authority. The new 'protector' role for the EU in respect to the 1998 Agreement could be seen as an effective reification of the previously abstract concept of constitutional pluralism, because, in the process of leaving the EU, the pluralising effect of membership on the UK constitution was not only exposed, in the case of Northern Ireland, but had to be accommodated as part of the 'constitutional requirements' that constrained the terms of withdrawal set out in the Withdrawal Agreement.

In addition to its relationship to the concept of constitutional pluralism, this first key research finding raises questions about the future of the EU–UK(NI) relationship as a new frontier of EU external governance. Being one of several 'privileged partnerships' with non-EU regions, the position of Northern Ireland under the Protocol is without precedent, particularly in view of the automaticity of its dynamic alignment to aspects of the EU legal *acquis* and the governing institutions set up to oversee its implementation (see Gstöhl and Phinnemore, 2019; Phinnemore, 2019). The operation of the EU's new 'protector' role in Northern Ireland in practice and going forward is an interesting area for research. Analysis of any legal action arising either under the Withdrawal Agreement dispute resolution mechanisms or under the EUWA 2018 (s7A) can also be expected to provide an important means of determining the tangible effect of the EU's 'protector' role in respect to the 1998 Agreement. More broadly, comparative research on the role of the EU in post-Brexit Northern Ireland and in other non-EU regions with 'privileged partnerships' could provide novel insights into the nature and extent of the EU's influence in external governance scenarios and therefore ought to be pursued.

Key Finding 2: Brexit has exposed and exacerbated discrepancies between domestic and international law provisions for the Northern Ireland constitution

A black letter reading of the Protocol reveals some notable discrepancies between domestic constitutional law in respect to Northern Ireland, and its new post-Brexit arrangement. As set out in Chapter 7, existing UK legal definitions for the 1998 Agreement (1998 Act s98) and the territory of Northern Ireland (*ibid.*) conflict with that used for the Agreement in the Protocol (*Preamble*: Recital 4) and its provisions for the territorial application of EU laws in Northern Ireland post-Brexit (Article 5(3)). The definition of the 1998 Agreement contained in the Protocol reflects Irish law rather than UK law. Although this discrepancy is unlikely to be judicially significant (see 7.2.1.1), it suggests a politically significant lack of detailed awareness of the 1998 Agreement and 1998 Act among UK negotiators. Such an apparent lack of familiarity with the particularities of the Northern Ireland constitution in the UK negotiating team is symptomatic of the 'Northern Ireland blindspot' evident in constitutional scholarship and dominant narratives of UK constitutional history identified in Chapter 2 of this book (see 2.1.1). A discrepancy between the definition of the territory of Northern Ireland in the Protocol (which excludes territorial waters) and the territory of Northern Ireland in domestic law (which includes territorial waters) (see 7.2.1.3) has more potential material significance in that it resulted in a new territorial scope of domestic legislation as it applies to and in Northern Ireland.

While, as noted, any black letter discrepancies between domestic law and the Protocol are not likely to be legislatively or judicially significant, the apparent lack of detailed familiarity with the Northern Ireland constitution demonstrated in withdrawal negotiations has important implications for its unique position in a post-Brexit UK. Continued application of aspects of the EU legal *acquis* in Northern Ireland under the Protocol will need to be accommodated in the UK internal market and UK trade policy and/or in specific free trade agreements (FTAs) with non-EU Third Countries. As such, post-Brexit, there will be an increasingly significant body of international law provisions that apply to the UK *in respect of Northern Ireland*. Findings from this research suggest that UK negotiators of future FTAs may not be sufficiently aware of Northern Ireland's unique obligations under (international) EU law, post-Brexit. The discrepancies between domestic and international law provisions for post-Brexit Northern Ireland identified here thus underline the importance of continued academic research and political attention regarding the extent to which Northern Ireland's unique position is recognised and accommodated in the post-Brexit UK market, trade policy, and trade agreements.

8.2 Brexit and the Principle of Consent

The constitutional principle of consent that underpins the 1998 Agreement received little attention during the UK's EU referendum campaign, yet it featured prominently in the landmark *Miller* case prior to triggering Article 50 and became a central issue in the latter stages of UK–EU withdrawal negotiations. As a result, the legal outcomes of the Brexit process on the principle of consent are significant and paradoxical. On one hand, a narrow understanding of the principle of (constitutional) consent has been reaffirmed while, on the other, a new form of (democratic) consent has been created which challenges aspects of the established consent principle (cross-community and popular consent), broadly understood.

Key Finding 3: Brexit has reaffirmed a narrow interpretation of the principle of constitutional consent

Affirmation of the principle of (constitutional) consent derives from domestic legal action and the Article 1 'objectives' of the Protocol. In *Miller* (2017) the Supreme Court adopted a narrow interpretation of domestic law provisions for the principle of consent (as set out in 1998 Act s1, Sch1). *Miller* therefore provided judicial affirmation of the constitutional consent principle in relation to any future 'border poll' or 'unification referendum' (*Miller*, 2017: 135) but simultaneously adopted an overly reductionist position on the matter of devolved legislative consent and the status of the 1998 Agreement in UK law (see 5.2.1). In doing so, the Supreme Court relied on an orthodox understanding of the 'British constitution' that failed to recognise the international legal basis of the Northern Ireland constitution or account for its multi-levelled structure of governance. While also reaffirming the principle of consent, the Protocol echoes the 1998 Agreement, not 1998 Act, by referring to 'any change' in the constitutional status of Northern Ireland (Article 1(1); CI 1(iii)) which could *prima facie* imply a broader interpretation of the principle of consent (i.e. constitutional, legislative and cross-community) than that affirmed in *Miller*. While discrepancies between the affirmation of the principle of consent in Article 1(1) of the Protocol and a similar affirmation on the part of the Supreme Court in *Miller* are, on one level, an unremarkable reflection of the UK's dualist legal system, they also underline tensions that exist between the status of the Northern Ireland constitution in international law and in domestic law respectively.

Key Finding 4: Brexit added a new dimension to the 'principle of consent' via the 'democratic consent mechanism'

The 'democratic consent principle' provided for in Article 18 of the Protocol (read alongside a 'Unilateral Declaration' by the UK Government) introduces a new form of consent to the constitutional landscape of Northern Ireland. By providing the Northern Ireland Assembly with the opportunity to vote on aspects of the Protocol in 2024 and at regular intervals thereafter, the 'democratic consent mechanism' amounts to an additional formulation (not a re-formulation) of the 1998 Agreement consent principle. Under this novel consent mechanism, the Northern Ireland legislature is granted a definitive vote on the continued application of Articles 5 to 10 of the Protocol; if passed by simple majority, another vote will be held in four years; if passed by a 'cross-community' majority, another vote will be held in eight years. The 'democratic consent mechanism' therefore prioritises parliamentary and majoritarian consent, whereas the provisions of the 1998 Agreement prioritised popular and cross-community consent (see 6.2.1.4). Furthermore, the domestic legislative implementation of this novel process departs from UK constitutional convention with regard to the balance between devolved and executive powers. By providing MLAs with a definitive vote on aspects of the Protocol (Articles 5 to 10) concerning devolved *and non-devolved* matters, the democratic consent mechanism is constitutionally unorthodox in respect to the balance of devolved vs executive competence in the Northern Ireland setting (see 7.2.1.4).

There is, therefore, an incongruity in the overall effect of Brexit on the principle of consent: reaffirmations of the consent principle provide legal reassurance of the constitutional status quo, yet the new 'democratic consent mechanism' introduces a degree of perpetual legal uncertainty as to the implementation of the Protocol while also providing for a political process that departs from domestic constitutional convention and is likely to be politically destabilising in Northern Ireland. Importantly, this latter novel provision for consent in the Protocol prioritises parliamentary consent and majoritarian decision-making, and therefore moves away from provisions for consent in the 1998 Agreement which prioritise popular consent and cross-community decision-making.

Taken together, the two key findings on the impact of Brexit on the principle of consent sit awkwardly with dominant scholarly discourses about the political constitution of UK, founded on a principle of parliamentary sovereignty. The Supreme Court reaffirmation of the principle of constitutional consent, narrowly understood, in *Miller*, read alongside its reaffirmation in Article 1(1) of the Protocol, reinforces one of those elements of the Northern Ireland constitution that challenges a conventional understanding of parliamentary sovereignty. The idea that the UK parliament could 'unmake' the principle of consent (Dicey, 1915: 40) provision in section 1 and Schedule 1 of the 1998 Act is, in view of its reaffirmation in (domestic/international) law, even less convincing post-Brexit than it was pre-Brexit. In this respect, findings regarding the principle of consent are relevant to debates over the extent to which UK withdrawal from the EU has, or has not, confirmed the principle of parliamentary sovereignty (see Elliott, 2018; Gordon, 2019). Based on findings from this research, parliamentary sovereignty is newly constrained by obligations to uphold commitments under the Protocol, with the UK being liable to legal sanction by the EU if it should fail to do so.

Affirmation of the principle of constitutional consent and the addition of a new dimension via the 'democratic consent mechanism' identified in this research also have implications for discussions about the constitutional future of Northern Ireland. On one level, the affirmation of the principle of constitutional consent, narrowly understood, challenges the idea, advocated by some Unionists in Northern Ireland, that the Protocol has wholly undermined the consent principle (see DUP, 2021b; 2021c; Foster in *PA Media*, 2021; Aiken in Harte 2021). On another level, however, the 'democratic consent mechanism' adds a new formulation to the already multifaceted principle of consent and, in so doing, adds another dimension to the already complex conversations regarding constitutional futures on the island of Ireland. In view of legal and political changes associated with Brexit, the prospect of a referendum on Irish unification in the short to medium term has, since 2016, increasingly come to the fore in public, political, and academic debates (see Garry et al., 2020; Renwick et al., 2020). Findings from this research on consent are relevant to said discussions because they highlight important new areas for empirical research including, for example, on the operation of the novel 'democratic consent mechanism' and the potential interaction of this process with any future 'border poll'.

8.3 Brexit and Devolved Government

The impact of Brexit on the devolved government dimension of the Northern Ireland constitution has two aspects: first, the process exposed the fragility of Strand One institutions to external political shocks; second, Brexit has weakened the Northern Ireland Executive and Assembly's capacity for democratic oversight in some areas of devolved competence, thereby strengthening the executive powers of the UK Government in respect to Northern Ireland. As set out in this section, key findings regarding Strand One of the Northern Ireland constitution intersect with two major domestic constitutional fault lines (see 1.1) that were exposed and exacerbated in the process of UK withdrawal from the EU: the first concerning the balance of executive vs parliamentary powers; the second, the balance of central government vs devolved government powers.

Key Finding 5: Political polarisation catalysed by Brexit exposed the fragility of devolved government in Northern Ireland to external shocks

After a brief period of consensus within the DUP and Sinn Féin-led Executive in the aftermath of the referendum (see 4.2.2), Strand One institutions collapsed in January 2017 amid the fallout over internal policy failures in the green energy RHI scheme. Although not directly caused by Brexit, the two parties' divergent perspectives on the issue contributed to the breakdown of power-sharing government by exacerbating an already very strained relationship (see 5.2.2). In the March 2017 Assembly election that followed, 28 seats were returned for the DUP and 27 seats for Sinn Féin; representing an increase in percentage support for both parties, the result affirmed the polarising effect of Brexit in Northern Ireland. A negligible difference between the two parties did little to incentivise compromise at inter-party talks. However, the likelihood of reaching sufficient consensus to form a power-sharing government decreased significantly in June 2017 when ten DUP MPs entered a confidence and supply arrangement with a minority Conservative Government led by Theresa May. The strategic position of the DUP at Westminster called into question the UK Government's ability to act with 'rigorous impartiality' (1998 Agreement, Article 1(v)) in respect to Northern Ireland as arrangements for post-Brexit Northern Ireland and its border with the Republic of Ireland became increasingly central in UK–EU withdrawal negotiations. These political machinations exposed the fragility of Strand One institutions in the face of external shocks. A breakdown in political consensus over Brexit did not only take place in Northern Ireland as this was a period of widespread political polarisation in the UK. The unique constitutional requirement for cross-community coalition government in Northern Ireland, however, rendered the effect of that polarisation all the more damaging, resulting in three years (2017–2020) without functioning devolved government.

The insight of this research regarding the vulnerability of the devolved Northern Ireland Government to collapse in the event of political polarisation—in this instance caused by the external shock of Brexit—is instructive for debates over the balance of competences in the UK constitution because of the government's approach to managing the Northern Ireland case. During the three-year (2017–2020) hiatus in the functioning of devolved government in Northern Ireland, central government's executive powers were expanded significantly: first, through the NI(EFEF) Acts granting legislative powers to civil servants, thereby severely constraining democratic oversight; and second, through the sweeping powers granted by the EUWA 2018 to UK Ministers to make changes to EU retained law (s5) and, later, to implement the Withdrawal Agreement and Protocol (s7A) by secondary legislation—meaning, in both respects, the UK Government demonstrated a preference for 'power-hoarding' approaches when dealing with political instability at the devolved level (see Anthony, 2018: 674). For current and future debates about the territorial constitution of the UK, this is an important (albeit arguably unsurprising) finding as, based on this research, Brexit has reinforced centripetal forces within the UK constitution, thereby strengthening executive and central government powers over parliamentary and devolved government powers.

Key Finding 6: Brexit has strengthened the executive powers of the UK Government vis-à-vis those of the devolved government in Northern Ireland through arrangements for oversight of implementing the Protocol

Under the Withdrawal Agreement and Protocol, aspects of the EU legal *acquis* continue to apply in post-Brexit Northern Ireland which remains in dynamic alignment with the EU single market *acquis* in respect of goods (see 6.2.2.1). The lack of any requirement for Strand One institutions to input into the three bodies established to oversee the implementation of the Withdrawal Agreement and Protocol—the UK–EU Joint Committee, Specialised Committee, and Joint Consultative Working Group—therefore risks creating a perpetual democratic deficit in Northern Ireland (see 6.2.2.2). A potential democratic deficit arises first from the dynamic alignment provision whereby currently applicable EU laws apply in Northern Ireland 'as amended or replaced' (Protocol Article 13(3)) without any UK (or UK(NI)) involvement in agreeing the given amendment or replacement; secondly, the addition of new parts of the EU *acquis* to those already applicable under the Protocol can be decided by the Joint Committee, withhout any Northern Ireland involvement in agreeing the given addition. As detailed in Chapters 6 and 7, the provisions of the Protocol and nature of its implementation have profound economic, social, and political implications for areas within the competence of the devolved administration. In view of the lack of requirement for Northern Ireland involvement in either amending/replacing applicable EU law or adding new EU law, the provisions of the Protocol depart from the level of competence envisaged for Strand One institutions in the 1998 Agreement whereby these are to 'exercise full legislative and executive authority' in devolved matters (S1: 3). Currently, the extent of Strand One institutions input on the implementation of the Protocol relies on UK Government commitments to facilitate Northern Ireland representation at relevant meetings of the three oversight bodies; such commitments are politically significant but ultimately contingent. As such, under the default governance framework for the continued application of aspects of EU law in post-Brexit Northern Ireland, the executive powers of the UK Government have been strengthened over the devolved powers available to the Strand One institutions.

Similar to the previous finding, this one also affirms the centripetal effect of Brexit on the UK constitution. That bodies established to oversee the implementation of the Protocol are not required to seek input from the Northern Ireland Executive or Assembly reinforces central government's executive powers by default. Ultimately, decision-making powers in policy areas covered by the Protocol now exist at the EU level (for 'amending and replacing' currently applicable laws) and at the UK–EU level (for adding new laws) (see 8.3), while, politically, there is significant scope for greater Northern Ireland Executive and Assembly involvement in the implementation oversight of the Protocol *if* the UK Government are amenable to adopting measures to this end. In this regard, it is important to note the UK Government commitment to ensure Northern Ireland Executive representation at Joint and Specialised Committee meetings if Irish Government representatives are also in attendance. This facilitates Northern Ireland input to UK–EU discussions on the Protocol but falls short of providing for scrutiny of decisions made as Executive representatives have no decision-making powers nor are there any transparency requirements (on UK or NI attendees) to report on matters discussed. These weak scrutiny provisions could be addressed by, for example, providing for consistent (official or political) Northern Ireland representation at all meetings of the Joint Committee, Specialised Committee, and/or JCWG; and establishing more robust domestic mechanisms for scrutiny of relevant decisions on an ongoing basis (via parliamentary select committees at devolved and/or central level). For this reason, this research finding as regards the strengthening of UK Government executive over devolved government powers in post-Brexit Northern Ireland again intersects with contemporary UK-wide debates about central vs devolved competencies. Any substantially increased role for Northern Ireland in post-Brexit UK governance could be viewed unfavourably by (in particular) the Scottish Government and the Welsh Government—meaning the extent of Northern Ireland input to the governance of the Protocol *could* become an additional source of tension in internal UK political debates about 'the Union' and its future.

8.4 Brexit and the North–South Dimension

Similar to the principle of consent, the impact of UK withdrawal from the EU on Strand Two of the Northern Ireland constitution is uneven in that it reaffirms the importance of North–South cooperation in general, provides strong legal guarantees for some specific areas but only limited legal guarantees for others. The effect of this uneven impact is to introduce an asymmetry to the Northern Ireland constitution, giving more legal weight to aspects of Strand Two over its other three components while, at the same time, incentivising a deepening of North–South cooperation to address gaps in post-Brexit governance frameworks on the island of Ireland.

In the early stages, outside of some political tensions between an Irish Government advocating for Remain and some pro-Leave Northern Ireland Unionists, notably the DUP, the impact of the UK's EU referendum on Strand Two relations and institutions was minimal. The possible implications of a vote to Leave on cross-border cooperation on the island of Ireland hardly featured during the campaign and the work of Strand Two institutions continued under the assumption of ongoing EU membership (see 4.2.3). In hindsight, the relative absence of North–South cooperation as a topic of debate during the referendum campaign is notable in view of the prominence granted post-Brexit arrangements for the land border and cross-border cooperation in withdrawal negotiations. For a brief period following the UK's EU referendum result, North–South cooperation was strengthened as politicians and officials in Belfast and Dublin worked together via the NSMC and on an ad hoc basis to map the potential repercussions of Brexit in both jurisdictions (see 5.2.3). However, after the collapse of the Northern Ireland Executive and dissolution of the Assembly in January 2017, potential avenues for cross-border cooperation at an official level were diminished as the NSMC could not meet. The mapping work that had begun on a North–South basis was instead carried forward in the international context of UK–EU negotiations. In retrospect, the necessary continuation of North–South mapping at a UK–EU level rather than on a North–South basis perhaps provided precedent for mechanisms subsequently agreed in the Protocol, allowing for the development of cross-border cooperation that is not contingent on a fully functioning Northern Ireland Executive and Assembly.

Key Finding 7: Brexit has resulted in more specific legal protections for aspects of Strand Two of the Northern Ireland constitution than for Strand One or Strand Three

The search for 'flexible and imaginative' solutions to ensure the 'necessary conditions for continued North–South cooperation' (Protocol Article 1(3)) and avoid a hard border became a key point of tension in UK–EU withdrawal negotiations. As Chapters 6 and 7 set out in detail, the outcome of prolonged UK–EU discussions on the issue and (sometimes dramatic) domestic political events was the signing of a Withdrawal Agreement and Protocol that prioritised maintaining conditions that allow for North–South cooperation in general and cross-border trade in goods in particular. This prioritisation of cross-border trade in goods arose from a political compromise between UK and EU negotiating objectives and the shared objective of avoiding a hard border on the island of Ireland—narrowly defined as avoiding physical infrastructure at the border—rather than arising directly from the 1998 Agreement (see 6.3.2.1). As a consequence of this compromise, the legal protections granted North–South trade under the Protocol have the effect of rebalancing the Northern Ireland constitution by adding new legal weight to Strand Two as a facilitator of cross-border trade in goods. In regard to other areas of existing North–South cooperation—excluding the single electricity market—the Protocol still reflects the logic of the 'Backstop' Protocol which sought a minimal framework for maintaining North–South cooperation 'unless and until' (2018, Article 1(4)) these could be superseded in the context of a 'deep and special' UK–EU future relationship agreement (HM Government, 2017a: 43) of the kind neither sought nor signed by the Johnson Government. This means that there are, in effect, gaps in the Protocol as it does not ensure the 'necessary conditions' for a significant portion of North–South cooperation, including 'in the areas of environment, health, agriculture, transport, education … justice and security, higher education and sport' (Article 11(1)) and thereby falls short on its stated objectives (*ibid.* Article 1(3)); this creates a policy incentive for a deepening of North–South cooperation via Strand Two bodies post-Brexit.

Key Finding 8: Brexit incentivised deeper North–South cooperation as a means of addressing 'gaps' in the Protocol

An indirect effect of gaps in the Protocol in respect to areas of existing North–South cooperation is to incentivise a deepening of cross-border cooperation via Strand Two institutions to make up for those areas not covered. In this respect, the provision for the NSMC and implementation bodies to input to the Specialised Committee (under Article 14(b)) appears to make this scenario probable. The prospect of deeper North–South cooperation *via Strand Two* could be reinforced by a discrepancy between provisions for the future development of North–South cooperation in the Protocol and similar provisions in UK implementing legislation (EUWA 2018 s10). Together, these create some uncertainty as to the process for ongoing North–South development because Article 11(1) of the Protocol enables the Joint Committee to agree new areas of cooperation, yet UK legislation prohibits this. As such, any deepening of North–South cooperation can only occur through the established mechanism of the NSMC and cross-border implementation bodies, not via the Joint or Specialised Committees.

Overall, as a consequence of Brexit, Strand Two of the Northern Ireland constitution enjoys more specific legal guarantees under the Withdrawal Agreement and Protocol than any of the other constitutional components. Continued frictionless NI–EU trade in goods is guaranteed by the Protocol (Articles 5–10) and underpinned by a robust system for oversight and enforcement. By contrast, GB–NI trade in goods faces new frictions due to (some limited) tariff and non-tariff barriers for 'East–West' movement across the Irish Sea; thus, new guarantees for the 'North–South' dimension challenge Northern Ireland's place in the UK internal market. Notwithstanding the new safeguards for cross-border trade, however, as a result of 'gaps' in the Protocol in respect of other areas of North–South cooperation, Brexit has created a policy incentive for deepening North–South cooperation in areas not specifically covered by the Withdrawal Agreement or TCA. As a result of provisions in the Protocol and in domestic implementing legislation, any development of North–South cooperation is likely to occur via Strand Two bodies.

The impact of Brexit on the North–South dimension of the Northern Ireland constitution is empirically important for current debates about the 'constitutional futures' of both jurisdictions on the island of Ireland. In the years since the UK's EU referendum, and as a knock-on effect of renewed attention on the Ireland/Northern Ireland land border, political debates in Northern Ireland and (to a lesser degree) Ireland can be said to have been 're-constitutionalised' in that the view that a referendum on Irish unification could, or should, be called in the short to medium term is now more widely held (Garry et al., 2020). Prospective academic research on procedural aspects of any future 'Irish unity' referendum has begun with a substantial collaborative report identifying the many still 'unanswered questions' (Renwick et al., 2020: 3.15) regarding the political and constitutional mechanics in the event of such a vote being called. To these ongoing conversations, the rebalancing effect of the Protocol on the 1998 Agreement whereby more specific legal protections now exist for aspects of Strand Two of the Northern Ireland constitution than those available to Strand One or Three is important. In view of the Protocol, relations between the two jurisdictions on the island of Ireland now have an EU-protected aspect in respect to, in particular, cross-border trade in goods (Articles 5–8), rights equivalence for British and Irish citizens (Article 2), cooperation in the supply of energy and electricity (Article 9), and an open-ended provision for North–South cooperation (Article 11). In view of the dynamic alignment provision (Article 13(8)) in the Protocol and 'gaps' in respect to North–South cooperation (Article 11(1); see 6.2.3.3), that new EU-protected aspect of North–South relations is likely to grow in scope and significance. At the same time, the democratic consent mechanism introduces a perpetual uncertainty to the development path of North–South cooperation post-Brexit with the potential for the Protocol's trade elements (Article 5 to 10) to be disapplied in future. Post-Brexit arrangements for Strand Two of the Northern Ireland constitution introduce a new complexity and contingency to conversations about constitutional futures.

Questions arise about the procedural and political implications of 'democratic consent mechanism' votes on any future 'Irish unity' referendum votes. For example: will 'democratic consent mechanism' votes be framed as proxy decisions on North–South cooperation and constitutional futures in keeping with the 're-constitutionalised' post-Brexit politics on the island of Ireland? What impact would a vote in favour of disapplication of Articles 5 to 10, or a simple majority vote in favour of continued application, have on conversations about future 'Irish unity' referenda? Policy-orientated questions also arise about the continued development of North–South cooperation in areas not covered by the Protocol. For example: will dynamic alignment provisions in the Protocol lead to an expansion of EU-protected aspects of North–South cooperation? Or will this development take place via Strand Two bodies, independent of Protocol oversight bodies? Alternatively, will there be a hollowing out of North–South cooperation in those areas not covered by the Protocol in the post-Brexit era? It is beyond the scope of this book to address all of these known unknowns; chapter 9 does however pick up on some of these questions in view of the first two years of full implementation.

Two additional, non-empirical implications of the impact on the North–South dimension are also worth noting. By revealing the extent to which cross-border cooperation had developed in the context of shared EU legal and policy frameworks, *prima facie* the North–South mapping exercise could be seen as an affirmation of neo-functionalist theory about the effect of European integration (see 6.2.3.1). The expansion of North–South cooperation from the twelve areas specified in the 1998 Agreement to the 142 identified in the mapping exercise, 96 of which were directly or indirectly underpinned by EU law, appears to affirm the neo-functionalist concept of 'positive spill-over' whereby integration in some areas leads to integration in others (see Haas, 2004 [1958]; Rosamond, 2000). That said, this would need to be caveated by understanding that the NSMC and all-island implementation bodies enable a degree of institutional cross-jurisdictional cooperation that is exceptional in the EU context. Comparative research could, usefully, illuminate the extent to which this development in North–South cooperation is generic or particular. Relatedly, findings from the mapping exercise and the UK–EU agreed approach to maintaining 'necessary conditions' (Article 1(1)) for future development of North–South cooperation (gaps notwithstanding) provides an important insight for Europeanisation theory as the policy-level integration revealed by the mapping exercise resulted in a polity-level agreement to maintain aspects of that cooperation, albeit only a minimal framework. Based on key findings on Strand Two of the 1998 Agreement, future research could usefully apply these two theories of European integration—neofunctionalism and Europeanisation—to the case of Northern Ireland and North–South cooperation, post-Brexit.

8.5 Brexit and the East–West Dimension

The impact of Brexit on East–West relations and institutions is significant but, primarily, indirect. The process of UK withdrawal from the EU has catalysed four important developments in respect to Strand Three of the Northern Ireland constitution: (1) a shift in the nature of UK and Ireland intergovernmentalism; (2) the creation of a new mechanism for managing non-devolved Northern Ireland issues previously under the purview of the BIIC; (3) greater legal clarification of East–West intergovernmental cooperation; and (4) a reframing of 'East–West' in political discourse to include GB–NI relations.

Key Finding 9: Brexit catalysed a shift in the nature of UK and Ireland approaches to Northern Ireland

Although Strand Three institutions were not engaged directly by the UK's EU referendum, the campaign marked the beginning of a shift away from an established consensus-based approach on the part of the UK and Ireland Governments on issues pertaining to Northern Ireland. Then Secretary of State for Northern Ireland, Theresa Villiers, campaigned as a leading Brexiteer and thereby contradicted the Irish Government's position on the negative implications of UK withdrawal for Northern Ireland. This diplomatic divergence constituted a step change in the post-1985 consensus-based British-Irish bilateralism on Northern Ireland issues (see Tannam, 2011; Murphy, 2018). East–West diplomatic divergence regarding the implications of Brexit for Northern Ireland was a consistent feature of UK–EU withdrawal negotiations as Ireland maintained a prominent and very influential role on the EU side.

Kay Finding 10: Brexit has resulted in a new mechanism for resolution of disputes over Northern Ireland in non-devolved areas

Alongside catalysing a change in bilateral British-Irish approaches to Northern Ireland, mechanisms for overseeing implementation of the Withdrawal Agreement and Protocol have resulted in a new process for resolving disputes previously within the purview of the BIIC. The first example of this was evident in the UK–EU dispute over the UKIM Bill during the transition period. The UK Government proposal to break international law and renege on aspects of the Protocol via the UKIM Bill strained bilateral relations. Notwithstanding the UK Government's removal of the proposed 'law-breaking' clauses before the UKIM Bill was enacted, damage to trust between the British and Irish Governments could not be wholly mitigated. The longevity, or otherwise, of any such damage to 'East–West' bilateral relations remains to be seen. The UKIM dispute also demonstrated a more fundamental shift in the means available for the resolution of disputes concerning 'non-devolved Northern Ireland matters' (1998 Agreement S3: 5) of interest to Ireland which were, previously, the sole purview of the BIIC. The fact that an international disagreement over Northern Ireland was resolved *not* by British-Irish bilateral diplomacy but by the UK–EU Joint Committee underlines a significant indirect implication of the Protocol's implementation, namely that protection of 'the 1998 Agreement in all its dimensions' (Article 1(3)) is no longer only a 'solemn commitment' (1998 Agreement, Article 2) on the part of the British and Irish Governments; the EU is now a 'protector' of those aspects of the 1998 Agreement that fall within the scope of the Protocol.

The introduction, via Brexit, of a mechanism for the resolution of disputes over Northern Ireland in non-devolved areas in the Joint Committee opens a new dimension in British-Irish relations as dialogues previously held bilaterally will now take place at a UK–EU level. This new procedural provision for dispute resolution could be said to follow from the shift away from a consensus-based bilateral UK and Ireland approach on Northern Ireland issues early in the Brexit process (see 4.2.4) and towards a new era of 'East–West' intergovernmentalism characterised by the management of divergence and possible dissent between the UK and Ireland on matters concerning Northern Ireland.

Key Finding 11: Brexit has led to some clarification of the nature of 'East–West' intergovernmental cooperation and incentivised putting aspects of British-Irish cooperation on a more secure legal footing

The particular attention on preserving Strand Two cooperation in UK–EU withdrawal negotiations contrasts with the comparative inattention on Strand Three. The text of the Protocol reflects this as 'East–West' relations are only mentioned once and neither the BIC nor BIIC are specifically mentioned. Yet, notwithstanding the lack of explicit provisions for Strand Three in the Protocol, it is covered by overarching commitments to ensure 'arrangements necessary ... to protect the 1998 Agreement *in all its dimensions*' (Article 1(3), *emphasis added*). Furthermore, the 'enduring nature' of the bilateral UK and Ireland relationship is recognised in Article 3 regarding the CTA (*Preamble*: Recital 1). This means, therefore, that although the Protocol provisions provide fewer legal guarantees in respect to Strand Three relations and institutions than is the case for, in particular, Strand Two, they also do not undermine or weaken the legal status of Strand Three of the Northern Ireland constitution; in this way, the *direct* impact of the Protocol on Strand Three is comparatively small. Furthermore, in the absence of specific provisions dedicated to preserving Strand Three in the Protocol, its impact on this component of the Northern Ireland constitution will depend on the way in which general commitments to the 1998 Agreement are interpreted and applied. It is therefore notable that, throughout UK–EU withdrawal negotiations, Strand Three institutions were used as fora for bilateral and multilateral engagement in such a way as to suggest that they could become more politically significant post-Brexit than pre-Brexit. In particular, intergovernmental engagement, via the BIIC, led to clarification of the substance of mutual UK and Ireland arrangements and commitments under the CTA, via a Memorandum of Understanding. Such an apparent renewed momentum for East–West cooperation via Strand Three institutions may prove to be an additional indirect impact of Brexit on this aspect of the Northern Ireland constitution.

Reflecting their absence in the Withdrawal Agreement and Protocol, Strand Three institutions are not mentioned in the relevant UK implementing legislation. Outside of a requirement, under the EUWA 2018 (as amended) for implementation of the Protocol to be compatible with the 1998 Act, there are no provisions that relate to either the BIC or BIIC explicitly. The legislative implementation of the Withdrawal Agreement and Protocol therefore has less of a direct effect on Strand Three than on the other components of the constitution. This notwithstanding, it is also true that the lack of consideration of Strand Three has an indirect effect given that the legal implementing of Brexit enables significant new divergence between member administrations of the BIC and the governments of the BIIC which is likely to make collaboration via the two institutions more difficult.

Taken together, the EU's new 'protector' role in respect to the 1998 Agreement (see 6.2), the powers granted the Joint Committee (6.2.2.1), and the potential for the European Council to approve any future bilateral UK–Ireland agreements in areas of exclusive EU competence (see 6.2.3.2), results in a new and indefinite EU dimension to Strand Three of the Northern Ireland constitution. Arguably, therefore, some aspects of post-Brexit UK–Ireland relations ought to be understood as a novel frontier of EU external relations, Ireland being an EU Member State with a unique arrangement for cooperation and integration with previous Member State now Third Country UK.

Key Finding 12: Brexit has caused a discursive reframing of 'East–West' relations to now include 'GB–NI'

A less legally material yet highly significant indirect impact of Brexit on Strand Three of the Northern Ireland constitution is the discursive reframing it has catalysed whereby 'East–West' relations are now understood to include Great Britain–Northern Ireland relations. There is arguably a link here to a UK Government tendency to frame issues pertaining to Northern Ireland *and* Ireland as two facets of the same problem which was clear from the early stages of the process (see 5.2.3). Notwithstanding the later assertions of the May Government that internal GB–NI divergence on matters of trade would threaten the 'constitutional integrity' of the UK and could not be tolerated (*BBC News*, 2018), the Johnson Government's subsequent ratification of a Withdrawal Agreement and Protocol that requires significant new frictions on GB–NI trade has changed the language and concept of 'East–West' cooperation. In the domestic political lexicon of post-Brexit UK, 'East–West' now incorporates internal GB–NI relations in a manner that does not arise from the 1998 Agreement or 1998 Act.

One of the contextual factors identified at the beginning of this research was the linguistic parallels between emerging discourses about 'Brexit's Northern Ireland problem' with similar historical discourses about 'the Troubles' during the 1969–1998 conflict and the so-called 'Irish question' that dominated early 19th-century British politics (see 1.3). This final key research finding serves to underline the continued importance of attending to changes in political language and thereby justifies the focus on discursive aspects of Brexit maintained throughout this research.

Following the entry into force of the Withdrawal Agreement, Protocol, and TCA, political debates in Northern Ireland focused on (respectively) Unionist opposition to the Protocol which they perceive as a threat to their place in the UK and a violation of the 1998 Agreement on the basis of consent and the damage done to 'East–West' relations, and Nationalist/Non-Aligned desire to develop 'easements' and 'adjustments' to 'make the Protocol work'. For the purpose of this research, the most important discursive shift that resulted from Brexit is the reframing of 'East–West' relations; whereas previously this referred to UK–Ireland intergovernmental relations and/or relations between the Member Administrations of the BIC, in contemporary political discourse 'East–West' now includes 'GB–NI'. This development in language provides an important context for academic analysis of the changing political demographics in Northern Ireland (see Hayward and McManus, 2018; Hayward and Rosher, 2020) in that a growing percentage of the population identify as 'Northern Irish' and/or as 'Neither' Unionist nor Nationalist. While this research offers only a preliminary finding, a reasonable hypothesis could be that a discursive shift that separates GB and NI in an 'East–West' frame indicates and/or results in an acceleration of those political demographic trends mentioned, leading a greater percentage of people in Northern Ireland to identify as 'Northern Irish' rather than, in particular, British.

8.6 Conclusion: What Impact Has Brexit Had on the Northern Ireland Constitution?

This analysis found that the impact of Brexit on the unique constitution of Northern Ireland has been multifaceted and profound. Twelve key findings emerged, and these can be stated, in short, as follows. Brexit established the EU as 'protector' of the 1998 Agreement. Brexit exposed and exacerbated discrepancies between domestic and international law provisions for the Northern Ireland constitution. Brexit reaffirmed a narrow interpretation of the principle of constitutional consent. Brexit added a new dimension to the principle of consent via the 'democratic consent mechanism'. The political polarisation catalysed by Brexit exposed the fragility of devolved government in Northern Ireland to external shocks. Brexit strengthened the executive powers of the UK Government vis-à-vis those of the devolved government in Northern Ireland through arrangements for oversight of the Protocol's implementation. Brexit resulted in more specific legal protections for aspects of Strand Two than for Strand One or Strand Three. Brexit has incentivised deeper North–South cooperation as a means of addressing 'gaps' in the Protocol and post-Brexit UK–EU relationship in general. Brexit catalysed a shift in the nature of UK and Ireland approaches to Northern Ireland. Brexit resulted in a new mechanism for resolution of disputes regarding Northern Ireland in non-devolved areas. Brexit has led to some clarification about the nature of 'East–West' intergovernmental cooperation and incentivised putting aspects of British-Irish cooperation on a more secure legal footing, and Brexit caused a discursive reframing of 'East–West' relations to now include 'GB–NI'.

Read together, the key findings of this research underline a fundamental fact, namely that the UK's decision to withdraw from the EU changed the political and legal environment in which the contemporary Northern Ireland constitution had existed for almost 25 years. Through the 'constructive ambiguity' of the 1998 Agreement on issues of national identity and statehood, the identities and concerns of both Unionists and Nationalists were recognised and accommodated. Following this, the 1998 Agreement had not solved the constitutional conflict but rather allowed it to be 'managed differently' (Phinnemore and Hayward, 2017a: 22) through a multi-levelled system of government within Northern Ireland (power-sharing devolution), on the island of Ireland (North–South cooperation) and between the islands of Ireland and Great Britain (East–West cooperation), all underpinned by a multifaceted principle of constitutional, popular, and cross-community consent. Recognising the 'constructively ambiguous' nature of the compromises that underpin the 1998 Agreement (and successor agreements) is a crucial first step on the road to understanding the significance of Brexit's impact in Northern Ireland. Only when read in the knowledge of a *still-in-process* peace does it become clear just how potentially transformative the specific constitutional impacts of UK withdrawal from the EU—as laid out in the key findings of this research—might be. By forcing a change in the way systems of government established under the 1998 Agreement operate, Brexit disrupted the 'constructively ambiguous' compromise that it represents and, thereby, has risked the stability and the still-processing peace of Northern Ireland.

When analysing the interaction of complex, multi-layered processes such as Brexit and the evolution of a post-conflict constitutional settlement, it is important to nuance any conclusions by noting their unavoidable contingency on events. Little about the Brexit process was inevitable and counterfactuals abound. Innumerable decisions made by the myriad of actors involved changed the overall impact which is, at the time of writing, still unfolding. This is especially so in Northern Ireland where the material implications of Brexit were destined to be most visible due to its unique vulnerability arising from its geographic, economic, political, and constitutional architecture. With these important disclaimers articulated, it is also true to say that one of the (few) methodological benefits of conducting legal and political research in real time is that it is possible to test research findings against reality after a relatively short period of time. This is what the next chapter of this book endeavours to do. Written from the perspective of January 2023, two years after the end of the transition period and the full entry into force of the Withdrawal Agreement, Protocol, and TCA, Chapter 9 enlists the benefit of hindsight to reflect on the veracity of the twelve key research findings in view of subsequent events. In concluding, Chapter 9 considers some of the likely and potential implications of Brexit for Northern Ireland in the medium and long term.

9
Northern Ireland's Brexit Problem

'What a fool I was. I was only a puppet, and so was Ulster, and so was Ireland, in the political game that was to get the Conservative Party into power ... Like everybody else, [this House] have betrayed Ulster.'

Lord Edward Carson, 1921[1]

'Prime Minister, you say that your commitment to Northern Ireland is unshakeable. But I speak for all of my constituents today when I tell you that the Protocol has betrayed us and made us feel like foreigners in our country.'

Ian Paisley Jnr, DUP MP, 2021[2]

One hundred years after the Ulster Unionist leader Edward Carson spoke of the 'betrayal' of Ulster by the Lloyd George Conservative Government over the signing of the Anglo-Irish Treaty, his words seemed once again apt. In the weeks following the 1 January 2021 entry into full legal force of the UK–EU Withdrawal Agreement, including the Protocol, Northern Ireland Unionist politicians were, once again, using the language of 'betrayal' to characterise the decision of a Conservative Party Government, this time led by Boris Johnson, to implement an untested set of arrangements that would result in divergence between post-Brexit Northern Ireland and post-Brexit Great Britain. Such an echo of history reflects what this analysis has demonstrated, namely that the constitution of Northern Ireland has been changed in and by the process of UK withdrawal from the EU.

While the long-term political, economic, and societal impacts of Brexit for Northern Ireland are still unfolding, this book has provided an original and substantive assessment of the immediate constitutional implications of the

---

[1] Carson, E. (2021) 'Address in Reply to His Majesty's Most Gracious Speech' HL Deb. 1921, 14 December. (*Hansard*: vol. 48, cc.45; 47.) Available: https://api.parliament.uk/historic-hansard/lords/1921/dec/14/address-in-reply-to-his-majestys-most.

[2] Paisley, I. (2021) 'Engagements' (*Hansard*, 3 February 1921: vol. 633.) Available: https://hansard.parliament.uk/Commons/2021-02-03/debates/2177E714-0248-4F3B-BE41-6EC94D176060/details) (Accessed 28 February 2021).

Brexit and the Northern Ireland Constitution. Lisa Claire Whitten, Oxford University Press.
© Lisa Claire Whitten (2023). DOI: 10.1093/oso/9780198881940.003.0009

unprecedented scenario of European *dis*integration on the part of the United Kingdom most exposed to its effects. In concluding, this chapter provides a descriptive account of relevant events in the two years that followed the entry into force of the Protocol. On this basis, the chapter then provides retrospective assessment of the twelve key research findings (see 8.6) while also considering their likely constitutional repercussions both within and beyond the (recently notorious) borders of Northern Ireland going forward.

9.1 Two Years of Implementation

The implementation of the Protocol in Northern Ireland has not been smooth. Practical difficulties with it—some expected and some less so—combined with political opposition to it—in Stormont and in Westminster—and diplomatic disputes over it—primarily between UK and EU but with intermittent contributions from the US—together amounted to a tumultuous 24 months. While not fully comprehensive, what follows is a high-level, chronological overview of relevant events; the subsequent section discusses their significance in relation to the key findings of this research and their possible constitutional consequences in the longer term.

9.1.1 Headline Events of the Protocol's First Two Years

In the first few weeks of January 2021, disruptions to supplies of certain goods due to new checks and controls on GB–NI movements were visible on the shelves of shops and supermarkets in Northern Ireland (see Andrews, 2021; Beesley, Nilsson, and Parker, 2021; Campbell, 2021; Carroll, 2021). Although a logical consequence of the very limited time allowed for businesses and traders to adapt to the untested arrangements of the Protocol and the TCA—the latter being concluded days prior and decisions on the former being concluded just weeks in advance—this very visible manifestation of the differentiation of Northern Ireland within the post-Brexit UK market arguably had lasting political effect.

Evident disruptions to the supply of certain goods prompted some Unionist politicians to call for the Protocol to be 'unilaterally disapplied', with select DUP representatives characterising its effect as 'unmitigated disaster' (Paisley in NIAC, 2021: Q378). Then First Minister and leader of the party Arlene Foster, however, initially struck a more conciliatory and nuanced tone regarding the Protocol, even noting the potential for a 'gateway of [economic] opportunity' to arise from it (*BBC News*, 2021a). DUP optimism did not last. As polls indicated a decline in support for the DUP under Foster (*Lucid Talk*, 2021), the party's position hardened while tensions on the ground escalated. On 1 February, the DUP Agriculture Minister Edwin Poots told council staff and officials carrying out checks at ports in Larne and Belfast not to attend their workplace due to security concerns (*@edwinpootsmla* 2021; *BBC News*, 2021b). The next day, the DUP launched its 'Free us from the Protocol' campaign accompanied by a five-point action plan (*BBC News*, 2021c; DUP, 2021a). This came in the wake of an EU move, on 29 January, to temporarily invoke the Protocol's Article 16 safeguard procedure in the course of drafting legislation regarding the supply of vaccines. Although widely condemned and swiftly withdrawn, the near invocation of Article 16 on the part of the European Commission exacerbated an already tense atmosphere in Northern Ireland (see Whitten, 2021d) and catalysed a change in the tone of UK–EU communications concerning the Protocol. Subsequent official UK Government statements and papers would cite the 'overwhelming' impact (Cabinet Office, 2021a) of the EU's non-move, suggesting it had had 'dramatic effect' on perceptions in Northern Ireland with 'significant political consequences' which 'continue[d] to reverberate' (HM Government, 2021: para. 24). An emergency meeting of the Joint Committee took place on 3 February and was attended by the First and deputy First Ministers of Northern Ireland. In a joint statement that followed, all parties 'condemned unreservedly' any threats or intimation of officials involved in conducting checks on goods, and the UK and EU committed to 'immediately work intensively to find solutions to outstanding issues' via the Joint Committee (Cabinet Office, 2021b).

Despite the intention to work together, consensus between the UK and EU was not forthcoming. On 3 March, the UK Government announced its decision to unilaterally extend the (initially) three-month grace period, agreed by the Joint Committee in December 2020, regarding export health certificates on GB–NI movements of plant and animal products (see Lewis, 2021). The action was framed by the UK as a 'temporary technical step' necessary for 'operational reasons' and to allow time for further discussions about the Protocol (Frost, 2021a). In response, the EU launched infringement proceedings against the UK on 15 March (European Commission, 2021a).

In Northern Ireland, tensions remained high. On 7 April, anger about the implications of the Protocol, together with some local frustrations, resulted in violent rioting in Unionist/Loyalist and interface areas of, primarily, Belfast (see *BBC News*, 2021d; Hayward, 2021; Whitten, 2021c). In view of the unrest, the Joint Committee called an informal meeting on 15 April. Subsequent separate UK and EU statements respectively noted the 'constructive' and 'solution-driven' atmosphere therein and both stated resolve to 'intensify' negotiations in coming weeks (see Cabinet Office, 2021c; European Commission, 2021b; Burchard, 2021). The riots in Northern Ireland ended after ten days during which nearly 90 police officers sustained injuries. Protests against the Protocol continued but these remained peaceful and represented an organised campaign on the part of Loyalist/Unionist activists.

Talks between the UK and EU about the implementation of the Protocol were ongoing throughout the spring of 2021. Issues of concern varied but, broadly, these related to the level of customs and/or sanitary and phytosanitary checks and controls either required or potentially required (pending the end of grace periods) on goods entering Northern Ireland from Great Britain, as well as, more specifically, the likely implications on the supplies of medicines and veterinary medicines to Northern Ireland once a relevant twelve-month grace period ended, and the involvement of local stakeholders and political representatives in the process of oversight and implementation. Other specific issues also arose; these included but were not limited to: pet passports, seed potatoes, bulbs and plants, agriculture equipment, tagging of live animals, car insurance green cards, groupage of lorry loads, tariff rate quotas, chilled meat products and the supply of kosher meat in particular.

In contrast to the unilateral extension of March 2021, the UK Government submitted a formal request to the EU on 16 June for a three-month extension to the grace period covering chilled meat products; the request was granted (European Commission, 2021c). In doing so, the EU also noted 'solutions' that had so far been found regarding the supply of human medicines, guide dogs, car insurance green cards, and movements of live animals (*ibid.*). Also in June, European Commission Vice-President and EU Co-Chair of the Joint Committee Maroš Šefčovič appeared before a Committee of the Northern Ireland Assembly to give evidence regarding the implementation of the Protocol (see NI Assembly, 2021a); this was an unprecedented occurrence from an EU standpoint in that a high-profile Commissioner appeared before a sub-state entity of a non-Member State. Weeks later Cabinet Office Minister and UK Co-Chair of the Joint Committee Lord David Frost gave evidence to the same NI Assembly Committee (NI Assembly, 2021b) in what was a similarly novel, although not totally unprecedented, occurrence in the UK context with a Minister of the Crown appearing before a committee in a devolved legislature. Not long after this, in July 2021, the UK Government published a Command Paper entitled *Northern Ireland Protocol: the way forward* in which it was stated that the Protocol was 'failing' to deliver on its objectives and therefore proposed 'significant changes' to it

(HM Government, 2021: 3). Raising an issue that had not previously been prominent in Protocol-related debates in Northern Ireland, the UK Command Paper characterised its enforcement provisions regarding the continued jurisdiction of the CJEU as 'highly unusual' and argued these had 'increased rather than reduced tensions' in the 'divided society' of Northern Ireland (*ibid.*: 68). A week later, the European Commission published proposals to address issues concerning medicines supplies and SPS measures at the same time as pausing the legal action taken against the UK in March following its unilateral extension of grace periods (*BBC News*, 2021e). In early September, the UK Joint Committee Co-Chair Lord Frost announced a(nother) unilateral extension of existing grace periods (Frost, 2021b); of this move the European Commission 'took note' but did not launch any new infringement proceedings 'for now' (European Commission, 2021d). The ninth meeting of the EU–UK Specialised Committee on the Protocol took place at the end of September, after which the UK and EU issued separate press releases (see Prime Minister's Office, 2021; European Commission, 2021e).

Parallel to the contentious unfolding of UK–EU talks on the Protocol, its effect continued to be evident in the politics of Northern Ireland. Application for judicial review launched by a cross-party group of Unionist politicians—in the case of *Re Allister and Others*—was dismissed by the High Court in Belfast on 30 June (see Judicial Communications Office, 2021 and 9.2.2 for discussion). Simultaneously, the largest Unionist party in Northern Ireland, the DUP, which was undergoing a tumultuous few months featuring a series of leadership changes, installed Sir Jeffery Donaldson on the same day as the *Re Allister* ruling and, as it happened, the EU's granting of the UK's request for a grace period extension (see Whitten, 2021d). Not long after these events, towards the end of September 2021, the four Unionist parties of Northern Ireland (DUP, UUP, TUV, and PUP) signed a declaration affirming their collective opposition to the Protocol and calling for it to be 'rejected and replaced' by arrangements which would 'fully respect' the integral position of Northern Ireland in the UK (see DUP, 2021b).

Speaking at the Conservative Party conference on 4 October 2021, the UK Co-Chair of the Joint Committee and Cabinet Office Minister Lord Frost warned that using 'the Article 16 safeguard mechanism … may in the end be the only way to protect our country, our people, our trade and our territorial integrity, the peace process' (Frost, 2021c). A similar message was reiterated eight days later by Frost in his 'observations on the present state of the nation' speech in which he characterised the Protocol as 'the biggest current problem' and 'source of mistrust' between the UK and the EU (Frost, 2021d). The following day, on 13 October, the EU published four 'non-papers' regarding the Protocol in which proposals for addressing 'the difficulties that people in Northern Ireland have been experiencing because of Brexit' were set out (European Commission, 2021f). The EU Non-Papers concerned SPS checks, customs formalities, engagement with Northern Ireland stakeholders, and security of medicines supplies. On the basis of, respectively, the UK Command Paper and the EU Non-Papers, so-called 'technical talks' between the UK and EU sides began and continued over the next few months. Somewhat regular meetings of the two Joint Committee Co-Chairs were held throughout this time. Progress was made on the issue of medicines with the EU publishing proposals on 17 December to amend relevant EU legislation so as to introduce various derogations designed to ease pressures on supply chains that would otherwise arise at the end of the applicable grace period (European Commission, 2021g). In relation to customs formalities, SPS checks, and governance, the two sides remained far apart, which fuelled speculation that the UK Government could actually act on its repeated threats to trigger Article 16 (see Connelly, 2021). No 'triggering' occurred. Lack of Article 16 drama was, perhaps, due to reports of the EU's willingness to take significant countermeasures, including potentially suspending the TCA. Instead, on 18 December, Lord Frost resigned citing 'concerns about the [general] direction of travel' of the government under Prime Minister Johnson (see *BBC News*, 2021f). Foreign Secretary Liz Truss took over responsibility as UK Co-Chair of the Joint Committee. Talks between the UK and the EU appeared more amicable in tone after Truss took up her new role and the two parties were able to agree an (almost) joint statement (see FCDO, 2022a; European Commission, 2022a). Notwithstanding a more cordial atmosphere the substantive issues and respective diverging positions remained the same, as did the UK Co-Chair's stated willingness to use Article 16.

The Protocol continued to be a focus of political contestation and Unionist ire in Northern Ireland. On 30 November 2021, the Court of Appeal in Belfast heard a challenge to the *Re Allister and Others* ruling on the lawfulness of the Protocol (see Campbell, 2021b). With the Appeal Court ruling still pending, on 2 February 2022, the DUP Agriculture Minister Edwin Poots ordered port officials to cease carrying out checks and controls required under the Protocol; this also led to legal action (see O'Carroll, 2022a). Judicial review proceedings were launched in relation to Minister Poots' decision; in the interim, the High Court in Belfast ordered officials to continue to carry out the relevant checks (*Law Society*, 2022). Against this backdrop, on 3 February, the DUP First Minister Paul Givan announced his resignation from office, thereby in effect collapsing the power-sharing Northern Ireland Executive

(Cousins, 2022; Maskey, 2022). Five days later, in Westminster, *the Northern Ireland (Ministers, Elections and Petitions of Concern) Act* 2022 (NI (MEPC) Act 2022) became law. Fulfilling commitments in the NDNA Agreement, this legislation replaced the previous fourteen- and seven-day time limits (in s16 of the 1998 Act) on Executive formation. Under the new provisions, Northern Ireland politicians would have up to four six-week periods for appointing Northern Ireland Ministers before another election would need to be called. Additionally, the NI (MEPC) Act 2022 introduced new provisions for Ministers in Departments that are not the Executive to remain in office for up to 24 weeks after an election, and for up to 48 weeks after the First or deputy First Minister stop holding office due to resignation (see NI 2022 (MEPC) Act s2 and 1998 Act s16A, as amended). These new legislative provisions were delivering part of a 'package of measures' designed to deliver 'sustainable' and 'resilient' institutions (New Decade New Approach, 2020: para. 14). Notably, however, without a First or deputy First Minister in office, no 'controversial or cross-cutting' decisions—including the passing of a budget—could be taken by the other Ministers who would remain in post in a 'caretaker capacity' (*ibid.* para. 18). In the run-up to the scheduled Northern Ireland Assembly election in May 2022, devolved government therefore continued to partially operate in this new and constrained manner.

At the end of February 2022, a Joint Committee meeting was held, the first since June 2021. A joint statement (this time genuine) was issued wherein the 'ongoing determination of both parties' to ensure 'outstanding issues' regarding Northern Ireland are addressed (FCDO, 2022b) was stated. A meeting of the Specialised Committee followed on 8 March (FCDO, 2022c). Despite these seemingly positive institutional activities, the UK and EU remained far apart on the substance of talks. The two parties' perspectives on the nature of the problem differed with the UK pursuing fundamental changes to the Protocol text and the EU pursuing technical fixes to arrangements for its implementation (see Whitten, 2022a). With limited prospects for significant progress in the short term and in view of the upcoming election in Northern Ireland, UK–EU talks were effectively paused at this time. The JCWG did, however, continue to carry out its operational functions.

Held on 5 May, the 2022 Northern Ireland Assembly election proved historic. For the first time, a Nationalist party—Sinn Féin—received the largest share of first preference votes (FPV) at 29% (+1.1%) and returned the most seats with 27 (no change). Support for Unionist parties was more divided than it had been in previous polls: the DUP were returned as the second largest party with 25 seats and 21.3% FPV representing a loss of three seats and −6.7% FPV. Lost first preference votes for the DUP appeared to go instead to the TUV party who adopt a harder line in relation to the Protocol and received 7.6% of FPV (an increase of 5.1%). Not being a 'transfer friendly' party, the increase in first preference votes for the TUV did not translate into seats with the party, only returning their established MLA Jim Wells. An additional dynamic in the results was the evident growth in support for the non-aligned Alliance Party who returned seventeen seats with 13.5% of FPV representing an increase of nine seats and 4.5% FPV respectively. Confirming trends from three elections in 2019, the increased electoral significance of Alliance arguably challenges the implicit premise of the Strand One institutional structure, namely that Northern Ireland society constitutes (only) 'two main communities' (1998 Agreement, S1: 5(c)). Politically, growing support for Alliance also raises questions for the moderate Unionist UUP and moderate Nationalist SDLP who returned nine seats (with 11.2% FPV) and eight seats (with 9.1% FPV) respectively representing a loss of one seat for the UUP (and −1.9% FPV) and four seats for the SDLP (and −2.9% in FPV).

The prospect of the first ever Sinn Féin First Minister did not incentivise Northern Ireland's largest Unionist party to reverse its pre-election policy of refusing to form a Northern Ireland Executive. The DUP instead maintained their stance and called for 'decisive action' on the Protocol (*RTÉ News*, 2022). Moreover, in the days that followed, the DUP took their abstentionist approach further by declining to support the election of an Assembly Speaker, which, in effect, blocked the new cadre of MLAs from taking their seats and/or the new Assembly from beginning its work (see McDonald, 2022).

Just a few weeks after the Assembly election, the UK Government introduced its *Northern Ireland Protocol Bill* (NIP Bill) which, if approved, would enable Ministers of the Crown to 'exclude' or disapply core elements of the Protocol in UK law—primarily those relating to trade in goods and to EU enforcement mechanisms. Additionally, if enacted, the NIP Bill would see *very* broad discretionary powers given to Ministers of the Crown to make regulations that would apply in Northern Ireland in any areas currently covered by the Protocol. The draft legislation also contained proposals for the creation of a 'dual regulatory regime' in Northern Ireland which would enable UK and/or EU regulations to apply alongside proposing a new system of 'red and green channels' for movement of goods GB–NI whereby goods not travelling on to Ireland/EU would enter via the green lane and thereby not be subject to the level of checks and controls currently required by the Protocol or, under the NIP Bill, required for goods entering via the red lane. Addressing existing provisions for enforcement, if enacted as introduced, the jurisdiction of the CJEU and related provisions for enforcement of EU law laid out in the Protocol would be 'excluded' or disapplied domestically, albeit with related powers given to Ministers of the Crown to (subject to their discretion) make relevant provisions, including potentially making provision for referrals to the CJEU.

In response to the introduction of the NIP Bill—which would amount to a wholesale change in the domestic legal effect of the Protocol if it became law—the EU revived existing and launched several new infringement proceedings—initially two, then an additional four—against the UK for alleged breaches of its obligations under the Protocol. As the NIP Bill began its parliamentary process, the European Commission launched a website on its *EUR-Lex* site dedicated to the Protocol and those EU laws it makes applicable to Northern Ireland (*EUR-Lex*, 2023). The EU announcement of more new infringement proceedings came two days after the NIP Bill passed its third reading in the House of Commons without amendment; it received 267 votes for and 195 against, a majority of 72 (Wheeler and Lynch, 2022). By the end of July, therefore, the EU had seven separate live legal cases against the UK (see European Commission, 2022b). Accompanying the announcement of the first new set of legal measures, the European Commission also published more detailed papers outlining its proposals for resolving issues regarding customs and SPS checks under the Protocol (see European Commission, 2022c). Notwithstanding oppositional developments in the realm of law, a change of personnel in Downing Street did appear to have a positive political effect, at least initially.

The departure of Boris Johnson and the arrival of Liz Truss as Prime Minister coincided with pronouncements of a UK desire to reach a negotiated settlement (Reuters, 2022). Under the rhetorical banner of a wider 're-set' in UK–EU relations, early October saw the newly installed Prime Minister Truss participating in an inaugural meeting of the European Political Community at the same time as 'good' first communications were taking place between new UK Co-Chair of the Joint Committee and Foreign Secretary James Cleverly and his EU counterpart Maroš Šefčovič (McGrath, 2022). A UK request for additional time to respond to infringement proceedings was also granted and the EU did not directly contest a UK announcement that existing 'grace periods' for checks and controls on GB–NI goods would be maintained (see O'Carroll, 2022). Yet, amid this more amicable political atmosphere, the UK and EU positions on the substantive issues that were the subject of talks between them had not changed and remained far apart. Although not directly related to the Protocol implementation, one of the early acts of the Truss Government was to introduce a long-awaited 'Brexit Freedoms' Bill in the form of the *Retained EU Law (Revocation and Reform) Bill* which proposes to disapply the majority of retained EU law by default at the end of 2023. If enacted as drafted, the REUL Bill had the potential to have a dramatic deregulatory effect on the UK statute book and create additional specific challenges in Northern Ireland. In particular, the REUL Bill could undermine areas of current and future North–South cooperation; areas of cooperation that are not specifically provided for in the Protocol rely to a large extent on the lingering equivalence between EU law in Ireland and retained EU law in Northern Ireland—the REUL Bill, as introduced, proposed to disapply the latter by default (see Clarke, Gravey, and Whitten, 2022; Phinnemore and Whitten, 2022b).

On 28 October, the legislative deadline for the formation of an Executive in Northern Ireland passed with no apparent progress to that end and, after another attempt to elect an Assembly Speaker, failed (see NI Assembly, 2022). Despite previously committing to immediately call an election, the NI Secretary initially prevaricated then confirmed that there would not be an election before the end of 2022 (Carroll, 2022a; 2022b). Instead, the government passed new legislation—the *Northern Ireland (Executive Formation etc) Act* 2022—to further extend the deadline for Executive formation and to grant exceptional powers to officials in Northern Ireland to carry out the 'exercise of functions' of government in the absence of Ministers (NI(EF) Act 2022, s3). With political parties in Northern Ireland united in their opposition to another election and the DUP holding firm to their Protocol-related abstentionism, the government further extended the deadline for Executive formation and/or calling an election until 19 January 2023.[3]

When the short-lived premiership of Liz Truss came to an end and, on 26 October, Rishi Sunak became the UK's first British Asian Prime Minister and third Conservative MP to hold the office in as many months. Yet another opportunity to 're-set' relations with the EU presented itself. Early contact between Prime Minister Sunak and European Commission President von der Leyen was characterised as 'encouraging' by the latter (von der Leyen in Pogatchnik, 2022) while communication between the Joint Committee Co-Chairs was unusually warm in nature (see @MarosSefcovic, 2022a). A separate but not unrelated sign of goodwill came in the form of Sunak's attendance at a summit meeting of the British-Irish Council in early November, the first time a UK Prime Minsiter had been present since 2007 (BIC, 2022b; DLUHC, 2022). Weeks later an in-person meeting of EU Co-Chair Šefčovič and UK Co-Chair Cleverly was said to be 'constructive' with both

---

[3] See *The Northern Ireland (Extension of Period for Making Ministerial Appointments) Regulations 2022* (SI 2022/1296). The 19 January 2023 deadline passed with no Executive formed. On 9 February 2023, the government introduced new legislation to again delay the obligation on the NI Secretary to call an election in Northern Ireland until 18 January 2024.

sides indicating their 'determination to find solutions' (@MarosSefcovic, 2022b; @JamesCleverly). Continuing in a spirit of accommodation, on 19 December, the European Commission announced an extension to an existing grace period until December 2025 for checks otherwise required under the Protocol on veterinary medicines entering Northern Ireland (European Commission, 2022d).

In the first weeks of 2023, another in-person meeting of the Joint Committee Co-Chairs Cleverly and Šefčovič—this time with NI Secretary Chris Heaton-Harris also joining—resulted in a joint statement wherein the meeting was described as 'cordial and constructive' (FCDO and NIO, 2023). Moreover, it was announced that an agreement had been reached between the two sides on 'the specific question of the EU's access to UK IT systems' which would provide a new basis for ongoing EU–UK discussions concerning the Protocol (*ibid.*). While positive, it is worth noting that such an 'access to data' agreement was anticipated in the text of the Protocol (see Article 12(2)). The fact that it had taken over two years to conclude a data access arrangement, and that this was considered significant progress, also indicates how slow-moving and how soured the UK–EU relationship became in the aftermath of Brexit and in the era of the Protocol.

9.2 Constitutional Consequences Within and Beyond Northern Ireland's Borders

In the 24 months after the Protocol entered fully into force, some findings from the initial research (see 8.3) have been more visible than others. The outworking of the EU's new role as protector of the 1998 Agreement and the vulnerability of Strand One institutions to external shocks have perhaps been the most prominent in the two years after 'getting Brexit done' became a reality. Other findings, such as the new democratic consent mechanism and the new incentives for North–South cooperation, have had less political significance so far and can only be expected to do so in time. Written from the perspective of January 2023, this section reflects on the events of the preceding two years in light of the findings from this research.

9.2.1 The New Protector: EU–NI Relations Post-Brexit

The EU has a greater role in Northern Ireland post-Brexit than it did pre-Brexit. This observation affirms and reflects the fact that, through the Brexit process and explicitly via the Protocol (Article 1(3)), the EU committed to 'protect the 1998 Agreement in all its dimensions'. Linked to the specific context of Brexit, the EU's protector role is distinct from, and less than, the 'guarantor' position of Ireland and the UK in respect to the 1998 Agreement (see 6.2). Nonetheless, the outworking of the EU's position in relation to Northern Ireland in the 24 months since the Protocol entered into force has been consequential and controversial. In substance, this post-Brexit EU–NI relationship has had a legal dimension and a political dimension. In respect to the former, a link has been established between EU law and NI law that flows directly from the Protocol's provision for the dynamic regulatory alignment with aspects of the EU *acquis*. In respect to the latter, as a consequence of UK withdrawal, and the Protocol it begot, the EU is more involved in Northern Ireland politics than was previously the case; this follows, at least in part, from its commitment to 'protect' the 1998 Agreement.

9.2.1.1 The Legal Dimension

The legal dimension of post-Brexit EU–NI relations is, to some extent, symbiotic. Although operationalising the Protocol primarily requires changes in UK(NI) law to reflect its dynamic regulatory alignment with aspects of the EU *acquis*, it has also resulted in changes in EU law to accommodate Northern Ireland (see Whitten, 2022c). So far, the most obvious example of EU legislative change arose due to concerns about the supply of medicines to Northern Ireland. A twelve-month 'grace period' arrangement regarding medicines formed part of the package of Joint Committee decisions reached just before the end of the transition period. Throughout 2021, however, consultations with pharmaceutical industry stakeholders underlined long-term risks to the supply of medicines to Northern Ireland if the requirement to comply with EU procedures under the Protocol were applied without amendment, primarily because of the small size of the UK(NI) market and prohibitive costs of UK(GB) suppliers developing separate UK(NI) production lines. With attempts to agree a UK–EU solution failing, the EU opted to unilaterally change its laws regarding medicines for human use that apply under the Protocol to address (at least some of) the issues pertaining to UK(NI). In April 2022, the European Parliament and Council approved legislation introducing derogations to address the post-Brexit supply of medicines for human use in Northern Ireland (European Commission, 2022e). From the UK perspective, there are some outstanding issues related to medicines supplies (see Cleverly, 2022); however, the process and fact of the EU adopting dedicated derogations for UK(NI) exemplifies the legal dimension of its commitment to uphold obligations under the Protocol. In the words of Co-Chair of the Joint Committee and European Commission Vice-President

Šefčovič, EU commitments under the Protocol involve ensuring 'predictability, legal certainty and the prosperity of all communities in Northern Ireland' (European Commission, 2022e). By referencing 'all communities', Šefčovič's terminology has echoes of that used in the 1998 Agreement; the language is also notably exclusive in stating the purpose of Šefčovič's ongoing work to be for prosperity in Northern Ireland alone.

Additionally, on the matter of legal certainty, the EU's launch in the summer 2022 of a new section on its official website of law—*EUR-Lex*—dedicated to the recording of those instruments that apply under the Protocol is another indicator of the novelty of the post-Brexit EU–NI relationship and its legal substance from an EU perspective. Responding to the launch of the new *EUR-Lex* section, the UK Foreign Secretary stated the government position that its contents were 'not endorsed' by the UK as it provided the 'the EU's view' of legislation that applies under the Protocol rather than one which is jointly agreed (Cleverly, 2022). There is no comprehensive record of Protocol-applicable law that *is* endorsed by the UK Government, and it has stated that it does not intend to publish one despite parliamentary pressure to do so (see *ibid.*; Ewelme, 2023). The UK position means that, notwithstanding its 'unilateral' nature, as the EU's website is the only comprehensive official and publicly available record of Protocol-applicable law, it provides an important resource for anyone involved in, or affected by, the implementation of the Protocol and could therefore be said to represent an additional dimension to the newly significant EU–NI relationship.

Given the unprecedented nature of the Protocol in EU law terms—the automaticity of alignment with and participation in the single market for goods—and the exceptional context of its implementation—in a post-Brexit UK actively pursuing divergence from the EU market—it is reasonable to assume that implementation will continue to involve amendments and/or derogations in Protocol-applicable law developed at the EU level. The political contestation surrounding the Protocol perhaps makes this even more probable because any UK non-compliance with its obligations to keep pace with Protocol-applicable acts could provide a catalyst for the adoption of legislative derogations or mitigations on the part of the EU. This scenario, which is even more pertinent following the introduction of the NIP Bill, raises questions about how much risk the EU is willing to tolerate to its single market, particularly if/when the UK diverges from the standards that it currently (largely) retains. As of January 2023, the EU has seven separate infringement proceedings against the UK for various issues of non-compliance or non-implementation of EU laws under the Protocol; the nature and timing of their resolution will be an important indicator of the EU's intended approach for managing risk in relation to the Protocol and its legal integrity. As time goes on and the respective regulatory orders of the UK and the EU chart separate paths, the potential for UK(NI) to fall behind EU law requirements under the Protocol will increase, whether intentionally in protest against its terms, or unintentionally due to its inherent complexity and constrained capacity in Northern Ireland to implement it. The operationalisation of the Protocol going forward thus constitutes a perpetual risk to the EU single market. The EU's commitment to 'protect' the 1998 Agreement is therefore likely to continue to necessitate consideration and accommodation of the unique position of UK(NI) in relevant EU law developments.

For Northern Ireland, the requirement to implement changes arising from its dynamic regulatory alignment under the Protocol flows (at the time of writing) through section 7A of the EUWA 2018. In the two years since the Protocol entered into force, changes arising from 'amendments and replacements' in Protocol-applicable EU law have been made by secondary legislation passed in Westminster (via statutory instruments) and in Stormont (via statutory rules). To date, due to the relative stability in retained EU law across the whole of the UK and the generally slow pace of development in EU law, there are only a handful of examples of domestic secondary legislation being used to implement changes arising from the Article 13(3) requirement for dynamic regulatory alignment (for detail see Whitten, 2022d).[4] This novel post-Brexit process for UK(NI) law-making—via Protocol Article 13(3) and section 7A of the EUWA 2018—can be expected to become more significant over time if, as anticipated, the EU regulatory order diverges from the UK regulatory order, and presuming UK(NI) continues to apply the former in areas covered by the Protocol. If enacted as drafted, the NIP Bill would undermine the present post-Brexit arrangement by decoupling what is currently Protocol-applicable EU law from EU legislative procedures and enforcement mechanisms by placing the power to amend UK versions of these instruments into the discretionary hands of central UK Government Ministers. Such a prospect links to another aspect of Brexit's impact identified in this analysis, namely that it has led to a strengthening of UK executive power

---

[4] Examples include: the Medical Devices (Northern Ireland Protocol) Regulations 2021 (SI 2021/905) brought in to implement EU Regulation 2017/745 on medical devices which came into effect in Northern Ireland, by dint of the Protocol, in May 2021; the Market Surveillance (Northern Ireland) Regulations 2021 (SI 2021/858) which implements Regulation (EU) 2019/1020 on Market Surveillance and Compliance (*Official Journal* 2019b) which came into effect in Northern Ireland under the Protocol in July 2021; the Hydrocarbon Oil and Biofuels (Northern Ireland Private Pleasure Craft) Regulations 2021 (SI 2021/780) is another example; this instrument prohibits the use of rebated fuel (red diesel) for use in private pleasure craft in Northern Ireland and marked the final step required to implement a 2018 ruling by the CJEU on the matter (Case C–503/17 *Commission v United Kingdom of Great Britain and Northern Ireland* [2018]); the same changes were not made in UK(GB) legislation.

and a corresponding weakening of devolved power in the Northern Ireland context. While this arises directly from the Protocol due to the lack of requirement for devolved input and the effective rebalancing of the proportion of international law vs domestic (including devolved) law that applies in Northern Ireland, this 'power-hoarding' dynamic has also been exacerbated by UK legislative initiatives introduced in 2022—including the NIP Bill which, as discussed, proposes to give Ministers of the Crown extensive discretionary powers. Moreover, although not directly related, the passing of the NI(EF) Act 2022 in reaction to steps taken to protest against the outworkings of Brexit gives law-making powers to officials in Northern Ireland subject only to a broad 'public interest' test and the oversight of the NI Secretary. The NI(EF) Act 2022 has therefore accelerated the increase in centralisation of arrangements for law and policy development that apply in post-Brexit Northern Ireland. Constraints on the law-making capacity in Northern Ireland arising from prolonged stalemate and the 'exceptional' provisions of the NI(EF) Act 2022 is *potentially* relevant in the context of the legally novel EU–NI relationship because it may have implications regarding the willingness and effectiveness of UK Ministers when it comes to implementing obligations that arise due to changes in EU laws that apply under the Protocol.

9.2.1.2 The Political Dimension

The EU has played a prominent role in Northern Ireland politics in the two years since the Protocol entered into force. Amidst the atmosphere of contestation over the Protocol, the level of EU engagement with Northern Ireland stakeholders has been notable. The primary context for direct contact of this nature has been between EU Co-Chair Vice-President Šefčovič alongside supporting officials in the European Commission on the one hand and representatives from Northern Ireland business, civic society, and political parties on the other.[5] In addition to ad hoc online meetings, Šefčovič and his officials visited Northern Ireland in September 2021 to hold in-person meetings with politicians from all sides of related debates as well as with business leaders, rights bodies, and civic groups; Šefčovič also delivered a speech about the Protocol during the trip (European Commission, 2021h; BBC News, 2021g). This visit came as a result of Šefčovič's appearance before the Executive Office Committee in the NI Assembly in June 2021 (NI Assembly, 2021a). Read in the context of EU external relations more broadly, both

---

[5] There have been numerous instances of direct contact between other EU institutions/representatives and Northern Ireland stakeholders/representatives throughout 2021 and 2022; some recent examples include a European Parliament trade delegation visit to NI (European Parliament, 2022) and a European Economic and Social Committee visit to NI (@EESC_REX, 2022).

instances exemplify the remarkably high level of attention being granted to a sub-state entity of a non-Member State on the part of the EU.

The clearest and most consequential demonstration of the new significance of relations with the EU as a political issue in Northern Ireland post-Brexit is the lack of a functioning NI Executive and Assembly due the DUP's ongoing protest against the Protocol. In stark contrast with previous political epochs in Northern Ireland, the nature of its relationship with the EU has been *the* predominant political issue since the end of the transition period (see 4.2.2). While this affirms the finding observed regarding the vulnerability of Strand One institutions to external shocks (see 5.2.2), it also raises (as yet unanswered) questions about their future viability. Regardless of if/how those questions are resolved, as a result of Brexit (and the Protocol it begot) ensuring that the principles and provisions of the 1998 Agreement endure is not only a duty undertaken by its co-guarantors—the UK and Ireland—the EU also has a role given its new commitment to 'protect' it 'in all dimensions'.

In the setting of Northern Ireland politics, it is worth stating that 'No Irish Sea Border' and expressions to that effect can currently be found in spray paint inscription on gable walls or printed on posters fastened to lampposts in many (majority Unionist/Loyalist) areas of Northern Ireland. Flags with anti-Protocol messages strung up in public places have featured the faces of senior EU representatives—most often Vice-President Šefčovič—throughout 2021 and 2022. Describing the content of flags and graffiti may seem frivolous to the unacquainted, but in Northern Ireland, political opinions, priorities, and demographics are often demarcated visually. The new EU/Protocol orientation of Northern Ireland street art is an indication of the increased political salience of the EU–NI relationship after Brexit.

9.2.2 Creation and Contestation: The Principle of Consent Post-Brexit

Amid the contested political atmosphere that followed the end of the UK transition period and in the two years thereafter, the reaffirmation of the principle of consent in Article 1(1) of the Protocol has largely been overlooked or discounted. Moreover, contrary to the 'without prejudice' guarantee in the text, the Protocol has been interpreted by Northern Ireland Unionist and some Eurosceptic Conservative representatives as having undermined the 'principle of consent', albeit with arguments based on a particular and, in some respects, novel interpretation of it. Contestation over the impact (or non-impact) of the Protocol on the principle of consent featured prominently in high-profile judicial review cases brought against the UK Government and challenging the lawfulness of its enactment. Given their direct relevance to the research findings, it is of value to set out the facts of the proceedings as they relate to the principle of consent in some detail before reflecting on their implications for the Northern Ireland constitution going forward.

In February 2021, judicial review proceedings challenging the lawfulness of the Protocol were brought against the Prime Minister, the NI Secretary, and the Chancellor of the Duchy of Lancaster by Mr Clifford Peeples. In March 2021, judicial review proceedings challenging the lawfulness of the Protocol were brought against the NI Secretary by a cross-party group of Unionists including TUV leader James Hugh Allister, former Conservative and Brexit Party MEP Benyamin Naeem Abib, Baroness Catherine Hoey of Lylehill and Rathlin, former UUP leader Steve Aiken, former DUP leader and First Minister Rt Hon Arlene Isobel Foster, and former UUP leader and First Minister Rt Hon Baron Trimble of Lisnagarvey. Both sets of proceedings were heard together and dismissed together by Colton J. on 30 June 2021 (*Allister and others* [2021] NIQB 64). Following appeal both proceedings were again heard together and dismissed together in the Court of Appeal on 14 March 2022 (*Allister and others* [2022] NICA 15). The appellants were granted leave to appeal to the UK Supreme Court on three of the issues considered by the lower courts where these were again dismissed on 8 February 2023 (*Allister and others* [2023] UKSC 5). Focusing on the arguments that came before the Supreme Court (these relate most directly to understandings of consent) the appellants contended as follows. First, that the Protocol conflicts with Article VI of the Acts of Union 1800 regarding the 'equal footing' of British and Irish citizens regarding 'privileges and bounties' and, therefore, the UK Government's use of the prerogative power in agreeing the Withdrawal Agreement and Protocol was unlawful. Second, that section 1(1) of the 1998 Act does not only regulate whether Northern Ireland should remain part of the UK or become part of Ireland but should be interpreted more widely such that any substantial diminution in the constitutional status of Northern Ireland—like unto (in the appellants view) that brought about by the Protocol—can only occur if approved by a poll held under Schedule 1 of the 1998 Act. Third, that the disapplication of section 42 of the 1998 Act (regarding cross-community 'petition of concern' protections) under the 'democratic consent mechanism' 2020 Regulations—made under section 8C of the EUWA 2018—was unlawful on the grounds that doing so is contrary to the 1998 Act and therefore *ultra vires* on the basis of section 10(1)(a) of the EUWA 2018 whereby exercise powers under the 2018 Act cannot be incompatible with the 1998 Act.

Addressing the first argument—concerning Article VI of the Acts of Union—the Court judged that the Protocol had 'modified' in part the 'equal footing' provision in Article VI of the Acts of Union (*Allister and others*, 2023 [67]) but not repealed it; moreover, the relevant statutory language in section 7A of EsUWA 2018 was clear, purposive, and therefore took precedence over any earlier enactments, including the 1800 Acts (*ibid.* [68]). Regarding the lawfulness of the UK Government use of the prerogative power to agree the Withdrawal Agreement (including the Protocol) in view of the second clause of Article VI of the Acts of Union (*ibid.* [6–10]), the Court dismissed the appellants' arguments on the basis that parliamentary authorisation was repeatedly given for the exercise of prerogative powers to this end (*ibid.* [73–76]). Addressing the second argument—concerning section 1(1) of the 1998 Act—the Court pointed to the conclusion and reasoning in *Miller* (2017) when a similar question was put regarding the potential unlawfulness of triggering Article 50 TEU without a poll being held in accordance with section 1(1) of the 1998 Act. As discussed in detail in Chapter 5 (see 5.2.1), the Court in *Miller* determined that the 1998 Act requirement for the exercise of popular consent did not regulate any change in the constitutional status of Northern Ireland other than whether it remains part of the UK or joins a UI (see 2017 [135]). Agreeing with the earlier judgments in *Miller* and that of the lower courts (see *Allister and others*, 2021 [127]; *Allister and others*, 2021 [222][410]), the second ground of appeal in *Allister and others* (2023) was dismissed. Addressing the third argument—concerning section 42 of the 1998 Act and the democratic consent mechanism 2020 Regulations—the Court acknowledged the 'potential force of the appellants' argument' (2023 [107]) that section 42 of the 1998 Act applies to 'a matter which is to be voted on by the Assembly' even if it is on a matter which is outside the legislative competence as is the case in relation to the continuation or cessation of Articles 5 to 10 of the Protocol; this would imply that section 42 was unlawfully disapplied by the 2020 Regulations. However, the Court determined that this matter was academic and not necessary to determine on the basis that section 7A of the EUWA 2018 had already modified the 1998 Act prior to the making of the 2020 Regulations to the effect that, at the time of their creation, the content of the 2020 Regulations was compatible with the amended 1998 Act and their making was therefore lawful (*Allister and others*, 2023 [108]).

Notwithstanding the judicial dismissal of the appellants in *Allister and others*, their substance, and the fact of their being brought by a group of high-profile, cross-party Unionist politicians, is noteworthy in light of this research; several points ought to be made. The 1998 Agreement principle of consent provisions can be, and have been, interpreted narrowly or broadly;

the former tends to give primacy to legal provisions for the exercise of consent while the latter tends to lean more on political commitments to it as a principle (see 3.2.2). As set out in Chapter 4, the case for viewing the UK's decision to withdraw from the EU as impinging on the principle of consent broadly understood did not enjoy prominence during the UK's EU referendum (see 4.2.1). As set out in Chapter 5, a broader interpretation of the principle of consent came to the fore in legal action taken regarding the triggering of Article 50 TEU (see 5.2.1). The Supreme Court in *Miller* (2017), however, favoured and affirmed a narrow interpretation of the 1998 Act provision for the exercise of consent, albeit while failing to engage with the broader question put by appellants regarding the possible relevance of the 1998 Agreement (*ibid.*). In view of its earlier judgment, the Supreme Court ruling on the question of constitutional consent in *Allister and others* is unsurprising, particularly given the sole reliance on provisions in the 1998 Act without reference to the 1998 Agreement on the part of the appellants which may (although also may not) have prompted the Court to clarify the relevance or otherwise of the international law dimension. The fact of the matter being raised, again, in relation to the outworking of Brexit is nonetheless important. In view of the findings of this research, it can be said that broad interpretations of the principle of consent now have more political purchase and profile in Northern Ireland than was the case prior to, and in the first stage of, the Brexit process. At the same time, and somewhat paradoxically, a narrow, legal interpretation of the principle of consent has, as a consequence of the Brexit process, been reinforced both in international law, as per the Protocol Article 1(1), and judicially in domestic case law, as per *Miller* and now also *Allister and others*.

In respect to arguments made by the appellants in *Allister and others* regarding cross-community consent (arising from 1998 Act s42), similar observations can be made about their premise on a broad understanding of the consent principle and its evident renewed political prominence in Northern Ireland. Notwithstanding parallels, there is a greater degree of novelty at work in arguments against the Protocol on the basis of cross-community consent. Arguments contending that the UK Government's negotiation and agreement to the terms of the Protocol, and its subsequent domestic ratification ought to have been made subject to securing cross-community consent in the NI Assembly—via the petition of concern mechanism provided for in section 42 of the 1998 Act—rely on an expansive (and arguably decontextualised) reading of the relevant provisions. As set out in Chapter 7 (see 7.2.1.4), the democratic consent mechanism is constitutionally innovative insomuch as it provides opportunity for the devolved legislature in Northern Ireland to take a definitive vote on an explicitly non-devolved matter—relations with the EU. The appellants in *Allister* proposed that the unconditional wording of section 42(1) of the 1998 Act regarding petitions of concern which can be presented on 'a matter which is to be voted on by the Assembly' renders irrelevant the fact that the democratic consent mechanism vote is on a non-devolved issue; it would follow that the petition of concern ought to apply. As noted above, the Court found 'potential force' [107] in the appellants position but found it unnecessary to decide definitively due to the implications of section 7A of the EUWA 2018 on the 1998 Act. As in *Miller* (see 5.2.1), the Supreme Court opted not to provide clarification on a matter of potential constitutional significance in Northern Ireland. On the substance of the argument, several points are worth making. Firstly, that introducing restrictions on the use of 'petitions of concern' such that only certain types of legislation and/or only legislation related to specified issues with a 'cross-community' dimension would be subject to section 42 of the 1998 Act was considered as an option during a review of the mechanism carried out by the NI Assembly (see Assembly and Executive Review Committee, 2014). As there was no consensus between political parties on the matter, no decision was taken; if one had been made, it is unlikely the appellants could have made the arguments they did regarding cross-community consent. Secondly, in regard to competence, it is noteworthy that petitions of concern can, at least in theory, be laid in relation to legislative consent motions (LCMs) (see Cabinet Office, 2022c: Appendix F); this is not, however, normal practice in the NI Assembly and changes introduced to the operation of the petitions of concern mechanism (by the *Northern Ireland (Ministers, Elections and Petitions of Concern) Act 2022*) make the (still hypothetical) timelines that would be involved in initiating a section 42 mechanism on an LCM extremely tight. Thirdly, it is worth making the point that *if* the reasoning of proponents in *Allister and others* were accepted, in theory any initiative successfully brought to the Assembly by a political party or by an MLA could be subject to cross-community consent regardless of whether or not it was within the competence of the Northern Ireland legislature and executive. While this could be an interesting exercise—one could imagine for example votes on the acceptability or otherwise of trade agreements negotiated by the UK Government—it could not have any bearing on legal enactments, at least not as a direct consequence of the result in the Assembly. This is because, regarding the legislative competence of the Assembly, the 1998 Act is unambiguous. Any provisions made by the Assembly that are outside its legislative competence 'are not law' (s6(1)) and competence is limited to that which is the law of Northern Ireland—any provision that would form part of the law of a country or territory other than Northern Ireland 'is outside that competence' (s6(2)(a)) as, of course, is any provision that 'deals with an excepted matter' (s6(2)(b)). Articles 5 to 10 of the Protocol make provisions that are applicable outside as well as inside the territory of Northern Ireland and they deal with 'international relations' which are explicitly excepted under the 1998 Act (Sch 2(3)). By implication, *if* the appellants argument had been accepted by the Supreme Court regarding the unlawfulness of the 2020 Regulations due to the necessity for the petition of concern to apply to any matter on which the Assembly voted regardless of competence, lack of cross-community consent would likely only ever be symbolic if/when votes were taken on matters that 'are not law' due to lack of competence. The UK Government would be lawfully able to ignore the absence of cross-community consent, just as is already the case in relation to LCMs and as the democratic consent mechanism already provides.

Regarding any direct impact of the democratic consent mechanism, this will not become clear until the first vote is held by the end of 2024 (see Phinnemore and Whitten, 2022a). While it is, therefore, only in time that the impact of its outworkings on the Northern Ireland constitution will become clear, in view of the deeply contested nature of the Protocol in its first two years, the holding of democratic consent mechanism votes every (presumably) four years can be expected to have a disruptive and divisive effect in the politics of Northern Ireland, at least in the medium term. Based on the results of the May 2022 Assembly elections, it appears likely that there would be a majority without cross-community consent in favour of the continued applicability of Articles 5 to 10 (*ibid.*). Notwithstanding the relative stability in respect to arrangements for trade and governance that this would affect, the collapse and prolonged absence of Strand One institutions due to opposition to the Protocol on the part of the DUP also suggests that Brexit and the Protocol it begot has not only stymied progress in the immediate term but is also likely to subject the deeply divided politics of Northern Ireland to routine, contentious votes that—reasonably or otherwise—will become proxies for politicians' preferences regarding the constitutional future of the place; this is unfortunate.

9.2.3 Exacerbating Fragility: Strand One Institutions Post-Brexit

Strand One institutions in contemporary Northern Ireland face the dual challenge of political stagnation and legal dynamism. As demonstrated during the Brexit process, the constraints of power-sharing devolution render the executive and legislature in Northern Ireland liable to collapse if/when either the largest Nationalist or the largest Unionist party decides to act to that end. Although this phenomena derives from the 1998 Agreement, not from Brexit or the Protocol, the changed context in which devolution must operate following UK withdrawal from the EU exacerbates its existing vulnerability to periods of stagnation while also changing, in part, the default legislative requirements that apply regardless of the functioning/non-functioning of devolved government. Events of 2021 and 2022 have reaffirmed that the existing fragility of Strand One institutions has been exacerbated by Brexit and its repercussions.

Previous instances of collapse and consequential hiatus in the functioning of devolved government in Northern Ireland have been rooted in and justified by developments in its own politics. By contrast, the resignation of the DUP First Minister in February 2022 and subsequent refusal of the party to re-establish the devolved institutions is rooted in and justified by developments in UK foreign policy and UK–EU relations. The DUP's reasoning behind its recent decision to collapse Strand One institutions is indicative of the fact that Brexit has catalysed an expansion and diversification of political debates in Northern Ireland while simultaneously making its legislative landscape more complex. Since the Protocol entered into force, discussions and divisions in Northern Ireland have centred on topics such as the level of customs controls and SPS checks applicable at its ports/airports, the construction of border control posts, the legitimacy or otherwise of the application of EU law and judicial oversight as well as the consequences of regulatory alignment and/or divergence with UK and/or EU rules. Technical and practical issues concerning the implementation of the Protocol are not *prima facie* linked to established divisions between Unionists and Nationalists in Northern Ireland. To a significant degree, however, since the Protocol took effect in January 2021, it and issues related to its implementation have become effective proxies for established ethno-nationalist divides in the politics of Northern Ireland—with Unionists generally against and Nationalists (and non-aligned) generally in favour. Formally, however, responsibility for implementing the Protocol and resolving related issues rests with, respectively, the central UK Government and the EU–UK Joint Committee. Taken together then, as a consequence of Brexit, the number of potentially polarising policy issues that power-sharing government in Northern Ireland is likely to need to overcome has increased while the capacity of its representatives to resolve those same issues has decreased; this renders the already fragile institutions of devolution even more vulnerable to collapse.

The legislative landscape in post-Brexit Northern Ireland is complex. Remaining dynamically aligned with EU single market rules that are in the scope of the Protocol while also remaining part of the UK internal market which is (at least under the current Conservative Party Government) in active pursuit of divergence from those same EU rules, poses challenges for Northern Ireland related to legal complexity, policy coherence, parliamentary scrutiny, and official capacity. To ensure adequate legal clarity and certainty, there is a need for politicians and officials in Northern Ireland to track developments in multiple spheres, including (but not limited to): Protocol-applicable EU law; (potentially) Protocol-related EU law; UK law developments in Great Britain (at national and at devolved level) corresponding to Protocol-applicable law in Northern Ireland; EU law (generally and its specific implementation in Ireland) and UK law (at national and devolved level) in areas of North–South cooperation that are not directly provided for in the Protocol; as well as any implications of new UK free trade agreements, particularly as regards trade in goods. Maintaining this degree of legislative monitoring is no small task; doing so without ministerial direction and/or parliamentary scrutiny in devolved areas (as is currently the case) will be even more difficult and is liable to lead to negative, unmanaged policy outcomes for Northern Ireland.

Due to the combined effect of political polarisation, institutional stagnation and legislative complexity, the relations and structures underpinning Strand One of the 1998 Agreement have to endure pressures in the post-Brexit era that were not envisaged when the agreement was signed. Whether or not devolved government can be restored in Northern Ireland in the near future, and/or the institutions and representatives of Strand One prove capable of managing the complexities and challenges of their post-Brexit circumstance, remains to be seen.

9.2.4 Complex and Contingent: The North–South Dimension Post-Brexit

Since the collapse of the Northern Ireland Executive in February 2022, the North–South Ministerial Council has not met. Similar to the three-year hiatus in functioning devolution during EU–UK withdrawal negotiations, the contingency of effective operation of Strand Two of the 1998 Agreement on effective operation of Strand One is once again (all too) evident. The last plenary meeting of the NSMC was in July 2021 (see NSMC, 2023a). In the absence of functioning Northern Ireland institutions, the work of N–S implementation bodies has also been stymied with the last formal meeting of one of the six taking place in November 2021 (NSMC, 2023b). However, as underlined by the mapping exercise undertaken during UK withdrawal (see 6.2.3.1), cooperation on the island of Ireland is not limited to that which takes place under 1998 Agreement institutions. In many areas, North–South cooperation has continued without discernible disruption notwithstanding the end of the UK transition period.

One area in which the continuation of N–S cooperation is particularly evident is in respect to trade. Data indicates that, since UK withdrawal from the EU, trade between Ireland and Northern Ireland has increased significantly while trade between Ireland and Great Britain has decreased in the same period. According to the Central Statistics Office (CSO), between the first quarter of 2019 and the first quarter of 2022, Ireland's exports to Northern Ireland as a share of its total exports to the UK increased from 16% to 23% while the share of imports increased from 12% to 18% over the same period (2022).[6] NISRA data reports similar trends with the total sales from Northern Ireland to Ireland in 2021 the highest on record at £5.2bn representing 6.7% of total NI sales and just over two fifths (42.5%) of NI sales outside the UK (NISRA, 2022). On one level, evident growth in N–S trade can be interpreted as *prima facie* evidence of the Protocol working as intended in respect to maintaining necessary conditions for N–S cooperation. While this may be so, it is also noteworthy that at least some of the growth in N–S trade is likely due to a reorientation of freight traffic rather than necessarily indicating substantive new business to business trading on the island of Ireland. Ports in Northern Ireland reported a substantial boost in profits after the end of the transition period with Belfast Harbour, for example, reporting that a record 25.6mn tonnes of cargo passed through the port in 2021 with a corresponding record turnover of £73.3m for the year, representing a 17% increase on previous figures (see Belfast Harbour Commissioners, 2022). Belfast Harbour Commissioners cited the impact of grace periods associated with the Protocol as well as 'some traffic diversion from Dublin port' services as contributing to its record profits (*ibid.*: 80). In view of the UK Government's 'unfettered access' guarantee for Northern Ireland businesses trading into Great Britain (New Decade New Approach, 2020: 10), the diversion of at least some freight

---

[6] CSO data indicates that exports from Ireland to Great Britain fell from €13.4bn in 2019 to €12.3bn in 2020 and recovered to €14.4bn in 2021; by contrast, exports from Ireland to Northern Ireland were around €2.5bn in 2019 and 2020 but increased to €3.7bn in 2021. Imports from Great Britain to Ireland fell from €18.2bn in 2019 to €15.4bn in 2021; imports from Northern Ireland to Ireland increased from €2.4bn in 2019 to €4bn in 2021 (see Central Statistics Office, 2023)

that, for example, travelled Dublin–Holyhead pre-Brexit to Belfast–Stranraer post-Brexit is to be expected.

Outside of cross-border trade are those areas of cooperation listed in Article 11 of the Protocol (see 6.2.3.3). Pre-Brexit, cooperation in many of these areas was facilitated by shared EU law and policy frameworks that no longer apply (as EU law) in Northern Ireland. In the post-Brexit paradigm, divergence in these areas of N–S cooperation is therefore possible; however, to date the potentiality of significant, widespread N–S divergence has not been realised; established cooperation has continued largely unhindered. This is partly due to the lingering equivalence of relevant law/policy on either side of the land border due to the continuation of EU law (in respect to Ireland) and the presence of corresponding retained EU law (in respect to Northern Ireland). If enacted, the REUL Bill would therefore change the legislative basis on which N–S cooperation in many areas has continued post-transition period. The REUL Bill's proposed 'sunsetting' of the majority of retained EU laws by default at the end of 2023 puts some areas of established North–South cooperation at risk through what would be the consequential automatic overnight divergence of standards and regulations on either side of the land border. In policy terms, the potential scope of the proposed default disapplication of large swathes of retained EU law in Northern Ireland is significant. Specifically for North–South cooperation, those areas which were underpinned by EU law/policy pre-Brexit but are not directly provided for in Protocol-applicable EU law/policy post-Brexit are particularly exposed—in substance this includes cooperation in the area of the environment, police and judicial cooperation, transport, sport, education, tourism, and healthcare (see Whitten, 2022b).

Under the REUL Bill, Ministers are to be granted the power to 'restate' any retained EU law before the sunset came into effect. While this restatement process could be used to mitigate the otherwise regressive impact of the Bill on North–South cooperation, it also raises questions regarding capacity of officials and politicians to identify and then 'restate' via regulations all relevant legislation in advance of the 2023 deadline. Without a functioning devolved government, the likelihood of the administration in Northern Ireland being able to adequately review and/or restate relevant laws is very slim indeed (see Clarke, Gravey, Whitten 2022). Moreover, the deregulatory preference of the REUL Bill, whereby any UK Minister seeking to restate or revise (what are currently) retained EU laws cannot do so if this would increase the regulatory burden on impacted stakeholders (see Gravey and Reid, 2022). This is particularly problematic when it comes to N–S cooperation given that Ireland, as an EU Member State, is not likely to follow a deregulatory trajectory. UK Ministers, under the REUL Bill, could not 'restate' any legislation in the scope of the 'sunset' even if doing so was a 'necessary condition' of continued N–S cooperation.

Alongside lingering legislative equivalence, evidence also suggests that mitigations of potential 'gaps' where shared EU law/policy previously underpinned N–S working have been undertaken on an iterative basis by industry as well as by government (for more detail see Whitten, 2022b). This applies, for example, in the area of family law and child protection cases. Prior to Brexit, the cross-jurisdictional recognition and enforcement of matters in family law between Ireland and Northern Ireland was underpinned by an instrument of EU law—Council Regulation EC 2201/2003 also known as 'Brussels IIa'—which no longer applies in Northern Ireland. In August 2021, a *Protocol between Northern Ireland and Ireland for Handling of Inter-Jurisdictional Child Cases* (Child Protection Protocol) was published. This Child Protection Protocol 2021 superseded a similar, earlier agreement[7] and set out revised arrangements for cross-border cooperation following the end of the UK transition period and the corresponding end to the application of Brussels IIa Regulation in Northern Ireland which could therefore no longer be used as a basis for progressing any new cross-border cases (Department of Health and Department of Children, Equality, Disability, Integration and Youth, 2021: para. 3.5). Instead, three international law conventions—the 1996 *Hague Convention on Jurisdiction, Applicable Law, Recognition, Enforcement and Co-operation in respect of Parental Responsibility and Measures for the Protection of Children*; the 2005 *Hague Convention on Choice of Court Agreements*; and the 2007 *Hague Convention on the International Recovery of Child Support and other Forms of Family Maintenance*—would underpin continued N–S cooperation in respect to child protection cases after 1 January 2021. As an EU Member State, the UK had been party to the three Hague Conventions by dint of their EU membership. Prior to the end of the transition period, the UK became a party in its own right with domestic effect being given to the Conventions in the *Private International Law (Implementation of Agreements) Act 2020* (PIL 2020, s1; EN: paras 8–9). The Child Protection Protocol 2021 also notes the importance of cross-jurisdictional data sharing for the purposes of child protection matters (2021: paras 3.7 and 3.8); in this respect EU decisions on the adequacy of the UK's data protection regime serves an essential facilitative function for continued N–S cooperation in child protection matters. While this example demonstrates the possibility for

---

[7] The *Inter-Jurisdictional Protocol for Transfer of Children's Social Care Cases between Northern Ireland and the Republic of Ireland*, agreed in November 2011.

continued N–S cooperation despite the decoupling of Ireland and Northern Ireland law and policy in areas previously covered by EU law in both jurisdictions, it also underlines the added complexity and piecemeal nature of 'necessary conditions' after Brexit.

For established areas of N–S cooperation and (very likely) any future areas of N–S cooperation that are not underpinned by Protocol-applicable EU law, continuation is contingent on the degree of complementarity of legal and policy developments between Ireland and Northern Ireland. By implication, in the post-Brexit era, the level of equivalence between the two jurisdictions on the island of Ireland is also likely to be influenced by any decisions taken on a UK-wide basis, on a bilateral UK–Ireland basis, on a unilateral Ireland basis, on a bilateral UK–EU basis as well as in the EU context to the extent of applicability in Ireland and/or Northern Ireland under the Protocol. Upholding the Protocol's objective to 'maintain necessary conditions' (Article 1(3)) for N–S cooperation broadly understood can therefore be assumed to be an inherently complex task and one that is more contingent and less certain in the post-Brexit era than at any time since the 1998 Agreement was signed almost 25 years ago.

9.2.5 Tensions and Inventions: The East–West Dimension Post-Brexit

Since the end of the UK transition period and the entry into full force of the Protocol (alongside the TCA), the institutions established under Strand Three of the 1998 Agreement have been marginally more active than they were during the Brexit process.

9.2.5.1 Interjurisdictional Relations and Institutions After Brexit

The British-Irish Council held four Summit meetings and seven Sectoral meetings in 2021 and 2022; this compares to three Summit meetings and four Sectoral meetings in 2019 and 2020 (see BIC, 2023a; 2023b). In November 2022, Rishi Sunak became the first UK Prime Minister in fifteen years to attend a BIC Summit meeting. Coming after years of strained relations between the UK Government and other BIC members—largely due to Brexit—Sunak's decision to take part in the BIC Summit was generally viewed as a positive and conciliatory step. In a statement, the UK Minister for Intergovernmental Relations, Rt Hon Michael Gove MP, said that 'the Prime Minister's attendance and constructive conversations with the First Ministers is a clear signal of our renewed ambition to work more closely together'

(DLUHC, 2022). The language used in respect to 'First Ministers' is notable for its focus on UK devolved administrations and its implicit exclusion of the Irish *Prime* Minister (or Taoiseach) and the Crown Dependencies *Chief* Ministers. Given that, in contrast to the other BIC members, Ireland is a separate state with no constitutional relationship to the UK Government, the rhetorical slippage on the part of Minister Gove arguably excludes (and/or insults) the Irish Taoiseach most directly. Without seeking to over-interpret one official statement, there are some noteworthy parallels between the language of the UK Government following the November 2022 BIC Summit and some similarly un-nuanced statements made in the run-up to and immediate aftermath of the UK's EU referendum in regard to their depiction and/or exclusion of Ireland (see 4.2.4).

Representing a progression of BIC discussions on activities of Member Administrations related 'to the UK's exit from the European Union' between 2016 and 2020 (see BIC, 2016a; 2016b; 2016c; 2017; 2018a; 2018b; 2019a; 2019b; 2020) since the end of UK transition period, Summit meetings of the BIC have discussed 'ongoing relations with the EU' (see BIC 2021a; 2021b; 2022a; 2022b). Although, prior to Brexit, the interaction of BIC activities with certain EU programmes were, at times, noted in Summit communiqués, 'relations' between the Member Administrations and the EU had not previously featured as a matter for the consideration of the Council.[8] Instead, extrapolating from the content of communiqués between 1999 and 2015, notwithstanding some variety in the nature of relations between the EU and each BIC Member, those differences did not appear to impinge on the activities of the Council; Brexit has changed this. As indicated in the findings of this research (see 6.2.4.2; 7.2.4.1; 8.5), the newly diverse, and (in most cases) newly distant, set of relations between BIC Member Administrations and the EU has resulted in those respective relations becoming a focus of, and constraint on, the work of the Council.

9.2.5.2 Intergovernmental Relations and Institutions After Brexit

The British Irish Intergovernmental Conference held four plenary meetings in 2021 and 2022; this compares to the three held in 2019 and 2020 (see Cabinet Office, 2019; 2021a; 2021b; 2022a; 2022b). At a meeting in March 2022, the Conference noted 'the importance of addressing the outstanding issues in the context of the Northern Ireland Protocol which is currently subject to [*sic*] continuing engagement between the EU and UK' (Cabinet Office, 2022a).

---

[8] The EU is not mentioned in BIC communiqués prior to 2007 but discussion of specific EU programmes and their interaction with Council work programmes is a feature of communiqués from 2008 onwards (see, for example, BIC, 2008; 2009; 2010).

A similar statement was made in October 2022 when the Conference 'noted the ongoing discussions to address issues around the Northern Ireland Protocol and to find an agreed way forward' (Cabinet Office, 2022b). Such statements underline one of the key findings of this research regarding the intergovernmental aspect of Strand Three of the Northern Ireland constitution whereby, as a consequence of Brexit, it is no longer the sole context for the resolution of disputes related to the 1998 Agreement and non-devolved issues in Northern Ireland.

Notwithstanding a marginal uptick in formal institutional interactions since the end of the UK transition period, political tensions between the UK and Ireland have continued to be evident, in addition to the parties' contrasting perspectives on the Protocol, a source of tension between the co-guarantor governments that has arisen since January 2021 arising from the implications of the *Nationality and Borders Act 2022* on the movement of people on the island of Ireland. Under the terms of the NABA 2022, non-Irish and non-British citizens, and those with no right of abode, who enter the UK—including those who travel from Ireland into Northern Ireland—will be required to complete an 'Electronic Travel Authorisation' (ETA) before doing so (s75). Due to enter into force at the end of 2024, the new scheme is 'a matter of concern' for the Irish Government (Coveney, 2022). The implications of the introduction of the ETA scheme for residents in border regions in Ireland as well as the potential chilling effect of the new requirement on the tourism industry have both featured prominently in related debates (see Rosher, 2022; Hoare, 2022; Jenrick, 2023. According to its Minister for Foreign Affairs Simon Coveney, these Irish Government concerns have 'been made clear' to the British Government and have been raised at BIIGC's held since the legislation was introduced (Coveney, 2022). Although the substance of the NABA 2022 was not necessitated by Brexit, insomuch as UK withdrawal from the EU enabled and required change in UK immigration law, the decision to introduce an ETA scheme is an indirect consequence of the process. The expected specific impacts of this UK law change in Ireland is dually indicative of the paradigmatic shift in the background for British-Irish relations post-Brexit and of a corresponding potential for tensions to develop therein.

9.2.5.3 Intra-UK 'East–West' *Relations* After Brexit

Although neither the 1998 Agreement nor the 1998 Act use the term 'East–West', since 1998 the terminology has been employed in academic, political, and public discussion to refer to institutions established under Strand Three of the 1998 Agreement, and the relationships they represent. As identified in this research (see 7.2.4.3), following the agreement of arrangements to address the 'unique circumstances' on the island of Ireland (Protocol, Article 1(3)) in the context of UK withdrawal from the EU and arising out of controversy surrounding the implementation of those arrangements, the language of 'East–West' has taken on a new and more expansive guise. While this rhetorical innovation did emerge in some quarters of Northern Ireland Unionism during the latter stages of the formal Brexit process, it only came to prominence in official UK Government statements after the coming into effect of the Protocol (and TCA) on 1 January 2021.

The timing of the emergence of the new concept of 'East–West' in UK Government language is worth noting. Writing in the forward to a UK Command Paper, Cabinet Office Minister Lord David Frost, and Secretary of State for Northern Ireland Brandon Lewis, stated their willingness to 'ensure that East–West processes are calibrated based on genuine risks, by removing undue frictions on goods remaining within the United Kingdom' (Frost and Lewis in HM Government, 2021: 6). Notably, the content of the relevant Command Paper, *Northern Ireland Protocol: the way forward*, went on to focus ostensibly on arrangements and relations between Great Britain and Northern Ireland. In the text, Strand Three of the 1998 Agreement was described as: 'the relationships between the UK and Irish governments, between their various jurisdictions, and the *broader links between Northern Ireland and Great Britain as part of one United Kingdom*' (HM Government, 2021: para. 6, *emphasis added*); the italicised characterisation does not reflect the 1998 Agreement text. Moreover, the idea that Strand Three relates to links between Northern Ireland and Great Britain is not supported by descriptions used earlier by the UK Government during withdrawal negotiations; a Position Paper published in 2017 stated: 'Strand 3 of the Agreement deals with East–West cooperation, recognising the importance of the strong relationship between the UK government and Irish government and between their various jurisdictions. *This is in addition to* the internal UK links between Northern Ireland and Great Britain that are part of Northern Ireland's status as an integral part of the United Kingdom' (HM Government, 2017b: para. 61, *emphasis added*). The difference between the 2017 and 2021 Command Papers is subtle but significant; in the earlier paper, GB–NI relations are set apart as distinct from Strand Three; in the later paper, GB–NI relations are incorporated into the UK Government description of Strand Three of the 1998 Agreement.

For Northern Ireland Unionist politicians, the new concept of 'East–West' tends to be employed in the course of critiques about the impact of implementing the Protocol on intra-UK trade and is also often linked to the idea of destabilisation, or failure, of the 1998 Agreement architecture. By way of demonstration, in evidence submitted to a House of Lords Committee, the DUP stated that, by requiring 'costly, complex and disproportionate customs and regulatory barriers for goods moving between *Great Britain and Northern Ireland*', the Protocol had 'dealt a damaging blow to historic *East–West trading relationships*' (DUP, 2021c). Addressing the 1998 Agreement more explicitly, the DUP's Lord Dodds stated that 'the Belfast agreement has been breached as far as protection of the third strand of relationships, namely *the east–west dimension*' (Dodds, 2021. Expressing a similar sentiment, DUP leader Sir Jeffery Donaldson has described the damaging effect of the Protocol on 'the East–West element' of the 'delicate political settlement' established by the 1998 Agreement and argued that North–South relations have been 'gravely undermined' as a result (Donaldson, 2022a; Donaldson, 2022b). The link between use, on the part of Unionist political leaders, of 'East–West' as a descriptor of GB-NI relations and the idea of 'damage' or 'breach' to the 1998 Agreement indicates that this discursive shift arises out of anger and a sense of betrayal over the differentiation of Northern Ireland in the Protocol. Arguably, therefore, while only a relatively minor change in the use of a term that is well established in political lexicons across 'these islands', the development of the new face of 'East–West' relations is symptomatic of a fundamental shift in the political typography of the UK, one that may prove to be among the most significant of all Brexit impacts.

9.3 Conclusion: Northern Ireland's Brexit Problem

Based on an interdisciplinary and systematic analysis of Brexit's impact on the part of the UK most exposed to its effects, this book has argued that the process of UK withdrawal from the EU has changed the constitution of Northern Ireland. Speaking of constitutional change in Northern Ireland is often controversial. In view of its history, this fact is understandable albeit also problematic. One of the consequences of the provisions that exist in international (read 1998 Agreement) and domestic (read 1998 Act) law for the constitutional status of Northern Ireland to potentially move from being part of the UK to becoming part of Ireland is that the language and concept of 'constitutional change' tends to connote (only) this specific sort of change. This is problematic because there are many ways in which constitutions can be altered that are short of the kind of wholesale shift in jurisdictional status that tends to overshadow related discussions in Northern Ireland; the constitutional changes engendered by Brexit are in that former category.

As has been detailed in this analysis, the constitutional status of Northern Ireland as an integral part of the United Kingdom has *not* been changed by Brexit. Moreover, the principle by which that status is maintained has been strengthened in international and in domestic law throughout the process of UK withdrawal from the EU. At the same time, however, because Brexit was (and is) an inherently constitutional process, it has resulted in constitutional change in the UK; this ought not to be surprising. Although not the only constitutionally unique part of the UK, from the outset, the 'constitutional arrangements' (as per Article 50 TEU) in the 'UK in respect of Northern Ireland' (as per Protocol Article 13) were considerably more particular than anywhere else in the state; this fact did not appear to be adequately understood or accounted for in the early stages of the Brexit process. In the outworking of UK withdrawal from the EU, however, those 'unique' (The Executive Office, 2016a) 'challenges' (European Council, 2017) and 'particular' (The Prime Minister, 2016) circumstances became apparent and both sides agreed on the necessity of accommodating them through specific arrangements (as per Protocol Article 1(3)). What this has meant is that the constitutional change engendered by Brexit in the UK as a whole has a dedicated, bespoke, novel, and complex Northern Ireland component.

As a consequence of the UK's decision to withdraw from the EU and the nature of the arrangements it agreed in that context, the stability (or otherwise) of the 1998 Agreement and its institutions are bound up with the regulation of the following: an external border of the EU single market for goods that is also an internal border of the UK (i.e. the GB–NI/Irish Sea Border) *and* an external border of the EU single market for services, people, and capital that is also an external border of the UK (i.e. the IRE–NI/Irish Land Border). This puts Northern Ireland and its evidently still fragile governing institutions in a pivotal position within the broader UK–EU relationship—arguably, for all parties involved such a setup is less than ideal. The dual forces of legal change and political disruption wrought by Brexit in and on Northern Ireland have undermined its unique constitutional arrangements and governing architecture. At time of writing, it is unclear how long it will be before fully functioning government, under the 1998 Agreement system, returns to Northern Ireland, or even if it will at all; this fact is an unfortunate consequence of Brexit.

Twenty-five years after the 1998 Agreement, the peace and prosperity of Northern Ireland is still in process. Brexit has had a regressive effect on the long, arduous, and iterative journey from conflict to reconciliation and beyond; this is regrettable. Nonetheless, Northern Ireland has overcome much in its 100 years of history and, while its current challenges are daunting, they need not be insurmountable. Looking to the post-Brexit future from within the (recently notorious) borders of Northern Ireland, there are many reasons for hope, just as there is no room at all for apathy.

Here's to hope.

10
The Windsor Framework

An Addendum

On 27 February 2023, the Prime Minister of the UK and President of the European Commission hailed the beginning of 'a new chapter' in UK–EU relations (von der Leyen, 2023; Sunak, 2023). Appearing together at a joint press conference, the two leaders announced that 'agreement in principle' had been reached on revised arrangements for the implementation of the *Protocol on Ireland/Northern Ireland* which 'should', thereafter, be known as 'the Windsor Framework' (Joint Declaration No 1/2023 in *Official Journal*, 2023).

Although not as yet legally confirmed, the changes due to be made to the Protocol by the Windsor Framework are both practically and politically significant. If, as anticipated, arrangements laid down in the Windsor Framework take effect, they will alter aspects of Brexit's overall impact in/on Northern Ireland going forward. Given the importance of these new arrangements, this short addendum reviews the content of the Windsor Framework and considers its provisions against the conclusions of the analysis set out in preceding chapters. Subject to the caveat that the revised terms for implementing (that formally known as) the Protocol have been neither legally ratified in full nor practically operationalised, it is nonetheless argued here that the Windsor Framework, provided it takes effect, stands to mitigate some of the negative impacts of Brexit on Northern Ireland while at the same time creating and/or exacerbating others.

10.1 A (Surprisingly Comprehensive) Agreement in Principle

Twenty-five months after the end of the UK transition period, the entry into force of the new UK–EU relationship, and the unique arrangements for Northern Ireland within it, the EU and UK published details of (yet another) deal reached between the two sides. Marking the conclusion of two years of intermittent and contested talks on the implementation of the Protocol (see 9.1), the package of measures branded (and hereafter referred to as) the

Windsor Framework was more comprehensive than most had anticipated. In this respect, the deal was received by many as a 'win', particularly for the still relatively new in office UK Prime Minister Rishi Sunak.

The legal underpinning for the array of political and legal documents that accompanied the inauguration of the Windsor Framework ('the Framework') is Article 164(5)(d) of the Withdrawal Agreement (see JC Decision 1/2023: *recital* (3) in HM Government, 2023a). In setting out the functions of the Joint Committee (or JC), the relevant clause enabled it to adopt decisions to amend the Withdrawal Agreement,[1] provided such amendments 'are necessary to correct errors, to address omissions or other deficiencies, or to address situations unforeseen' when it was signed; however, any such decisions could 'not amend essential elements' of the Withdrawal Agreement (WA, 2020: Article 164(5)(d)). No specific errors or omissions in the Protocol (as was) are cited in the Framework texts. Use of Article 164(5)(d) as the premise for the revised arrangements therefore relies on characterising the changes brought in as necessary to address 'deficiencies' in the agreed text and/or 'situations unforeseen' when it was signed. From the perspective of the Northern Ireland constitution, the Framework's legal basis is notable because, as set out in preceding chapters (see particularly 6.2 and 7.2), the political and constitutional destabilisation that followed the implementation of the Protocol (alongside the Trade and Cooperation Agreement (TCA)) was arguably not that difficult to foresee. The other relevant justification, that the Framework addresses 'deficiencies' in the previous version, is notable insomuch as it amounts to an admission of at least some fallibility by both sides. In view of the numerous leadership changes in the UK Government and the Conservative Party prior to the Framework announcement, the implications of its implicit critique of the earlier iteration of the Protocol are perhaps more significant in UK politics as Prime Minister Sunak, through the Framework, is effectively distancing himself from decisions of his predecessor(s).

By most measures, characterising the extent of change brought about by the Framework as addressing 'errors' or 'unforeseen' 'deficiencies' is a bit of a stretch. Nonetheless, pragmatism appeared to prevail. Reflecting the awkward combination of the Article 164(5)(d) restriction regarding agreeing to change 'essential elements' of the Withdrawal Agreement together with the political importance of securing revisions sufficient to address the concerns of those opposed to the Protocol in the UK (most particularly in Northern Ireland), the substance of the Framework is spread across an extensive

---

[1] Parts One, Four, and Six of the Withdrawal Agreement are excluded from JC powers to amend the text under Article 164(5)(d), and these expire four years after the end of the transition period (i.e. on 1 January 2025).

collection of different legal and political instruments. Related publications included: a UK Government Command Paper and UK legal position; a Joint Committee draft decision on the overall Framework; two Joint Committee draft recommendations (one on Article 13(3)(a) and one on market surveillance and enforcement); five Joint Committee draft declarations (on the title of the Windsor Framework, on mechanisms for dialogue, on VAT, on the application of Article 10(1), and on the application of new Article 13(3)(a)); five unilateral UK declarations (on Article 18, export procedures and strengthening enforcement, on enforcement action regarding parcel carriers specifically and, annexed to the draft JC decision, on the involvement of 1998 Agreement institutions); and one JCWG draft decision (on amending its terms of reference). Additional publications on the EU side included: a European Commission press release, factsheet, and question and answer resource; two proposals for Council Decisions (one on the EU position to be taken in the Joint Committee and the other in the JCWG); three proposals for new Regulations concerning SPS measures, medicines for human use, and tariff rate quotas; one Implementing Regulation on certain high-risk plants; one Delegated Regulation on simplified customs formalities for trusted GB – NI parcel carriers; four unilateral declarations 'taking note' of UK declarations' (excluding that annexed to the draft JC Decision); two Commission position papers (on customs and on agrifood, plants, and pets) and one Commission statement on arrangements for the enhanced involvement of Northern Ireland stakeholders. Additionally, both the UK and EU published an agreed political declaration on the Framework. The provisions contained across all these Windsor Framework documents are detailed, complex and, at the time of writing, many are still in draft form, which means they are still potentially subject to change. Although it is unlikely the Framework legislative texts will undergo extensive amendment during their respective ratification processes in the UK and EU systems, their implementation will require additional (largely secondary/implementing) laws to be made; these are not yet published but may be significant for the impact of the Framework overall. What follows in the analytical sections of this addendum is therefore only an *initial* and a high-level assessment of the content of the Windsor Framework and its possible constitutional consequences for Northern Ireland.

10.2 The Windsor Framework: An Overview

In substance, the provisions in the Windsor Framework relate primarily to arrangements for the movement of goods—particularly from GB to NI—as well as to arrangements for governance and implementation—particularly regarding Northern Ireland stakeholders' involvement in it. Taking each in turn.

10.2.1 Amendments and Provisions Related to Goods

One of the key innovations of the Windsor Framework (and one of the most widely anticipated in advance) is the introduction of easements for the movement of goods between Great Britain and Northern Ireland based on differentiation according to destination. Goods moved by trusted traders for end use or consumption in Northern Ireland will be able to avail of a 'green lane' process whereby considerably fewer customs checks, and regulatory controls, will apply.[2] By contrast, goods moving into Northern Ireland that are at risk of moving on into the EU will enter through a 'red lane' process where full customs checks, and regulatory controls, will apply. In substance, the agreed easements address two specific sets of issues: customs rules and checks and SPS rules and checks on movements of agri-food goods; the former are due to be fully operational in October 2024 and the latter are to be introduced in October 2023.

On customs, traders authorised to avail of the green lane process will be able to submit simplified customs paperwork and to do so monthly rather than for each movement of goods; additionally, physical checks on those goods will only take place if smuggling or fraud is suspected, rather than as a matter of routine. Businesses with an annual turnover of less than £2,000,000 and/or who are moving goods for the sole purpose of selling them as food products or retail goods; or installing them in a permanent structure; or using them in the provision of health and social care services, or in non-profit activities, or as animal feed *in Northern Ireland* will be able to avail of the simplified customs paperwork and be subject to 'intelligence-led' rather than routine physical checks (JC Decision 1/2023: Article 6). To avail of the green lane easements, traders will be obliged to obtain authorisation. The details of the trader authorisation process are still pending, however, provisions in the Framework texts expand the pool of those able to apply: traders located in Great Britain that have 'an indirect customs representative' in Northern Ireland will now be eligible to become 'authorised' and therefore use the green lane system (*ibid.*: Article 10); this was not the case under the previous Protocol arrangements. Customs requirements are also due to be eased for

---

[2] This 'green lane and red lane' terminology is used in UK Government documents and communications regarding the Framework; EU documents and communications instead refer to an 'express lane' or simply easements.

authorised parcel operators. As a result of the Framework, all parcels moved by authorised parcel carriers and transit operators will be considered 'not at risk' of moving on into the EU and therefore not subject to 'routine' checks nor obliged to fulfil full customs declarations as was previously the case under the unamended Protocol (*ibid.*: Article 7).

On SPS rules and checks, additional easements are agreed for 'retail goods' covering pre-packaged products of animal or plant origin (e.g., fresh meat, fresh vegetables), food and food contact goods (e.g., food packaging, cutlery, kitchen equipment), plants (other than for planting), pet food as well as composite food products (e.g. ready-made meals or sandwiches). Those retail goods (as defined) entering NI via the green lane process will not be required to comply fully with EU law instruments that otherwise apply to goods placed on the Northern Ireland market. Of the 300 or so pieces of EU law that otherwise apply to goods being moved into or produced in Northern Ireland under Article 5 and Annex 2 of the Protocol, approximately 65 will not apply to goods entering via the green lane. Although characterised by the UK Government as a 'disapplication' of relevant EU laws (HM Government, 2023f: para. 29), it is important to underline that these instruments only do not apply to certain goods being moved in accordance with specific conditions—from GB–NI, by trusted traders and subject to safeguards and labelling requirements—the same EU laws continue to apply in Northern Ireland generally as well as to goods being moved into Northern Ireland that do not meet the green lane process threshold. The continued application of EU law in Northern Ireland notwithstanding, it is also the case that goods which fall within the scope of these most generous green-lane conditions—primarily pre-packaged agri-food goods—are not required to fully conform to EU standards. This arrangement arguably, in effect, establishes a dual regulatory system for those goods within the scope of this aspect of the green lane process, albeit one that is contingent on data sharing, record keeping, and labelling requirements for participating traders. This is also in lieu of a more general system of dual regulation as was proposed by the UK Government in the *Northern Ireland Protocol Bill* (see 9.2) which, as a consequence of this new UK–EU agreement, has been withdrawn (*Joint Political Declaration*, European Commission, 2023d; HM Government, 2023e: 4).

The agreed easements for GB–NI movements of goods are achieved by and reflected in an amendment to Article 6(2) of the Protocol text concerning Northern Ireland's place in the UK internal market[3] which is provided for in a

---

[3] Under Article 1 of the JC decision, the following sentence will be added to Article 6(2) of the Protocol: 'This includes specific arrangements for the movement of goods within the United Kingdom's internal market, consistent with Northern Ireland's position as part of the customs territory of the United Kingdom in accordance with this Protocol, where goods are destined for final consumption or final use in Northern

Joint Committee decision which also repeals the previous definition of goods 'at risk' (provided for in Decision 4/2020; see 6.2.2.2) and replaces it with the more streamlined definition which allows for differentiation by destination (see JC Decision 1/2023: Section 2 in HM Government, 2023a). Additionally, changes to EU legislation necessary to implement the revised approach are set out in the proposals for new EU Regulations published as part of the Framework texts, most particularly in the one concerning SPS measures (see European Commission, 2023e).

The Windsor Framework also contains specific provisions regarding VAT and excise. Amendments are made to the terms of application of four EU law instruments[4] to the UK in respect of Northern Ireland under Article 8 and Annex 3 of the Framework. The relevant changes introduce derogations exempting NI from certain EU law requirements so as to enable the UK to apply reduced VAT rates on goods installed in immovable properties in Northern Ireland while also allowing for Northern Ireland participation in UK excise provisions related to sales of alcohol, so long as these do not contravene EU minimum duty rates (see JC Decision 1/2023: Article 3 in HM Government, 2023a). The derogations also exempt Northern Ireland from the EU's new VAT scheme for small enterprises on condition of the UK scheme respecting EU rules on annual turnover thresholds.

Several provisions agreed in the Framework address specific issues that had arisen since the Protocol entered into force; these include the supply of medicines and the movement of pets. On medicines for human use, building on derogations introduced unilaterally by the EU in April 2022 to relevant EU law instruments applicable under the Protocol (see 9.1.1), some additional exemptions have been negotiated between the two sides. Under the new agreement, when the changes are enacted, any new or innovative medicines developed in the UK will be eligible for circulation in Northern Ireland on the basis of approval by UK authorities—the Medicines and Healthcare products Regulatory Agency (MHRA)—and according to UK regulations; this would not have been possible under the previous arrangements. Additionally, the requirement for packages of medicinal products to have an EU stamp when placed on the NI market will be disapplied; this will allow manufacturers in the UK to produce a single package labelled 'UK only'. In substance, measures regarding human medicines are to take the form of a new EU Regulation which, when adopted, will amend established EU Directive 2001/83/EC (see

---

Ireland and where the necessary safeguards are in place to protect the integrity of the Union's internal market and customs union' (Decision 1/2023).

[4] Council Directive 2006/112/EC; Regulation (EU) No 904/2010 and Council Directive 92/84/EEC and Council Directive 92/83/EEC.

Official Journal, 2001) that applies to Northern Ireland under the Framework (see EC Proposal 2023/0064 in European Commission, 2023b).

Notably, the new Framework derogations only relate to medicines for human use; for veterinary medicines, there exists a grace period allowing UK-authorised medicines to be sold in Northern Ireland until 2025 after which, according to current provisions, these must comply with EU standards. On a not unrelated matter, under the previous Protocol arrangement, anyone seeking to bring a pet from Great Britain to Northern Ireland would have been required (every time) to secure an animal health certificate, signed by a vet, and to verify that their pet was microchipped, vaccinated against rabies, and treated for tapeworm. Instead, under the Framework, those wishing to travel GB–NI with their pet will be required to acquire one travel document that will remain valid for the lifetime of the animal, and which confirms that it is microchipped and will not move into the EU. For Northern Ireland pet owners, an EU pet passport will still be required to move their pet into Ireland or elsewhere in the EU, but there will be no administrative requirements when travelling to and from Great Britain. Easements regarding movements of pets are also to be implemented through changes in relevant EU law instruments that apply in Northern Ireland (see EC Proposal 2023/0062 in European Commission, 2023c).

An area of consistent UK Government concern had been the potential scope of Article 10 of the Protocol regarding the application of EU State Aid rules. Building on an EU unilateral declaration on the matter in December 2020, of which the UK 'took note' (see 7.1.2 and European Commission, 2021i), the Framework contains an additional declaration, this time joint, setting out further guarantees regarding the specific scope of Article 10 (see HM Government, 2023b). The content of the Joint Declaration (re)affirms that only subsidies that have a material effect on Northern Ireland beneficiaries are to be subject to EU rules under Article 10.

10.2.2 Amendments and Provisions Related to Governance

The other significant area of change introduced by the Windsor Framework to the Protocol (as was) relates to its governance. Whereas, under the Protocol, there was no requirement for NI representation at nor involvement in structures established to oversee its implementation (see 6.2.2.2; 7.2.2.1, and 7.2.2.2), the Framework proposes to establish multiple new avenues for Northern Ireland input. New arrangements for involvement of Northern

Ireland representatives and stakeholders in the implementation of the Framework fall into three categories: provisions for direct EU to NI engagement; provisions for NI involvement in joint UK–EU bodies; and domestic provisions granting NI representatives and institutions a greater role in related UK legislative and policy processes.

10.2.2.1 EU–NI engagement

Asserting the 'paramount importance' (European Commission, 2023a) of stakeholder engagement in Northern Ireland, in the Framework, the EU commit to: providing an annual presentation on the Commission Work Programme to Northern Ireland stakeholders; publishing new and upcoming EU initiatives and public consultations, relevant to Northern Ireland, on the dedicated *EUR-Lex* Protocol (Framework) webpage; providing information sessions and/or workshops on new initiatives to NI stakeholders if/when requested by them; and to providing a dedicated overview of any Northern Ireland stakeholders' input in any impact assessments of new EU policy initiatives relevant to Northern Ireland. From the perspective of EU external relations, the proposed new level of engagement between the Commission and stakeholders from a sub-national region of a third country is both novel and remarkable. Although in the immediate aftermath this aspect of the new arrangements for governance and implementation of the Framework garnered less attention than other aspects, *if* this strand of new engagement processes is made to work effectively, it has the potential to render the more constitutionally novel domestic aspects of the Framework governance provisions (i.e. the Stormont Break(s)) less practically, and therefore politically, significant.

10.2.2.2 EU–UK Institutions

In a Joint Declaration on dialogue and goods, the UK and EU 'restate' their shared commitment 'to make full use of the [Withdrawal Agreement] structures', namely the Joint Committee, Specialised Committee, and the JCWG (Joint Declaration No 2/2023 in HM Government, 2023c). To this end, the two parties agreed that the Specialised Committee 'may convene in a specific composition' to be known as the 'Special Body on Goods' at which exchanges of views can take place on 'any future UK legislation regarding goods' that is relevant to the operation of the Framework (*ibid.*). Where appropriate, representatives from business or civic society may be invited to attend relevant meetings. Joint Declaration No 2/2023 also contains a (re)commitment on the part of the UK to ensure full participation of the First and deputy First Ministers in the UK delegation to the Joint Committee (*ibid.*); this reflects and reiterates a similar commitment set out in the New Decade, New Approach agreement (NDNA, 2020: Annex A: 9).

In addition to the Special Body on Goods, the UK and EU agreed to establish a 'forward-looking coordination mechanism' in the area of VAT and excise to address any future issues that may arise concerning the unique position of Northern Ireland regarding the dual application of aspects of EU and UK rules on VAT and excise (*Joint Political Declaration*: 2; see also JC Decision 1/2023: *recital* (14)). Section 3 of JC Decision 1/2023 on the Framework sets out that the 'Enhanced Coordination Mechanism' on VAT and excise will also function under the remit of the Specialised Committee with 'specific meetings' being convened by the Committee according to necessity (JC Decision 1/2023: Section 3 Article 19(1) in HM Government, 2023a). Tasks of the mechanism are to: assist the Joint Committee by providing a forum for exchange of information on relevant EU and/or UK legislation; provide assessments of its potential impact; discuss practical difficulties related to the application of VAT and excise rules in NI under the Framework; adopt decisions or recommendations related to the application of EU rules listed in Annex 3 of the Framework, and/or to discuss and adopt any other appropriate measures arising from the implementation of the same (*ibid*. Section 3 Article 18).

Among the Framework documents, there is a proposal for a decision to be taken in the Joint Consultative Working Group (JCWG) to amend its rules of procedure so as to 'better ensure' that the UK is able to discuss its views on EU acts in that body 'on the basis of input provided by stakeholders in NI' (see European Commission, 2023e: Annex: *recital* (3)). To this end, the JCWG is to change its rules of operation so that 'structured sub-groups' composed of UK and EU officials could be established (*ibid*.: Annex (3)) under its auspices. Both the UK and EU have indicated that these sub-groups could involve business and civil society representatives; details about how these groups will work and/or who may be involved have not yet been published.

As is the case in regard to new procedures for EU–NI engagement, *if* the proposed revisions to the UK–EU architecture for implementation and oversight of the Framework can be operationalised effectively, they will be innovative in terms of both EU external relations and UK domestic governance. For the EU, the new setup will, at least potentially, give officials, business, and civic representatives from a sub-national entity of a third country state means of regularly inputting to and receiving information from EU law-making processes. For the UK, the new level of access granted NI representatives on bodies designed to implement and oversee an international treaty is novel in regard to the balance between reserved and devolved competence.

10.2.2.3 UK Unilateral Measures

One of the least expected and most remarked upon aspects of the Windsor Framework is the so-called 'Stormont Brake' for which it makes provision. Inserting new Article 13(3)(a) into what was Article 13(3) of the Protocol, this new 'Stormont Brake' procedure will enable the UK to deviate from the otherwise automatic 'dynamic regulatory alignment' of UKNI with EU rules on goods on the instruction of Members of the Legislative Assembly (MLAs) in Northern Ireland. In legislating for the implementation of the 'Stormont Brake' procedure in domestic law, the UK Government introduced an additional new process which is linked to Article 13(4) of the Framework according to which the UK and EU can, by agreement, add new EU instruments to those that already apply to Northern Ireland if the new act is agreed to be within the scope of its objectives. Thus, in effect, the 'Stormont Brake' comes in two forms—the associated procedures of both aspects are complex.

10.2.2.3.1 Article 13(3): Stormont Brake on Amended or Replaced EU Acts

Under Article 13(3) of the Protocol, those EU acts within its scope applied to the UK in respect of NI 'as amended or replaced' (see 9.2.1.1; Whitten, 2022d). Borrowing from the Northern Ireland 'petition of concern' constitutional procedure for its threshold, under Article 13(3)(a) of the Framework, 30 MLAs from two or more political affiliations can 'notify' the UK Government of their desire for the 'brake' to be applied to a specific amendment or replacement to an EU act which would otherwise apply in Northern Ireland under Article 5 and Annex 2. Notification on the part of MLAs is subject to several conditions. Firstly, the case must be convincingly made by notifying MLAs that the relevant change would have a 'significant impact specific to everyday life of communities in Northern Ireland' and one that is 'liable to persist' (JC Decision 1/2023: Article 2 in HM Government, 2023a). Secondly, notifying MLAs must be able to demonstrate compliance with the NDNA restrictions on the use of the Petition of Concern, principally that any petition or, in this case, notification is 'only being made in the most exceptional circumstances and as a last resort' (JC Decision 1/2023: Annex 1(c)(i)). Thirdly, notifying MLAs will need to be able to demonstrate that: they have sought 'prior substantive discussion' with the UK Government and with (or within) the Northern Ireland Executive to 'examine all possibilities in relation to the [relevant specific] Union act'; they have 'taken steps to consult' businesses, traders, or civic society representatives affected by the relevant EU act; and they have made 'all reasonable use of applicable consultation processes' provided by the EU for new acts of relevance to Northern Ireland (*ibid.*: Annex

1(c)(iii)). Finally, any notification must be given within two months of the relevant change being published in the *Official Journal* of the EU.

The scope of this aspect of the Stormont Brake procedure is limited to that EU law made applicable by Article 5(2) of the Framework and which is listed in Annex 2, excluding those EU instruments listed under subheadings 2 to 6 (representing 32 instruments) which relate, primarily, to trade defence measures and bilateral safeguards.[5] Based on the original agreed text, this leaves 256 instruments listed under subheadings 1 and 7 to 47 of Annex 2 within the scope of the Stormont Brake procedure which is subject to notification on the part of 30 MLAs from two or more political affiliations. Crucially, only if/when the Northern Ireland Assembly and Executive are fully restored does this new Stormont Brake procedure become available. Thereafter, if the institutions collapse again, only those MLAs seeking 'individually and collectively' to operate the institutions 'in good faith' would be able to avail of the procedure (JC decision 1/2023: Annex 1 (a) in HM Government, 2023a). The specific mechanisms by which the brake would operate in this scenario, particularly as regards the process for possible Assembly recall and/or the criteria by which the 'good faith' test would be determined, remains unclear.

10.2.2.3.2 Article 13(4): Stormont Brake on New EU Acts

Under Article 13(4) of the Protocol, any new acts adopted by the EU considered to be within the scope of the Protocol could be brought to the Joint Committee and, by agreement, added to the body of EU laws that already apply to the UK in respect of Northern Ireland. Importantly, this procedure for additions is subject to mutual consent; it thereby gives the UK 'a veto' on any expansion in EU law terms of the agreed scope. While the Framework makes no amendment to the text of Article 13(4), the UK Command Paper indicated that new domestic procedures would be introduced to allow greater Northern Ireland involvement in the related process (HM Government, 2023f: para. 68). In the event, the publication of a statutory instrument setting out the legislative provisions for the Stormont Brake in UK law included a new domestic legislative process related to Article 13(4) of the Framework and the addition of any new EU instruments.

According to the (still draft) *Windsor Framework (Democratic Scrutiny) Regulations* (the *Draft Regulations*), a UK Minister will be unable to agree to the addition of a new EU act to Northern Ireland in the Joint Committee unless the NI Assembly has passed a motion in favour of doing so

---

[5] Subheadings 2 to 6 of Annex 2 cover: protection of the Union's financial interests; trade statistics; general trade-related aspects (such as generalised tariff preferences, common rules for exports, etc.); trade defence instruments; and regulations on bilateral safeguards.

(2023 c18(1)) *or* 'exceptional circumstances' apply (c18(2)). Importantly, any 'applicability motion' tabled to this end can only pass if cross-community consent is achieved (c19(6)). While the determination of the presence of 'exceptional circumstances' is left to the discretion of the UK Minister, it is stated that if the application of the new EU act would not create a new regulatory GB–NI border, the condition of exceptionality is reached; no reference is made to consideration of IRE–NI regulatory, or divergence, implications of decisions taken.

Similar to the Article 13(3)(a)-related process, the Article 13(4)-related process will only become available if/when the devolved institutions are fully restored, and a new Executive is sitting. Notwithstanding the similarity, in contrast to the brake for amendments or replacements, the brake for new EU acts would, on present provisions, *not* be available for use in the event of a subsequent collapse of devolved government in Northern Ireland; the draft statutory instrument is explicit in this regard. One of the possible 'exceptional circumstances' that could lead a Secretary of State to ignore the absence of cross-community consent for the application of a new EU act is lack of a sitting Executive (*Draft Regulations* 2023 c18(5)).

While the scope of the Article 13(3)(a)-related brake is limited to changes or updates made to (the majority of) those EU laws that apply under Article 5 and Annex 2 of the Framework, the Article 13(4)-related brake is not limited. Any proposal for a new EU act to be added to the Framework under any of its provisions could, potentially, be subject to the Article 13(4)-related 'applicability motion' procedure in the Assembly, *if* devolved government in Northern Ireland is up and running.

10.3 Brexit, the Windsor Framework, and the Northern Ireland Constitution

The extent and nature of the impact that the revisions brought about by the Windsor Framework on the Northern Ireland constitution are still largely unknown. That said, and building on the analysis set out in preceding chapters, several initial and/or likely implications (pending implementation) can be observed.

10.3.1 EU–NI Relationship Consolidated

The Protocol established a new relationship between the EU and Northern Ireland (see 9.2.1); the Framework reflects and, at least potentially, reinforces this fact. By introducing a range of new mechanisms and requirements for direct engagement between stakeholders in Northern Ireland and the European Commission, changes introduced in the Framework effectively consolidate the novel EU–NI relationship begotten by Brexit. Notwithstanding the potential for regular and substantive EU to Northern Ireland consultation in and through the new Framework procedures—including the Commission Work Programme briefings and any ad hoc policy workshops requested—and bodies—including the Special Body on Goods, the Enhanced Coordination Mechanism, and the JCWG structured sub-groups—much still depends on the manner in which these are implemented.

Operationalising the new EU–NI consultative mechanisms, alongside the new and related scrutiny requirements of/for Northern Ireland stakeholders, raises questions of capacity. To make full use of, for example, the possibility of dedicated briefings from the European Commission, stakeholders in Northern Ireland will need to have a level of awareness of developments in EU law and policy processes sufficient to enable them to request briefings on relevant aspects. While this presents a significant and unique opportunity for a sub-national entity of a non-Member State, it is also not something that Northern Ireland stakeholders or officials have previously had reason to do. Whether or not there will be sufficient resource and/or desire amongst officials, businesses, or civil society in Northern Ireland to carry out the monitoring work that is likely to be required to keep on top of relevant changes so as to make full use of the possible consultative mechanisms is an as yet unanswered question.

10.3.2 Democratic Deficit Mitigated

A strong case can be made that the Windsor Framework addresses much of the 'democratic deficit' impacts of the Protocol (as was) and Brexit more generally in Northern Ireland. Although its governance measures are still to be implemented in practice, by (at least in theory) introducing mechanisms for the involvement of Northern Ireland business, civic society, and political representatives at various levels of related EU and UK law-making processes, the Framework changes amount to a very important shift in regard to the impact of Brexit on Northern Ireland and, in particular, on Strand One of its constitution. The possibility, and probability, of elected representatives of the Northern Ireland Assembly being able to have open channels of communication with the European Commission on the development of policy of relevance to the unique setup for Northern Ireland alignment with, and access to, the EU single market in goods is exceptional. From the perspective of EU external relations, the degree of potential access to the Commission reflected in the option for dedicated briefings and impact assessments is remarkable. So too, from the perspective of UK constitutional arrangements, these measures constitute a graduation of existing Northern Ireland constitutional exceptionalism from, prior to Brexit, being essentially bound to the unique arrangements for Northern Ireland to Ireland bilateralism (reflected in particular in Schedule 2(3) of the 1998 Act) to now constituting, at least potential, Northern Ireland agency on the EU stage if/when either the Stormont Brake procedure is legitimately exercised and/or stakeholders successfully input to EU legislative developments at an earlier stage such that use of any 'Brake' is avoided through consideration of Northern Ireland particularities in the drafting of relevant EU law.

Although unlikely to satisfy the now deeply engrained ire of the Protocol's most vocal opponents—namely the TUV and factions of the DUP alongside prominent Loyalist/Unionist activists—the introduction of green lane processes, via the Framework, *could* be said to go some way to addressing critiques and concerns regarding Article VI of the 1800 Acts of Union. By enabling Northern Ireland consumers access, contingent on the extent of traders' participation, to (primarily agri-food) goods available in Great Britain while also easing the bureaucratic burden for movements GB–NI and expanding the criteria for trader authorisation such that GB-based businesses can apply, the Framework comes (at least) close to complying with the 'equal footing' guarantee set out in the Sixth Article of the Acts of Union (see 9.1.1). Notwithstanding such arguments being made possible as a result of the amended Framework terms for the implementation of the Protocol, in the polarised context of post-Brexit Northern Ireland politics, these are very unlikely to prove convincing for the constituency most vehemently opposed to the Protocol come Framework.

10.3.3 Dual Divergence Guaranteed

The introduction of the green lane process and with it the effective creation of a dual regulatory environment for the sale of certain goods in Northern Ireland has the potential to have both positive and negative impacts on the local economy. On the one hand, consumers in Northern Ireland can be expected to have the choice of EU-standard goods without additional associated costs that may apply in the rest of the UK due to lack of single market access, as well as GB-standard goods without or with limited additional associated costs due to simplified green lane processes for GB–NI movements. On the other hand,

and in the same context, Northern Ireland producers face the new risk of undercutting insomuch as they must continue to comply with EU standards on goods, under the Framework, but are now, due to the changes it introduces, going to have to compete with producers in Great Britain who need only comply with UK(GB) standards which are, on the current trajectory, likely to be lower. The extent to which this risk is realised depends to a very large degree on decisions yet to be taken in the UK system. If, for example, the *Retained European Union Law Bill* is enacted, the automatic disapplication of a majority of (previously EU, now) retained EU law rules on goods that apply in Great Britain has the potential to exert significant divergence pressure on the GB to NI axis. If, alternatively, the UK Government was to negotiate significant new trade agreement(s), for example with the US, which contained deregulatory measures in respect to goods, this could, again, be expected to exert divergence pressures on Northern Ireland as less regulated goods from Great Britain could be sold on its supermarket shelves alongside those produced locally and still subject to compliance with EU regulations. What the actual economic impact of the green lane–red lane system proves to be remains to be seen.

Another divergence-related *potential* implication of the Framework relates to North–South cooperation. Introducing, via the Stormont Brake(s), the possibility of Northern Ireland opting *not* to align with new or updated EU standards on goods creates the potential for divergence in, and disruption of, cross-border supply chains in affected areas. Again, the extent to which this (currently hypothetical) scenario is realised is not yet clear. Operationalisation of the Stormont Brake is contingent, first, on the return of devolved government in Northern Ireland, which, at the time of writing, does not seem imminent. Additionally, it is worth underlining that the thresholds and conditions introduced under the Brake procedure(s) are high; therefore, even in the contested political context of Northern Ireland, regardless of the number of attempted uses, instances of the Stormont Brake(s) being 'pulled' legitimately are likely to be rare. Thus, the risk to established North–South cooperation that is currently protected under the Protocol, but which could be exposed to divergence that results from successful exercise of the Brake procedure(s), is arguably minimal.

10.4 An Inconclusive Conclusion

Viewed from Northern Ireland, the most important dimension of the most recent UK–EU agreement is the very fact that it is *agreed*. Brexit has set Northern Ireland up as the touching point between the internal markets and regulatory orders of the EU and the UK. One of the implications of this newly unique constitutional arrangement for/in Northern Ireland is that there can be expected to be a correlation between the health (or unhealth) of UK–EU relations and the stability (or instability) of Northern Ireland. Such a scenario creates responsibilities for all involved parties.

In the wake of the Windsor Framework, perhaps the most pressing issue for Northern Ireland representatives and stakeholders will be capacity building. The extent of monitoring of the parallel evolution of both EU law and UK law that is likely to be required to make the Windsor Framework mechanisms work to the benefit of Northern Ireland is significant. In the short term, if devolved government is not restored, this burden can be expected to fall on officials and stakeholders in business and civic society, with some assistance perhaps coming from central government. For the UK more generally, the now more settled arrangement for post-Brexit Northern Ireland comes with obligations for its consideration in the broader landscape of policy and legislative development after Brexit. An upcoming test case in this regard is the *Retained EU Law Bill*. The degree to which Northern Ireland particularities, under the Windsor Framework, are recognised and accommodated in the anticipated ratification and/or implementation of the REUL Bill/Act will likely serve as an omen for what is to come. For the EU, the inauguration of the Windsor Framework reaffirms the exceptional position of Northern Ireland in the context of EU external relations. The manner in which new EU–NI mechanisms for consultation are established and operate will be crucial. If, as it appears to be intended, the outworking of the new arrangements leads to a focus on the technical details of legislative amendments, this can be expected to be interpreted as a victory in/for the EU system. If, as is still possible, the outworking of the new arrangements leads to further polarisation and politicisation of the EU–NI relationship, this can be expected to be interpreted as, and in reality amount to, a loss in/for the EU and Northern Ireland.

At the time of writing—March 2023—the implications of the most recent development—the Windsor Framework—in the saga of Brexit and Northern Ireland are, largely, pending. While this results in a, perhaps dissatisfying, inconclusive conclusion, it also befits the subject. After seven years (and ten book chapters), the story of Brexit and Northern Ireland is, it seems, still unfolding.

Table of Cases

Allister and others v Northern Ireland Secretary [2021] NIQB 64 (30 June 2021) Available: https://www.judiciaryni.uk/judicial-decisions/2021-niqb–64

Allister and others v Northern Ireland Secretary [2022] NICA 15 (14 March 2022) Available: https://www.judiciaryni.uk/judicial-decisions/summary-judgment-re-jim-allister-and-others-eu-exit-ca

Allister and others v Northern Ireland Secretary [2023] UKSC 5 (8 February 2023) Available: https://www.supremecourt.uk/cases/docs/uksc-2022-0089-0093-judgment.pdf

Buick, Re Judicial Review [2018b] NICA 26 (6 July 2018) Available: https://www.bailii.org/nie/cases/NICA/2018/26.html

Pham v Secretary of State for the Home Department [2015] UKSC 19 (25 March 2015) Available: https://www.supremecourt.uk/cases/docs/uksc-2013-0150-judgment.pdf

Miller v Secretary of State for Exiting the EU [2017] UKSC 5 (24 January 2017) Available: https://www.supremecourt.uk/cases/docs/uksc-2016-0196-judgment.pdf

Re Allister and others [2021] NIQB (30 June 2021) Available: https://www.judiciaryni.uk/judicial-decisions/summary-judgment-re-jim-allister-and-others-eu-exit

Re Buick [2018a] NIQB 43 (14 May 2018) Available: https://www.judiciaryni.uk/judicial-decisions/2018-niqb–43

Re Jackson v Attorney-General [2005] UKHL 56 (13 October 2005) Available: https://www.bailii.org/uk/cases/UKHL/2005/56.html

Re McComb [2003] NIQB 47 (30 June 2003) Available: https://www.bailii.org/nie/cases/NIHC/QB/2003/47.html

Re McCord [2019] NICA 49 (17 September 2019) Available: https://www.bailii.org/nie/cases/NICA/2019/49.html

Robinson v Secretary of State [2002] UKHL 32 (25 July 2002) Available: https://publications.parliament.uk/pa/ld200102/ldjudgmt/jd020725/robin-1.htm

Secretary of State for the Home Department v Mr Jake Parker de Souza [2019] UKUT 335 (IAC) (14 October 2019) Available: https://www.bailii.org/uk/cases/UKUT/IAC/2019/355.html

Van Gen den Loos v Nederlandse Administatie der Belastingen ECLI:EU:C:1963:1 (5 February 1963) Available: https://eur-lex.europa.eu/legal-content/EN/TXT/?uri=CELEX%3A61962CJ0026

Commission v United Kingdom of Great Britain and Northern Ireland ECLI:EU:C:2018:83 (7 October 2018) Available: https://eur-lex.europa.eu/legal-content/en/TXT/?uri=CELEX:62017CJ0503

Table of Legislation

International Treaties

United Nations. (1958) *Convention on the Territorial Sea and the Continuous Zone* vol. 516, p. 205. Available: https://treaties.un.org/pages/ViewDetails.aspx?src=TREATY&mtdsg_no=XXI-1&chapter=21 (Accessed 14 April 2021)

World Trade Organization. (1994) *General Agreement on Tariffs and Trade* [Article XXIV] Available: https://www.wto.org/english/tratop_e/region_e/region_art24_e.htm (Accessed 10 February 2021)

Hague Conference on Private International Law. (2005) *Convention on Choice of Court Agreements* Available: https://assets.hcch.net/docs/510bc238-7318-47ed-9ed5-e0972510d98b.pdf (Accessed 20 January 2023)

Hague Conference on Private International Law. (1996) *Convention on Jurisdiction, Applicable Law, Recognition, Enforcement and Cooperation in Respect of Parental Responsibility and Measures for the Protection of Children* Available: https://assets.hcch.net/docs/f16ebd3d-f398-4891-bf47-110866e171d4.pdf (Accessed 2 February 2023)

Hague Conference on Private International Law. (2007) *Convention on the International Recovery of Child Support and Other Forms of Family Maintenance* Available: https://assets.hcch.net/docs/14e71887-0090-47a3-9c49-d438eb601b47.pdf (Accessed 2 February 2023)

European Union Legislation

Official Journal (1979) *Council Directive 79/7/EC of 19 December 1978 on the progressive implementation of the principle of equal treatment for men and women in matters of social security.* L6 10 January 1979 p. 24. Available: https://eur-lex.europa.eu/legal-content/EN/TXT/?uri=celex%3A32004L0113 (Accessed 19 April 2021)

Official Journal (2000a) *Council Directive 2000/43/EC of 29 June 2000 implementing the principle of equal treatment between persons irrespective of racial or ethnic origin.* L180 19 July 2000 p. 22. Available: https://eur-lex.europa.eu/legal-content/EN/TXT/?uri=CELEX%3A32006L0054 (Accessed 19 April 2021)

Official Journal (2000b) *Council Directive 2000/78/EC of 27 November 2000 establishing a general framework for equal treatment in employment and occupation.* L303 2 December 2000 p. 16. Available: https://eur-lex.europa.eu/legal-content/EN/TXT/?uri=uriserv%3AOJ.L_.2000.180.01.0022.01.ENG&toc=OJ%3AL%3A2000%3A180%3ATOC (Accessed 19 April 2021)

Official Journal (2000c) *Directive 2000/60/EC of the European Parliament and of the Council of 23 October 2000 establishing a framework for Community action in the field of water policy.* L327, 22 December 2000 pp. 1–73. Available: https://eur-lex.europa.eu/legal-content/EN/TXT/?uri=CELEX%3A32000L0060&qid=1618737684531 (Accessed 14 April 2021)

Official Journal (2001) *Directive 2001/83/EC of the European Parliament and of the Council of 6 November 2001 on the Community code relating to medicinal products for human use.* L311,

Table of Legislation 263

28 November 2001 pp. 67–128. Available: https://eur-lex.europa.eu/legal-content/en/TXT/?uri=CELEX%3A32001L0083 (Accessed 7 June 2023)

Official Journal (2003) *Regulation (EC) No 998/2003 of the European Parliament and of the Council of 26 May 2003 on the animal health requirements applicable to the non-commercial movement of pet animals and amending Council Directive 92/65/EEC.* L146, 13 June 2003 pp. 1–21. Available: https://eur-lex.europa.eu/legal-content/en/ALL/?uri=CELEX%3A32003R0998 (Accessed 14 April 2021)

Official Journal (2004) *Council Directive 2004/113/EC of 13 December 2004 implementing the principle of equal treatment between men and women in the access to and supply of goods and services.* L373 21 December 2004 p. 37. Available: https://eur-lex.europa.eu/legal-content/EN/TXT/?uri=uriserv%3AOJ.L_.2000.303.01.0016.01.ENG&toc=OJ%3AL%3A2000%3A303%3ATOC (Accessed 19 April 2021)

Official Journal (2006) *Directive 2006/54/EC of the European Parliament and of Council of 5 July 2006 on the implementation of the principle of equal opportunities and equal treatment of men and women in matters of employment and occupation.* L204 26 July 2006 p. 23. Available: https://eur-lex.europa.eu/legal-content/EN/TXT/?uri=uriserv%3AOJ.L_.2010.180.01.0001.01.ENG&toc=OJ%3AL%3A2010%3A180%3ATOC (Accessed 19 April 2021)

Official Journal (2007) *Treaty of Lisbon amending the Treaty on European Union and the Treaty establishing the European Community, signed at Lisbon, 13 December 2007.* C306, 17 December 2007 pp. 1–271. Available: https://eur-lex.europa.eu/legal-content/EN/TXT/?uri=celex%3A12007L%2FTXT (Accessed 14 April 2021)

Official Journal (2010) *Directive 2010/41/EU of the European Parliament and of the Council of 7 July 2010 on the application of the principle of equal treatment between men and women engaged in an activity in a self-employed capacity and repealing Council Directive 86/613/EEC.* L180 15 July 2010 p. 1. Available: https://eur-lex.europa.eu/legal-content/EN/TXT/?uri=uriserv%3AOJ.L_.1979.006.01.0024.01.ENG&toc=OJ%3AL%3A1979%3A006%3ATOC (Accessed 19 April 2021)

Official Journal (2013) *Regulation (EU) No 952/2013 of the European Parliament and of the Council of 9 October 2013 laying down the Union Customs Code.* L269 10 October 2013 pp. 1–101. Available: https://eur-lex.europa.eu/eli/reg/2013/952/oj (Accessed 15 April 2021)

Official Journal (2015) *Regulation (EU) 2015/479 of the European Parliament and of the Council of 11 March 2015 on common rules for exports.* L83 27 March 2015 pp. 34–40. Available: https://eur-lex.europa.eu/legal-content/EN/TXT/?uri=CELEX%3A32015R0479 (Accessed 20 April 2021)

Official Journal (2016) *Consolidated Versions of the Treaty on European Union and the Treaty on the Functioning of the European Union.* C326, 26 October 2012 pp. 47–390. Available: https://eur-lex.europa.eu/legal-content/EN/TXT/?uri=celex%3A12012E%2FTXT (Accessed 14 April 2021)

Official Journal (2019a) *Agreement on the withdrawal of the United Kingdom of Great Britain and Northern Ireland from the European Union and the European Atomic Energy Community.* C661 19 February 2019 pp. 1–184. Available: https://eur-lex.europa.eu/legal-content/EN/TXT/?uri=uriserv%3AOJ.CI.2019.066.01.0001.01.ENG&toc=OJ%3AC%3A2019%3A066I%3ATOC (Accessed 15 April 2021)

Official Journal (2019b) *Regulation (EU) 2019/1020 of the European Parliament and of the Council of 20 June 2019 on market surveillance and compliance of products and amending Directive 2004/42/EC and Regulations (EC) No 765/2008 and (EU) No 305/2011.* L169/1 26 June 2019 p. 1. Available: https://eur-lex.europa.eu/legal-content/EN/TXT/?uri=celex:32019R1020 (Accessed 20 January 2023)

Official Journal (2020a) *Agreement on the withdrawal of the United Kingdom of Great Britain and Northern Ireland from the European Union and the European Atomic Energy Community.* L29 31 January 2020 pp. 7–187. Available: https://eur-lex.europa.eu/legal-content/EN/TXT/?uri=uriserv%3AOJ.L_.2020.029.01.0007.01.ENG&toc=OJ%3AL%3A2020%3A029%3ATOC (Accessed 14 April 2021)

Official Journal (2020b) *Council Decision (EU) 2020/135 of 30 January 2020 on the conclusion of the Agreement on the withdrawal of the United Kingdom of Great Britain and Northern Ireland from the European Union and the European Atomic Energy Community.* L29, 31 January 2020 pp. 1–6. Available: https://eur-lex.europa.eu/legal-content/EN/TXT/?uri=uriserv%3AOJ.L_.2020.029.01.0001.01.ENG&toc=OJ%3AL%3A2020%3A029%3ATOC (Accessed 14 April 2021)

Official Journal (2020b) *Council Decision (EU) 2020/1599 of 23 October 2020 on the position to be taken on behalf of the European Union in the Joint Consultative Working Group established by the Agreement on the withdrawal of the United Kingdom of Great Britain and Northern Ireland from the European Union and the European Atomic Energy Community as regards the adoption of its rules of procedure.* L365, 3 November 2020 pp. 3–8. Available: https://eur-lex.europa.eu/legal-content/EN/TXT/?uri=CELEX%3A32020D1599 (Accessed 15 April 2021)

Official Journal (2020c) *Decision No 3/2020 of the Joint Committee established by the Agreement on the withdrawal of the United Kingdom of Great Britain and Northern Ireland from the European Union and the European Atomic Energy Community of 17 December 2020 amending the Protocol on Ireland and Northern Ireland to the Agreement on the withdrawal of the United Kingdom of Great Britain and Northern Ireland from the European Union and the European Atomic Energy Community.* L443, 30 December 2020 pp. 3–5. Available: https://eur-lex.europa.eu/legal-content/EN/TXT/?uri=uriserv%3AOJ.L_.2020.443.01.0003.01.ENG&toc=OJ%3AL%3A2020%3A443%3ATOC (Accessed 14 April 2021)

Official Journal (2020d) *Decision No 4/2020 of the Joint Committee established by the Agreement on the withdrawal of the United Kingdom of Great Britain and Northern Ireland from the European Union and the European Atomic Energy Community of 17 December 2020 on the determination of goods not at risk.* L443, 30 December 2020 pp. 6–12. Available: https://eur-lex.europa.eu/legal-content/EN/TXT/?uri=uriserv%3AOJ.L_.2020.443.01.0006.01.ENG&toc=OJ%3AL%3A2020%3A443%3ATOC (Accessed 14 April 2021)

Official Journal (2020e) *Decision No 5/2020 of the Joint Committee established by the Agreement on the withdrawal of the United Kingdom of Great Britain and Northern Ireland from the European Union and the European Atomic Energy Community of 17 December 2020 determining the initial maximum exempted overall annual level of support and the initial minimum percentage referred to in Article 10(2) of the Protocol on Ireland/Northern Ireland to the Agreement on the withdrawal of the United Kingdom of Great Britain and Northern Ireland from the European Union and the European Atomic Energy Community.* L443, 30 December 2020 pp. 13–15. Available: https://eur-lex.europa.eu/legal-content/EN/TXT/?uri=uriserv%3AOJ.L_.2020.443.01.0013.01.ENG&toc=OJ%3AL%3A2020%3A443%3ATOC (Accessed 14 April 2021)

Official Journal (2020f) *Decision No 6/2020 of the Joint Committee established by the Agreement on the withdrawal of the United Kingdom of Great Britain and Northern Ireland from the European Union and the European Atomic Energy Community of 17 December 2020 providing for the practical working arrangements relating to the exercise of the rights of Union representatives referred to in Article 12(2) of the Protocol on Ireland/Northern Ireland.* L443, 30 December 2020 pp. 16–21. Available: https://eur-lex.europa.eu/legal-content/EN/TXT/?uri=uriserv%3AOJ.L_.2020.443.01.0016.01.ENG&toc=OJ%3AL%3A2020%3A443%3ATOC (Accessed 14 April 2021)

Official Journal (2020g) *Political declaration setting out the framework for the future relationship between the European Union and the United Kingdom.* C34, 31 January 2020 pp. 1–16. Available: https://eur-lex.europa.eu/legal-content/EN/TXT/?uri=uriserv:OJ.C_.2020.034.01.0001.01.ENG (Accessed 14 April 2021)

Official Journal (2020h) *Trade and Cooperation Agreement between the European Union and the European Atomic Energy Community, of the One Part, and the United Kingdom of Great Britain and Northern Ireland, of the Other Part.* L444, 31 December 2020 pp. 14–1462. Available: https://eur-lex.europa.eu/legal-content/EN/TXT/?uri=uriserv%3AOJ.L_.2020.444.01.0014.01.ENG&toc=OJ%3AL%3A2020%3A444%3AFULL (Accessed 14 April 2021)

Official Journal (2023) *Decision No 1/2023 of the Joint Committee established by the Agreement on the withdrawal of the United Kingdom of Great Britain and Northern Ireland from the European Union and the European Atomic Energy Community of 24 March 2023 laying down arrangements relating to the Windsor Framework.* L102/61, 17 April 2023 pp 61–83. Available: https://eur-lex.europa.eu/legal-content/EN/TXT/?uri=CELEX:22023D0819 (Accessed 15 June 2023)

Official Journal (2023) *Joint Declaration No 1/2023 of the Union and the United Kingdom in the Joint Committee Established by the Agreement on the Withdrawal of the United Kingdom of Great Britain and Northern Ireland from the European Union and the European Atomic Energy Community.* L102/87, 17 April 2023 pp. 87–87. Available: https://eur-lex.europa.eu/legal-content/EN/TXT/?uri=uriserv%3AOJ.L_.2023.102.01.0087.01.ENG&toc=OJ%3AL%3A2023%3A102%3ATOC (Accessed 6 June 2023)

Ireland Legislation

Government of Ireland (2000) *Agreement between the Government of Ireland and the Government of the United Kingdom of Great Britain and Northern Ireland.* Treaty Series 2000 N° 18 Available: https://www.dfa.ie/media/dfa/alldfawebsitemedia/treatyseries/uploads/documents/treaties/docs/200018.pdf (Accessed 12 December 2020)

United Kingdom Legislation

Act of Union (Ireland) 1800 c. 38 Available: https://www.legislation.gov.uk/aip/Geo3/40/38/contents (Accessed 20 April 2021)

Agreement between the Government of the United Kingdom of Great Britain and Northern Ireland and the Government of Ireland (British-Irish Agreement) Treaty Series 050/2000 [Cm 4292] Available: http://foto.archivalware.co.uk/data/Library2/pdf/2000-TS0050.pdf (Accessed 10 February 2021)

Agreement between the Government of the United Kingdom of Great Britain and Northern Ireland and the Government of Ireland establishing a British-Irish Council Treaty Series 055/2000 [Cm 4296] Available: http://foto.archivalware.co.uk/data/Library2/pdf/2000-TS0055.pdf (Accessed 10 February 2021)

Agreement between the Government of the United Kingdom of Great Britain and Northern Ireland and the Government of Ireland establishing a British-Irish Intergovernmental Conference Treaty Series 054/2000 [Cm 4295] Available: http://foto.archivalware.co.uk/data/Library2/pdf/2000-TS0054.pdf (Accessed 10 February 2021)

Agreement between the Government of the United Kingdom of Great Britain and Northern Ireland and the Government of Ireland establishing Implementation Bodies Treaty Series 051/2000 [Cm 4293] Available: http://foto.archivalware.co.uk/data/Library2/pdf/2000-TS0051.pdf (Accessed 10 February 2021)

Agreement between the Government of the United Kingdom of Great Britain and Northern Ireland and the Government of Ireland establishing a North/South Ministerial Council Treaty Series 053/2000 [Cm 4294] Available: http://foto.archivalware.co.uk/data/Library2/pdf/2000-TS0053.pdf (Accessed 10 February 2021)

Assembly and Executive Reform (Assembly Opposition) Act (Northern Ireland) 2016 c. 10 Available: https://www.legislation.gov.uk/nia/2016/10/contents (Accessed 20 April 2021)

British Nationality Act 1981 c. 61 Available: https://www.legislation.gov.uk/ukpga/1981/61 (Accessed 15 April 2021)

Civil Authority (Special Powers) Act 1922 1949 No. 147 Available: https://cain.ulster.ac.uk/hmso/spa1922.htm (Accessed 10 February 2023)

Civil Authorities (Special Powers) 1971 No. 309 Available: https://www.legislation.gov.uk/nisro/1971/309/contents/made (Accessed 14 February 2023)

Early Parliamentary General Election Act 2019 c. 29 Available: https://www.legislation.gov.uk/ukpga/2019/29/enacted (Accessed 8 February 2021)

European Communities Act 1972 c. 68 Available: https://www.legislation.gov.uk/ukpga/1972/68/contents (Accessed 11 December 2020)

European Union Act 2011 c. 12 Avilable: https://www.legislation.gov.uk/ukpga/2011/12/contents (Accessed 6 June 2023)

European Union (Referendum) Act 2015 c.36 Available: https://www.legislation.gov.uk/ukpga/2015/36/contents/enacted (Accessed 5 June 2023)

European Union (Future Relationship) Act 2020 c. 29 Available: https://www.legislation.gov.uk/ukpga/2020/29/enacted (Accessed 10 February 2021)

European Union (Withdrawal Agreement) Act 2020 c. 1 Available: https://www.legislation.gov.uk/ukpga/2020/1/contents/enacted (Accessed: 10 December 2020)

European Union (Withdrawal) Act 2018 c. 16 Available: https://www.legislation.gov.uk/ukpga/2018/16/contents/enacted (Accessed: 10 December 2020)

Fixed-term Parliaments Act 2011 c. 14 Available: https://www.legislation.gov.uk/ukpga/2011/14/contents/enacted (Accessed 12 March 2021)

Government of Ireland Act 1920 c. 67 Available: https://www.legislation.gov.uk/ukpga/1920/67/pdfs/ukpga_19200067_en.pdf (Accessed 16 April 2021)

Government of Wales Act 2006 c. 32 Available: https://www.legislation.gov.uk/ukpga/2006/32/contents (Accessed 12 April 2021)

Human Rights Act 1998 c. 42 Available: https://www.legislation.gov.uk/ukpga/1998/42/contents (Accessed 12 April 2021)

Interpretation Act (Northern Ireland) 1954 c. 33 Available: https://www.legislation.gov.uk/apni/1954/33/section/7 (Accessed 2 March 2021)

Memorandum of Understanding between the Government of the United Kingdom of Great Britain and Northern Ireland and the Government of Ireland concerning the Common Travel Area and associated reciprocal rights and privileges. 2019, May 8 Available: https://assets.publishing.service.gov.uk/government/uploads/system/uploads/attachment_data/file/800280/CTA-MoU-UK.pdf (Accessed 2 March 2021)

Nationality and Borders Act 2022 c. 36 Available: https://www.legislation.gov.uk/ukpga/2022/36/contents/enacted (Accessed 20 January 2023)

Northern Ireland Act 1998 c. 47 Available: https://www.legislation.gov.uk/ukpga/1998/47/introduction (Accessed: 10 December 2020)

Northern Ireland Act 1974 c. 28 Available: https://www.legislation.gov.uk/ukpga/1974/28/enacted (Accessed 17 February 20230
Northern Ireland Assembly Act 1973 c. 17 Available: https://www.legislation.gov.uk/ukpga/1973/17/enacted (Accessed 15 February 2023)
Northern Ireland Constitution Act 1973 c. 36 Available: https://www.legislation.gov.uk/ukpga/1973/36/contents (Accessed 15 April 2021)
Northern Ireland (Elections) Act 1998 c. 12 Available: https://www.legislation.gov.uk/ukpga/1998/47 (Accessed 21 April 2021)
Northern Ireland (Executive Formation and Exercise of Functions) Act 2018 c. 28 Available: https://www.legislation.gov.uk/ukpga/2018/28/enacted (Accessed 8 December 2020)
Northern Ireland (Executive Formation etc.) Act 2019 c. 22 Available: https://www.legislation.gov.uk/ukpga/2019/22/enacted (Accessed 8 December 2020)
Northern Ireland (Executive Formation etc.) Act 2022 c. 48 Available: https://www.legislation.gov.uk/ukpga/2022/48/contents/enacted (Accessed 20 January 2023)
Northern Ireland (Extension of Period for Executive Formation) Regulations 2019 (SI 2019/616) Available: https://www.legislation.gov.uk/uksi/2019/616/made (Accessed 12 December 2020)
Northern Ireland (Extension of Period for Executive Formation) (No. 2) Regulations 2019 (SI 2019/1364) Available: https://www.legislation.gov.uk/uksi/2019/1364/made (Accessed 12 December 2020)
Northern Ireland (Ministerial Appointments and Regional Rates) Act 2017 c. 24 Available: https://www.legislation.gov.uk/ukpga/2017/24/section/1/enacted (Accessed 12 December 2020)
Northern Ireland (Ministers, Elections and Petitions of Concern) Act 2022 c. 2 Available: https://www.legislation.gov.uk/ukpga/2022/2/contents/enacted (Accessed 20 January 2023)
Northern Ireland (Temporary Provisions) Act 1972 c. 22 Available: https://www.legislation.gov.uk/ukpga/1972/22/enacted (Accessed 10 February 2023)
Planning Act (Northern Ireland) 2011 c. 25 Available: https://www.legislation.gov.uk/nia/2011/25/contents (Accessed 21 April 2021)
Private International Law (Implementation of Agreements) Act 2020 c. 24 Available: https://www.legislation.gov.uk/ukpga/2020/24/notes/division/3/index.htm (Accessed 20 January 2023)
Scotland Act 1998 c. 46 Available: https://www.legislation.gov.uk/ukpga/1998/46/contents (Accessed 12 April 2021)
Taxation (Cross-Border Trade) Act 2018 c. 22 Available: https://www.legislation.gov.uk/ukpga/2018/22/contents (Accessed 2 February 2021)
Taxation (Post-transition Period) Act 2020 c. 26 Available: https://www.legislation.gov.uk/ukpga/2020/26/contents/enacted (Accessed 3 February 2021)
The Conflict Minerals (Compliance) (Northern Ireland) (EU Exit) Regulations 2020 (SI 2020/1664) Available: https://www.legislation.gov.uk/uksi/2020/1664/made (Accessed 15 January 2021)
The Definition of Qualifying Northern Ireland Goods (EU Exit) Regulations 2020 (SI 2020/1454) Available: https://www.legislation.gov.uk/uksi/2020/1454/made (Accessed 12 December 2020)
The Departments (Northern Ireland) Order 1999 NIOC No. 283 (N.I. 1) Available: https://www.legislation.gov.uk/nisi/1999/283/article/2/made (Accessed 12 December 2020)
The Excise Goods (Sales on Board Ships and Aircraft) Regulations 1999 (SI 1999/1565) Available: https://www.legislation.gov.uk/uksi/1999/1565/made (Accessed 15 January 2021)
The Northern Ireland Constitution Act 1973 c. 36 Available: https://www.legislation.gov.uk/ukpga/1973/36/section/1/enacted (Accessed 7 March 2021)

The Northern Ireland (Extension of Period for Making Ministerial Appointments) Regulations 2022 (SI 2022/1296) https://www.legislation.gov.uk/uksi/2022/1296/introduction/made (Accessed 20 January 2023)

The Protocol on Ireland/Northern Ireland (Democratic Consent Process) (EU Exit) Regulations 2020 (SI 2020/1500). Available: https://www.legislation.gov.uk/uksi/2020/1500/made (Accessed: 10 December 2020)

The Travellers' Allowances and Miscellaneous Provisions (Northern Ireland) (EU Exit) Regulations 2020 (SI 2020/1619) Available: https://www.legislation.gov.uk/uksi/2020/1619/made#f00003 (Accessed 15 January 2021)

The Windsor Framework (Democratic Scrutiny) Regulations 2023 Available: https://www.legislation.gov.uk/ukdsi/2023/9780348246322 (Accessed 27 March 2023)

Union with England Act 1707 c. 7 Available: https://www.legislation.gov.uk/aosp/1707/7/contents (Accessed 20 April 2021)

United Kingdom Internal Market Act 2020 c. 27 Available: https://www.legislation.gov.uk/ukpga/2020/27/contents/enacted (Accessed 2 February 2021)

Bibliography

@DUPleader 2019 *Arlene Foster* 2019, October 16 *Twitter* Available: https://twitter.com/DUPleader/status/1184447621106143234 (Accessed 10 December 2020)

@edwinpootsmla 2021 *Edwin Poots* 2021, February 1 *Twitter* Available: https://twitter.com/edwinpootsmla/status/1356368473090363395?s=20&t=Y4nz6BTtTGS4nAGI4VwbjA (Accessed 16 January 2023)

@EESC_REX 2022 *EESC External Relations* 2022, October 21 *Twitter* Available: https://twitter.com/EESC_REX/status/1583469167793295361 (Accessed 22 January 2023)

@JamesCleverly 2022 *James Cleverly* 2022, December 15 *Twitter* Available: https://twitter.com/JamesCleverly/status/1603392863437553666 (Accessed 19 January 2023)

@JoeBiden 2020 *Joe Biden* 2020, September 16 *Twitter* Available: https://twitter.com/joebiden/status/1306334039557586944?lang=en (Accessed 10 December 2020)

@MarosSefcovic 2022a *Maroš Šefčovič* 2022, December 1 *Twitter* Available: https://twitter.com/JamesCleverly/status/1598335967525576708 (Accessed 19 January 2023)

@MarosSefcovic 2022b *Maroš Šefčovič* 2022, December 15 *Twitter* Available: https://twitter.com/MarosSefcovic/status/1603386004299288576 (Accessed 19 January 2023)

@rdanielkeleman 2020 'The Brexit Trilemma' *Daniel Keleman* 2020, September 20 *Twitter* Available: https://twitter.com/rdanielkelemen/status/1344316160699846657/photo/1 (Accessed 8 January 2021)

Ackerman, B. A. (1993) *We the People vol. 1, Foundations*. Cambridge, Massachusetts: Harvard University Press.

Ackerman, B. A. (1998) *We the People vol. 2, Transformations* London: Belknap Press.

Adelman, P. (1996) *Great Britain and the Irish question, 1800–1922* London: Hodder & Stoughton.

Allen, M., Downing, E., Edwards, T., Seaton, N., and Semple, M. (2014) 'Cap Reform 2014–20: EU Agreement and Implementation in the UK and in Ireland' *RaISe paper* Available: http://www.niassembly.gov.uk/globalassets/Documents/RaISe/Publications/2014/dard/allen10314.pdf (Accessed 05 January 2019)

Alliance (2010) 'Alliance Works: Working for You at Westminster. The Alliance Party of Northern Ireland' *CAIN* Available: https://cain.ulster.ac.uk/issues/politics/docs/apni/apni060510man.pdf (Accessed 10 March 2020)

Alliance (2016) 'Forward. Faster. Manifesto 2016: An agenda to increase the speed of change in Northern Ireland' *CAIN* Available: https://cain.ulster.ac.uk/issues/politics/docs/apni/apni_2016-04-19_nia-man.pdf (Accessed 22 May 2019)

Alliance (2017) 'How to change Northern Ireland. For good: Manifesto 2017' *CAIN* Available: https://cain.ulster.ac.uk/issues/politics/docs/apni/apni_2017-02-21_nia-man.pdf (Accessed 14 April 2021)

Andrews, C. (2021) 'Brexit: Why are the shelves empty in some supermarkets' 2021, January 7. *BBC News* Available: https://www.bbc.co.uk/news/uk-northern-ireland-55575988 (Accessed 16 January 2023)

Anthony, G. (2008) 'The St Andrews Agreement and the Northern Ireland Assembly' *European Public Law*, 14(2): 151–64.

Bibliography

Anthony, G. (2017) 'Brexit and the Irish Border: Legal and Political Questions'. *The British Academy* Available: https://www.thebritishacademy.ac.uk/publications/europe-brexit-and-irish-border-legal-and-political-questions/ (Accessed 31 March 2021)

Anthony, G. (2018) 'Brexit and the Common Law Constitution' *European Public Law*, 24(4): 673–94.

Anthony, G. (2018) 'Sovereignty, Consent and Constitutions: The Northern Ireland References' in Elliott, M., Williams, J., and Young, A. L. *The UK Constitution after Miller: Brexit and Beyond*. Oxford: Hart Publishing 181–202.

Anthony, G. (2021) 'The Quartet Plus Two: Judicial Review in Northern Ireland' in Arvind, T. T., Kirkham, R., Mac Sítigh, D., and Stirton, L. (eds.) *Executive Decision-Making and the Courts: Revisiting the Origins of Modern Judicial Review*. Oxford: Hart Publishing 261–77.

Anushka, A., Mason, R., and Elgot, J. (2016) 'Andrea Leadsom pulls out of Conservative leadership race' 2016, July 11. *The Guardian* Available: https://www.theguardian.com/politics/2016/jul/11/conservative-leadership-andrea-leadsom-pulls-out-of-race (Accessed 6 June 2020)

Anushka, A., McDonald, H., and Carrell, S. (2017) 'Theresa May faces backlash from Scotland and Wales over £1bn Tory-DUP deal'. *The Guardian* 2017, June 26. Available: https://www.theguardian.com/politics/2017/jun/26/tories-and-the-dup-reach-deal-to-prop-up-minority-government (Accessed 14 April 2021)

Aristotle (350 BCE) *Rhetoric* (trans.) by Rhys Roberts, W. Available: http://classics.mit.edu/Aristotle/rhetoric.1.i.html (Accessed 12 April 2021)

Assembly and Executive Review Committee (2014) 'Review of Petitions of Concern' *niassembly.gov.uk* Available: http://www.niassembly.gov.uk/globalassets/documents/assembly-and-executive-review-2011—2016/reports/review-of-petitions-of-concern.pdf (Accessed 10 February 2023)

Associated Press (1998) 'Sinn Fein's delegates endorse North Ireland peace agreement' 1998, May 11. *Associated Press* Available: https://www.deseret.com/1998/5/11/19379325/sinn-fein-s-delegates-endorse-north-ireland-peace-agreement (Accessed 4 March 2021)

Aveyard, S. (2014) '"We couldn't do a Prague": British government responses to loyalist strikes in Northern Ireland 1974–77' *Irish Historical Studies*, 39(153): 91–111.

Bagehot, W. (1867) *The English Constitution*. London: Chapman and Hall.

Bailey, D., and Budd, L. (2017) *The Political Economy of Brexit*. Newcastle upon Tyne: Agenda.

Bale, T. (2018) 'Who leads and who follows? The symbiotic relationship between UKIP and the Conservatives—and populism and Euroscepticism' *Politics*, 38(3): 263–77.

Banks, A. (2016) *The Bad Boys of Brexit*. London: Biteback.

Barker, R. (2000) 'Hooks and hands, interests and enemies: political thinking as political action' *Political Studies*, 48(2): 223–38

Barnard, C. (2017) 'Law and Brexit' *Oxford Review of Economic Policy*, 33(S1): S4–S11.

BBCMarkSimpson 2016 *Mark Simpson* 2016, May 6 *Twitter* Available: https://twitter.com/BBCMarkSimpson/status/728833017599430656 (Accessed 6 May 2016)

BBC News (2015) 'SNP bid for "quadruple lock" on EU referendum vote rejected' 2015, June 16. *BBC News* Available: https://www.bbc.co.uk/news/uk-scotland-scotland-politics-33150080 (Accessed 12 April 2019)

BBC News (2016a) 'EU referendum: Row over Turkey's membership bid escalates' 2016, May 24. *BBC News* Available: https://www.bbc.co.uk/news/uk-politics-eu-referendum-36353013 (Accessed 14 April 2020)

BBC News (2016b) 'Major and Blair say an EU exit could split the UK' 2016, June 9. *BBC News* Available: https://www.bbc.co.uk/news/uk-politics-eu-referendum-36486016 (Accessed 5 April 2019)

BBC News (2016c) 'Reality Check: Would Brexit mean border controls for NI?' 2016, June 7. *BBC News* Available: https://www.bbc.co.uk/news/uk-politics-eu-referendum-36462023 (Accessed 05 April 2019)

BBC News (2016d) 'Andrea Leadsom 'motherhood' comments spark row' 2016, July 9. *BBC News* Available: https://www.bbc.co.uk/news/uk-politics-36752865 (Accessed 6 June 2020)

BBC News (2016e) 'Andrea Leadsom apologises to Theresa May over motherhood remark' 2016, July 11. *BBC News* Available: https://www.bbc.co.uk/news/uk-politics-36760986 (Accessed 6 June 2016)

BBC News (2016f) 'PM-in-waiting Theresa May promises 'a better Britain'' 2016, 11 July. *BBC News* Available: https://www.bbc.co.uk/news/uk-politics-36768148 (Accessed 6 June 2020)

BBC News (2016g) 'Michael Gove: Boris Johnson wasn't up to the job' 2016, June 30. *BBC News* Available: https://www.bbc.co.uk/news/uk-politics-36677028 (Accessed 14 June 2020)

BBC News (2016h) 'EU referendum: NI reaction to referendum result' 2016, July 11. *BBC News* Available: https://www.bbc.co.uk/news/uk-northern-ireland-36617314 (Accessed 6 June 2020)

BBC News (2017a) 'Martin McGuinness resigns as NI deputy First Minister' 2017, January 10. *BBC News* Available: https://www.bbc.co.uk/news/uk-northern-ireland-38561507 (Accessed 20 May 2019)

BBC News (2017b) 'Michelle O'Neill calls for "urgent" referendum on Irish unity' 2017, March 13. *BBC News* Available: https://www.bbc.co.uk/news/uk-northern-ireland-politics-39249929 (Accessed 10 June 2020)

BBC News (2018) 'Theresa May rejects EU's draft option for Northern Ireland' 2018, February 28. *BBC News* Available: https://www.bbc.co.uk/news/uk-politics-43224785 (Accessed 15 April 2021)

BBC News (2019a) 'Theresa May Quits: UK set for new PM by end of July' 2019, May 24. *BBC News* Available: https://www.bbc.co.uk/news/uk-politics-48395905 (Accessed 13 April 2021)

BBC News (2019b) 'Merkel: Backstop alternative "possible within 30 days"' 2019, August 21. *BBC News* Available: https://www.bbc.co.uk/news/uk-politics-49427674 (Accessed 9 January 2020)

BBC News (2019c) 'Brexit: Boris Johnson and Leo Varadkar "can see pathway to a deal"' 2019, October 10. *BBC News* Available: https://www.bbc.co.uk/news/uk-politics-49995133 (Accessed 8 January 2020)

BBC News (2019d) 'Brexit: EU and UK reach deal but DUP refuses support' 2019, October 17. *BBC News* Available: https://www.bbc.co.uk/news/uk-politics-50079385 (Accessed 14 April 2021)

BBC News, (2019e) 'Brexit: PSNI chief says potential for loyalist disorder if Brexit threatens union' 2019, October 23. *BBC News* (https://www.bbc.co.uk/news/uk-northern-ireland-50157743) (Accessed 8 March 2020)

BBC News (2021a) 'Brexit: Arlene Foster sees "gateway of opportunity" in UK–EU trade deal' 2021, January 3. *BBC News* Available: https://www.bbc.co.uk/news/uk-northern-ireland-55521248 (Accessed 16 January 2023)

BBC News (2021b) 'Brexit: Animal-based food checks at ports suspended' 2021, February 2. *BBC News* Available: https://www.bbc.co.uk/news/uk-northern-ireland-55895276 (Accessed 16 January 2023)

BBC News (2021c) 'Brexit: DUP vows to send "strong message" to Irish Government over NI Protocol' 2021, February 2. *BBC News* Available: https://www.bbc.co.uk/news/uk-northern-ireland-55910506 (Accessed 16 January 2023)

BBC News (2021d) 'NI riots: What is behind the violence in Northern Ireland' 2021, April 14. *BBC News* Available: https://www.bbc.co.uk/news/uk-northern-ireland-56664378 (Accessed 16 January 2023)

BBC News (2021e) 'Brexit: EU pauses legal action against UK over NI Protocol "breaches"' 2021, July 27. *BBC News* Available: https://www.bbc.co.uk/news/uk-northern-ireland-57986307 (Accessed 16 January 2023)

BBC News (2021f) 'Lord Frost's resignation letter in full' 2021, December 18. *BBC News* Available: https://www.bbc.co.uk/news/uk-politics-59714710 (Accessed 18 January 2023)

BBC News (2021g) 'NI Protocol: Five things we learned from Šefčovič visit' 2021, September 12. *BBC News* Available: https://www.bbc.co.uk/news/uk-northern-ireland-58531492 (Accessed 20 January 2023)

BBC News (2021h) 'NI 100: The King's speech to the Northern Ireland Parliament' 2021, June 22. *BBC News* Available: https://www.bbc.co.uk/news/uk-northern-ireland-57526224 (Accessed 22 August 2021)

BBC Two (2019) 'We Quit' Episode 1 in *Inside Europe: Ten Years of Turmoil*. Available: https://www.dailymotion.com/video/x71isj8 (Accessed 15 April 2021)

Beesley, A. Nilsson, P., and Parker, G. (2021) 'Northern Ireland shoppers face empty shelves as Brexit snags supply chains' 2021, January 11. *Financial Times* Available: https://www.ft.com/content/c1215859-db02-42f3-a12e-3039137377cb (Accessed 16 January 2023)

Belfast Harbour Commissioners (2022) 'Annual Report and Accounts 2021' *belfast-harbour.co.uk* Available: https://www.belfast-harbour.co.uk/wp-content/uploads/2022/06/ANNUAL-REPORT-FINAL.pdf (Accessed 3 February 2023)

Belfast Telegraph (2015a) 'EU referendum: DUP's Sammy Wilson gives backing to Ukip Brexit campaign, blasting David Cameron's "pathetic" demands' 2015, November 25. *Belfast Telegraph* Available: https://www.belfasttelegraph.co.uk/news/politics/eu-referendum-dups-sammy-wilson-gives-backing-to-ukip-brexit-campaign-blasting-david-camerons-pathetic-demands-34233078.html (Accessed 20 May 2019)

Belfast Telegraph (2015b) 'Sinn Fein to protect EU membership' 2019, April 20. *Belfast Telegraph* Available: https://www.belfasttelegraph.co.uk/news/northern-ireland/sinn-fein-to-protect-eu-membership-31156231.html (Accessed 20 May 2019)

Belfast Telegraph (2016a) 'First Minister Arlene Foster: 'Our nation is safe and Northern Ireland will be front and centre of Brexit negotiations' 2015, June 24. *Belfast Telegraph* Available: https://www.belfasttelegraph.co.uk/news/brexit/first-minister-arlene-foster-our-nation-is-safe-and-northern-ireland-will-be-front-and-centre-of-brexit-negotiations-34829817.html (Accessed 24 May 2019)

Belfast Telegraph (2016b) 'Northern Ireland whacked by Brexit, says Bill Clinton' 2016, April 1. *Belfast Telegraph* Available: https://www.belfasttelegraph.co.uk/news/world-news/northern-ireland-whacked-by-brexit-says-bill-clinton-34589412.html (Accessed 12 April 2021)

Belfast Telegraph (2016c) 'Enda Kenny urges Irish-born voters to back Remain in visit to UK' 2016, June 16. *Belfast Telegraph* Available: https://www.belfasttelegraph.co.uk/news/republic-of-ireland/enda-kenny-urges-irish-born-voters-to-back-remain-in-visit-to-uk-34808080.html (Accessed 12 April 2021)

Belfast Telegraph (2018) 'Boris Johnson backs DUP in demanding Brexit backstop scrapped' 2018, November 24. *Belfast Telegraph* Available: https://www.belfasttelegraph.co.uk/news/brexit/boris-johnson-backs-dup-in-demanding-brexit-backstop-is-scrapped-37561720.html (Accessed 18 April 2021)

Belfast Telegraph (2019a) 'Brexit: DUP backs Boris Johnson's offer but Sinn Féin hits out at Stormont veto plans' 2019, October 2. *Belfast Telegraph* Available: https://www.

belfasttelegraph.co.uk/news/brexit/brexit-dup-backs-boris-johnsons-offer-but-sinn-fein-hits-out-at-stormont-veto-plans-38556510.html (Accessed 10 December 2020)

Belfast Telegraph (2019b) 'Brexit: Foster dismisses as "nonsense" claims DUP accepts proposal on Stormont consent' 2019, October 16. *Belfast Telegraph* Available: https://www.belfasttelegraph.co.uk/news/northern-ireland/brexit-foster-dismisses-as-nonsense-claims-dup-accepts-proposal-on-stormont-consent-38601523.html (Accessed 8 December 2020)

Bell, C. (2014) 'Constitutional transitions: the peculiarities of the British constitution and the politics of comparison' *Public Law*, 446: 1–20.

Bell, C. and Cavanaugh, K. (1999) 'Constructive Ambiguity or Internal Self-Determination—Self-Determination, Group Accommodation, and the Belfast Agreement' *Fordham International Law Journal*, 22: 1345–72.

Bell, J. (2019) 'Brexit deal: DUP says Johnson's agreement isn't in Northern Ireland's interests and undermines the Union' 2019, October 17. *Belfast Telegraph* (https://www.belfasttelegraph.co.uk/news/brexit/brexit-deal-dup-says-johnsons-agreement-isnt-in-northern-irelands-interests-and-undermines-union-38604720.html) Accessed 2 March 2020.

Bellamy, R. (2007) *Constitutionalism: A Republican Defence of the Constitutionality of Democracy*. Cambridge: Cambridge University Press.

Berridge, G. R. and James, A. (2003) *A Dictionary of Diplomacy*. 2nd ed. New York: Palgrave Macmillan.

BIC (2008) 'British-Irish Council Communiqué' 2008, September 26. *British Irish Council* Available: https://www.britishirishcouncil.org/sites/default/files/communiqués/11%20-%20Eleventh%20Summit%20Meeting%20-%20Scotland%20-%2026%20Sep%202008.pdf (Accessed 6 February 2023)

BIC (2009) 'British-Irish Council Communiqué' 2009, November 13. *British Irish Council* Available: https://www.britishirishcouncil.org/sites/default/files/communiqués/13%20-%20Thirteenth%20Summit%20-%20Jersey%20-%2013%20Nov%202009.pdf (Accessed 6 February 2023)

BIC (2010) 'British-Irish Council Communiqué' 2010, December 13. *British Irish Council* Available: https://www.britishirishcouncil.org/sites/default/files/communiqués/15%20-%20Fifteenth%20Summit%20-%20Isle%20of%20Man%20-%2013%20Dec%202010.pdf (Accessed 6 February 2023)

BIC (2016a) 'British-Irish Council Communiqué' 2016, June 17. *British Irish Council* Available: https://www.britishirishcouncil.org/sites/default/files/communiqués/Twenty%20Sixth%20Summit%20-%20Glasgow%20-%2017062016.pdf (Accessed 6 June 2020)

BIC (2016b) 'British-Irish Council Communiqué Extraordinary Summit' 2016, July 22. *British Irish Council* Available: https://www.britishirishcouncil.org/sites/default/files/communiqués/Extraordinary%20Summit%20-%20Cardiff%20-%2022072016.pdf (Accessed 6 June 2020)

BIC (2016c) 'British-Irish Council Communiqué' 2016, November 25. *British Irish Council* Available: https://www.britishirishcouncil.org/sites/default/files/communiqués/Twenty%20Eighth%20Summit%20-%20Cardiff%20-%2025112016.pdf (Accessed 6 June 2016)

BIC (2017) 'British-Irish Council Communiqué' 2017, November 10. *British Irish Council* Available: https://www.britishirishcouncil.org/sites/default/files/communiqués/29th%20Summit%20-%20Jersey.pdf (Accessed 12 April 2021)

BIC (2018a) 'British-Irish Council Communiqué' 2018, June 22. *British Irish Council* Available: https://www.britishirishcouncil.org/sites/default/files/communiqués/Thirtieth%20Summit%20Comminique%20-%20Guernsey_3.pdf (Accessed 12 April 2021)

BIC (2018b) 'British-Irish Council Communiqué' 2018, November 9. *British Irish Council* Available: https://www.britishirishcouncil.org/sites/default/files/communiqués/Thirty%20First%20Summit%20Comminique%20-%20Isle%20of%20Man_0.pdf (Accessed 12 April 2021)

BIC (2019a) 'British-Irish Council Communiqué' 2019, June 28. *British Irish Council* Available: https://www.britishirishcouncil.org/sites/default/files/communiqués/Thirty%20Second%20Summit%20-%20UK%20-%2028%2006%2019.pdf (Accessed 12 April 2021)

BIC (2019b) 'British-Irish Council Communiqué' 2019, November 15. *British Irish Council* Available: https://www.britishirishcouncil.org/sites/default/files/communiqués/33rd%20Summit%20Held%20in%20Dublin%20Communique.pdf (Accessed 12 April 2021)

BIC (2020) 'British-Irish Council Communiqué' 2020, November 6. *British Irish Council* Available: https://www.britishirishcouncil.org/sites/default/files/communiqués/Thirty%20Fourth%20Summit%20-%20Scotland%20-%2006%2011%2020.pdf (Accessed 6 February 2023)

BIC (2021a) 'British-Irish Council Communiqué' 2021, June 11. *British Irish Council* Available: https://www.britishirishcouncil.org/sites/default/files/communiqués/Thirty%20Fifth%20Summit%20-%20Northern%20Ireland%20-%2011%2006%2021_0.pdf (Accessed 6 February 2023)

BIC (2021b) 'British-Irish Council Communiqué' 2021, November 19. *British Irish Council* Available: https://www.britishirishcouncil.org/sites/default/files/communiqués/Thirty%20Sixth%20Summit%20-%20Wales%20-%2019%2011%2021_1.pdf (Accessed 6 February 2023)

BIC (2022a) 'British-Irish Council Communiqué' 2022, July 8. *British Irish Council* Available: https://www.britishirishcouncil.org/sites/default/files/communiqués/FINAL%20BIC%20Summit%20Communique_0.pdf (Accessed 6 February 2023)

BIC (2022b) 'British-Irish Council Communiqué' 2022, November 11. *British Irish Council* Available: https://www.britishirishcouncil.org/sites/default/files/communiqués/38th%20BIC%20Summit%20-%20Communique%20-%20Final.pdf (Accessed 20 January 2023)

BIC (2023a) 'Communiqués' *British-Irish Council* Available: https://www.britishirishcouncil.org/bic/summits (Accessed 4 February 2023)

BIC (2023b) 'Publications' *British-Irish Council* Available: https://www.britishirishcouncil.org/publications (Accessed 4 February 2023)

Blair, T. (2010) 'Tony Blair: Northern Ireland peace is an inspiration to the world' 2010, September 2. *The Belfast Telegraph* Available: http://www.belfasttelegraph.co.uk/news/local-national/northern-ireland/tony-blair-northern-ireland-peace-is-an-inspiration-to-the-world-28556892.html (Accessed 27 November 2020)

Bogdanor, V. (1999) *Devolution in the United Kingdom*. Oxford: Oxford University Press.

Bogdanor, V. (2007) 'Our new Constitution' *Gresham College*. 2007, May 29. Available: https://www.gresham.ac.uk/lectures-and-events/our-new-constitution-0 (Accessed 12 February 2021)

Bogdanor, V. (2019) *Beyond Brexit: Towards a British Constitution*. London: I. B. Tauris.

Bolingbroke, H. (1841) *The Works of Lord Bolingbroke with A Life: vol. II*. Philadelphia: Carey and Hart.

Bowers, P. (2005) 'The Sewel Convention' SN/PC/2084. *HC Library* Available: https://researchbriefings.parliament.uk/ResearchBriefing/Summary/SN02084 (Accessed 02 December 2018)

Boyce, D. G. (1996) *The Irish Question and British Politics, 1868–1996*. 2nd ed. Basingstoke: Macmillan.

British Election Study (2016) 'Wave 9 of the 2014–2018 British Election Study Panel (2016 EU Referendum Study, Post-election survey)' *britishelectionstudy.com* Available: https://www.britishelectionstudy.com/data-object/wave-9-of-the-2014-2017-british-election-study-internet-panel-2016-eu-referendum-study-post-election-survey/ (Accessed 12 April 2021)

British Social Attitudes. (2016) 'Technical Details' Issue 34 *bas.natcen.ac.uk* Available: https://www.bsa.natcen.ac.uk/media/39143/bsa34_technical-details_fin.pdf (Accessed 14 April 2021)

Brownlow, G. and Budd, L. (2019) 'Sense making of Brexit for economic citizenship in Northern Ireland' *Contemporary Social Science*, 14(2): 294–311.

Bruschi, A. (2017) 'Measurement in social research: some misunderstandings' *Qual Quant*, 51: 2219–43.

Buchan, L. (2019) 'Brexit: Boris Johnson accused of misleading parliament after saying there would be "no checks" between Northern Ireland and Britain' 2019, October 23. *Independent* Available: https://www.independent.co.uk/news/uk/politics/brexit-boris-johnson-northern-ireland-sea-border-checks-steve-barclay-latest-a9167651.html (Accessed 9 March 2020)

Buckland, P. (1980) 'Who Governed Northern Ireland? The Royal Assent and the Local Government Bill 1922' *Irish Jurist*, 15(2): 326–40.

Buckledee, S. (2018) *The Language of Brexit: How Britain Talked its Way Out of the European Union*. London: Bloomsbury.

Budd, L. (2015) 'The consequences for the Northern Ireland economy from a United Kingdom exit from the European Union' 2015, March. *NI Assembly*. Available: https://crossborder.ie/site2015/wp-content/uploads/2015/11/2015-03-22-brexit-ceti-specialist-advisor.pdf (Accessed 30 March 2021)

Burchard, H. (2021) 'EU, UK vow to "intensify" talks on Northern Ireland border checks' 2021, April 16. *politico.eu* Available: https://www.politico.eu/article/eu-and-uk-vow-to-intensify-talks-on-northern-ireland-border-checks/ (Accessed 16 January 2023)

Burke, E. (2016) 'Who will speak for Northern Ireland? The looming danger of an Ulster Brexit' *RUSI Journal*, 161(2): 4–12.

Burton, M. (2022) 'Northern Ireland Assembly Election: 2022' CBP 9549 *House of Commons Library* Available: https://commonslibrary.parliament.uk/research-briefings/cbp-9549/ (Accessed 19 January 2023)

Bussey, K. and Stone, J. (2015) 'David Cameron says he could give Scotland more powers after meeting with Nicola Sturgeon' 2015, May 15. *Independent* Available: https://www.independent.co.uk/news/uk/politics/david-cameron-considering-giving-scotland-more-powers-after-meeting-with-nicola-sturgeon-10253335.html (Accessed 10 March 2019)

Cabinet Office (2011) 'The Cabinet Manual: A guide to laws, conventions and rules on the operation of government' *assets.publishing.service.gov.uk* Available: https://assets.publishing.service.gov.uk/government/uploads/system/uploads/attachment_data/file/60641/cabinet-manual.pdf (Accessed 1 April 2021)

Cabinet Office (2012) 'Devolution: memorandum of understanding and supplementary agreement' *assets.publishing.service.gov.uk* Available: https://www.gov.uk/government/publications/devolution-memorandum-of-understanding-and-supplementary-agreement (Accessed 2 December 2019)

Cabinet Office (2017) 'The Government's Response to the Electoral Commission's Reports on the EU Referendum' *assets.publishing.service.gov.uk* Available: https://assets.publishing.service.gov.uk/government/uploads/system/uploads/attachment_data/file/669702/Gov_Response_to_EC_Report_on_EU_Referendum.pdf (Accessed 12 April 2021)

Cabinet Office (2018a) 'Joint Communiqué of the British-Irish Intergovernmental Conference 25 July 2018' 2018, July 25 *gov.uk(archived)* Available: https://cain.ulster.ac.uk/issues/politics/conference/biic_2018-07-25_communique.pdf (Accessed 20 April 2021)

Cabinet Office (2018b) 'Joint Communiqué of the British-Irish Intergovernmental Conference 2 November 2018' 2018, November 2 *gov.uk(archived)* Available: https://cain.ulster.ac.uk/issues/politics/conference/biic_2018-11-02_communique.pdf (Accessed 20 April 2021)

Cabinet Office (2019) 'Joint Communiqué of the British-Irish Intergovernmental Conference 8 May 2019' 2019, May 8 *gov.uk* Available: https://www.gov.uk/government/publications/joint-communique-of-the-british-irish-intergovernmental-conference-8-may-2019 (Accessed 4 February 2023)

Cabinet Office (2019) 'Memorandum of Understanding between the Government of the United Kingdom of Great Britain and Northern Ireland and the Government of Ireland concerning the Common Travel Area and associated reciprocal rights and privileges' 2019, May 8 *gov.uk* Available: https://assets.publishing.service.gov.uk/government/uploads/system/uploads/attachment_data/file/800280/CTA-MoU-UK.pdf (Accessed 4 June 2023)

Cabinet Office (2020a) 'The Northern Ireland Protocol' 2020, December 31 *assets.publishing.service.gov.uk* Available: https://assets.publishing.service.gov.uk/government/uploads/system/uploads/attachment_data/file/950601/Northern_Ireland_Protocol_-_Command_Paper.pdf (Accessed 15 April 2021)

Cabinet Office (2020b) 'The UK's Approach to the Northern Ireland Protocol' 2020, May 20 *assets.publishing.service.gov.uk* Available: https://assets.publishing.service.gov.uk/government/uploads/system/uploads/attachment_data/file/887532/The_UK_s_Approach_to_NI_Protocol_Web_Accessible.pdf (Accessed 20 September 2020)

Cabinet Office (2021a) 'Joint Communiqué of the British-Irish Intergovernmental Conference 24 June 2021' 2021, June 24 *gov.uk* Available: https://www.gov.uk/government/news/joint-communique-of-the-british-irish-intergovernmental-conference (Accessed 4 February 2023)

Cabinet Office (2021b) 'Joint Communiqué of the British-Irish Intergovernmental Conference 2 December 2021' 2021, December 2 *gov.uk* Available: https://www.gov.uk/government/news/joint-communique-of-the-british-irish-intergovernmental-conference—3 (Accessed 4 February 2023)

Cabinet Office (2021c) 'Statement following the meeting between Lord Frost and Vice President Šefčovič' 2021, April 16 *gov.uk* Available: https://www.gov.uk/government/news/statement-following-the-meeting-between-lord-frost-and-vice-president-sefcovic-16-april-2021 (Accessed 16 January 2023)

Cabinet Office (2022a) 'Joint Communiqué of the British-Irish Intergovernmental Conference 23 March 2022' 2022, March 23 *gov.uk* Available: https://www.gov.uk/government/news/joint-communique-of-the-british-irish-intergovernmental-conference—5 (Accessed 4 February 2023)

Cabinet Office (2022b) 'Joint Communiqué of the British-Irish Intergovernmental Conference 7 October 2022' 2022, October 7 *gov.uk* Available: https://www.gov.uk/government/news/joint-communique-of-the-british-irish-intergovernmental-conference—7 (Accessed 4 February 2023)

Cabinet Office (2022c) 'Guide to Making Legislation' *gov.uk* Available: https://assets.publishing.service.gov.uk/government/uploads/system/uploads/attachment_data/file/1099024/2022-08_Guide_to_Making_Legislation_-_master_version__4_.pdf (Accessed 20 February 2023)

Calvert, H. (1968) *Constitutional Law in Northern Ireland: A Study in Regional Government.* London: Stevens.

Cameron, Lord D. S. C. (1969) 'Disturbances in Northern Ireland: Report of the Commission appointed by the Governor of Northern Ireland' Cmd. 532 Available: https://cain.ulster.ac.uk/hmso/cameron.htm (Accessed 13 February 2023)

Cameron, D. (2013) 'EU Speech at Bloomberg' 2013, January 23 *assets.publishing.service.gov.uk* Available: https://www.gov.uk/government/speeches/eu-speech-at-bloomberg (Accessed 4 February 2018)

Cameron, D. (2016) 'PM speech at Vauxhall on the EU Referendum: 10 March 2016 (Archived)' 2016, March 10 *assets.publishing.service.gov.uk* Available: https://www.gov.uk/government/speeches/pm-speech-at-vauxhall-on-the-eu-referendum-10-march-2016 (Accessed 10 April 2020)

Campbell, C., Ní Aoláin, F., and Harvey, C. (2003) 'The Frontiers of Legal Analysis: Reframing the Transition in Northern Ireland' *The Modern Law Review*, 66(3): 317–45.

Campbell, J. (2021) 'Brexit: Some lorries delayed at NI border control posts' 2021, January 3. *BBC News* Available: https://www.bbc.co.uk/news/uk-northern-ireland-55521239 (Accessed 16 January 2023)

Campbell, J. (2021b) 'Brexit: NI Protocol 'not shattering' for the union, court told' 2021, November 30. *BBC News* Available: https://www.bbc.co.uk/news/uk-northern-ireland-59478818? (Accessed 18 January 2023)

Canning, M. (2016) 'EU referendum: Vote Leave to regain control of Northern Ireland's future, Foster urges' 2016, June 17. *belfasttelegraph.co.uk* Available: https://www.belfasttelegraph.co.uk/news/brexit/eu-referendum-vote-leave-to-regain-control-of-northern-irelands-future-foster-urges-voters-34808922.html (Accessed 12 April 2021)

Carrell, S. (2016) 'David Cameron points to risk of Scotland leaving UK after Brexit' 2016, June 8. *The Guardian* Available: https://www.theguardian.com/politics/2016/jun/08/david-cameron-raises-risk-scotland-leaving-uk-after-brexit (Accessed 15 April 2020)

Carroll, R. (2021) 'Northern Ireland facing food supply disruption over Brexit, MP's told' 2021, January 6. *The Guardian* Available: https://www.theguardian.com/uk-news/2021/jan/06/northern-ireland-facing-food-supply-disruption-over-brexit-mps-told (Accessed 16 January 2023)

Carroll, R. (2022a) 'Northern Ireland secretary plays for time by failing to name election date' 2022, October 28. *The Guardian* Available: https://www.theguardian.com/politics/2022/oct/28/northern-ireland-secretary-plays-for-time-by-failing-to-name-election-date (Accessed 20 January 2023)

Carroll, R. (2022b) 'Groundhog Day: why another Northern Ireland election looks like insanity' 2022, October 28. *The Guardian* Available: https://www.theguardian.com/politics/2022/oct/28/northern-ireland-elections-voters-groundhog-day-polls-dup-sinn-fein (Accessed 20 January 2023)

Carroll, R. and O'Carroll, L. (2019) 'Rival unionists accuse DUP of catastrophic miscalculation' 2019, October 17. *The Guardian* Available: https://www.theguardian.com/politics/2019/oct/17/rival-unionists-accuse-dup-of-catastrophic-brexit-miscalculation (Accessed 14 April 2021)

Carson, E. (2021) 'Address in Reply to His Majesty's Most Gracious Speech' HL Deb. 1921, 14 December. (*Hansard*: vol. 48, cc.45; 47.) Available: https://api.parliament.uk/historic-hansard/lords/1921/dec/14/address-in-reply-to-his-majestys-most.

Central Statistics Office (2023) 'Ireland's Trade in Goods 2021' *cso.ie* Available: https://www.cso.ie/en/releasesandpublications/ep/p-ti/irelandstradeingoods2021/tradewiththeuk/ (Accessed 21 January 2023)

Clarke, H., Goodwin, M., and Whiteley, P. (2017) *Brexit: Why Britain Voted to Leave the European Union*. Cambridge: Cambridge University Press.

Clarke, J., Gravey, V., and Whitten, L. C. (2022) 'Ten questions for the REUL Bill in Northern Ireland' 2022, October 17. *Brexit & Environment* Available: https://www.brexitenvironment.co.uk/2022/10/17/ten-questions-for-the-reul-bill-in-northern-ireland/ (Accessed 20 January 2023)

Cleverly, J. (2022) 'Official Correspondence: Northern Ireland Protocol and Medicines Supply' 2022, March 28. *parliament.uk* Available: https://committees.parliament.uk/publications/21851/documents/162782/default/ (Accessed 20 January 2023)

Cleverly, J. (2023) 'EUR-Lex database on the Northern Ireland Protocol' 2022, October 13. *Foreign, Commonwealth and Development Office*. Available: https://committees.parliament.uk/publications/30368/documents/175454/default/ (Accessed 10 February 2023)

Coakley, J. and Garry, J. (2016) 'Northern Ireland: The challenge of public opinion' 2016, December 9 *qpol.qub.ac.uk* Available: http://qpol.qub.ac.uk/public-opinion-challenge-ni/ (Accessed 1 April 2021)

Coakley, J. and Todd, J. (2020) *Negotiating a Settlement in Northern Ireland, 1969–2019*. Oxford: Oxford University Press.

Coghlin, P., O'Brien, U., and MacLean, K. (2020) 'The Report of the Independent Public Inquiry into the Non-domestic Renewable Heat Incentive (RHI) Scheme' *Department of Finance*. Available: https://www.rhiinquiry.org/sites/rhi/files/media-files/Introduction.pdf (Accessed 12 January 2021)

Connelly, T. (2018) *Brexit and Ireland: The Dangers, the Opportunities, and the Inside Story of the Irish Response*. 2nd ed. London: Penguin.

Connelly, T. (2021) 'Article 16: The threats, the retaliation, the risks' 2021, November 13. *RTE* Available: https://www.rte.ie/news/brexit/2021/1113/1259634-tony-connelly-brexit/ (Accessed 18 January 2023)

Conservative Home (2018) 'Interview. The Brexit negotiation—Dodds warns against the "annexation" of Northern Ireland' 2018, April 25. *Conservative Home* Available: https://www.conservativehome.com/highlights/2018/04/interview-the-brexit-negotiation-dodds-warns-against-the-annexation-of-northern-ireland.html (Accessed 23 May 2019)

Conservative Party. (2010) 'Invitation to Join the Government of Britain: The Conservative Manifesto 2010'. *issuu* Available: https://issuu.com/conservatives/docs/cpmanifesto2010_hires (Accessed 1 April 2021)

Cousins, G. (2022) 'Full statement from Paul Givan as he announces resignation as Northern Ireland's First Minister' 2022, February 3. *News Letter* Available: https://www.newsletter.co.uk/news/politics/full-statement-from-paul-givan-after-resignation-3554405 (Accessed 18 January 2023)

Coveney, S. (2022) 'Visa Agreements: Dáil Éireann Debate: Tuesday—25 October 2022'. *oireachtas.ie* Available: https://www.oireachtas.ie/en/debates/question/2022-10-25/347/ (Accessed 4 February 2023)

Crace, J. (2016) 'Owen Paterson hunts the Brussels badgers in the smoke of falling empire' 2016, April 25. *The Guardian* Available: https://www.theguardian.com/politics/2016/apr/25/cometh-the-hour-cometh-owen-paterson-for-leave-campaign (Accessed 15 April 2021)

Craig, P. (2011) 'The European Union 2011: Locks, Limits and Legality' *Common Market Law Review*, 48: 1881–910.

Craig, P. (2016) 'Brexit: A Drama in Six Acts' *European Law Review*, 41(4): 447–68.

Craig, P. (2017a) 'The process: Brexit and the anatomy of article 50' in Fabbrini, F. (ed.) *The Law and Politics of Brexit*. Oxford: Oxford University Press (Chapter 3).

Craig, P. (2017b) 'Brexit, A Drama: The Interregnum' *Yearbook of European Law*, 26: 3–45.

Craig, P. (2017c) 'Casting aside Clanking Medieval Chains: Prerogative, Statute and Article 50 after the EU Referendum' *Modern Law Review*, 79(6): 1041–63.

Craig, P. (2019) 'Constitutional Principle, the Rule of Law and Political Reality: The European Union (Withdrawal) Act 2018' *Modern Law Review*, 82(2): 319–66.
Craig, Sir J. (1934) 'Unionist Party' *Northern Ireland House of Commons*. 1934, April 22. vol. XVI, cols. 1091–95.
Cromie, C. (2015) 'EU referendum: DUP's Sammy Wilson gives backing to Ukip Brexit campaign, blasting David Cameron's "pathetic" demands"' 2015, November 25. *Belfast Telegraph* Available: https://www.belfasttelegraph.co.uk/news/politics/eu-referendum-dups-sammy-wilson-gives-backing-to-ukip-brexit-campaign-blasting-david-camerons-pathetic-demands-34233078.html (Accessed 12 April 2021)
Cunningham, S. (2016) 'Arlene Foster's Brexit comments "irresponsible", opponents blast' 2016, May 16. *The Irish News* Available: http://www.irishnews.com/news/politicalnews/2016/05/16/news/arlene-foster-s-brexit-comments-irresponsible-opponents-blast-520924/ (Accessed 15 April 2020)
Curtis, J. (2021) 'Northern Ireland Protocol: Article 16 and EU vaccine export controls' 2021, February 2. *House of Commons Library* Available: https://commonslibrary.parliament.uk/northern-ireland-protocol-article-16-and-eu-vaccine-export-controls/ (Accessed 16 January 2023)
Daly M. E. (2017) 'Brexit and the Irish Border: Historical Context'. *The British Academy* Available: https://www.thebritishacademy.ac.uk/publications/europe-brexit-and-irish-border-historical-context/ (Accessed 30 March 2021)
Davis, D. (2016) 'Ireland does not have to choose between the UK and the EU' 2016, September 8. *Irish Times* Available: https://www.irishtimes.com/opinion/ireland-does-not-have-to-choose-between-the-uk-and-the-eu-1.2783042 (Accessed 8 August 2020)
Davis, D. (2016a) 'David Davis: "We don't want hard border post Brexit, Northern Ireland still open for business"' 2016, September 1. *Belfast Telegraph* Available: https://www.belfasttelegraph.co.uk/news/northern-ireland/david-davis-we-don't-want-hard-border-post-brexit-northern-ireland-still-open-for-business-35011702.html (Accessed 8 August 2020)
Davis, D. (2017, May 14) in @Jack_Blanchard_ 2017, June 19. *Twitter* (Accessed 16 April 2019)
de Búrca, G. and Weiler, J. H. H. (2012) 'Introduction' in Búrca, Gráinne de and Weiler, J. H. H. (eds.) *The Worlds of European Constitutionalism*. Cambridge: Cambridge University Press: 1–10.
de Mars, S., Murray, C., O'Donoghue, A., and Warwick, B. (2018) *Bordering Two Unions: Northern Ireland and Brexit*. Bristol: Policy Press.
Department for Levelling Up, Housing and Communities (2022) 'UK government hosts British-Irish Council in Blackpool to bring islands closer together' 2022, November 11. *gov.uk* Available: https://www.gov.uk/government/news/uk-government-hosts-british-irish-council-in-blackpool-to-bring-islands-closer-together (Accessed 20 January 2023)
Department of Agriculture and Rural Development (2016) 'Farm Incomes in Northern Ireland 2014–15' *DARD* Available: (https://www.daera-ni.gov.uk/sites/default/files/publications/dard/farm-incomes-in-northern-ireland-2014-15-final.PDF) Accessed 8 July 2016
Department for Exiting the European Union Interviewee (2020) 'DExEU Protocol Team Interview' interviewed by Whitten, L. C. on 8 January 2020, London.
Department of Foreign Affairs and Trade (2015) 'Minister Flanagan addresses Chatham House in London on Brexit' 2015, September 7. *DFAT* Available: https://www.dfa.ie/news-and-media/speeches/speeches-archive/2015/september/flanagan-addresses-chatham-house-on-brexit,-london/ (Accessed 12 April 2020)
Department of Foreign Affairs (2019) 'Joint Communiqué of the British-Irish Intergovernmental Conference' 2019, May 8. *dfa.ie* Available: https://www.dfa.ie/news-and-media/

press-releases/press-release-archive/2019/may/joint-communique-of-the-british-irish-intergovernmental-conference.php (Accessed 20 April 2021)

Department of Health and Department of Children, Equality, Disability, Integration and Youth (2021) 'Protocol between Northern Ireland and Ireland for Handling Inter-Jurisdictional Child Cases' 2021, August 1. *health-ni.gov.uk* Available: https://www.health-ni.gov.uk/sites/default/files/publications/health/doh-north-south-protocol-inter-child-cases.pdf (Accessed 20 January 2023)

Department of the Taoiseach (2016) 'EU–UK Relations: Statements' 2016, April 21. *Dáil Éierann* Available: https://www.oireachtas.ie/en/debates/debate/dail/2016-04-21/2/ (Accessed 12 April 2020)

Diamond, P., Nedergaard, P., and Rosamond, B. (2018) *The Routledge Handbook of the Politics of Brexit*. London: Routledge.

Dicey. A. V. (1915) *An Introduction to the Study of the Law of the Constitution*. 8th ed. London: Palgrave Macmillan.

Dodds, N. (2021) 'UK Government Union Capability' vol. 813. 2021, July 1. *HL Hansard*. Available: https://hansard.parliament.uk/lords/2021-07-01/debates/706E179A-50BB-46F4-B2A8-7C79FAC4BA80/UKGovernmentUnionCapability# (Accessed 12 February 2023)

Doherty, B., Temple Lang, J., McCrudden, C., McGowan, L., Phinnemore, D., and Schiek, D. (2017) 'Northern Ireland and Brexit: The European Economic Area option' *European Policy Centre*. Available: http://www.epc.eu/documents/uploads/pub_7576_northernirelandandbrexit.pdf?doc_id=1842 (Accessed 12 February 2021)

Donaldson, J. (2022a) 'Sir Jeffery: NI should not be used as a pawn in a diplomatic chess match' 2022, February 28 *mydup.com* Available: https://mydup.com/news/sir-jeffrey-ni-should-not-be-used-as-a-pawn-in-a-diplomatic-chess-match (Accessed 2 April 2022)

Donaldson, J. (2022b) 'Jeffery Donaldson—The Protocol on Ireland/Northern Ireland: The DUP Perspective' 2022, February 24 *IIEA* Available: https://www.youtube.com/watch?v=FHMJumfInuM (Accessed 2 April 2022)

Donaldson, J. (2023) 'Protocol must be replaced with arrangements unionists can support' 2023, February 8 *mydup.com* Available: https://mydup.com/news/protocol-must-be-replaced-with-arrangements-unionists-can-support (Accessed 9 February 2023)

Donnelly, K.J. (2016) 'Report by the Comptroller and Auditor General for Northern Ireland: Department of Enterprise, Trade and Investment Resource Accounts 2015–16' *Northern Ireland Audit Office*. Available: https://www.niauditoffice.gov.uk/sites/niao/files/media-files/Final%20CAG%20Report%2028%20June%202016%20%28after%20typo%20correction%29.pdf (Accessed 22 May 2019)

Donohue, C. (2016) 'The Northern Ireland Question: All-Ireland Self-Determination Post-Belfast Agreement' *Victoria University Wellington Law Review*, 47: 41–72.

Dorling, D., Stuart, B., and Stubbs, J. (2016) 'Brexit, inequality and the demographic divide' 2016, December 22 *blog.lse.ac.uk* Available: https://blogs.lse.ac.uk/politicsandpolicy/brexit-inequality-and-the-demographic-divide/ (Accessed 14 April 2021)

Dougan, M. (2020) 'So Long, Farewell, Auf Wiedersehen, Goodbye: The UK's Withdrawal Package' *Common Market Law Review*, 57: 631–704.

DUP (2010) 'Manifesto 2010: Let's Keep Northern Ireland Moving Forward' *mydup.com* Available: https://cain.ulster.ac.uk/issues/politics/docs/dup/dup060510man.pdf (Accessed 11 March 2021)

DUP (2016a) 'Our Plan for Northern Ireland: The DUP Manifesto for the 2016 Northern Ireland Assembly Election' 2016, April 4 *mydup.com* Available: http://www.mydup.com/images/uploads/publications/DUP_Manifesto_2016_v8_LR.pdf (Accessed 22 May 2019)

DUP (2017) 'Standing Strong for Northern Ireland' *mydup.com* Available: http://www.mydup.com/publications/view/2017-westminster-manifesto (Accessed 13 July 2019)

DUP (2021a) 'DUP – free us from the Protocol' 2021, February 2 *mydup.com* Available: https://mydup.com/news/dup-free-us-from-protocol (Accessed 31 March 2021)

DUP (2021b) 'Joint Unionist Declaration in opposition to the Northern Ireland Protocol' 2021, September 28 *mydup.com* Available: https://mydup.com/news/joint-unionist-declaration-in-opposition-to-the-northern-ireland-protocol (Accessed 16 January 2023)

DUP (2021c) 'DUP Written Evidence IIO0025—Introductory inquiry into the operation of the Protocol on Ireland/Northern Ireland' 2021, June 18 *parliament.uk* Available: https://committees.parliament.uk/writtenevidence/36883/pdf/ (Accessed 13 February 2023)

Dustmann, C. and Frattini, T. (2014) 'The Fiscal Effects of Immigration to the UK' *Economic Journal*, 124(580): F593–F643.

Eeckhout, P. and Frantziou, E. (2017) 'Brexit and Article 50 TEU: A constitutionalist reading' *Common Market Law Review*, 54(3): 695–733.

Elliott, M. (2015) 'The Principle of Parliamentary Sovereignty in Legal, Constitutional, and Political Perspective' in Jowell, J., Oliver, D., and O'Cinneide, C. (eds.) *The Changing Constitution*. 8th ed. Oxford: Oxford University Press (Chapter 2).

Elliott, M. (2017) 'A "Blatant Power Grab"? The Scottish Government on the EU (Withdrawal) Bill' 2017, August 10. *Public Law for Everyone*. Available: https://publiclawforeveryone.com/2017/08/10/a-blatant-power-grab-the-scottish-government-on-the-eu-withdrawal-bill/ (Accessed 3 March 2018)

Elliott, M. (2018) 'Sovereignty, Primacy and the Common Law Constitution: What Has EU Membership Taught Us?' in Elliott, M., Williams, J., and Young A. L. (eds.) *The UK Constitution after Miller: Brexit and Beyond*. Oxford: Hart Publishing 221–48.

Elliott, M. and Thomas, R. (2020) *Public Law*. 4th ed. Oxford: Oxford University Press.

Elliott, M. and Tierney, S. (2019) 'Political Pragmatism and Constitutional Principle: The European Union (Withdrawal) Act 2018' *Public Law*, 1: 37–60.

Elliott, M., Williams, J., and Young A. L. (2018) *The UK Constitution after Miller: Brexit and Beyond*. Oxford: Hart Publishing.

Embury-Denis, T. (2018) 'Northern Ireland secretary admits she did not realise nationalists refuse to vote for unionist parties when she took the job' 2018, September 6. *Independent* Available: https://www.independent.co.uk/news/uk/politics/northern-ireland-karen-bradley-secretary-nationalists-unionists-sinn-fein-dup-elections-a8526466.html (Accessed 12 February 2021)

EONI (2021) 'Elections 2016' *eoni.org.uk* Available: https://www.eoni.org.uk/Elections/Election-results-and-statistics/Election-results-and-statistics-2003-onwards/Elections-2016 (Accessed 14 April 2021)

EUR-Lex (2023) 'Protocol on Ireland/Northern Ireland' *eur-lex.europa.eu* Available: https://eur-lex.europa.eu/content/news/index.html (Accessed 20 January 2023)

European Commission (2017a) 'Directives for the negotiation of an agreement with the United Kingdom of Great Britain and Northern Ireland setting out the arrangements for its withdrawal from the European Union' 21009/17 BXT 16 ADD 1. 2017, May 22 *ec.europa.eu* Available: https://www.consilium.europa.eu/media/21766/directives-for-the-negotiation-xt21016-ad01re02en17.pdf (Accessed: 11 December 2020)

European Commission (2017b) 'Guiding Principles for the Dialogue on Ireland/Northern Ireland' TF50. 2017, September 20 *ec.europa.eu* Available: https://ec.europa.eu/commission/sites/beta-political/files/dialogue_ie-ni.pdf (Accessed: 10 December 2020)

European Commission (2018) 'European Commission Draft Withdrawal Agreement on the withdrawal of the United Kingdom of Great Britain and Northern Ireland from the

European Union and the European Atomic Energy Community' TF50 33. 2018, February 28 *ec.europa.eu* Available: https://commission.europa.eu/publications/european-commission-draft-withdrawal-agreement-withdrawal-united-kingdom-great-britain-and-northern_en (Accessed 14 April 2021)

European Commission (2020b) 'Guidance Note: Withdrawal of the United Kingdom and EU Rules in the Field of Customs, Including Preferential Origin' REV3. 2020, July 14 *ec.europa.eu* Available: https://ec.europa.eu/info/sites/info/files/brexit_files/info_site/guidance-customs-procedures_en_0.pdf (Accessed 20 November 2020)

European Commission (2020c) 'Guidance Note: Withdrawal of the United Kingdom and EU Rules in the Field of Customs, Including Preferential Origin' REV4. 2020, December 23 *ec.europa.eu* Available: https://ec.europa.eu/info/sites/info/files/brexit_files/info_site/guidance-customs-procedures_en_0_0.pdf (Accessed 12 January 2021)

European Commission (2020d) 'Joint statement by the co-chairs of the EU-UK Joint Committee' 2020, December 8 *ec.europa.eu* Available: https://ec.europa.eu/commission/presscorner/detail/en/STATEMENT_20_2346 (Accessed 10 February 2021)

European Commission (2020e) 'Statement by the European Commission following the extraordinary meeting of the EU-UK Joint Committee' 2020, September 10 *ec.europa.eu* Available: https://ec.europa.eu/commission/presscorner/detail/en/statement_20_1607 (Accessed 4 February 2021)

European Commission (2020f) 'Technical note on the implementation of the Protocol on Ireland / Northern Ireland' UKTF16. 2020, April 30 *ec.europa.eu* Available: https://ec.europa.eu/info/publications/technical-note-implementation-protocol-ireland-northern-ireland_en (Accessed 4 February 2021)

European Commission (2020g) 'Withdrawal Agreement: European Commission sends letter of formal notice to the United Kingdom for breach of its obligations' 2020, October 1 *ec.europa.eu* Available: https://ec.europa.eu/commission/presscorner/detail/en/IP_20_1798 (Accessed 6 February 2021)

European Commission (2020h) 'Data protection: Commission adopts adequacy decisions for the UK' 2021, June 28 *ec.europa.eu* Available: https://ec.europa.eu/commission/presscorner/detail/ro/ip_21_3183 (Accessed 20 January 2023)

European Commission (2021a) 'Withdrawal Agreement: Commission sends letter of formal notice to the United Kingdom for breach of its obligations under the Protocol on Ireland and Northern Ireland' 2021, March 15 *ec.europa.eu* Available: https://ec.europa.eu/commission/presscorner/detail/en/ip_21_1132 (Accessed 16 January 2023)

European Commission (2021b) 'Statement by Vice-President Maroš Šefčovič following his meeting with Lord David Frost' 2021, April 16 *ec.europa.eu* Available: https://ec.europa.eu/commission/presscorner/detail/en/statement_21_1801 (Accessed 16 January 2023)

European Commission (2021c) 'EU–UK relations: solutions found to help implementation of the Protocol on Ireland and Northern Ireland' 2021, June 30 *ec.europa.eu* Available: https://ec.europa.eu/commission/presscorner/detail/en/ip_21_3324 (Accessed 16 January 2023)

European Commission (2021d) 'Statement by the European Commission following the UK announcement regarding the operation of the Protocol on Ireland / Northern Ireland' 2021, September 6 *ec.europea.eu* Available: https://ec.europa.eu/commission/presscorner/detail/en/STATEMENT_21_4586 (Accessed 16 January 2023)

European Commission (2021e) 'Statement by the European Commission following the ninth meeting of the Specialised Committee on the implementation of the Protocol on Ireland and Northern Ireland' 2021, September 24 *ec.europea.eu* Available: https://commission.europa.eu/publications/statement-european-commission-following-ninth-meeting-specialised-committee-implementation-protocol_en (Accessed 18 January 2023)

European Commission (2021f) 'Protocol on Ireland/Northern Ireland: Commission proposes bespoke arrangements to benefit Northern Ireland' 2021, October 13 *ec.europa.eu* Available: https://ec.europa.eu/commission/presscorner/detail/en/IP_21_5215 (Accessed 18 January 2023)

European Commission (2021g) 'EU–UK relations: Commission delivers on promise to ensure continued supply of medicines to Northern Ireland as well as Cyprus, Ireland and Malta' 2021, December 17 *ec.europa.eu* Available: https://ec.europa.eu/commission/presscorner/detail/en/ip_21_6911 (Accessed 18 January 2023)

European Commission (2021h) 'Press speaking points by Vice-President Maroš Šefčovič in Belfast, following his two-day visit to Northern Ireland' 2021, September 10 *ec.europa.eu* Available: https://ec.europa.eu/commission/presscorner/detail/en/speech_21_4674 (Accessed 20 January 2023)

European Commission (2021i) 'Unilateral Declarations of the EU and the UK (on the application of the Union's State Aid rules under Article 10 of the IE/NI Protocol)' 2021, January 8 *commission.europa.eu* Available: https://commission.europa.eu/publications/unilateral-declarations-eu-and-uk-application-unions-state-aid-rules-under-article-10-ieni-protocol_en

European Commission (2022a) 'Joint Statement by Vice-President Maroš Šefčovič and UK Foreign Secretary Liz Truss' 2022, January 14 *ec.europa.eu* Available: https://ec.europa.eu/commission/presscorner/detail/en/statement_22_362 (Accessed 18 January 2023)

European Commission (2022b) 'Commission launches infringement proceedings against the UK for breaking international law and provides further details on possible solutions to facilitate the movement of goods between Great Britain and Northern Ireland' 2022, June 15 *ec.europa.eu* Available: https://ec.europa.eu/commission/presscorner/detail/en/ip_22_3676 (Accessed 20 January 2023)

European Commission (2022c) 'Questions and Answers: Commission launches four new infringement procedures against the UK' 2022, July 22 *ec.europa.eu* Available: https://ec.europa.eu/commission/presscorner/detail/en/QANDA_22_4664 (Accessed 20 January 2023)

European Commission (2022d) 'Statement by Vice-President Maroš Šefčovič on the movement of veterinary medicines from Great Britain to Northern Ireland, Cyprus, Ireland and Malta' 2022, December 19 *ec.europa.eu* Available: https://ec.europa.eu/commission/presscorner/detail/en/statement_22_7831 (Accessed 20 January 2023)

European Commission (2022e) 'EU–UK relations: European Union ensures continued supply of medicines to Northern Ireland, as well as Cyprus, Ireland and Malta' 2022, April 12 *ec.europa.eu* Available: https://ec.europa.eu/commission/presscorner/detail/en/ip_22_2385 (Accessed 20 January 2023)

European Commission (2023a) 'Enhanced engagement with Northern Ireland stakeholders' 2023, February 27 *commission.europa.eu* Available: https://commission.europa.eu/system/files/2023-02/statement%20stakeholders%20engagement.pdf

European Commission (2023b) 'Proposal for a Regulation of the European Parliament and of the Council on specific rules relating to medicinal products for human use intended to be placed on the market of Northern Ireland' 2023/0064(COD) 2023, February 27 *commission.europea.eu* Available: https://commission.europa.eu/system/files/2023-02/COM_2023_122_1_EN_ACT_part1_v2.pdf

European Commission (2023c) 'Proposal or a Regulation of the European Parliament and of the Council on specific rules relating to the entry into Northern Ireland from other parts of the United Kingdom of certain consignments of retail goods, plants for planting, seed potatoes, machinery and certain vehicles operated for agricultural or forestry purposes, as well as non-commercial movements of certain pet animals into Northern Ireland' 2023/0062(COD) 2023, February 27 *commission.europea.eu* Available: https://eur-lex.europa.eu/legal-content/EN/TXT/?uri=CELEX:52023PC0124

European Commission (2023d) 'Proposal for a Council Decision on the position to be taken on behalf of the European Union in the Joint Consultative Working Group established by the Agreement on the withdrawal of the United Kingdom of Great Britain and Northern Ireland from the European Union and the European Atomic Energy Community as regards the amendment of its rules of procedure' 2023/0065 (NLE) 2023, February 27 *commission.europea.eu* Available: https://commission.europa.eu/system/files/2023-02/COM_2023_120_1_EN_ACT_part1_v1%20%28003%29.pdf

European Commission (2023e) 'Proposal for a Regulation of the European Parliament and of the Council on specific rules relating to the entry into Northern Ireland from other parts of the United Kingdom of certain consignments of retail goods, plants for planting, seed potatoes, machinery and certain vehicles operated for agricultural or forestry purposes as well as non-commercial movements of certain pet animals into Northern Ireland' 2023/0062 (COD) 2023, February 27 *commission.europea.eu* Available: https://eur-lex.europa.eu/resource.html?uri=cellar:ea6d9b16-b6b9-11ed-8912-01aa75ed71a1.0001.02/DOC_1&format=PDF

European Council (2015) 'Letter by President Donald Tusk to the European Council on the issue of a UK in/out referendum' *consilium.europa.eu* Available: https://www.consilium.europa.eu/en/press/press-releases/2015/12/07/tusk-letter-to-28ms-on-uk/ (Accessed 14 March 2020)

European Council (2016) 'European Council Conclusions EUCO 1/16, Annex I "A New Settlement for the United Kingdom within the European Union"' 2016, February 19 *consilium.europa.eu* Available: https://www.consilium.europa.eu/media/21787/0216-euco-conclusions.pdf (Accessed 12 March 2020)

European Council (2017) 'European Council (Art. 50) guidelines for Brexit negotiations' EUCO XT 20004/17. 2017, April 29 *consilium.europa.eu* Available: http://www.consilium.europa.eu/en/press/press-releases/2017/04/29/euco-brexit-guidelines/ (Accessed 12 December 2020)

European Council (2018) 'European Council (Art. 50) Conclusions' EUCO 788/18. 2018, December 13 *consilium.europa.eu* Available: https://www.consilium.europa.eu/en/press/press-releases/2018/12/13/european-council-art-50-conclusions-13-december-2018/pdf (Accessed 12 October 2020)

European Council (2019) 'European Council, 20–21 June 2019' *consilium.europa.eu* Available: https://www.consilium.europa.eu/en/meetings/european-council/2019/06/20-21/ (Accessed 9 January 2021)

European Council (2020) 'ANNEX to COUNCIL DECISION authorising the opening of negotiations with the United Kingdom of Great Britain and Northern Ireland for a new partnership agreement' 5870/20 ADD 1 REV 3. 2020, February 25 *consilium.europa.eu* Available: https://www.consilium.europa.eu/media/42736/st05870-ad01re03-en20.pdf (Accessed 2 November 2020)

European Parliament (2017a) 'European Parliament resolution of 5 April 2017 on negotiations with the United Kingdom following its notification that it intends to withdraw from the European Union' (2017/2593(RSP)). 2017, April 5 *europarl.europa.eu* Available: http://www.europarl.europa.eu/sides/getDoc.do?pubRef=-//EP//TEXT+TA+P8-TA-2017-0102+0+DOC+XML+V0//EN (Accessed 11 December 2020)

European Parliament (2017b) 'Outcome of the special European Council (Article 50) meeting of 29 April 2017' 2017, May 3 *europarl.europa.eu* Available: https://www.europarl.

europa.eu/RegData/etudes/ATAG/2017/603226/EPRS_ATA%282017%29603226_EN.pdf (Accessed 15 October 2020)

European Parliament (2019) 'Brexit: recent UK proposals do not offer the safeguards the EU and Ireland need' 2019, October 3 *europarl.europa.eu* Available: https://www.europarl.europa.eu/news/en/press-room/20191003IPR63303/brexit-recent-uk-proposals-do-not-offer-the-safeguards-the-eu-and-ireland-need (Accessed 9 December 2020)

European Parliament (2020) 'Statement of the UK Coordination Group and the leaders of the political groups of the EP' *europarl.europa.eu* Available: https://www.europarl.europa.eu/news/en/press-room/20200907IPR86513/statement-of-the-uk-coordination-group-and-ep-political-group-leaders (Accessed 11 February 2021)

European Parliament (2022) 'Parliamentary trade delegation to visit Northern Ireland' 2022, October 12 *europarl.europa.eu* Available: https://www.europarl.europa.eu/unitedkingdom/en/news-and-press-releases/news/2022/october2022/tradedelegationni.html (Accessed 20 January 2023)

Evans, A. (2020) 'A Tale as Old as (Devolved) Time? Sewel, Stormont, and the Legislative Consent Convention' *The Political Quarterly*, 91(1): 165–72.

Evans, G. and Menon, A. (2017) *Brexit and British Politics*. Cambridge: Polity Press.

Ewelme, J. (2023) 'UK Government log of regulatory divergence between Northern Ireland and Great Britain arising from EU and domestic legislation' 2023, February 9. *House of Lords European Affairs Sub-Committee on the Protocol on Ireland/Northern Ireland*. Available: https://committees.parliament.uk/publications/33942/documents/186049/default/ (Accessed 12 February 2023)

Fella, S. (2020) 'The UK–EU Withdrawal Agreement: dispute settlement and EU powers' Briefing Paper Number 9016. 2020, October 2 *HC Library* Available: https://commonslibrary.parliament.uk/research-briefings/cbp-9016/ (Accessed 28 March 2021)

Fella, S., Ferguson, D., Webb, D., Jozepa, I., Ares, E., and Kennedy, S. (2020) 'The UK–EU Trade and Cooperation Agreement: summary and implementation' Briefing Paper No. 09106. 2020, December 30 *HC Library* Available: https://commonslibrary.parliament.uk/research-briefings/cbp-9106-2/ (Accessed 28 March 2021)

Ferguson, A. (2016) 'McGuinness urges vote on united Ireland in event of Brexit' 2016, March 11. *Irish Times* Available: https://www.irishtimes.com/news/politics/mcguinness-urges-vote-on-united-ireland-in-event-of-brexit-1.2569500 (Accessed 27 April 2020)

Ferriter, D. (2019) *The Border: The Legacy of a Century of Anglo-Irish Politics*. London: Profile Books Ltd.

Finalyson, A. (2004) 'Political science, political ideas and rhetoric' *Economy and Society*, 33(4): 528–49.

Finlayson, A. (2006) '"What's the Problem": Political Theory, Rhetoric and Problem-Setting' *Critical Review of International Social and Political Philosophy*, 9(4): 541–7.

Finnis, J. and Larkin, J. (2020) 'Introducing the Internal Market bill isn't unconstitutional' 2020, September 10. *The Spectator*.

Fontaine, L. (2017) 'The Early Semantics of the Neologism BREXIT: a lexicogrammatical approach' *Functional Linguistics*, 4(6).

Foreign and Commonwealth Office (2012) 'Review of the Balance of Competences between the United Kingdom and the European Union' Cm 8415. July 2012 *gov.uk* Available: https://www.gov.uk/guidance/review-of-the-balance-of-competences (Accessed 28 March 2021)

Foreign, Commonwealth and Development Office (2022a) 'Northern Ireland Protocol and UK–EU relations: UK and EU joint statement' 2022, January 24 *gov.uk* Available: https://www.gov.uk/government/news/northern-ireland-protocol-and-uk-eu-relations-uk-and-eu-joint-statement-24-january (Accessed 18 January 2023)

Foreign, Commonwealth and Development Office (2022b) 'Joint statement on the meeting of the Withdrawal Agreement Joint Committee' 2022, February 21 *gov.uk* Available: https://www.gov.uk/government/news/joint-statement-on-the-meeting-of-the-withdrawal-agreement-joint-committee-21-february-2022 (Accessed 18 January 2023)

Foreign, Commonwealth and Development Office (2022c) 'Tenth meeting of the Specialised Committee on the implementation of the Protocol on Ireland and Northern Ireland: joint statement' 2022, March 8 *gov.uk* Available: https://www.gov.uk/government/news/tenth-meeting-of-the-specialised-committee-on-the-implementation-of-the-protocol-on-ireland-and-northern-ireland-joint-statement (Accessed 18 January 2023)

Foreign, Commonwealth and Development Office and Northern Ireland Office (2023) 'Northern Ireland Protocol meeting, 9 January 2023: joint statement from the Foreign Secretary and Vice President Šefčovič' 2023, January 9 *gov.uk* Available: https://www.gov.uk/government/news/joint-statement-from-foreign-secretary-james-cleverly-and-vice-president-maros-seHvic (Accessed 19 January 2023)

Foster, A. (2016a) 'DUP to "recommend vote to leave the EU"' 2016, February 20. *Newsletter* Available: https://www.newsletter.co.uk/news/dup-to-recommend-vote-to-leave-the-eu-1-7224491 (Accessed 20 May 2019)

Foster, A. (2016b) 'First Minister's Statement to Assembly Following EU Referendum Result' 2016, June 27 *mydup.com* Available: http://www.mydup.com/news/article/first-ministers-statement-to-assembly-following-eu-referendum-result (Accessed 18 May 2019)

Foster, A. (2017a) 'Arlene Foster: Assembly poll a wake-up call for unionism—only a vote for DUP can get us back on track' 2017, June 4. *Belfast Telegraph* Available: https://www.belfasttelegraph.co.uk/news/general-election-2017/comment/arlene-foster-assembly-poll-a-wake-up-call-for-unionism-only-a-vote-for-dup-can-get-us-back-on-track-35779675.html (Accessed 6 June 2020)

Foster, A. (2017b) 'Foster: 'Northern Ireland must leave on the same terms as the UK'' 2017, December 4. *Irish Times* Available: https://www.irishtimes.com/news/politics/foster-northern-ireland-must-leave-the-eu-on-the-same-terms-as-the-uk-1.3315089 (Accessed 14 April 2021)

Foster, A. and McGuiness, M. in Davenport, M. (2016) 'Foster and McGuinness in Brexit talks call' 2016, August 10. *BBC News* Available: https://www.bbc.co.uk/news/uk-northern-ireland-37039683 (Accessed 15 January 2019)

Foucault, M. (1999) 'Truth and Power' in Rabinow, P. (ed.) *The Foucault Reader*. New York: Penguin 51–75.

Freeman, E. (1873) *The Growth of the English Constitution from the Earliest Times*. 2nd ed. London: Macmillan.

Fresh Start Agreement (2015) 'A Fresh Start: The Stormont Agreement and Implementation Plan' 2015, November 17 *assets.publishing.service.gov.uk* Available: https://assets.publishing.service.gov.uk/government/uploads/system/uploads/attachment_data/file/479116/A_Fresh_Start_-_The_Stormont_Agreement_and_Implementation_Plan_-_Final_Version_20_Nov_2015_for_PDF.pdf (Accessed 22 April 2021)

Frost, D. (2021a) 'Lord Frost call with European Commission Vice President Maroš Šefčovič' 2021, March 3 *gov.uk* Available: https://www.gov.uk/government/news/lord-frost-call-with-european-commission-vice-president-maros-sefcovic-3-march-2021 (Accessed 16 January 2023)

Frost, D. (2021b) 'Northern Ireland Update' 2021, September 6 *parliament.uk* Available: https://questions-statements.parliament.uk/written-statements/detail/2021-09-06/hlws257 (Accessed 16 January 2023)

Frost, D. (2021c) 'Lord Frost: Conference Speech' 2021, October 4 *policymogul.com* Available: https://policymogul.com/key-updates/19214/lord-frost-conference-speech (Accessed 18 January 2023)

Frost, D. (2021d) 'Lord Frost speech: Observations on the present state of the nation' 2021, October 12 *gov.uk* Available: https://www.gov.uk/government/speeches/lord-frost-speech-observations-on-the-present-state-of-the-nation-12-october-2021 (Accessed 18 January 2023)

Garry, J. (2016) 'The EU referendum vote in Northern Ireland: Implications for our citizens' political views and behaviour' *Northern Ireland Assembly* Available: https://niassembly.tv/eu-referendum-vote-northern-ireland-implications-understanding-citizens-political-views-behaviour/ (Accessed 28 March 2021)

Garry, J., McNicholl, K., O'Leary, B., and Pow, J. (2018) 'Northern Ireland and the UK's Exit from the EU: What do people think?' *The UK in a Changing Europe* Available: https://ukandeu.ac.uk/partner-reports/northern-ireland-and-the-uks-exit-from-the-eu-what-do-people-think/ (Accessed 30 March 2021)

Garry, J., O'Leary, B., Coakley, J., Pow, J., and Whitten, L. (2020) 'Public attitudes to different possible models of a United Ireland: evidence from a citizens' assembly in Northern Ireland' *Irish Political Studies*, 35(3): 422–50.

Gee, G. and Webber G. C. N. (2010) 'What Is a Political Constitution?' *Oxford Journal of Legal Studies*, 30(2): 273–99.

George, S. (1996) *An Awkward Partner: Britain in the European Community*. 2nd ed. Oxford: Oxford University Press.

Gillespie, G. (1998) 'The Sunningdale agreement: lost opportunity or an agreement too far?' *Irish Political Studies* 13(1): 100–114.

Glencross, A. (2016) *Why the UK Voted for Brexit: David Cameron's Great Miscalculation*. Basingstoke: Palgrave.

Goldsworthy, J. (2010) *Parliamentary Sovereignty: Contemporary Debates*. Cambridge: Cambridge University Press.

Goodwin, M. and Heath, O. (2016) 'A tale of two countries: Brexit and the "left behind" thesis' 2016, July 25 *blogs.lse.ac.uk* Available: https://blogs.lse.ac.uk/politicsandpolicy/brexit-and-the-left-behind-thesis/ (Accessed 14 April 2021)

Gordon, M. (2015) *Parliamentary Sovereignty in the UK Constitution: Process, Politics and Democracy*. London: Hart Publishing.

Gordon, M. (2019) 'Parliamentary Sovereignty and the Political Constitution(s): From Griffith to Brexit' *King's Law Journal*, 30(1): 125–47.

Gordon, T. (2017) 'Nicola Sturgeon publishes full list of 111 powers vulnerable to Brexit "power grab"' 2017, September 19. *The Herald* Available: https://www.heraldscotland.com/news/15544320.nicola-sturgeon-publishes-full-list-of-111-powers-vulnerable-to-brexit-power-grab/ (Accessed 10 December 2020)

Gormley-Heenan, C. and Aughey, A. (2017) 'Northern Ireland and Brexit: Three effects on 'the border in the mind' *British Journal of Politics and International Relations*, 19(3): 497–511.

Gormley-Heenan, C., Aughey, A., and Devine, P. (2017) 'Waking up in a different country: Brexit and Northern Ireland' *ARK Research Update No. 116* Available: https://www.ark.ac.uk/ARK/sites/default/files/2018-07/update%20116.pdf (Accessed 3 March 2021)

Gove, M. (2016) 'Statement from Michael Gove MP, Secretary of State for Justice, on the EU Referendum' 2016, February 26 *voteleavetakecontrol.org* Available: http://www.voteleavetakecontrol.org/statement_from_michael_gove_mp_secretary_of_state_for_justice_on_the_eu_referendum.html (Accessed 12 April 2021)

Gove, M. (2020) 'Withdrawal Agreement Update' 2020, December 9 *gov.uk* Available: https://www.gov.uk/government/speeches/withdrawal-agreement-update (Accessed 10 January 2021)

Gove, M. and Raab, D. (2016) 'Gove and Raab: EU membership makes us less safe' 2016, June 8 *Vote Leave* Available: http://www.voteleavetakecontrol.org/gove_and_raab_eu_membership_makes_us_less_safe.html (Accessed 11 March 2020)

Gravey, V. and Reid C. (2022) 'Retained EU Law Bill and Devolution: reigniting tensions in post-Brexit intergovernmental relations' 2022, October 10. *Brexit & Environment* Available: https://www.brexitenvironment.co.uk/2022/10/10/reul-bill-devolution/ (Accessed 20 January 2023)

Gravey, V. and Whitten, L. (2021) 'The NI Protocol & the Environment: The Implications for Northern Ireland, Ireland and the UK' 2021, March. *Brexit & Environment* Available: https://www.brexitenvironment.co.uk/research-projects/egii/ (Accessed 3 January 2023)

Greaves, H. R. G. (1938) *The British Constitution*. London: Allen and Unwin.

Green Party in Northern Ireland (2016) 'A Zero Waste Strategy for Northern Ireland: The Green Party Manifesto for the Northern Ireland Assembly Election 2016' *cain.ulster.ac.uk* Available: https://cain.ulster.ac.uk/issues/politics/docs/green/gp_2016-04-21_nia-man.pdf (Accessed 23 May 2019)

Griffith, J. A. G. (1979) 'The Political Constitution' *Modern Law Review*, 42.

Griffith, J. A. G. (2001) 'The Common Law and the Political Constitution' *Law Quarterly Review*, 117: 42–67.

Gstöhl, S. and Phinnemore, D. (eds.) (2019) *The Proliferation of Privileged Partnerships Between the European Union and its Neighbours*. Oxon: Routledge.

Haas, E. B. (ed.) (2004 [1958]) *The Uniting of Europe: Political, Social, and Economic Forces, 1950–1957*. 3rd ed. Notre Dame, Indiana: University of Notre Dame Press.

Hadfield, B. (1989) *The Constitution of Northern Ireland*. Belfast: SLS Legal Publications.

Hadfield, B. (1992) 'The Northern Ireland Constitution' in Hadfield, B. (ed.) *Northern Ireland: Politics and the Constitution*. Buckingham: Open University Press 1–12.

Hague, W. in Elgot, J. (2016) 'William Hague: leaving EU risks fragmenting western world' 2016, June 8. *The Guardian* Available: https://www.theguardian.com/politics/2016/jun/08/william-hague-leaving-eu-risks-fragmenting-western-world (Accessed 26 March 2020)

Hainsworth, P. (1983) 'Direct rule in Northern Ireland: The European Community dimension 1972-79' *Administration*, 31: 53–69.

Hansard (1976) 'Northern Ireland (Constitutional Convention)' vol. 903. 1976, January 12 *parliament.uk* Available: https://hansard.parliament.uk/commons/1976-01-12/debates/8b295c83-fca3-4cad-9264-220933d14620/NorthernIreland(ConstitutionalConvention) (Accessed 20 February 2023)

Hansard (2016) 'Outcome of the EU Referendum' vol. 612. 2016, June 27 *parliament.uk* Available: https://hansard.parliament.uk/commons/2016-06-27/debates/1606275000001/OutcomeOfTheEUReferendum (Accessed 14 April 2021)

Hansard (2017) 'Article 50' vol. 620. 2017, January 24 *parliament.uk* Available: https://hansard.parliament.uk/Commons/2017-01-24/debates/D423AEE6-BE36-4935-AD6A-5CA316582A9C/Article50 (Accessed 14 April 2021)

Hansard. (2019) 'Brexit Negotiations' vol. 664. 2019, October 3 *parliament.uk* Available: https://hansard.parliament.uk/commons/2019-10-03/debates/585F872D-9372-4448-A32F-5CEC0FD49FB7/BrexitNegotiations (Accessed 12 January 2021)

Hansard. (2019a) 'Withdrawal Agreement: Legal Opinion' vol. 656. 2019, March 12 *parliament.uk* Available: https://hansard.parliament.uk/commons/2019-03-12/debates/2071A524-04FF-4629-8EDB-50AD54C25026/WithdrawalAgreementLegalOpinion (Accessed 15 October 2020)

Hansard. (2019b) 'Brexit Readiness: Operation Yellowhammer' vol. 664. 2019, September 25 *parliament.uk* Available: https://hansard.parliament.uk/commons/2019-09-25/debates/B2BCE472-527C-4549-B23F-A34C4D8F4160/BrexitReadinessOperationYellowhammer (Accessed 8 January 2020)

Hansard. (2020a) 'Northern Ireland Protocol: UK Legal Obligations' vol. 679. 2020, September 8 *parliament.uk* Available: https://hansard.parliament.uk/Commons/2020-09-08/debates/2F32EBC3-6692-402C-93E6-76B4CF1BC6E3/NorthernIrelandProtocolUKLegal Obligations?highlight=specific%20limited%20way#contribution-C5C04D42-8987-4DDD-A764-67E95E23966D (Accessed 4 February 2021)

Hansard (2020b) 'EU Withdrawal Agreement' vol. 685. 2020, December 9 *parliament.uk* Available: https://hansard.parliament.uk/Commons/2020-12-09/debates/F5A28792-DDD8-4D10-A254-FE777E6703FC/EUWithdrawalAgreement (Accessed 15 April 2021)

Hansard (2020c) 'UK Internal Market: White Paper' vol. 678. 2020, July 16 *parliament.uk* Available: https://hansard.parliament.uk/commons/2020-07-16/debates/807F5D47-BCDB-46EB-8C02-BE8935534502/UKInternalMarketWhitePaper (Accessed 22 April 2021)

Hart (2012 [1961]) *The Concept of Law*. 2nd ed. Oxford: Oxford University Press.

Harte, L. (2021) 'UUP and EU in separate legal moves on NI Protocol' 2021, March 15. *Belfast Telegraph* Available: https://www.belfasttelegraph.co.uk/news/northern-ireland/uup-and-eu-in-separate-legal-moves-on-ni-protocol-40197205.html (Accessed 31 March 2021)

Harvey, A. (2020) 'A Legal Analysis of Incorporating Into UK Law the Birthright Commitment under the Belfast (Good Friday) Agreement 1998' *Northern Ireland Human Rights Commission and Irish Human Rights and Equality Commission*. Available: https://www.nihrc.org/uploads/publications/Birthright-Commitment-Report.pdf (Accessed 8 January 2021)

Harvey, C. (2012) 'Reconstructing the 'Political Constitution' of Northern Ireland' *UK Constitutional Law Blog* 2012, August 2. Available: https://ukconstitutionallaw.org/2012/08/02/colin-harvey-reconstructing-the-political-constitution-of-northern-ireland/ (Accessed 9 September 2017)

Harvey, C. (2017) 'Uniting and Sharing the Island: Normalising Good Friday Agreement Constitutionalism' 2017, August 23 *qpol.qub.ac.uk* Available: http://qpol.qub.ac.uk/normalising-gfa-constitutionalism/ (Accessed 29 March 2019)

Harvey, C. (2020) 'Designing a Special Arrangement for Northern Ireland: The Irish Protocol in Context' *Brexit Institute Working Paper Series*. No 6/2020.

Harvey, J. and Bather, L. (1963) *The British Constitution*. London: Macmillan.

Haughey, S. (2020) 'Back to Stormont: The New Decade, New Approach Agreement and What it means for Northern Ireland' *The Political Quarterly*, 91(1): 134–40.

Hayward, K. (2021) 'Who's responsible for the violence in Northern Ireland?' 2021, April 9. *Politico* Available: https://www.politico.eu/article/northern-ireland-oped/ (Accessed 4 April 2022)

Hayward, K. and Komorova, M. (2019) 'The Irish Border as a European Union Frontier: The Implications for Managing Mobility and Conflict' *Geopolitics*, 24(3): 541–64.

Hayward, K. and McManus, C. (2018) 'Neither/Nor: The rejection of Unionist and Nationalist identities in post-Agreement Northern Ireland' *Capital and Class*, 43(1): 139–55.

Hayward, K. and Murphy, M. (2018) 'The EU's Influence on the Peace Process and Agreement in Northern Ireland in Light of Brexit' *Ethnopolitics*, 17(3): 276–91.

Hayward, K. and Phinnemore, D. (2020) 'What does the "New Decade, New Approach" (NDNA) agreement mean for Northern Ireland's Brexit?' 2020, January 16 *qpol.qub.ac.uk* Available: http://qpol.qub.ac.uk/what-does-the-new-decade-new-approach-ndna-agreement-mean-for-northern-irelands-brexit/ (Accessed 8 December 2020)

Hayward, K. and Rosher, B. (2020) 'Political Attitudes at a Time of Flux' ARK Research Update. No. 133 *ark.ac.uk* Available: https://www.ark.ac.uk/ARK/sites/default/files/2020-06/update133.pdf (Accessed 8 August 2020)

Hayward, K. and Whitten, L. (2018) 'What is Northern Ireland saying about Brexit—key slides' *qpol.qub.ac.uk* Available: http://qpol.qub.ac.uk/northern-ireland-saying-brexit-key-slides/ (Accessed 12 March 2021)

Hazell, R. (2000) *The State and the Nations: The First Year of Devolution in the United Kingdom*. Thorverton: Imprint Academic.

HC (2015a) 'European Union Referendum Bill: Committee of the Whole House, Tuesday 16 June 2015' *parliament.uk* Available: https://publications.parliament.uk/pa/bills/cbill/2015-2016/0002/amend/pbc021606m.pdf (Accessed 10 August 2019)

HC (2015b) 'European Union Referendum Bill: Supplement to the Votes and Proceedings, Tuesday 16 June 2015' *parliament.uk* Available: https://publications.parliament.uk/pa/bills/cbill/2015-2016/0002/pro021606p.21-27.html (Accessed 10 August 2019)

HC (2015c) 'European Union Referendum Bill: Explanatory Notes HCB-2 EN' 2015, May 28 *parliament.uk* Available: https://publications.parliament.uk/pa/bills/cbill/2015-2016/0002/en/16002en.pdf (Accessed 10 February 2020)

HC (2020) 'European Union (Withdrawal Agreement) Bill: Amendments as of 8 January'. 2020, January 8 *parliament.uk* Available: https://publications.parliament.uk/pa/bills/cbill/58-01/0001/amend/euwithdrawal_daily_cwh_0107.1-7.html (Accessed 11 January 2021)

Helm, T. (2015) 'Lords accuse Tories of 'burying' review that cleared EU of interference' 2015, March 28. *The Observer* Available: https://www.theguardian.com/world/2015/mar/28/lords-accuse-tories-burying-eu-powers-review (Accessed 20 March 2020)

Heppell, T. (2008) *Choosing the Tory Leader: Conservative Party Leadership Elections from Heath to Cameron*. London: IB Tauris.

Hewitt, J. (1986) *The Irish Question*. Hove: Wayland.

HL (1998) 'Scotland Bill: HL Deb 21 July 1998 vol. 592 cc.798–800' 1998, July 21 *parliament.uk* Available: https://api.parliament.uk/historic-hansard/lords/1998/jul/21/scotland-bill (Accessed 12 April 2021)

HL Constitution Committee (2018) 'European Union (Withdrawal) Bill' HL 69 *parliament.uk* Available: https://publications.parliament.uk/pa/ld201719/ldselect/ldconst/69/69.pdf (Accessed 30 March 2021)

HL EU Committee (2015) 'The Review of the Balance of Competences between the UK and the EU' HL Paper 140. 2015, March 25 *parliament.uk* Available: https://publications.parliament.uk/pa/ld201415/ldselect/ldeucom/140/140.pdf (Accessed 2 April 2021)

HM Government (1916) 'Headings of a settlement as to the Government of Ireland' (LG/D/15/1/7) *Parliamentary Archives* Available: https://discovery.nationalarchives.gov.uk/details/r/8e0f1d06-1f43-4d06-ab52-ad2f2271b50a (Accessed 26 September 2021)

HM Government (2010) 'The Coalition: our programme for government' 2010, May 20 *gov.uk* Available: https://assets.publishing.service.gov.uk/government/uploads/system/uploads/attachment_data/file/78977/coalition_programme_for_government.pdf (Accessed 20 March 2020)

HM Government (2014a) 'Review of the balance of competences' 2014, December 18 *gov.uk* Available: https://www.gov.uk/guidance/review-of-the-balance-of-competences (Accessed 10 March 2020)

HM Government (2014b) 'Review of the Balance of Competences between the United Kingdom and the European Union: Cohesion Policy' 2014, July 22 *gov.uk* Available: https://assets.publishing.service.gov.uk/government/uploads/system/uploads/attachment_data/file/355455/BIS_14_981__Review_of_the_Balance_of_Competences_between_the_United_Kingdom_and_the_European_Union.pdf (Accessed 12 March 2021)

HM Government (2014c) 'Review of the Balance of Competences between the United Kingdom and the European Union: Single Market Free Movement of Goods' 2014, February 17 *gov.uk* Available: https://assets.publishing.service.gov.uk/government/uploads/system/uploads/attachment_data/file/288194/2901479_BoC_SingleMarket_acc5.pdf (Accessed 12 March 2021)

HM Government (2014d) 'Review of the Balance of Competences between the United Kingdom and the European Union: Animal Health and Welfare and Food Safety Report' 2013, July 22 *gov.uk* Available: https://assets.publishing.service.gov.uk/government/uploads/system/uploads/attachment_data/file/227367/DEF-PB13979-BalOfComp-HMG-WEB.PDF (Accessed 12 March 2021)

HM Government (2016a) 'The process for withdrawing from the European Union' CM 9216. 2016, February 22 *assets.publishing.service.gov.uk* Available: https://assets.publishing.service.gov.uk/government/uploads/system/uploads/attachment_data/file/504216/The_process_for_withdrawing_from_the_EU_print_ready.pdf (Accessed 14 April 2021)

HM Government (2016b) 'HM Treasury Analysis: The Long-term Economic Impact of EU Membership and the Alternatives' Cm 9250. 2016, April 13 *assets.publishing.service.gov.uk* Available: https://assets.publishing.service.gov.uk/government/uploads/system/uploads/attachment_data/file/517415/treasury_analysis_economic_impact_of_eu_membership_web.pdf (Accessed 28 March 2021)

HM Government (2016c) 'The best of both worlds: The United Kingdom's special status in a reformed European Union' 2016, February 22 *gov.uk* Available: https://assets.publishing.service.gov.uk/government/uploads/system/uploads/attachment_data/file/504220/The_best_of_both_worlds_the_UKs_special_status_in_a_reformed_EU_print_ready.pdf (Accessed 8 August 2019)

HM Government (2016d) 'Why the Government Believes that Voting to Remain in the EU is the Best Decision for the UK' 2016, April 6 *assets.publishing.service.gov.uk* Available: https://assets.publishing.service.gov.uk/government/uploads/system/uploads/attachment_data/file/515068/why-the-government-believes-that-voting-to-remain-in-the-european-union-is-the-best-decision-for-the-uk.pdf (Accessed 9 August 2019)

HM Government (2017a) 'The United Kingdom's exit from, and partnership with, the European Union' 2017, February 2 *assets.publishing.service.gov.uk* Available: https://www.gov.uk/government/publications/the-united-kingdoms-exit-from-and-new-partnership-with-the-european-union-white-paper/the-united-kingdoms-exit-from-and-new-partnership-with-the-european-union—2#ensuring-free-trade-with-european-markets (Accessed 12 September 2020)

HM Government (2017b) 'Northern Ireland and Ireland: position paper' 2017, August 16 assets.publishing.service.gov.uk Available: https://assets.publisFdavidhing.service.gov.uk/government/uploads/system/uploads/attachment_data/file/638135/6.3703_DEXEU_Northern_Ireland_and_Ireland_INTERACTIVE.pdf (Accessed 12 September 2020)

HM Government (2018) 'Guidance on decision-making for Northern Ireland Departments during the period for Northern Ireland Executive formation' Cm 9725. 2018, November 5 *gov.uk* Available: https://assets.publishing.service.gov.uk/government/uploads/system/uploads/attachment_data/file/754029/Cm9725_Guidance_on_decision-making_for_NI_Dpts.pdf (Accessed 10 December 2020)

HM Government (2019a) 'UK Government Commitments to Northern Ireland and Its Integral Place in the United Kingdom' 2019, January 9 *gov.uk* Available: https://assets.publishing.service.gov.uk/government/uploads/system/uploads/attachment_data/file/769954/NI_unilateral_commitments_-_9_January_FINAL.pdf (Accessed 10 December 2020)

HM Government (2019b) 'Explanatory Note: UK Proposals for an Amended Protocol on Ireland/Northern Ireland' 2019, October 2 *gov.uk* Available: https://assets.publishing.service.gov.uk/government/uploads/system/uploads/attachment_data/file/836116/Explanatory_Note_Accessible.pdf (Accessed 11 December 2020)

HM Government (2019c) 'Operation Yellowhammer: HMG Reasonable Worst Case Planning Assumptions As of 2 August 2019' 2019, August 2 *gov.uk* Available: https://assets.publishing.service.gov.uk/government/uploads/system/uploads/attachment_data/file/831199/20190802_Latest_Yellowhammer_Planning_assumptions_CDL.pdf (Accessed 8 January 2021)

HM Government (2019d) 'Declaration by Her Majesty's Government of the United Kingdom of Great Britain and Northern Ireland concerning the operation of the 'Democratic consent in Northern Ireland' provision of the Protocol on Ireland/Northern Ireland' 2019, October 19 *gov.uk* Available: https://assets.publishing.service.gov.uk/government/uploads/system/uploads/attachment_data/file/840232/Unilateral_Declaration_on_Consent.pdf (Accessed 11 December 2020)

HM Government (2020a) 'The Future Relationship with the EU: The UK's Approach to Negotiations' 2020, February 27 *gov.uk* Available: https://www.gov.uk/government/publications/our-approach-to-the-future-relationship-with-the-eu (Accessed 31 March 2021)

HM Government (2020b) 'HMG Legal Position: UKIM Bill and Northern Ireland Protocol' 2020, September 9 *gov.uk* Available: https://assets.publishing.service.gov.uk/government/uploads/system/uploads/attachment_data/file/916702/UKIM_Legal_Statement.pdf (Accessed 7 June 2023)

HM Government (2021) 'Northern Ireland Protocol: the way forward' 2021, July 21 *gov.uk* Available: https://assets.publishing.service.gov.uk/government/uploads/system/uploads/attachment_data/file/1008451/CCS207_CCS0721914902-005_Northern_Ireland_Protocol_Web_Accessible__1_.pdf (Accessed January 2023)

HM Government (2023a) 'Decision of the Withdrawal Agreement Joint Committee on laying down arrangements relating to the Windsor Framework' 2023, March 24 *gov.uk* Available: https://assets.publishing.service.gov.uk/government/uploads/system/uploads/attachment_data/file/1145694/Decision_of_the_Withdrawal_Agreement_Joint_Committee_on_laying_down_arrangements_relating_to_the_Windsor_Framework.pdf (Accessed 27 March 2023)

HM Government (2023b) 'Joint Declaration of the Union and the United Kingdom in the Joint Committee Established by the Agreement on the Withdrawal of the United Kingdom of Great Britain and Northern Ireland from the European Union and the European Atomic Energy Community of 24 March 2023 on the application of Article 10(1) of the Windsor Framework' 2023, March 24 *gov.uk* Available: https://assets.publishing.service.gov.uk/government/uploads/system/uploads/attachment_data/file/1145697/Joint_Declaration_by_the_United_Kingdom_of_Great_Britain_and_he_European_Union_in_the_Withdrawal_Agreement_Joint_Committee_on_the_application_of_Article_10_1_.pdf (Accessed 27 March 2023)

HM Government (2023c) 'Joint Declaration No 2/2023 of the Union and the United Kingdom in the Joint Committee Established by the Agreement on the Withdrawal of the United Kingdom of Great Britain and Northern Ireland from the European Union and the European Atomic Energy Community of 24 March 2023' 2023, March 24 *gov.uk* Available: https://assets.publishing.service.gov.uk/government/uploads/system/uploads/attachment_data/file/1145698/Joint_Declaration_by_the_United_Kingdom_of_Great_Britain_and_Northern_Ireland_and_the_European_Union_in_the_Withdrawal_Agreement_Joint_Committee_on_dialogue_and_goods.pdf

HM Government (2023d) 'Joint declaration by the United Kingdom of Great Britain and Northern Ireland and the European Union in the Withdrawal Agreement Joint Committee on dialogue and goods' 2023, March 24 *gov.uk* Available: https://assets.publishing.service.gov.uk/government/uploads/system/uploads/attachment_data/file/1145698/Joint_Declaration_by_the_United_Kingdom_of_Great_Britain_and_Northern_Ireland_and_the_European_Union_in_the_Withdrawal_Agreement_Joint_Committee_on_dialogue_and_goods.pdf

HM Government (2023f) *The Windsor Framework: A New Way Forward*. CP 806. Available: https://assets.publishing.service.gov.uk/government/uploads/system/uploads/attachment_data/file/1138989/The_Windsor_Framework_a_new_way_forward.pdf (Accessed 27 March 2023)

Hoare, S. (2022) 'Correspondence: Issues relating to Electronic Travel Authorisation (ETA) and the Common Travel Area' *HC Northern Ireland Affairs Committee*. Available: https://committees.parliament.uk/publications/33896/documents/185462/default/ (Accessed 25 January 2023)

Hobolt, S. (2016) 'The Brexit vote: a divided nation, a divided continent' *Journal of European Public Policy*, 23(9): 1259–77.

Honeycombe-Foster, M. (2019) 'Boris Johnson vows to deliver Brexit "do or die" by 31 October' 2019, June 25. *Politics Home* Available: https://www.politicshome.com/news/article/boris-johnson-vows-to-deliver-brexit-do-or-die-by-31-october (Accessed 14 April 2021)

Hooton, C. and Stone, J. (2016) 'Brexit: Article 50 Was Never Actually Meant to Be Used, Says Its Author' 2016, July 26. *Independent* Available: https://www.independent.co.uk/news/uk/politics/brexit-eu-referendum-britain-theresa-may-article-50-not-supposed-meant-to-be-used-trigger-giuliano-a7156656.html (Accessed 6 June 2020)

Hopkinson, M. (1990) 'The Craig-Collins Pacts of 1922: Two Attempted Reforms of the Northern Ireland Government' *Irish Historical Studies* 27(106): 145–58

Humphreys, R. (2018) *Beyond the Border: The Good Friday Agreement and Irish Unity After Brexit*. Newbridge: Merrion Press.

Irish Government (2017) 'Ireland and the negotiations on the UK's withdrawal from the European Union: The Government's Approach' 2017, May 2 *dfa.ie* Available: https://www.dfa.ie/brexit/brexit-negotiations/key-documents/ (Accessed 20 April 2021)

Irish News (2017) 'The funeral of Martin McGuinness was one of a kind' 2017, March 3. *The Irish News* Available: http://www.irishnews.com/news/northernirelandnews/2017/03/23/news/thousands-attend-funeral-of-martin-mcguinness-in-derry-974818/ (Accessed 10 August 2020)

Irish Times (2016) 'McGuinness urges vote on united Ireland in event of Brexit' 2016, March 11. *Irish Times* Available: https://www.irishtimes.com/news/politics/mcguinness-urges-vote-on-united-ireland-in-event-of-brexit-1.2569500 (Accessed 12 March 2020)

Ipsos Mori (2016) 'How Britain voted in the 2016 EU referendum' 2016, September 5 *Ipsos.com* Available: https://www.ipsos.com/ipsos-mori/en-uk/how-britain-voted-2016-eu-referendum (Accessed 14 April 2021)

Ipsos Mori (2016) 'How Britain voted in the 2016 EU referendum' 2016, September 5 *Ipsos.com* Available: https://www.ipsos.com/ipsos-mori/en-uk/how-britain-voted-2016-eu-referendum (Accessed 14 April 2021)

Ipsos Mori (2016) 'How Britain voted in the 2016 EU referendum' 2016, September 5 *Ipsos.com* Available: https://www.ipsos.com/ipsos-mori/en-uk/how-britain-voted-2016-eu-referendum (Accessed 14 April 2021)

Jeffery, D., Heppell, T., Hayton, R., and Crines, A. (2018) 'The Conservative Party Leadership Election of 2016: An Analysis of the Voting Motivations of Conservative Parliamentarians' *Parliamentary Affairs*, 71(2): 263–82.

Jennings, I. (1971) *The British Constitution*. 5th ed. London: Cambridge University Press.

Jenrick, R. (2023) 'Ministerial Correspondence: Electronic Travel Authorisations' *Home Office* Available: https://committees.parliament.uk/publications/33897/documents/185463/default/ (Accessed 6 February 2023)

Joint Committee on European Union Affairs (2015) 'UK/EU future relationship: Implications for Ireland' *oireachtas.ie* Available: https://ec.europa.eu/dgs/secretariat_general/relations/relations_other/npo/docs/ireland/own_initiative/oi_uk_eu_relations_and_the_implications_for_ie/oi_uk_eu_relations_and_the_implications_for_ie_oireachtas_opinion_en.pdf (Accessed 12 April 2021)

Joint Committee on Jobs, Enterprise, and Innovation (2016) 'Report on the All-Island Economy' 31 JEI 023. 2016, January *oireachtas.ie* Available: https://webarchive.oireachtas.ie/parliament/media/committees/jobsenterpriseandinnovation/all-island-economy—final.pdf (Accessed 10 April 2021)

Joint Ministerial Committee (2016) 'Joint Ministerial Committee Communiqué' 2016, October 24 *northernireland.gov.uk* Available: https://www.northernireland.gov.uk/sites/default/files/publications/newnigov/joint-ministerial-committee-communique-24-october-2016.pdf (Accessed 6 June 2020) *Joint [Windsor Framework] Political Declaration*:

European Commission (2023d) 'Windsor Political Declaration by the European Commission and the Government of the United Kingdom' 2023, February 27 *gov.uk* Available: https://commission.europa.eu/system/files/2023-02/political%20declaration.pdf

HM Government (2023e) 'Political Declaration by the European Commission and the Government of the United Kingdom' 2023, February 27 *gov.uk* Available: https://assets.publishing.service.gov.uk/government/uploads/system/uploads/attachment_data/file/1139420/Political_Declaration_by_the_European_Commission_and_the_Government_of_the_United_Kingdom.pdf

Joint Report of Negotiators (2017) 'Joint report from the Negotiators of the European Union and the United Kingdom Government on progress during phase 1 of negotiations under Article 50 TEU on the United Kingdom's orderly withdrawal from the European Union' TF40 19. 2017, December 8 *europa.ec* Available: https://ec.europa.eu/commission/sites/beta-political/files/joint_report.pdf (Accessed 11 December 2020)

Johnson, B. (2019) 'Boris Johnson says single market access after Brexit is "great deal" for Northern Ireland'. 2019, November 8. *The Independent* Available: https://www.independent.co.uk/news/uk/politics/brexit-deal-boris-johnson-northern-ireland-speech-general-election-single-market-a9194476.html (Accessed 20 September 2020)

Judicial Communications Office (2021) 'Court Dismisses Challenge to EU Exit Protocol: Summary of Judgment' 2021, June 30 *judiciaryni.uk* Available: https://www.judiciaryni.uk/sites/judiciary/files/decisions/Summary%20of%20judgment%20-%20In%20re%20Jim%20Allister%20and%20others%20%28EU%20Exit%29%20-%20300621.pdf (Accessed 16 January 2023)

Karlsson, L. (2017) 'Smart Border 2.0 Avoiding a hard border on the island of Ireland for Customs control and the free movement of persons' *europarl.europa.eu* Available: http://www.europarl.europa.eu/RegData/etudes/STUD/2017/596828/IPOL_STU(2017)596828_EN.pdf (Accessed 2 March 2018)

Kavanagh, A. (2019) 'Recasting the Political Constitution: From Rivals to Relationships' *King's Law Journal*, 30(1): 43–73.

Kelly, B. (2019) 'Dominic Raab's ignorant indifference to the Good Friday Agreement is an insult to Northern Irish people like me' 2019, February 1. *Independent* Available: https://www.independent.co.uk/voices/dominic-raab-good-friday-agreement-brexit-irish-border-a8758076.html (Accessed 12 February 2021)

Kelly, R. (2016) 'Statutory Instruments' HC Library. 2016, December 15 parliament.uk Available: https://researchbriefings.files.parliament.uk/documents/SN06509/SN06509.pdf (Accessed 5 June 2023)

Ker-Lindsay, J. (2016) 'Turkey's EU accession as a factor in the 2016 Brexit referendum' *Turkish Studies*, 19(1): 1–22.

King, A. (2001) *Does the United Kingdom Still Have a Constitution?* London: Sweet & Maxwell.

King, A. (2009) *The British Constitution*. Oxford: Oxford University Press.

Kolodko, G. (2016) 'Political economy of Brexit, or Brexitology' *Transformation, Integration and Globalization Economic Research Working Paper Series*, 134: 1–5.

Komarova, M. and Hayward, K. (2019) 'The Irish Border as a European Union Frontier Implications for Managing Mobility and Conflict' *Geopolitics*, 24(3): 541–64.

Larkin, J. (2018) 'Miller and Northern Ireland: The Northern Ireland Constitution Before the UK Supreme Court' *UK Supreme Court Yearbook*, 8: 282–98.

Lawrence, R. (1965) *The Government of Northern Ireland: Public Finance and Public Services 1921–1964*. Oxford: Clarendon Press.

Law Society (2022) 'Judge suspends Poot's border-checks order' 2022, February 3 *lawsociety.ie* Available: https://www.lawsociety.ie/gazette/top-stories/2022/february/judge-blocks-poots-order-on-border-checks (Accessed 18 January 2023)

Lewis, B. (2021) 'Northern Ireland Protocol: Implementation' vol. 690: 3 March 2021. HC Hansard Available: https://hansard.parliament.uk/commons/2021-03-03/debates/21030327000007/NorthernIrelandProtocolImplementation (Accessed 16 January 2023)

Lewis, B. (2021a) 1 January. @BrandonLewis. Available: https://twitter.com/brandonlewis/status/1345057483887411200?lang=en (Accessed 9 March 2021)

Lewis, B. (2021b) 4 March. 'Our lawful steps are consistent with a good faith implementation of the Northern Ireland Protocol' *The Telegraph*. Available: https://www.telegraph.co.uk/politics/2021/03/04/lawful-steps-consistent-good-faith-implementation-northern-ireland/ (Accessed 9 March 2021)

Liberal Democrats (2010) 'Liberal Democrat Manifesto 2010' *markpack.co.uk* Available: https://www.markpack.org.uk/files/2015/01/Liberal-Democrat-manifesto-2010.pdf (Accessed 10 April 2021)

Lloyd G. (1921a) *Correspondence Between His Majesty's Government and the Prime Minister of Northern Ireland Relating to the Proposals for an Irish Settlement*. Parliamentary Papers, Session 1921, vol. I, p.83. Available: https://archive.org/details/op1256877-1001/page/n7 (Accessed 9 October 1921)

Lloyd G. (1921b) in *Hansard* 'Ulster' HC Deb. 1921, December 14. vol. 149 cc.38–9. Available: https://api.parliament.uk/historic-hansard/commons/1921/dec/14/ulster#S5CV0149P0_19211214_HOC_76 (Accessed 9 October 2021)

Loughlin, M. (2018) 'The British Constitution: Thoughts on the Cause of the Present Discontents' *New Zealand Journal of Public and International Law*, 16: 1–20.

Loughlin, M. (2019) 'The Political Constitution Revisited' *King's Law Journal*, 30(1): 11–14.

Loveland. I. (2012) *Constitutional Law, Administrative Law, and Human Rights: A Critical Introduction*. 6th ed. Oxford: Oxford University Press.

Lucid Talk (2021) 'LT NI quarterly 'Tracker' Poll—Winter 2021' *lucidtalk.co.uk* Available: https://www.lucidtalk.co.uk/single-post/lt-ni-quarterly-tracker-poll-winter-2021 (Accessed 16 January 2023)

Mac Síthigh, D. (2018) 'Official status of languages in the United Kingdom and Ireland' *Common Law World Review*, 47(1): 77–102.

MacCormick, N. (1999) *Questioning Sovereignty: Law, State and Nation in the European Commonwealth*. Oxford: Oxford University Press.

MacFlynn, P. (2016) The Economic Implications of BREXIT for Northern Ireland' *Nevin Economic Research Institute*. Available: https://www.nerinstitute.net/download/pdf/brexit_wp_250416.pdf (Accessed 17 December 2017)

Madden, A. (2021) 'Chief Constable Simon Byrne urges public to 'step back from the brink' over NI Protocol tensions' 2021, February 4. *Belfast Telegraph* Available: https://www.belfasttelegraph.co.uk/news/northern-ireland/chief-constable-simon-byrne-urges-public-to-step-back-from-the-brink-over-ni-protocol-tensions-40051593.html (Accessed 16 January 2023)

Maher, I. (2017) 'The Common Travel Area: More Than Just Travel'. *The British Academy* Available: https://www.thebritishacademy.ac.uk/documents/319/common-travel-area-more-just-travel.pdf (Accessed: 10 April 2021)

Major, J. (2016) 'Article on the EU Referendum—19 March 2016' *johnmajorarchive.org.uk* Available: https://johnmajorarchive.org.uk/2016/03/19/article-on-the-eu-referendum-19-march-2016/ (Accessed 14 April 2021)

Mance, H. (2017) 'David Davis warns Brexit timetable will be "row of the summer"' 2017, May 14 *Financial Times*.

Maskey, A. (2022) 'Resignation of the First Minister, Paul Givan MLA' 2022, February 3 *niassembly.gov.uk* Available: http://www.niassembly.gov.uk/assembly-business/office-of-the-speaker/correspondence/resignation-of-the-first-minister-paul-givan-mla/ (Accessed 18 January 2023)

Matthews, F. (2017) 'Whose Mandate is it Anyway? Brexit, the Constitution and the Contestation of Authority' *The Political Quarterly*, 88(4): 603–11.

Matthews, N. and Pow, J. (2017) 'A fresh start? The Northern Ireland Assembly election 2016' *Irish Political Studies*, 32(2): 311–26.

Matti, J. and Zhou, Y. (2017) 'The political economy of Brexit: explaining the vote' *Applied Economics Letters*, 24(16): 1131–4.

May, T. (2016a) 'Theresa May's launch statement: full text' 2016, June 30. *Conservative Home* Available: https://www.conservativehome.com/parliament/2016/06/theresa-mays-launch-statement-full-text.html (Accessed 3 March 2018)

May, T. (2016b) 'Theresa May: First speech as Prime Minister—BBC News' 2016, July 13 *youtube.com* Available: https://www.youtube.com/watch?v=FDyZ8trge2E (Accessed 14 April 2021)

May, T. (2016c) 'Theresa May's keynote speech at Tory conference in full' 2016, October 5. *Independent* Available: https://www.independent.co.uk/news/uk/politics/theresa-may-speech-tory-conference-2016-in-full-transcript-a7346171.html (Accessed 8 June 2020)

May, T. (2017) 'The government's negotiating objectives for exiting the EU: PM speech' 2017, January 17 *gov.uk* Available: https://www.gov.uk/government/speeches/the-governments-negotiating-objectives-for-exiting-the-eu-pm-speech (Accessed 1 March 2019)

McBride, S. (2019) *Burned: The Inside Story of the "Cash-For-Ash" Scandal and Northern Ireland's Secretive New Elite*. Kildare: Merrion Press.

McConalogue, J. (2019) 'The British constitution resettled? Parliamentary sovereignty after the EU Referendum' *British Journal of Politics and International Relations*, 21(2): 439–58.

McCormack, J. (2019a) 'Brexit deal: NI firms must declare goods heading to rest of the UK' 2019, October 22. *BBC News* Available: https://www.bbc.co.uk/news/uk-northern-ireland-50137320 (Accessed 3 March 2020)

McCrudden, C. (2004) 'Northern Ireland, the Belfast Agreement, and the British Constitution' in Jowell J. and Oliver, D. (eds.) *The Changing Constitution*. 5th ed. Oxford: Oxford University Press: 227–270.

McCrudden, C. (2017) 'The Good Friday Agreement, Brexit, and Rights'. *The British Academy* Available: https://www.ria.ie/news/policy-and-international-relations/ria-british-academy-brexit-briefing-paper-series (Accessed 12 December 2017)

McCrudden, C. (ed.) (2022) *The Law and Practice of the Ireland-Northern Ireland Protocol.* Cambridge: Cambridge University Press.

McCrudden, C. and Halberstam, D. (2017) 'Miller and Northern Ireland: A Critical Constitutional Response' *The UK Supreme Court Yearbook*, 8 (575): 299–343.

McDonald, H. (2016a) 'Sinn Fein calls for vote on Irish reunification if UK backs Brexit' 2016, March 11. *The Guardian* Available: https://www.theguardian.com/politics/2016/mar/11/sinn-fein-irish-reunification-vote-brexit-eu-referendum (Accessed 4 May 2019)

McDonald, H. (2016b) 'Theresa May tries to ease 'hard border' fears on Northern Ireland visit' 2016, July 25. *The Guardian* Available: https://www.theguardian.com/uk-news/2016/jul/25/theresa-may-hard-border-fears-northern-ireland-visit-brexit (Accessed 12 April 2021)

McDonald, H. (2016c) 'SDLP fights for survival in Derry in face of Sinn Féin onslaught' 2016, May 3. *The Guardian* Available: http://www.theguardian.com/politics/2016/may/03/ (Accessed 10 September 2020)

McDonald, H. (2017) 'Northern Ireland power-sharing government expected to collapse' 2017, January 16. *The Guardian* Available: https://www.theguardian.com/uk-news/2017/jan/16/northern-ireland-power-sharing-government-expected-to-collapse-sinn-fein-cash-for-ash (Accessed 5 June 2020)

McDonald, H. (2022) 'Jeffery Donaldson: DUP will not nominate a speaker when Assembly meets' 2022, May 13. *News Letter* Available: https://www.newsletter.co.uk/news/politics/sir-jeffrey-donaldson-dup-will-not-nominate-a-speaker-when-assembly-meets-3692315

McDowell, L. (2017) 'Martin McGuinness funeral: They came from far and wide … but Arlene Foster made the toughest journey' 2017, March 24. *Belfast Telegraph* Available: https://www.belfasttelegraph.co.uk/news/northern-ireland/martin-mcguinness-funeral-they-came-from-far-and-wide-but-arlene-foster-made-toughest-journey-35560306.html (Accessed 16 August 2020)

McEvoy, K., Bryson, A., and Kramer, A. (2020) 'The Empire Strikes Back: Brexit, The Irish Peace Process, and the Limitations of Law' *Fordham International Law Journal*, 43(3): 608–68.

McGee, H. (2016) 'Most Irish political parties take active role in Brexit debate' 2016, June 22. *Irish Times* Available: https://www.irishtimes.com/news/politics/most-irish-political-parties-take-active-role-in-brexit-debate-1.2693651 (Accessed 20 April 2020)

McGrath, D. (2022) '"Good" call between Cleverly and Šefčovič amid ongoing Protocol row' 2022, September 30. *Independent* Available: https://www.independent.co.uk/news/uk/european-commission-liz-truss-government-dup-london-b2184502.html (Accessed 18 January 2023)

McHarg, A. (2018) 'Navigating without maps: Constitutional silence and the management of the Brexit crisis' *International Journal of Constitutional Law*, 16(3): 952–68.

McKenzie, L. (2017) 'The class politics of prejudice: Brexit and the land of no-hope and glory' *British Journal of Sociology*, 68(1): 265–80.

McLoughlin, P. (2009) 'The SDLP and the Europeanization of the Northern Ireland problem' *Irish Political Studies*, 24: 603–19.

Mills, E. and Colvin, C. (2016) 'Why did Northern Ireland vote to Remain?' 2016, July 18 *qpol.qub.ac.uk* Available: http://qpol.qub.ac.uk/northern-ireland-vote-remain/ (Accessed 2 April 2021)

Mitchell D. (2009) 'Cooking the Fudge: Constructive Ambiguity and the Implementation of the Northern Ireland Agreement, 1998–2007' *Irish Political Studies*, 24(3): 321–36.

Morgan, A. (2000) *The Belfast Agreement: A Practical Legal Analysis*. London: The Belfast Press Ltd.

Moriarty, G. (2016) 'DUP chastises Kenny over Brexit warning on Northern Ireland' 2016, January 27. *Irish Times* Available: https://www.irishtimes.com/news/politics/dup-chastises-kenny-over-brexit-warning-on-northern-ireland-1.2511487 (Accessed 10 March 2021)

Murphy, M. (2007) 'Europeanisation and the sub-national level: Changing patterns of governance in Northern Ireland', *Regional and Federal Studies*, 17(3): 293–315.

Murphy M. (2011) 'Regional Representation in Brussels and multi-level governance: Evidence from Northern Ireland' *British Journal of Politics and International Relations*, 13(4): 551–66.

Murphy, M. C. (2009) 'Pragmatic politics: The Ulster Unionist Party and the European Union' *Irish Political Studies*, 24: 589–602.

Murphy, M. C. (2014) *Northern Ireland and the European Union: The Dynamics of a Changing Relationship*. Manchester: Manchester University Press.

Murphy, M. C. (2016a) 'The EU Referendum in Northern Ireland: Closing borders, re-opening border debates' *Journal of Contemporary European Research*, 12(4): 844–53.

Murphy, M. C. (2016b) 'Northern Ireland and the EU referendum: The outcome, options and opportunities' *Journal of Cross Border Studies of Ireland*, 11: 18–31.

Murphy, M. C. (2018) *Europe and Northern Ireland's Future: Negotiating Brexit's Unique Case* Newcastle Upon Tyne: Agenda Publishing.

Murphy, M. C. (2019) 'The Brexit crisis, Ireland, and British-Irish relations: Europeanisation and/or de-Europeanisation? *Irish Political Studies*, 34(4): 530–50.

Murray, C. (2022) 'A New Period of "Indirect" Direct Rule – The Northern Ireland (Executive Formation etc) Bill' 2022, 29 November *U.K. Const. L. Blog* Available: https://ukconstitutionallaw.org/2022/11/29/colin-murray-a-new-period-of-indirect-direct-rule-the-northern-ireland-executive-formation-etc-bill/ (Accessed 4 January 2023).

Nedergaard, P. and Henriksen, M. F. (2018) 'Brexit and British Exceptionalism' in P. Diamond, P. Nedergaard, and B. Rosamond (eds.) *Routledge Handbook of the Politics of Brexit*. Oxon: Routledge: 134–46.

New Decade New Approach (2020) January 8 *gov.uk* Available: https://assets.publishing.service.gov.uk/government/uploads/system/uploads/attachment_data/file/856998/2020-01-08_a_new_decade__a_new_approach.pdf (Accessed 12 December 2020)

News Letter (2016a) 'DUP to 'recommend vote to leave the EU' 2016, February 20 *newsletter.co.uk* Available: https://www.newsletter.co.uk/news/dup-recommend-vote-leave-eu-1265866 (Accessed 14 April 2021)

News Letter (2016b) 'UUP Grandees urge party's supporters to quit 'out of control' EU' 2016, June 18 *newsletter.co.uk* Available: https://www.newsletter.co.uk/news/uup-grandees-urge-partys-supporters-quit-out-control-eu-1229096 (Accessed 2 April 2020)

NIAC (2016a) 'Northern Ireland Affairs Committee Oral Evidence: Northern Ireland and the EU Referendum, HC 760' 2016, March 2 *parliament.uk* Available: http://data.parliament.uk/writtenevidence/committeeevidence.svc/evidencedocument/northern-ireland-affairs-committee/northern-ireland-and-the-eu-referendum/oral/30043.html (Accessed 6 June 2023)

NIAC (2016b) 'Northern Ireland Affairs Committee Oral Evidence: Northern Ireland and the EU Referendum, HC 760' 2016, February 3 *parliament.uk* Available: http://data.parliament.uk/writtenevidence/committeeevidence.svc/evidencedocument/northern-ireland-affairs-committee/northern-ireland-and-the-eu-referendum/oral/28395.html (Accessed 6 June 2023)

NIAC (2021) 'Northern Ireland Affairs Committee Oral Evidence: Brexit and the Northern Ireland Protocol, HC 767' 2021, January 6 *parliament.uk* Available: https://committees.parliament.uk/oralevidence/1471/pdf/ (Accessed 16 January 2023)

NICS Board (2016a) 'NICS Board 16 December 2016, The Glasshouse Minutes' 2016, December 16 *executiveoffice-ni.gov.uk* Available: https://www.executiveoffice-ni.gov.uk/sites/default/files/publications/execoffice/nics-board-161216-minutes.pdf (Accessed 6 June 2020)

NICS Board (2016b) 'NICS Board 28 October 2016, Orchard House Draft Minutes' 2016, October 28 *executiveoffice-ni.gov.uk* Available: https://www.executiveoffice-ni.gov.uk/sites/default/files/publications/execoffice/nics-board-281016-minutes.pdf (Accessed 6 June 2020)

NICS Board (2016c) 'NICS Board 30 September 2016, Glasshouse, Stormont Castle Minutes' 2016, September 30 *executiveoffice-ni.gov.uk* Available: https://www.executiveoffice-ni.gov.uk/sites/default/files/publications/execoffice/nics-board-300916-minutes.pdf (Accessed 6 June 2020)

NICS Board (2016d) 'NICS Board 26 August 2016, Glasshouse, Stormont Castle Minutes' 2016, August 26 *executiveoffice-ni.gov.uk* Available: https://www.executiveoffice-ni.gov.uk/sites/default/files/publications/execoffice/nics-board-260816-minutes.pdf (Accessed 6 June 2020)

NICS Board (2016e) 'NICS Board 24 June 2016, Glasshouse, Stormont Castle Minutes' 2016, 24 June *executiveoffice-ni.gov.uk* Available: https://www.executiveoffice-ni.gov.uk/sites/default/files/publications/execoffice/nics-board-240616-minutes.pdf (Accessed 6 June 2020)

NICS Board (2016f) 'NICS Board 29 July 2016, Glasshouse, Stormont Castle Draft Minutes' 2016, July 29 *executiveoffice-ni.gov.uk* Available: https://www.executiveoffice-ni.gov.uk/sites/default/files/publications/execoffice/nics-board-290716-minutes.pdf (Accessed 6 June 2020)

NILT (2016) 'Northern Ireland Life and Times Survey 2016' *ARK* Available: https://www.ark.ac.uk/nilt/2016/Political_Attitudes/ (Accessed 6 June 2020)

NILT (2020) 'Northern Ireland Life and Times, Module: Political Attitudes' *ARK* Available: https://www.ark.ac.uk/nilt/results/polatt.html (Accessed 2 August 2020)

NIO (2020) 'The First Report on the Use of the Petition of Concern Mechanism in the Northern Ireland Assembly' CP 252 *publishing.service.gov.uk* Available: https://assets.publishing.service.gov.uk/government/uploads/system/uploads/attachment_data/file/901146/First_Report_on_the_Use_of_the_Petition_of_Concern_Mechanism_in_the_Northern_Ireland_Assembly.pdf_-_Copy.pdf (Accessed 25 February 2021)

NISRA (2020) 'Overview of Northern Ireland Trade' 2020, July 15 *nisra.gov.uk* Available: https://www.nisra.gov.uk/publications/overview-northern-ireland-trade-0 (Accessed 12 January 2021)

NISRA (2022) 'Northern Ireland Economic Trade Statistics 2021' 2022, December 15 *nisra.gov.uk* Available: https://datavis.nisra.gov.uk/economy-and-labour-market/northern-ireland-economic-trade-statistics-2021.html (Accessed 20 January 2023)

Northern Ireland Affairs Committee (2016) 'Northern Ireland and the EU referendum' *publications.parliament.uk* Available: https://publications.parliament.uk/pa/cm201617/cmselect/cmniaf/48/48.pdf (Accessed 6 April 2020)

Northern Ireland Assembly (2016b) 'Official Report (Hansard) Tuesday 7 March 2016 Volume 113, No 6' *niassembly.gov.uk* Available: http://data.niassembly.gov.uk/HansardXml/plenary-08-03-2016.pdf (Accessed 12 April 2021)

Northern Ireland Assembly (2016a) 'Official Report (Hansard) Monday 13 June 2016 Volume 114, No 6' *niassembly.gov.uk* Available: http://data.niassembly.gov.uk/HansardXml/plenary-13-06-2016.pdf (Accessed 12 April 2021)

Northern Ireland Assembly (2016c) 'Official Report (Hansard) Tuesday 13 September 2016 Volume 115, No 2' *niassembly.gov.uk* Available: http://data.niassembly.gov.uk/HansardXml/plenary-13-09-2016.pdf (Accessed 12 April 2021)

Northern Ireland Assembly (2016d) 'Official Report (Hansard) Monday 17 October 2016 Volume 116, No 5' *niassembly.gov.uk* Available: http://aims.niassembly.gov.uk/officialreport/report.aspx?&eveDate=2016/10/17&docID=276626 (Accessed 12 June 2020)

Northern Ireland Assembly (2017) 'Official Report (Hansard) Tuesday 17 January 2017 Volume 123, No 2' *niassembly.gov.uk* Available: http://data.niassembly.gov.uk/HansardXml/plenary-17-01-2017.pdf (Accessed 10 June 2020)

Northern Ireland Assembly (2020a) 'Official Report (Hansard) Monday 20 January 2020 Volume 125, No 3' *niassembly.gov.uk* Available: http://data.niassembly.gov.uk/HansardXml/plenary-20-01-2020.pdf (Accessed 10 January 2021)

Northern Ireland Assembly (2020b) 'Official Report (Hansard) 21 September 2020 Volume 130 No 6' *niassembly.gov.uk*. Available: http://data.niassembly.gov.uk/HansardXml/plenary-21-09-2020.pdf (Accessed 10 January 2021)

Northern Ireland Assembly (2020c) 'Official Report (Hansard) Tuesday 22 September 2020 Volume 130 No 7' *niassembly.gov.uk* Available: http://data.niassembly.gov.uk/HansardXml/plenary-22-09-2020.pdf (*niassembly.gov.uk*. Available: http://data.niassembly.gov.uk/HansardXml/plenary-22-09-2020.pdf (Accessed 15 January 2021)

Northern Ireland Assembly (2020d) 'Official Report (Hansard) Monday 14 December 2020 Volume 134 No 1' *niassembly.gov.uk* Available: http://aims.niassembly.gov.uk/officialreport/reportssearchresultsreport.aspx?&eveDate=2020/12/14&rID=319621&hwcID=3159309&aID=0&pg=3&sesID=23&dID=0&init=B#3159309 (Accessed 10 January 2021)

Northern Ireland Assembly (2020e) 'Official Report (Hansard) Brexit: Oireachtas Joint Committee on European Union Affairs' 2020, November 25 *niassembly.gov.uk* Available: http://data.niassembly.gov.uk/HansardXml/committee-24318.pdf (Accessed 12 January 2021)

Northern Ireland Assembly (2021a) 'Official Report: Minutes of Evidence. Committee for The Executive Office' 2021, June 28 *niassembly.gov.uk* Available: http://aims.niassembly.gov.uk/officialreport/minutesofevidencereport.aspx?AgendaId=27071&eveID=14534 (Accessed 16 January 2023)

Northern Ireland Assembly (2021b) 'Official Report: Minutes of Evidence. Committee for The Executive Office' 2021, July 9 *niassembly.gov.uk* Available: http://aims.niassembly.gov.uk/officialreport/minutesofevidencereport.aspx?AgendaId=27187&eveID=14594 (Accessed 16 January 2023)

Northern Ireland Assembly (2022) 'Official Report' 2022, October 27 *niassembly.gov.uk* Available: http://aims.niassembly.gov.uk/officialreport/report.aspx?&eveDate=2022/10/27&docID=385403 (Accessed 20 January 2023)

Northern Ireland Executive (2016a) 'Letter to the Prime Minister' 2016, August 10 *executiveoffice.-ni.gov.uk* Available: https://www.executiveoffice-ni.gov.uk/sites/default/files/publications/execoffice/Letter%20to%20PM%20from%20FM%20%26%20dFM.pdf (Accessed 14 April 2020)

Northern Ireland Executive (2016b) 'Draft programme for government framework 2016–2021' *northernireland.gov.uk* Available: https://www.northernireland.gov.uk/sites/default/files/consultations/newnigov/draft-pfg-framework-2016-21.pdf (Accessed 10 April 2021)

Northern Ireland Executive (2016c) 'Programme for Government Consultation Document' *northernireland.gov.uk* Available: https://www.northernireland.gov.uk/sites/default/files/consultations/newnigov/pfg-consulation-document.PDF (Accessed 20 May 2019)

Northern Ireland Office and Department of Foreign Affairs (2001) 'Implementation Plan issues by the British and Irish Governments on 1 August 2001' *cain.ulster.ac.uk* Available: https://cain.ulster.ac.uk/events/peace/docs/bi010801.htm (Accessed 6 June 2023)

Northern Ireland Office (2010) 'Hillsborough Castle Agreement' 2010, February 5 *gov.uk* Available: https://www.gov.uk/government/publications/hillsborough-castle-agreement (Accessed 20 February 2023)

Northern Ireland Office (2014) 'Stormont House Agreement' 2014, December 23 *gov.uk* Available: https://www.gov.uk/government/publications/the-stormont-house-agreement (Accessed 20 February 2023)

Northern Ireland Office (2015) 'A Fresh Start: the Stormont Agreement and Implementation Plan' 2015, November 17 *gov.uk* Available: https://www.gov.uk/government/news/a-fresh-start-for-northern-ireland (Accessed 20 February 2023)

Norton, P. (2014) 'The Changing Constitution' in Jones, B. and Norton, P. (eds.) *Politics UK*. 8th ed. Oxon: Routledge 251–71

NSMC (2015) 'North South Ministerial Council Twenty-First Plenary Meeting' 2015, December 11 *northsouthministerialcouncil.org* Available: https://www.northsouthministerialcouncil.org/sites/northsouthministerialcouncil.org/files/publications/%5Bcurrent-domain%3Amachine-name%5D/Twenty%20First%20Plenary%20Joint%20Communiqué%20-%2011%20December%202015.pdf (Accessed 10 March 2020)

NSMC (2016a) 'North South Ministerial Council Inland Waterways Meeting' 2016, June 24 *northsouthministerialcouncil.org* Available: https://www.northsouthministerialcouncil.org/sites/northsouthministerialcouncil.org/files/publications/Inland%20Waterways%20Joint%20Communiqué%2024%20June%202016_0.pdf (Accessed 12 March 2020)

NSMC (2016b) 'North South Ministerial Council North South Language Body Meeting' 2016, June 24 *northsouthministerialcouncil.org* Available: https://www.northsouthministerialcouncil.org/sites/northsouthministerialcouncil.org/files/publications/Language%20Joint%20Communiqué%20-%2024%20June%202016.pdf (Accessed 12 March 2020)

NSMC (2016c) 'PAPER NSMC P1 (16) JC North South Ministerial Council Twenty-Second Plenary Meeting' 2016, July 4 *northsouthministerialcouncil.org* Available: https://www.northsouthministerialcouncil.org/sites/northsouthministerialcouncil.org/files/publications/Plenary%20Joint%20Communique%20-%20English%20-%2004%20Jul-16.pdf (Accessed 6 June 2020)

NSMC (2016d) 'Paper NSMC P2 (16) JC North South Ministerial Council Twenty-Third Plenary Meeting' 2016, November 18 *northsouthministerialcouncil.org* Available: https://www.northsouthministerialcouncil.org/sites/northsouthministerialcouncil.org/files/publications/Paper%20NSMC%20P2%20%2816%29%20JC%20-%20Joint%20Communiqué%2018%20Nov%202016_0.pdf (Accessed 6 June 2020)

NSMC (2023a) 'Plenary Meetings' *northsouthministerialcouncil.org* Available: https://www.northsouthministerialcouncil.org/plenary-meetings-0 (Accessed 20 January 2023)

NSMC (2023b) 'Publications' *northsouthministerialcouncil.org* Available: https://www.northsouthministerialcouncil.org/publications (Accessed 20 January 2023)

Ó Beacháin, D. (2019) *From Partition to Brexit: The Irish Government and Northern Ireland*. Manchester: Manchester University Press.

O'Carroll, L. (2019) 'DUP dismisses May's Brexit pledge to consult Stormont as meaningless' 2019, January 9. *The Guardian* Available: https://www.theguardian.com/politics/2019/jan/09/dup-dismisses-may-brexit-pledge-to-consult-stormont-as-meaningless (Accessed 8 December 2020)

O'Carroll, L. (2022a) 'Northern Ireland minister orders halt to Brexit agri-food checks' 2022, February 2. *The Guardian* Available: https://www.theguardian.com/politics/2022/feb/02/

northern-ireland-minister-orders-halt-to-brexit-agri-food-checks (Accessed 18 January 2023)

O'Carroll, L. (2022b) 'UK to unilaterally continue suspending Northern Ireland border checks' 2022, September 15. *The Guardian* Available: https://www.theguardian.com/politics/2022/sep/15/uk-to-unilaterally-continue-suspending-northern-ireland-border-checks (Accessed 18 January 2023)

O'Carroll, L. and Rankin, J. (2019) 'Northern Ireland Brexit impact "mapping exercise" finally released' 2019, June 20. *The Guardian* Available: https://www.theguardian.com/politics/2019/jun/20/northern-ireland-brexit-impact-study-finally-released (Accessed 14 January 2021)

O'Donovan, G. (2017) 'Theresa v Boris: How May Became PM review: an odd yet ambitious concoction' 2017, 18 June. *The Telegraph* Available: https://www.telegraph.co.uk/tv/2017/06/18/theresa-v-boris-may-became-pm-review-odd-yet-ambitious-concotion/ (Accessed 28 March 2019)

O'Halloran, M. and Bray, J. (2019) 'Brexit: Ireland will not "countenance" deal involving customs checks—Varadkar' 2019, October 3. *Irish Times* Available: https://www.irishtimes.com/news/politics/brexit-ireland-will-not-countenance-deal-involving-customs-checks-varadkar-1.4038886 (Accessed 6 June 2020)

O'Leary, B. (1998) 'The nature of the Agreement', 9th John Whyte Memorial Lecture, 1998, November 26. Queen's University Belfast.

O'Leary, B. (2017) 'Detoxifying the UK's exit from the EU: a multi-national compromise is possible' 2017, 27 June *blogs.lse.ac.uk* Available: https://blogs.lse.ac.uk/brexit/2016/06/27/detoxifying-the-uks-eu-exit-process-a-multi-national-compromise-is-possible/ (Accessed 17 February 2020)

O'Leary, B. (2019) *A Treatise on Northern Ireland, vol. III: Consociation and Confederation.* Oxford: Oxford University Press.

O'Leary, N., Staunton, D., and Leahy, P. (2020) 'EU threatens legal action if UK does not withdraw treaty "violation" by end of month' 2020, September 11. *Irish Times* Available: https://www.irishtimes.com/news/world/europe/eu-threatens-legal-action-if-uk-does-not-withdraw-treaty-violation-by-end-of-month-1.4351946#.X1sT4fy3Qfo.twitter (Accessed 11 January 2021)

O'Rourke, K. (2019) *A Short History of Brexit: From Brentry to Backstop.* London: Pelican Books.

O'Toole, M. (2017) 'Ireland an afterthought during Brexit campaign when I was Cameron adviser' 2017, October 4. *Irish Times* Available: https://www.irishtimes.com/opinion/ireland-an-afterthought-during-brexit-campaign-when-i-was-cameron-adviser-1.3242732 (Accessed 5 April 2019)

Obama, B. M. in McDonald, M. (2013) 'Obama: Northern Ireland peace process blueprint to solve conflicts' 2013, June 17. *The Guardian* Available: https://www.theguardian.com/uk/2013/jun/17/obama-northern-ireland-peace-blueprint (Accessed 5 January 2019)

Oliver, C. (2016) *Unleashing Demons: The Inside Story of Brexit.* London: Hodder & Stoughton.

Oliver, T. (2019) 'Brexitology: delving into the books on Brexit' *International Politics Reviews*, 7: 1–24.

Oxford Economics (2016) *Assessing the Economic Implications of Brexit.* Oxford: Oxford Economics.

PA Media. (2021) 'DUP leadership starts legal challenge against Northern Ireland protocol' 2021, February 21. *The Guardian* Available: https://www.theguardian.com/uk-news/2021/feb/21/dup-leadership-starts-legal-challenge-against-northern-ireland-protocol (Accessed 31 March 2021)

Paisley, I. (2021) 'Engagements' (*Hansard*, 3 February 1921: vol. 633) Available: https://hansard.parliament.uk/Commons/2021-02-03/debates/2177E714-0248-4F3B-BE41-6EC94D176060/details) (Accessed 28 February 2021)

Papazian, C. (2018) 'The White Paper's Answer to the "Brexit Trilemma"' (Part I) 2018, July 19 *dcubrexitinstitute.eu* Available: http://dcubrexitinstitute.eu/2018/07/the-white-papers-answer-to-the-brexit-trilemma-part-i/ (Accessed 8 January 2021)

Parliament Live (2020) 'Eighth Delegated Legislation Committee' 2020, November 26 *parliamentlive.tv* Available: https://parliamentlive.tv/Event/Index/a83aeaab-7c3a-4a7d-a345-fb11d2c04eb6 (Accessed 20 February 2021)

Parpworth, N. (2018) *Constitutional and Administrative Law*. 10th ed. Oxford: Oxford University Press.

Permanent Secretaries Group (2016a) 'Permanent Secretary Group Meeting' 2016, November 4 *executiveoffice-ni.gov.uk* Available: https://www.executiveoffice-ni.gov.uk/sites/default/files/publications/execoffice/psg-041116-minutes.pdf (Accessed 6 June 2020)

Permanent Secretaries Group (2016b) 'Permanent Secretary Group Meeting' 2016, November 11 *executiveoffice-ni.gov.uk* Available: https://www.executiveoffice-ni.gov.uk/sites/default/files/publications/execoffice/psg-111116-minutes.pdf (Accessed 6 June 2020)

Permanent Secretaries Group (2016c) 'Permanent Secretary Group Meeting' 2016, November 18 *executiveoffice-ni.gov.uk* Available: https://www.executiveoffice-ni.gov.uk/sites/default/files/publications/execoffice/psg-181116-minutes.pdf (Accessed 6 June 2020)

Phinnemore, D. (2019) 'UK withdrawal from EU membership: the quest for cake' in Gstöhl, S. and Phinnemore, D. (eds.) *The Proliferation of Privileged Partnerships Between the European Union and its Neighbours*. Oxon: Routledge: 157–74.

Phinnemore, D. (2020) 'Northern Ireland: A "Place Between" in UK–EU Relations?' *European Foreign Affairs Review*, 25(4): 631–50.

Phinnemore, D., Galligan, Y., McGowan, L., and Murphy, M. C. (2015) *To Remain or Leave? Northern Ireland and the EU Referendum*. Belfast: Centre for Democracy and Peace Building. Available: https://pureadmin.qub.ac.uk/ws/files/17978177/briefing_paperNI_and_EU.pdf (Accessed 12 April 2021)

Phinnemore, D. and Hayward, K. (2017) 'UK Withdrawal ("Brexit") and the Good Friday Agreement" *europarl.europa.eu* Available: https://www.europarl.europa.eu/RegData/etudes/STUD/2017/596826/IPOL_STU(2017)596826_EN.pdf (Accessed 17 February 2020)

Phinnemore, D. and Hayward, K. (2018) 'Brexit and the backstop' *ukandeu.ac.uk* Available: http://ukandeu.ac.uk/explainers/brexit-and-the-backstop/ (Accessed 4 January 2019)

Phinnemore, D. and McGowan, L. (2016) *After the Referendum: Establishing the Best Outcome for Northern Ireland*. Belfast: Centre for Democracy and Peace Building. Available: https://core.ac.uk/reader/74406024 (Accessed 12 April 2021)

Phinnemore, D. and Whitten, L. C. (2022a) 'Democratic Consent and the Protocol on Ireland/Northern Ireland' 2022, June. *Post-Brexit Governance NI* Available: https://www.qub.ac.uk/sites/post-brexit-governance-ni/ProjectPublications/Explainers/DemocraticConsentandtheProtocolonIrelandNorthernIreland/ (Accessed 4 February 2023)

Phinnemore, D. and Whitten, L. C. (2022b) 'On the Legislative Complexity to Come: Reflections on What the Northern Ireland Protocol Bill and Retained EU Law Bill could mean for Northern Ireland' 2022, November. *Post-Brexit Governance NI* Available: https://cmst4.qub.ac.uk/terminalfour/preview/15/en/296306 (Accessed 4 February 2023)

Pogatchnik, S. (2022) 'Von der Leyen 'encouraged' by positive vibes from Sunak over EU–UK Brexit row' 2022, December 1 *politico.eu* Available: https://www.politico.eu/article/

commission-ursula-von-der-leyen-says-europe-encouraged-by-positive-uk-vibes-from-pm-rishi-sunak/ (Accessed 20 January 2023)

Poptcheva, E. and Eatcock, D. (2016) 'The UK's "New Settlement" in the European Union: Renegotiation and Referendum' PE 577.983 *europarl.europa.eu* Available: https://www.europarl.europa.eu/RegData/etudes/IDAN/2016/577983/EPRS_IDA(2016)577983_EN.pdf (Accessed 10 April 2020)

Press Association (2016) 'Gove's leadership bid statement in full' 2016, June 30. *The Guardian* Available: https://www.theguardian.com/politics/2016/jun/30/goves-leadership-bid-statement-in-full (Accessed 6 June 2020)

Prime Minister's Office (2021) 'Statement following the ninth meeting of the Specialised Committee on the implementation of the Protocol on Ireland and Northern Ireland' 2021, September 24 *gov.uk* Available: https://www.gov.uk/government/news/statement-following-the-ninth-meeting-of-the-specialised-committee-on-the-implementation-of-the-protocol-on-ireland-and-northern-ireland-24-september (Accessed 18 January 2023)

PUP (2016) 'PUP Country Before Party: Manifesto 2016' *pupni.com* Available: http://pupni.com/assets/images/articles/manifesto.pdf (Accessed 10 April 2020)

Quekett, A. (1928) *The Constitution of Northern Ireland Part I: The Origin and Development of the Constitution*. Belfast: HM Stationary Office.

Quinn, A. (2021) 'NI Protocol—"If loyalists have to physically fight then so be it" David Campbell—Sammy Wilson describes protocol as "poison to the people of Northern Ireland"—MLA uses attack on US Capitol and Donald Trump to emphasise why people must "dial down rhetoric" concerning NI Protocol' 2021, February 3. *Newsletter* Available: https://www.newsletter.co.uk/news/politics/live-updates-ni-protocol-if-loyalists-have-to-physically-fight-then-so-be-it-warns-david-campbell-sammy-wilson-describes-protocol-as-poison-to-the-people-of-northern-ireland-mla-uses-attack-on-us-capitol-and-donald-trump-to-3122278 (Accessed 10 February 2023)

Rawlings, R. (2017) *Brexit and the Territorial Constitution: Devolution, Reregulation, and Intergovernmental Relations*. London: The Constitution Society.

Renwick, A., Doyle, O., Garry, J., Gillespie, P., Gormley-Heenan, C., Hayward, K., Hazell, R., Kenny, D., McCrudden, C., O'Leary, B., Tannam, E., and Whysall, A. (2020) 'Working Group on Unification Referendums on the Island of Ireland: Interim Report' *ucl.ac.uk* Available: https://www.ucl.ac.uk/constitution-unit/sites/constitution-unit/files/wgurii_interim_report_nov_2020.pdf (Accessed 10 April 2021)

Reuters (2016a) 'David Cameron's full resignation speech: "I'll go before the autumn"—video' 2016, 24 June. *The Guardian* Available: //www.theguardian.com/politics/video/2016/jun/24/david-camerons-full-resignation-speech-i-will-go-before-the-autumn-video (Accessed 03 June 2020)

Reuters (2016b) 'Northern Ireland leader says special status for province possible after Brexit' 2016, October 29 *reuters.com* Available: https://www.reuters.com/article/us-britain-eu-nireland/northern-ireland-leader-says-special-status-for-province-possible-after-brexit-idUSKCN12T0JI (Accessed 13 July 2019)

Reuters (2022) 'UK's new PM Truss wants negotiated solution on N. Ireland Protocol' 2022, September 7 *reuters.com* Available: https://www.reuters.com/world/uk/uks-new-pm-truss-wants-negotiated-solution-northern-ireland-protocol-2022-09-07/ (Accessed 18 January 2023)

Rodgers, I. (2017) 'The inside story of how David Cameron drove Britain to Brexit' 2017, November 25. *Prospect Magazine* Available: https://www.prospectmagazine.co.uk/politics/the-inside-story-of-how-david-cameron-drove-britain-to-brexit (Accessed 20 March 2020)

Rosamond, B. (2000) *Theories of European Integration*. New York: St Martin's Press.

Rose, N. (1999) *Powers of Freedom: Reframing Political Thought*. Cambridge: Cambridge University Press.

Rosher, B. (2022) 'Rebordering Northern Ireland after Brexit: Electronic Travel Authorisation' 2022, June 9. *DCU Brexit Institute* Available: https://dcubrexitinstitute.eu/2022/06/rebordering-northern-ireland-after-brexit-electronic-travel-authorisation/ (Accessed 6 February 2023)

RTÉ News (2018) 'Foster says no deal better than EU "annexation" of Northern Ireland' 2018, October 13 *rte.ie* Available: https://www.rte.ie/news/2018/1013/1002900-brexit/ (Accessed 21 July 2019)

RTÉ News (2022) 'DUP will not nominate ministers without "decisive action" on Protocol—Donaldson' 2022, May 9 *rte.ie* Available: https://www.rte.ie/news/player/2022/0509/22094787-dup-will-not-nominate-ministers-without-decisive-action-on-protocol-donaldson/ (Accessed 19 January 2023)

Schiek, D. (2018) 'Brexit on the island of Ireland: beyond unique circumstances' *Northern Ireland Legal Quarterly*, 69(3): 367–95.

Scottish Legal News (2015) 'EU Referendum Top Priority for UK Government' 2015, 19 May. *Scottish Legal News* Available: https://www.scottishlegal.com/article/eu-referendum-top-priority-for-uk-government (Accessed 14 March 2020)

SDLP (2010) 'For Your Future: SDLP Westminster Manifesto' *cain.ulster.ac.uk* Available: https://cain.ulster.ac.uk/issues/politics/docs/sdlp/sdlp060510man.pdf (Accessed 12 April 2020)

SDLP (2016) 'Build a Better Future: SDLP Manifesto 2016' *sdlp.ie* Available: https://www.sdlp.ie/site/assets/files/43032/sdlp_manifesto_web-1.pdf (Accessed 23 May 2019)

SDLP (2017) 'Securing our Place in Europe: Proposals for a Special Status for Northern Ireland within the EU' *sdlp.ie* Available: https://www.newry.ie/attachments/article/4720/eustatus.pdf (Accessed 12 July 2019)

Shipman, T. (2016) *All Out War: The Full Story of How Brexit Sank Britain's Political Class*. Glasgow: William Collins.

Shipman, T. (2018) *Fall Out: A Year of Political Mayhem*. Glasgow: William Collins.

Shirlow, P. and Coulter, C. (2014) 'Northern Ireland: Twenty years after the ceasefires' *Studies in Conflict and Terrorism*, 39(9): 713–19.

Sinn Féin (2010) '2010 Westminster Election Manifesto' *cain.ulster.ac.uk* Available: https://cain.ulster.ac.uk/issues/politics/docs/sf/sf060510man.pdf (Accessed 10 April 2020)

Sinn Féin (2016) 'Better with Sinn Féin: Sinn Féin Manifesto: Assembly Election 2016' *sinnfein.ie* Available: https://www.sinnfein.ie/files/2017/2016_Assembly_Manifesto.pdf (Accessed 23 May 2019)

Sinn Féin (2017) 'Securing designated special status for the North within the EU' *sinnfein.ie* Available: https://www.sinnfein.ie/files/2017/BrexitMiniDocs_April2017_Final.pdf (Accessed 12 July 2019)

Smyth, P. (2019) 'Tusk "fully behind Ireland" as MEPs reject UK Brexit proposals' 2019, October 3. *Irish Times* Available: https://www.irishtimes.com/news/world/europe/tusk-fully-behind-ireland-as-meps-reject-uk-brexit-proposals-1.4039133 (Accessed 10 December 2020)

SNP (2015) 'Stronger for Scotland: SNP Manifesto 2015' *Lancaster University Centre for Computer Research on Language*. Available: http://ucrel.lancs.ac.uk/wmatrix/ukmanifestos2015/localpdf/SNP.pdf (Accessed 10 February 2020)

Sobolewska, M. and Ford, R. (2020) *Brexit Land*. Cambridge: Cambridge University Press.

Sparrow, A. (2011) 'Politics Live with Andrew Sparrow: EU referendum Commons vote—Monday 24 October 2011'. *The Guardian* Available: https://www.theguardian.com/politics/2011/oct/24/eu-referendum-commons-vote-live-coverage (Accessed 10 March 2020)

Staunton, D. and Leahy, P. (2017) 'Brexit summit: EU accepts united Ireland declaration' 2017, April 29. *Irish Times* Available: https://www.irishtimes.com/news/world/europe/brexit-summit-eu-accepts-united-ireland-declaration-1.3066569 (Accessed 15 October 2020)

Stennett, A. (2016) 'The EU Referendum and potential implications for Northern Ireland' 2016, January 21 *nisra.gov.uk* Available: http://www.niassembly.gov.uk/globalassets/documents/raise/publications/2016/eti/2116.pdf (Accessed 12 April 2021)

Stephens, P. (2013) 'Facts Finally Collide with Answers' 2013, July 22. *Financial Times* Available: https://www.ft.com/content/96074de6-f2d9-11e2-a203-00144feabdc0 (Accessed 12 March 2020)

Stewart, H. and Elgot, J. (2016) 'Boris Johnson rules himself out of Tory leadership race' 2016, 30 June. *The Guardian* Available: https://www.theguardian.com/politics/2016/jun/30/boris-johnson-rules-himself-out-of-tory-leadership-race-brexit-eu-referendum (Accessed 6 June 2020)

Stone, J. (2020) 'Ireland says it will block Brexit trade deal unless Boris Johnson backs down on Internal Market Bill' 2020, November 15. *Independent* Available: https://www.independent.co.uk/news/uk/politics/brexit-trade-deal-eu-ireland-internal-market-bill-b1723174.html (Accessed 15 February 2021)

Sturgeon, N. and Jones, C. (2017) 'EU (Withdrawal) Bill' 2017, July 13 *gov.scot* Available: https://www.gov.scot/news/eu-withdrawal-bill/ (Accessed 22 February 2021)

Sumption, J. (2020) 'Brexit and the British Constitution: Reflections on the Last Three years and the Next Fifty' *The Political Quarterly*, 91(1): 107–19.

Sunak, R. (2023) 'PM speech on the Windsor Framework: February 2023' 2023, February 27 *gov.uk* Available: https://www.gov.uk/government/speeches/pm-speech-on-the-windsor-framework-february-2023#:~:text=Today's%20agreement%20is%20about%20preserving,the%20people%20of%20Northern%20Ireland (Accessed 16 March 2023)

Swales, K. (2016) 'Understanding the Leave Vote' *NatCen Social Research* Available: http://whatukthinks.org/eu/wp-content/uploads/2016/12/NatCen_Brexplanations-report-FINAL-WEB2.pdf (Accessed 1 March 2021)

Syal, R. and Walker, P. (2017) 'John Major: Tory-DUP deal risks jeopardising Northern Ireland peace' 2017, June 13. *The Guardian* Available: https://www.theguardian.com/politics/2017/jun/13/john-major-tory-dup-deal-could-jeopardise-northern-ireland-peace (Accessed 10 April 2021)

Tannam, E. (2011) 'Explaining British-Irish cooperation' *Review of International Studies*, 37(3): 191–214.

Task Force 50 Interviewee (2019) 'Task Force 50 Council Secretariat Interview' interviewed by Whitten, L. C. on 21 November 2019, Brussels.

Temple Lang, J. (2017) 'Brexit and Ireland—Legal, Political and Economic Considerations' *europarl.europa.eu* Available: http://www.europarl.europa.eu/RegData/etudes/STUD/2017/596825/IPOL_STU(2017)596825_EN.pdf (Accessed 2 January 2018)

The Electoral Commission (2016) 'The 2016 EU Referendum: Report on the 23 June 2016 Referendum on the UK's Membership of the European Union, September 2016' *electoralcommission.org.uk* Available: https://www.electoralcommission.org.uk/sites/default/files/pdf_file/2016-EU-referendum-report.pdf (Accessed 10 February 2020)

The Electoral Commission (2019) 'Results and turnout at the EU referendum' *electoralcommission.org.uk* Available: https://www.electoralcommission.org.uk/who-we-are-and-what-we-do/elections-and-referendums/past-elections-and-referendums/eu-referendum/results-and-turnout-eu-referendum (Accessed 6 June 2023)

The Executive Office (2016a) 'Letter to the Prime Minister, The Rt Hon Theresa May MP' 2016, August 10 *executiveoffice-ni.go.uk* Available: https://www.executiveoffice-ni.gov.uk/publications/letter-prime-minister-rt-hon-theresa-may-mp (Accessed 12 July 2019)

The Executive Office (2016b) 'The Executive Office Departmental Plan 2016/17' 2016, September 12 *executiveoffice-ni.gov.uk* Available: https://www.executiveoffice-ni.gov.uk/sites/default/files/publications/execoffice/TEO%20Departmental%20Plan%202016-17.pdf (Accessed 6 June 2020)

The Executive Office (2018a) 'A Report On Decisions Taken During November 2018 By Northern Ireland Departments In Accordance With The Guidance Issued By The Secretary Of State For Northern Ireland Under The Provisions Of The Northern Ireland (Executive Formation And Exercise Of Functions) Act 2018' 2018, November *executiveoffice-ni.go.uk* Available: https://www.executiveoffice-ni.gov.uk/sites/default/files/publications/execoffice/decisions-taken-by-ni-dpts-summary-report-nov-2018.pdf (Accessed 22 April 2021)

The Executive Office (2018b) 'A Report On Decisions Taken During December 2018 By Northern Ireland Departments In Accordance With The Guidance Issued By The Secretary Of State For Northern Ireland Under The Provisions Of The Northern Ireland (Executive Formation And Exercise Of Functions) Act 2018' 2018, December *executiveoffice-ni.go.uk* Available: https://www.executiveoffice-ni.gov.uk/sites/default/files/publications/execoffice/decisions-taken-by-ni-dpts-summary-report-dec-2018._0.pdf (Accessed 22 April 2021)

The Executive Office (2019a) 'A Report On Decisions Taken During January 2019 By Northern Ireland Departments In Accordance With The Guidance Issued By The Secretary Of State For Northern Ireland Under The Provisions Of The Northern Ireland (Executive Formation And Exercise Of Functions) Act 2018' 2019, January *executiveoffice-ni.go.uk* Available: https://www.executiveoffice-ni.gov.uk/sites/default/files/publications/execoffice/decisions-taken-by-ni-dpts-summary-report-jan-2019.pdf (Accessed 22 April 2021)

The Executive Office (2019b) 'A Report On Decisions Taken During March 2019 By Northern Ireland Departments In Accordance With The Guidance Issued By The Secretary Of State For Northern Ireland Under The Provisions Of The Northern Ireland (Executive Formation And Exercise Of Functions) Act 2018' 2019, March *executiveoffice-ni.go.uk* Available: https://www.executiveoffice-ni.gov.uk/sites/default/files/publications/execoffice/decisions-taken-by-ni-dpts-summary-report-march-2019_0.pdf (Accessed 22 April 2021)

The Executive Office (2019c) 'A Report On Decisions Taken During September 2019 By Northern Ireland Departments In Accordance With The Guidance Issued By The Secretary Of State For Northern Ireland Under The Provisions Of The Northern Ireland (Executive Formation And Exercise Of Functions) Act 2018' 2019, September *executiveoffice-ni.go.uk* Available: https://www.executiveoffice-ni.gov.uk/sites/default/files/publications/execoffice/decisions-taken-by-ni-dpts-summary-report-sept-2019.pdf (Accessed 22 April 2021)

The Executive Office (2019d) 'A Report On Decisions Taken During November 2019 By Northern Ireland Departments In Accordance With The Guidance Issued By The Secretary Of State For Northern Ireland Under The Provisions Of The Northern Ireland (Executive Formation And Exercise Of Functions) Act 2018' 2019, November *executiveoffice-ni.go.uk* Available: https://www.executiveoffice-ni.gov.uk/sites/default/files/publications/execoffice/decisions-taken-by-ni-dpts-summary-report-nov-2019.pdf (Accessed 22 April 2021)

The Executive Office (2020a) 'Executive Committee Dealing with EU Exit Matters: Terms of Reference' 2020, April 22 *niassembly.gov.uk* Available: http://www.niassembly.gov.uk/globalassets/committee-blocks/executive-office/2017—2022/20200622-executive-committee-dealing-with-eu-exit-matters—terms-of-reference.pdf (Accessed 10 October 2020)

The Executive Office (2020b) 'TEO COMMITTEE—BREXIT ISSUES' 2020, September 29 *niassembly.gov.uk* Available: http://www.niassembly.gov.uk/globalassets/committee-blocks/executive-office/2017—2022/20200918-the-executive-office—brexit-issues.pdf (Accessed 10 October)

The Executive Office (2020c) 'BRIEFING—EU EXIT' 2020, April 24 *niassembly.gov.uk* Available: http://www.niassembly.gov.uk/globalassets/committee-blocks/executive-office/2017—2022/20200424-the-executive-office—eu-exit.pdf (Accessed 10 October 2020)

The Executive Office (2020d) 'Implications of the Withdrawal Agreement' 2020, November 5 *rte.ie* Available: https://www.rte.ie/documents/news/2020/11/letter-to-european-commission-05.11.2020.pdf (Accessed 15 April 2021)

The Guardian (2017) 'Martin McGuinness funeral—in pictures' 2017, March 23. *The Guardian* Available: https://www.theguardian.com/politics/gallery/2017/mar/23/martin-mcguinness-funeral-in-pictures (Accessed 16 August 2020)

The Labour Party (2010) 'The Labour Party Manifesto 2010: A future fair for all' *cpa.org.uk* Available: http://www.cpa.org.uk/cpa_documents/TheLabourPartyManifesto-2010.pdf (Accessed 14 April 2021)

The Prime Minister (2015) 'EU reform: PM's letter to President of the European Council Donald Tusk' 2015, November 10 *gov.uk* Available: https://www.gov.uk/government/publications/eu-reform-pms-letter-to-president-of-the-european-council-donald-tusk (Accessed 14 March 2020)

The Prime Minister (2016) 'Letter to the First Minister, Arlene Foster and the deputy First Minister, Martin McGuinness from the Prime Minister, The Rt Hon Theresa May MP' 2016, October 14 *executiveoffice-ni.gov.uk* Available: https://www.executiveoffice-ni.gov.uk/publications/letter-first-minister-arlene-foster-and-deputy-first-minister-martin-mcguinness-prime-minister-rt (Accessed 12 July 2019)

The Prime Minister (2017) 'Triggering Article 50' 2017, March 29 *publishing.service.gov.uk* Available: https://assets.publishing.service.gov.uk/government/uploads/system/uploads/attachment_data/file/604079/Prime_Ministers_letter_to_European_Council_President_Donald_Tusk.pdf (Accessed 8 August 2019)

The Prime Minister (2019a) 'Prime Minister's press statement in Strasbourg: 11 March 2019' *gov.uk* Available: https://www.gov.uk/government/speeches/prime-ministers-press-statement-in-strasbourg-11-march-2019 (Accessed 15 October 2020)

The Prime Minister (2019b) 'A Fair and Reasonable Compromise: UK Proposals for A New Protocol on Ireland/Northern Ireland' 2019, October 2 *gov.uk* Available: https://assets.publishing.service.gov.uk/government/uploads/system/uploads/attachment_data/file/836029/PM_letter_to_Juncker.pdf (Accessed 11 December 2020)

The UK Statistics Authority (2016) 'Press Statement on Use of Official Statistics on Contributions to the EU' 2016, May 27 *statisticsauthority.gov.uk* Available: https://www.statisticsauthority.gov.uk/news/uk-statistics-authority-statement-on-the-use-of-official-statistics-on-contributions-to-the-european-union/ (Accessed 10 March 2020)

Thompson, B. and Gordon, M. (2017) *Cases and Materials on and Administrative Law*. 12th ed. Oxford: Oxford University Press.

Tierney, S. (2013) 'The Three Hundred- and Seven-Year Itch': Scotland and the 2014 Independence Referendum' in Qvortrup, M. (ed.) *The British Constitution: Continuity and Change: A Festschrift for Vernon Bogdanor*. Oxford: Hart Publishing: 141–52.

Tierney, S. (2019) 'The Territorial Constitution and the Brexit Process' *Current Legal Problems*, 72(1): 59–83.

Tonge, J. (2000) 'From Sunningdale to the Good Friday Agreement: Creating Devolved Government in Northern Ireland' *Contemporary British History*, 14(3): 39–60.

Torrance, D. (2020) 'EU powers after Brexit: 'Power grab' or 'power surge'?' *commonslibrary.parliament.uk* Available: https://commonslibrary.parliament.uk/eu-powers-after-brexit-power-grab-or-power-surge/ (Accessed 11 December 2020)

TUV (2016) 'Assembly Election Manifesto 2016: Straight talking. Principled politics' *cain.ulster.ac.uk* Available: https://cain.ulster.ac.uk/issues/politics/docs/tuv/tuv_2016-04-13_nia-man.pdf (Accessed 22 May 2019)

UK Government (2017) 'North–South Cooperation Scoping Exercise' *parliament.uk* Available: https://www.parliament.uk/globalassets/documents/commons-committees/Exiting-the-European-Union/17-19/Correspondence/UK-Government-scoping-document-1.pdf (Accessed 12 January 2021)

UK Government (2018a) 'Devolution Settlement: Northern Ireland' *gov.uk* Available: https://www.gov.uk/guidance/devolution-settlement-northern-ireland (Accessed 8 March 2018)

UK Government (2018b) 'Technical Explanatory Note: North-South Cooperation Mapping Exercise' *gov.uk* Available: https://assets.publishing.service.gov.uk/government/uploads/system/uploads/attachment_data/file/762820/Technical_note_-_North-South_cooperation_mapping_exercise__2_.pdf (Accessed 11 January 2021)

UK Government (2020) 'The Northern Ireland Protocol' 2020, December 10 *gov.uk* Available: https://assets.publishing.service.gov.uk/government/uploads/system/uploads/attachment_data/file/950601/Northern_Ireland_Protocol_-_Command_Paper.pdf (Accessed 12 January 2021)

UKIP (2016) 'It's Time for Real Change: 2016 UKIP Assembly Election Manifesto' *cain.ulster.ac.uk* Available: https://cain.ulster.ac.uk/issues/politics/docs/ukip/ukip_2016-04-06_nia-man.pdf (Accessed 22 May 2019)

UUP (2010) 'Invitation to Join the Government of the United Kingdom: Conservatives and Unionist Manifesto 2010'. *Conservative Party and Ulster Unionist Party*. Available: https://uup.org/assets/images/featured/Invitation%20to%20join%20the%20Government%20of%20the%20United%20Kingdom.pdf (Accessed 12 April 2021)

UUP (2016a) 'Statement from the Ulster Unionist Party' 2016, May 5 *uup.org* Available: http://uup.org/news/4155/21/Statement-from-the-Ulster-Unionist-Party#.XOKeXi-ZPfY (Accessed 20 May 2019)

UUP (2016b) 'A Vision for Northern Ireland outside the EU' *uup.org* Available: https://uup.org/assets/images/a%20vision%20for%20ni%20outside%20the%20eu.pdf (Accessed 19 July 2019)

UUP (2017a) 'A manifesto for real partnership: A plan for a better Northern Ireland: Manifesto 2017' *CAIN* Available: https://cain.ulster.ac.uk/issues/politics/docs/uup/uup_2017-02-14_nia-man.pdf (Accessed 14 April 2021)

UUP (2017b) 'A vision for Northern Ireland outside the EU' *uup.org* Available: https://uup.org/assets/policies/a%20vision%20for%20ni%20outside%20the%20eu.pdf (Accessed 14 April 2021)

Villiers, T. (2016a) 'Democracy was the reason I had to back Leave campaign' 2016, June 25. *The Guardian* Available: https://www.theguardian.com/commentisfree/2016/jun/25/theresa-villiers-democracy-was-the-reason-i-backed-brexit (Accessed 12 April 2021)

Villiers, T. (2016b) 'Vote Leave, and take back control', Speech to the Financial Times Future of Europe conference. 2016, April 16 *Vote Leave* Available: https://www.theresavilliers.co.uk/news/vote-leave-and-take-back-control-speech-theresa-villiers (Accessed 12 April 2021)

Von der Leyen, U. in Connelly, T. (2020) 'Von der Leyen contradicts Johnson on Brexit checks'. 2020, January 31. *RTÉ* Available: https://www.rte.ie/news/2020/0131/1112284-brexit-europe/ (Accessed 28 January 2021)

Von der Leyen, U. (2023) 'Statement by President von der Leyen at the joint press conference with UK Prime Minister Sunak' 2023, February 27 *ec.europa.eu* Available: https://ec.europa.eu/commission/presscorner/detail/en/STATEMENT_23_1270 (Accessed 16 March 2023)

Walker, N. (2014) 'Our Constitutional Unsettlement' *Public Law*, 2014 (Jul): 529–548.

Walker, N. (2016) 'Constitutional Pluralism Revisited' *European Law Journal*, 22(3): 333–55

Wall, E. (2019) 'Leo Varadkar points out "major obstacles" in Boris Johnson's Brexit plan and enrages Brexiteers with suggestions' 2019, October 3 *extra.ie* Available: https://extra.ie/2019/10/03/news/brexit/leo-varadkar-obstacles-brexit-plan (Accessed 8 January 2021)

Watson, M. (2017) 'Brexit, the left behind and the let-down: the political abstraction 'the economy' and the UK's EU referendum' *British Politics*, 13: 17–30.

Weatherill, S. (2020) 'The Protocol on Ireland/Northern Ireland: protecting the EU's internal market at the expense of the UK's' *European Law Review*, 45(2): 222–36.

Wheeler, R. and Lynch, D. (2022) 'Protocol Bill clears the Commons with UK Government "top priority" pledge' 2022, July 20. *Belfast Telegraph* Available: https://www.belfasttelegraph.co.uk/news/northern-ireland/ni-protocol-bill-clears-the-commons-with-uk-government-top-priority-pledge-41856037.html (Accessed 20 January 2023)

Whittaker, N. J. 2017. 'The Island race: Ontological security and critical geopolitics in British parliamentary discourse' *Geopolitics*, 23(4): 954–85.

Whitten, L. C. (2018) 'Unenvied, Unrecognised, Lingering Victors' 2018, August 27. *Northern Slant* Available: https://www.northernslant.com/unenvied-unrecognised-lingering-victors/ (Accessed 16 June 2020)

Whitten, L. C. (2020) 'Breaking Walls & Norms: A Report on the UK general election in Northern Ireland, 2019' *Irish Political Studies*, 35(2): 313–30.

Whitten, L. C. (2021a) 'Northern Ireland and Brexit: An Explanation' 2021, November 1. *The Constitution Society* Available: https://consoc.org.uk/wp-content/uploads/2021/10/Northern-Ireland-An-Explanation-Lisa-Claire-Whitten.pdf (Accessed 6 January 2022).

Whitten, L. C. (2021b) 'Northern Ireland: The United Kingdom's Non-Nation' 2021, July 20. *Centre on Constitutional Change* Available: https://www.centreonconstitutionalchange.ac.uk/news-and-opinion/northern-ireland-united-kingdoms-non-nation (Accessed 6 January 2022).

Whitten, L. C. (2021c) 'Northern Ireland: What's the Problem?' 2021, April 10. *Northern Slant* Available: https://www.northernslant.com/northern-ireland-whats-the-problem/ (Accessed 12 April 2022)

Whitten, L. C. (2021d) 'The politics of the Northern Ireland Protocol' 2021, February 9. *UK in a Changing Europe* Available: https://ukandeu.ac.uk/the-politics-of-the-northern-ireland-protocol/ (Accessed 16 January 2023).

Whitten, L. C. (2021e) 'Sir Jeffery Donaldson and the DUP: parties, polls, and promises' 2021, July 7. *UK in a Changing Europe* Available: https://ukandeu.ac.uk/sir-jeffery-donaldson-northern-ireland/ (Accessed 16 January 2023).

Whitten, L. C. (2022a) 'In search of a landing zone for the Protocol on Ireland/Northern Ireland' Issue 486. *Fortnight Magazine* Available: https://fortnightmagazine.org/articles/in-search-of-a-landing-zone-for-the-protocol-on-ireland-northern-ireland/ (Accessed 19 January 2023)

Whitten, L. C. (2022b) 'North–South Cooperation in the Post-Brexit Era: A Complex and Contingent Future' *The Journal of Cross Border Studies in Ireland*, 17: 18–34.

Whitten, L. C. (2022c) 'Post-Brexit Dynamism: the dynamic regulatory alignment of Northern Ireland under the Protocol on Ireland/Northern Ireland' *Northern Ireland Legal Quarterly*, 73 S2: 37–64.

Whitten, L. C. (2022d) 'Dynamic Regulatory Alignment and the Protocol on Ireland/Northern Ireland—Eighteen Months' July 2022. *Post-Brexit Governance NI* Available: https://www.qub.ac.uk/sites/post-brexit-governance-ni/ProjectPublications/Explainers/DynamicRegulatoryAlignmentandtheProtocolonIrelandNorthernIreland-EighteenMonths/ (Accessed 20 January 2023)

Wingfield, D. (2016) 'The Brexit case: Does the constitution have a place for democracy?' University of *Queensland Law Journal*, 35(2): 343–8.

Wintour, P. (2016) 'Irish leader to campaign in UK for Remain vote' 2015, May 13. *The Guardian* Available: https://www.theguardian.com/politics/2016/may/13/irish-leader-enda-kenny-campaign-uk-remain-vote-eu-referendum (Accessed 12 April 2020)

Wollaston, S. (2017) 'Theresa vs Boris: How May Became PM review—a timely mix of treachery and Mayhem' 2017, June 19. *The Guardian* Available: https://www.theguardian.com/tv-and-radio/2017/jun/19/theresa-vs-boris-how-may-became-pm-review-a-timely-mix-of-treachery-and-mayhem (Accessed 28 March 2019)

Working Group (2016) 'North South Cooperation on Criminal Justice Matters: Work Programme 2016–17' 2016, October 26 *justice-ni.gov.uk* Available: https://www.justice-ni.gov.uk/sites/default/files/publications/justice/inter-governmental-agreement-work-programme-2016%2017.pdf (Accessed 6 June 2020)

Yeats, W. B. (1989) *The Collected Poems of W. B. Yeats*. Hertfordshire: Wordsworth Editions Limited.

Yorke, H. (2021) 'Unionist legal challenge over Northern Ireland Protocol set for High Court hearing' 2021, March 29. *The Telegraph* Available: https://www.telegraph.co.uk/politics/2021/03/29/unionist-legal-challenge-northern-ireland-protocol-set-high/ (Accessed 31 March 2021)

YouGov (2016) 'YouGov/Times Survey Results—Conservative Members' 2016, July 5 *YouGov* Available: https://d25d2506sfb94s.cloudfront.net/cumulus_uploads/document/dgak27s1eh/TimesResults_160704_ConservativeMembers.pdf (Accessed 6 June 2020)

Young, A. (2017) 'The Constitutional Implications of Brexit' *European Public Law*, 23(4): 757–86.

Zhang, A. (2018) 'New Findings on Key Factors Influencing the UK's Referendum on Leaving the EU' *World Development*, 102: 304–14.

Index

1998 Belfast 'Good Friday' Agreement: 2–3, 8–12, 14–15, 27, 31–32 n.18, 38, 41, 50–62, 72–87, 99–139, 155–157, 159–187, 192, 209, 222–242, 256–259
  Strand One: 6–7, 9, 13–15, 27–29, 56, 63, 77, 82, 87, 110–115, 140–141, 170–176, 188–189, 197, 232
  Institutions of
    Northern Ireland Assembly (*see also* 'Northern Ireland, Executive of'):3–4, 9, 14–15, 27–28, 56–57, 59, 69–70, 77, 110, 115, 170–176, 181–182, 189, 221, 245
    Northern Ireland Executive (*see also* 'Northern Ireland, Assembly of'): 9, 14–15, 25–29, 56–57, 59, 77, 108–110, 115, 170–176, 181–182, 189, 217–218, 221, 245
  Strand Two: 9, 28–29, 40–41, 44, 59, 63–64, 82, 87–88, 116, 121–131, 141, 178, 188, 201, 234
  Institutions of
    North-South Ministerial Council: 9, 28–29, 59–60, 82–86, 179–180, 183–184, 188, 201–205, 234–235
  Strand Three: 9, 28–29, 40–41, 44, 61, 64, 84, 87–88, 133–138, 141–142, 182–186, 188–189, 205, 238
  Institutions of
    British-Irish Council: 9, 84–86, 138, 188, 206–208, 221–222
    British-Irish Intergovernmental Conference: 9, 136, 188, 206–208
  Principle of Consent: 8–9, 14–15, 32–33, 39–40, 44, 51, 62–63, 72, 101–107, 140, 160–169, 187, 195, 227
  History: 19
Acts of Union 1800: 1–2, 8, 17 n.1–2, 227, 258
Allister and others v Northern Ireland Secretary: 197, 216, 217–218, 227

Anglo-Irish Agreement 1985: 61, 64
Anglo-Irish Treaty 1921: 8, 20–21, 212

Bloomberg Speech: 44
Border Poll: 51, 78, 195, 197, 204
Brexit
  Definition: 1–2 n.3, 37–38, 42
  Analysis: 44–245

Common Travel Area: 47–48 n.6, 54, 62, 68, 80–83, 85–86, 94–96, 138–139, 153–154
Constitution: 1, 34, 35
  Ireland: 9–10 n.9, 17
  Northern Ireland: 8, 10, 13–14, 16, 38–41, 44–245
    definition: 2–3, 8, 10, 38, 42
  Traditional British: 3–4 n.5, 11, 29, 195
  United Kingdom: 1–4, 10–13, 29–30, 257–258
Constitutionalism
  Legal: 30–31
  Political: 30–31, 35, 191–192
Constitutional Pluralism: 36–37, 193
Court of Justice of the European Union: 67–68, 99–100, 111, 112–115, 154–155, 158–159, 215–216

European Commission: 92–97, 156–157, 213, 223–226, 245
  Representatives of
    Šefčovič, Maroš: 156–157, 215–216, 220–227
    Von der Leyen, Ursula: 245
European Communities Act 1972: 31–32, 72–73, 146, 147
European Council: 92–93, 223–224
  Representatives of
    Tusk, Donald: 71–72, 92–93
European Integration (*theories of*): 36–37, 45, 193, 204–205
European Parliament: 156–157, 223–224

Index   313

European Union Act 2011: 45–46
European Union (Referendum) Act2015 (*see also* 'UK's 2016 EU Referendum'): 38, 45, 47–49 n.7, 51–52, 55, 59, 60–61 n.15, n.15
European Union (Notification of Withdrawal) Act 2017: 38, 66, 71–72
European Union (Withdrawal) Act 2018: 37–38, 147–152, 160–187, 227
European Union (Withdrawal Agreement) Act 2020: 37–38, 96–97, 147–152, 160–187

Government of Ireland Act 1920: 17 n.4, 19, 21; 23–24, 30–32

Ireland: 86, 238–239
  Constitution: 9–10 n.9
  Government: 60–64, 83, 85–86, 150–151, 177–178, 182–186, 205–208, 240
    Irish Taoisigh: 86, 238–239
      Kenny, Enda: 60–61
      Lynch, Jack: 25
      Varadkar, Leo: 97–98
  History: 17, 19, 21
  Law: 234
'Irish Border'
  Land (*Ireland–Northern Ireland*): 7, 54–55, 61, 62, 68, 89–95, 121–125, 198, 201–202, 236
  Sea (*Northern Ireland–Ireland*): 131, 190–191, 213, 227

Jackson v Attorney General: 3–4, 31–32

Lancaster House Speech: 67–68

Miller v Secretary of State for Exiting the EU: 4–5, 36, 65–66 n.3, 66–67, 71, 83–84, 86–87, 195, 229–230

Northern Ireland
  Act 1998: 2–3, 9–10, 40–41, 74–77, 106–109, 118–119, 147–150, 184–185, 227
  Assembly: 3–4, 9, 14–15, 27–28, 56–57, 59, 69–70, 77, 110, 115, 170–176, 181–182, 189, 221, 245
    Election, 2016: 56–58
    Election, 2017: 69, 77
    Election, 2022: 218–220
  Blindspot: 7, 12–14, 16, 21, 31–32, 63, 107, 187, 194
  Executive: 9, 14–15, 25–29, 56–57, 59, 77, 108–110, 115, 170–176, 181–182, 189, 217–218, 221, 245
  History: 8, 16
  Parliament (*1920–1972*): 8, 19–21
  Political Parties
    Alliance Party: 56–59, 98–99, 218–219
    Democratic Unionist Party: 6–7, 24–25, 28, 49–50, 56–58, 60–61, 63–64, 69–71, 77, 93, 95–99, 213–214, 218–219, 221, 241–242, 258
    Green Party NI: 57–59
    Progressive Unionist Party: 58, 216
    Sinn Féin: 27–28, 51, 56–59, 62–63, 69–71, 77, 99, 218–219
    Social Democratic and Labour Party: 56–59, 80–81, 83–84, 98–99, 218–219
    Traditional Unionist Voice: 57–58, 98–99, 216, 218–219, 258
    Ulster Unionist Party: 49–51, 56–58, 80–81, 98–99, 216, 218–219
  Prime Minister: 23
    Craig, James: 8, 22–23
    Faulkner, Brian: 25–26
  Troubles: 8, 23, 29

Parliamentary Sovereignty: 3–4, 32–33, 36, 71, 197
PEACE Funding: 57, 59–60
  PEACE IV: 7, 59–60
Protocol on Ireland/Northern Ireland: 6–7, 14–15, 89–245
  Articles
    Article 1: 101, 105–107, 113–114, 121, 135, 143–144, 222, 227–228, 240–241
    Article 2: 103, 135, 153–154
    Article 3: 153–154
    Article 5: 113–114, 117–120, 125, 131, 173–175
    Article 6: 116–117, 125, 131
    Article 8: 116–117
    Article 10: 113–114, 116–117, 155–158, 175–176
    Article 11: 116–117, 128, 178, 183, 188

Protocol on Ireland/Northern Ireland:
(*Continued*)
Article 12: 111–112, 116–117
Article 13: 106–107, 111, 112, 243
Article 14: 116
Article 15: 116–117
Article 16: 116–117, 213
Article 18: 107, 110–111, 135, 173, 187, 196–197, 230–232
Backstop Protocol: 6–7, 89–91, 94–95, 97, 124–125, 178–179
Stormont Brake: 255
Windsor Framework: 15, 245

Robinson v Secretary of State for Northern Ireland: 2–3, 9–10, 32–33, 41, 191–192

Scotland: 48–49, 69–70, 73–74, 184
First Minister: 86
Government/Parliament: 3–4, 51–52, 56–57, 170–171, 200–201
Political Parties
Scottish National Party: 48, 51–54, 62–63
Scotland Act 1998: 75
Sewel Convention: 5, n.6, 23, 51–52, 73–74, 76–77
Stormont Brake (*see also* 'Protocol, Stormont Brake' and 'Protocol, Article 13'):255

Treaty on the European Union: 1–2
Article 50(1): 1–4, 6–7, 13, 14, 34, 65, 243

UK's 2016 EU Referendum: 44
Campaign: 6, 48, 53
In Northern Ireland: 56
European Union (Referendum) Act 2015: 38, 45, 47–49 n.7, 51–52, 55, 59, 60–61 n.15, n.15
Result: 3, 48–49
In Northern Ireland: 49, 78
Turnout: 6 n.8
In Northern Ireland: 6
United Kingdom
General Election
2015: 47–48
2017: 93
2019: 98–99, 152–153

Political Parties
Conservative Party: 4, 45–48, 67, 69–70, 79–80, 89–91, 93, 97, 99, 198, 212, 216–217, 246
Labour Party: 48
Liberal Democrats: 45–46, 48
UKIP: 45, 48, 57–58
Green Party: 48
Prime Ministers
Asquith, Herbert: 18
Blair, Tony: 54–55
Cameron, David: 3, 44, 45, 47–48, 53–54, 60–61, 67
Heath, Edward: 25
Johnson, Boris: 4, 6–7, 48, 89–91, 97–99, 156–157, 178–179, 181–182, 212
Lloyd George, David: 19–20, 212
Major, John: 53–55
May, Theresa: 4, 6–7, 48–49, 67–70, 79–80, 89–97, 178–179, 181–182, 198, 220–221
Sunak, Rishi: 221–222, 238–239, 245–246
Truss, Liz: 220–221, 9P20

Wales: 48–49, 69–70, 73–74, 184
Assembly/Government: 3–4, 51–52, 56–57, 170–171, 200–201
First Minister: 86
Government of Wales Act 2006: 75
Political Parties
Plaid Cymru: 48, 51–52
Windsor Framework (*see also* 'Protocol, Windsor Framework'):15, 245
Withdrawal Agreement: 6–7, 13, 14–15, 89, 143, 252, 256
Institutions of
Joint Committee: 96, 115–120, 126–127, 150–151, 157–158, 176, 179–180, 199–201, 206–208, 218, 223, 246–247, 252, 255–256
Joint Consultative Working Group: 96, 115–116, 150–151, 176, 199–201, 218, 223, 246–247, 252, 256
Specialised Committee: 96, 115–116, 150–151, 176, 199–201, 223, 252, 256